Guy Wilbor
1881 Lyman Ct.
Highland Park
Illinois

1.70

D1274140

CONSTRUCTIVE ENGLISH

DERIVATION, SPELLING, PRONUNCIATION
GRAMMAR, USAGE, CAPITALIZATION
PUNCTUATION, AND LETTER
WRITING, WITH EXERCISES

BY

FRANCIS KINGSLEY BALL

The foundation of every state is the education of the youth.

DIOGENES

GINN AND COMPANY

BOSTON · NEW YORK · CHICAGO · LONDON
ATLANTA · DALLAS · COLUMBUS · SAN FRANCISCO

The Athenæum Press

GINN AND COMPANY · PRO-
PRIETORS · BOSTON · U.S.A.

PREFACE

Reading maketh a full man, conference a ready man, and writing an exact man. And therefore if a man write little, he had need have a great memory, if he confer little, he had need have a present wit, and if he read little, he had need have much cunning, to seem to know that he doth not.— LORD BACON.

This book aims to present, in the most useful form for reference and study, those principles which are essential to effectiveness in speaking and writing. The purpose has been to provide definite help on such points as usually cause difficulty to anybody who is seeking correct, clear, and forcible expression of his ideas.

To accomplish this end, the scope of the book has been made comprehensive. Grammar, effective diction and sentence structure, punctuation and capitalization, spelling, and letter writing are each carefully treated in a detailed but simple manner. The many illustrative sentences under each point, collected during a period of some years, show correct usage more clearly than can any amount of explanation. Thus the student cannot fail to know what is right and why it is right.

That this fund of material may be easily accessible to all, the book has been organized with the greatest care, even in its unusually complete table of contents and its detailed index. The helpful system of cross references has made it possible to treat subjects in their proper places ; for example, a point of grammar under grammar, with a cross reference under rhetoric when necessary.

To drive home the practical application of these various principles, numerous exercises have been added (Chapter XI); and thus, without interrupting the continuity of the subject matter, this handbook becomes a *vade mecum* for students in school and college. In using "Constructive English" as a textbook, teachers have only to turn to pages 364–394 and follow the course of study marked out there. A Teachers' Manual, obtainable from the publishers, plans the daily work, and suggests methods of treating the subject matter.

Especial thanks are due to the generous scholars and teachers who have improved the book by their suggestions and painstaking criticism. For the letter on page 153 the author is indebted to Mr. Ernest Cobb, of Newton Upper Falls. For permission to reprint the letter on page 344, from Letters of James Russell Lowell, edited by Charles Eliot Norton, he is indebted to the courtesy of the publishers, Harper and Brothers. For the reading of the manuscript he is indebted to Mr. George W. Lee, librarian of Stone and Webster, to Doctor D. O. S. Lowell, formerly Head Master of the Roxbury Latin School, to Mr. Clarence W. Gleason, senior master of the Roxbury Latin School, and to Mr. Homer K. Underwood, Head Master of the Bulkeley School, New London, Connecticut. For the reading of the galley proof he is indebted to Doctor Lowell, to Professor James Arthur Tufts, of The Phillips Exeter Academy, to Mr. F. W. C. Hersey, Instructor in English in Harvard University, to Professor William Marshall Warren, of Boston University, and to the Reverend Jones I. J. Corrigan, S. J., Professor of Social Ethics at Boston College. For the reading of the page proof he is indebted to Doctor E. Charlton Black, of Boston University.

FRANCIS KINGSLEY BALL.

CONTENTS

CHAPTER III. GRAMMAR AND RHETORIC (CONTINUED)

CONTENTS

CHAPTER III. GRAMMAR AND RHETORIC (Continued)

THE ADJECTIVE (CONTINUED)

CHAPTER III. GRAMMAR AND RHETORIC (Continued)

CONTENTS

The Verb (Continued)

CHAPTER III. GRAMMAR AND RHETORIC (Continued)

CONTENTS

CHAPTER III. GRAMMAR AND RHETORIC (Continued)

CHAPTER IV. RHETORIC: STYLE

CHAPTER V. THE DERIVATION OF WORDS

CHAPTER VIII. CAPITAL LETTERS (Continued)

CHAPTER VI. USES AND ABUSES OF WORDS

CHAPTER VII. WORDS OFTEN MISPRONOUNCED

CHAPTER VIII. CAPITAL LETTERS

CONTENTS

CHAPTER IX. PUNCTUATION AND OTHER MARKS
(Continued)

CHAPTER IX. PUNCTUATION AND OTHER MARKS
(CONTINUED)

CHAPTER X. LETTER WRITING

CHAPTER XII. THE DEVELOPMENT OF ENGLISH
(CONTINUED)

CONSTRUCTIVE ENGLISH

CHAPTER I

THE ART OF SPEAKING

Rhetoric, or the art of speaking, is, in Plato's language, the government of the souls of men; and her chief business is to address the affections and passions, which are as it were the strings and keys to the soul, and require a skillful and careful touch to be played on as they should be. — PLUTARCH.

1. Rhetoric. The ancient Greeks tempered their life by heeding that famous maxim "Do nothing too much." If, for example, they were building a temple, they refrained from making one part out of proportion to another, or from putting ornament where it should not be, or from trying to make marble express more than it was capable of expressing.

In their language, too, they observed the same rule of symmetry and simplicity. They sought the most appropriate expression for their thought, that the thought might not be disfigured by the words. They felt that words, however beautiful or effective, if ill chosen or ill placed, were like misused marble, inharmonious and uncouth.

If we would attain the art of speaking, or the government of the souls of men, we also should study the nature, uses, and arrangement of words. "Vulgar, coarse, and ill-chosen words", says Lord Chesterfield, in a letter to his son, "will deform the best thoughts, as much as rags and dirt will the best figure." (Exercises I, II, §§ 546, 547.)

CHAPTER II

WORD, SENTENCE, PHRASE, CLAUSE

POLONIUS. What dost thou read, my lord?
HAMLET. Words, words, words.

SHAKESPEARE.

2. Word, idea. A word represents the mental picture, or idea, of a person or thing, and serves to recall that picture. For example, the word *Edwin* recalls to the mind the picture of a person ; the word *write* recalls the picture of an action.

3. Thought, sentence. By properly grouping words, as in *Edwin writes*, we can say something about a person or thing, and thus express a thought. A group of words expressing a thought is called a sentence.

4. Subject and predicate. A sentence consists of two parts, called the subject and the predicate. The subject (as, *Edwin*) names the person or thing spoken of ; the predicate (as, *writes*) says something about the subject.

NOTE. A group of words like *the beautiful blue Danube* is not a sentence ; for although it may suggest a thought, it does not express one, since it does not contain both a subject and a predicate. Nor is *before he thinks* a sentence, although it contains both a subject and a predicate ; see §§ 7 and 8. But in connected speech or writing, if the context supplies the words needed to complete the thought, either *the beautiful blue Danube* or *before he thinks* may be an elliptical sentence. Study § 347.

5. Parts of speech. In the sentence *Edwin writes* there are two kinds of words, each of which has its own use. In the English language there are eight kinds of words. Since each kind forms a part of the language, the eight kinds are grouped in eight classes, called the parts of speech. The eight parts of speech are the noun, pronoun, adjective, verb, adverb, preposition, conjunction, and interjection (§§ 10–319).

6. Phrase. In the sentence *Edwin writes* each part of speech is a single word. But instead of using a single word, we may use a group of words as a part of speech. Instead of *Edwin* we may use *Edwin Grey* ; and instead of *writes* we may use *is writing*. A group of words used as a part of speech, but not containing both a subject and a predicate, is called a phrase : *Edwin Grey* ; *is writing*.

Again, we may say *Edwin writes thoughtlessly*, or *Edwin writes without thinking*. In the first sentence the word *thoughtlessly* is another part of speech. It suggests the way in which Edwin writes. In the second sentence the phrase *without thinking* is used instead of the single word *thoughtlessly*.

7. Clause. We may also say *Edwin writes before he thinks*. In this sentence the group of words *before he thinks* is used instead of the single word *thoughtlessly*. But this group of words is not a phrase (like *without thinking*), because it contains both a subject (*he*) and a predicate (*thinks*). Such a group of words is called a clause. (A clause is but a part of a sentence, and the name should not be given to a sentence as a whole.)

8. Principal clause ; subordinate clause. In the sentence *Edwin writes before he thinks* the group of words *Edwin writes* is also a clause ; for it contains both a subject and a predicate. But this clause would make sense by itself, and might stand alone ; hence it is called a principal clause. The clause *before he thinks* would not make sense by itself ; it depends on the principal clause, *Edwin writes* ; hence it is called a subordinate clause. A principal clause is a clause which may stand alone as a sentence : *Edwin writes*. A subordinate clause is a clause which depends on a principal clause : *before he thinks* (§§ 329–332). Study § 347. (Exercise III, § 548.)

CHAPTER III

GRAMMAR AND RHETORIC

The first thing you should attend to is, to speak whatever language you do speak, in the greatest purity, and according to the rules of Grammar; for we must never offend against Grammar; nor make use of words which are not really words. — LORD CHESTERFIELD.

And practise Rhetoric in your common talk. — SHAKESPEARE.

9. Grammar and rhetoric. Grammar teaches correctness in the forms and the uses of words, by presenting the usages of the best speakers and the best writers. By its aid we may not only speak and write correctly, but get a clearer meaning of what we read. Rhetoric teaches correctness and effectiveness in the choice and the arrangement of words.

Words, as we have seen, are divided into eight classes, which are called the parts of speech (§ 5).

THE NOUN

10. Noun. A noun is the name of a person or a thing:

1. James, farmer, Indian.
2. House, iron, village.

11. Noun phrase; noun clause. A phrase or a clause (§§ 6–8) may be used as a noun:

1. *Escape* was impossible. (Noun.)
2. *To escape* was impossible. (Noun phrase.)
3. *That we should escape* was impossible. (Noun clause.)
4. Post office; dining room; commander in chief. (Noun phrases; see §§ 498–500.)

4

12. Compound word. Many nouns are compound words, the parts being united directly or by means of the hyphen (see §§ 498–500):

1. Schoolhouse, bookcase, windowpane, whippoorwill, grasshopper, railroad, nickname, afternoon, inside, overcoat, outlaw, bypath, goldenrod, grandmother.
2. Quarter-deck, self-control, well-wisher, forget-me-not, jack-o'-lantern, man-of-war, good-by.

13. Adjective as noun. Adjectives are often used as nouns:

1. The little girl wore *blue*.
2. It did me *good* to see him. (See § 238, *a*, 10.)

14. Abstract noun. When a noun is the name of a quality, action, or state, considered apart from any person or thing, it is called an abstract noun:

1. Sweetness, redness. (From the adjectives *sweet* and *red*.)
2. Reading, sleeping. (From the verbs *read* and *sleep*.)
3. Friendship, girlhood. (From the nouns *friend* and *girl*.)

15. Concrete noun. A concrete noun is any noun which denotes a person or a thing. Some nouns which in one meaning are abstract (that is, refer to ideas) may in another meaning be concrete (that is, refer to material things), and may then have a plural:

1. *Beauty* lives with *kindness*. (Abstract.)
2. The *beauties* of nature (as, *green hills*, *flowers*). (Concrete.)

16. Classification. There are two general classes of nouns, proper and common. A proper noun (or proper name) is the name of a particular person or thing; a common noun is a name which may be applied to any one of a class of persons or things:

1. James, Baltimore, Bible, Spain. (Proper nouns.)
2. Man, city, book, Spaniard (§ 431, N.). (Common nouns.)

17. Capital letters. A proper noun begins with a capital letter; a common noun generally begins with a small letter (see §424).

18. Gender. A noun denoting a male is masculine (or of the masculine gender); a noun denoting a female is feminine (or of the feminine gender); a noun denoting neither a male nor a female is neuter (or of the neuter gender):

1. Man, boy, tiger. (Masculine.)
2. Woman, girl, tigress. (Feminine.)
3. Tree, brook, chair. (Neuter.)

19. Gender indicated. Masculine and feminine gender may be indicated in several ways:

a. By the use of different words:

MASCULINE	FEMININE	MASCULINE	FEMININE
bachelor	spinster, maid	buck	doe
brother	sister	drake	duck
king	queen	horse	mare
monk	nun	gander	goose
sir	madam	hart (or stag)	hind

b. By the addition of masculine or feminine words:

boy cousin	girl cousin (§ 149)	———	milkmaid [3]
cash boy	cash girl	milkman [4]	———
draftsman	draftswoman	salesman	saleswoman
fisherman [1]	———	cock sparrow	hen sparrow
fish man [1]	fishwife [2]	he-goat	she-goat
man clerk	woman clerk (§ 149)	peacock	peahen
manservant	maidservant	turkey cock	hen turkey

[1] A *fisherman* is a man who catches fish; a *fish man* is a man who sells or delivers fish.

[2] A *fishwife* is a woman who sells fish.

[3] A *milkmaid* is a girl who does the milking.

[4] A *milkman* is a man who sells or delivers milk.

c. By the addition of an ending, usually to designate the feminine; sometimes there is a slight change of form:

actor	actress	host	hostess
bridegroom	bride	Joseph	Josephine
duke	duchess	master	mistress
emperor	empress	shepherd	shepherdess
executor	executrix	testator	testatrix
heir	heiress	waiter	waitress
hero	heroine	widower	widow

20. Gender not indicated. Many nouns do not show by their form whether they are masculine or feminine: *cousin, friend, schoolmate.*

NOTE. Nouns like *cousin, friend,* and *schoolmate* are sometimes said to be of common gender.

21. Gender of animals. A large animal, such as the horse, dog, lion, or eagle, we often call *he,* and a small animal or a child we call *it,* without regard to sex; but usage varies according to our feelings.

22. Personification. We may speak of things as if they were persons. If they are noted for strength, grandeur, or terror, we usually consider them masculine; if for gentleness, beauty, or fertility, feminine; countries and cities we usually consider feminine (for capitalization, see §§ 433, 434):

1. Lo, steel-clad *War his* gorgeous standard rears.
2. *Earth* with *her* thousand voices praises God.
3. Ancient Rome was called the *mistress* of the world. (Exercises IV, V, §§ 549, 550.)

23. Number. That form of a noun which indicates one person or thing is called the singular; that form which indicates two or more is called the plural:

1. Toy, city, glass, fox, horse. (Singular.)
2. Toys, cities, glasses, foxes, horses. (Plural.)

24. Formation of plural. Nouns regularly form their plural by adding *s* or *es* to the singular; they add *es* when their singular ends in an *s*-sound (*ch, s, sh, x,* or *z*):

1. Girl, *girls*; shoe, *shoes*; valley, *valleys*; cameo, *cameos*; curio, *curios*; oratorio, *oratorios* (see § 28).
2. Church, *churches*; dress, *dresses*; Lewis, *Lewises*; Jones, *Joneses*; bush, *bushes*; box, *boxes*; topaz, *topazes*.

25. Nouns in -ey, -y. Nouns ending in *ey* form their plural regularly, by adding *s* (§ 24); nouns ending in *y* preceded by a consonant change *y* to *ie* (an old form), and add *s*; proper names ending in *y* preceded by a consonant form their plural in either *ies* (preferred by Webster) or *s* (preferred by the Oxford University Press):

1. Valley, *valleys*; turkey, *turkeys*; monkey, *monkeys*.
2. Story, *stories*; lady, *ladies*; monarchy, *monarchies*.
3. Mary, *Maries* (or *Marys*); Cary, the *Carys*; Merry, the *Merrys*. (But some long-established forms are invariable: the *Ptolemies*; the Two *Sicilies*.)

26. Nouns in -f, -fe. Most nouns ending in *f* or *fe* form their plural regularly, by adding *s* (as, roof, *roofs*; fife, *fifes*); but the following important nouns change *f* or *fe* to *ve*, and add *s* (as, beef, *beeves*):

beef	half	life	sheaf	wharf
calf	knife	loaf	shelf	wife
elf	leaf	self	thief	wolf

NOTE. The plural of *wharf* is usually *wharves* in the United States; in England it is more commonly *wharfs*. The plural of *staff* is *staves*, except when used in a military sense or when denoting a body of assistants (as in a hospital or on a newspaper), in which case it is *staffs*.

27. Nouns in -ful. Nouns ending in *ful* (from the adjective *full*) denote quantity or measure; they form their plural regularly, by adding *s* (§ 24):

1. Cupful, *cupfuls*; basketful, *basketfuls*; bucketful, *bucketfuls*; spoonful, *spoonfuls*; mouthful, *mouthfuls*.

2. Give me two *teaspoonfuls* of cream. (' Two teaspoons full of cream ' means ' two separate teaspoons filled with cream '.)

28. Nouns in -o. Nouns ending in *o* preceded by a vowel form their plural regularly, by adding *s* (§ 24).

Most nouns ending in *o* preceded by a consonant form their plural by adding *es*; some of the most important add *s*; a few add either *es* or *s*:

a. By adding *es*: echo, embargo, hero, innuendo, manifesto, mosquito, motto, potato, tomato, tornado, torpedo, veto, etc.

b. By adding *s*:

alto	casino	Eskimo	piano	solo
banjo	chromo	Filipino	proviso	soprano
basso	contralto	junto	quarto	torso
burro	duodecimo	lasso	silo	trio
canto	dynamo	octavo	sirocco	two

c. By adding *es* or *s* (the Oxford University Press prefers *es*):

bravo (*cheer*)	calico	fresco	memento	salvo
buffalo	cargo	halo	portico	volcano

29. Peculiar plurals. Some nouns have peculiar plurals:

Foot, *feet*; goose, *geese* (§ 30); mouse, *mice*; tooth, *teeth*; man, *men*; woman, *women*; ox, *oxen*; child, *children*.

30. Two plurals. Some nouns have two plurals, usually with different meanings; one of the plurals is sometimes like the singular, but is used in a collective sense (§ 36):

1. Brother, *brothers*; or *brethren* (members of a society, etc.).

2. Cloth, *cloths* (pieces of cloth); or *clothes* (dress).

3. Fish, *fishes* (individually); or *fish* (collectively: ' Few *fish* are caught here ').

4. Genius, *genii* (nature demons); or *geniuses* (persons of unusual mental power).

5. Goose, *geese* (fowls); or *gooses* (tailors' smoothing irons).
6. Head, *heads*; or *head*: 'There *are* a thousand *head* of cattle'.
7. Sail, *sails*; or *sail*: 'Twenty *sail were* in view'.

31. Plural like singular. Some nouns have the same form for the singular and the plural:

Sheep, trout, Chinese, corps (§ 39), molasses, Sioux (§ 423).

32. Plural as singular. Some nouns which are plural in form are singular in meaning (§ 205):

Mathematics, news, physics, acoustics, measles.

33. Plural or singular wanting. Some nouns naturally have no plural; others have no singular:

1. Gold, integrity, wisdom, music, pride.
2. Goods (§ 417), scissors, teens, tongs, riches.

34. Compound nouns. In compound nouns the sign of the plural is usually put at the end, as in other nouns; sometimes it is attached to the first part of the word; rarely it is attached to both parts:

1. Bookcase, *bookcases*; handful, *handfuls*; horsewoman, *horsewomen*; Frenchman, *Frenchmen*; forget-me-not, *forget-me-nots*.
2. Son-in-law, *sons-in-law*; hanger-on, *hangers-on*; court-martial, *courts-martial*; knight-errant, *knights-errant*; notary public, *notaries public*.
3. Knight Templar, *Knights Templars*; manservant, *menservants*.

NOTE. Such words as *Brahman, German, Mussulman, Ottoman, Roman, talisman*, and *Turkoman* are not compounded with *man*, and have the plural in *-s* (as, *Brahmans*). The word *Norman*, although originally a compound of *man*, has the plural *Normans*.

35. Letters, figures, signs. The plural of letters, figures, signs, and the like is generally formed by the addition of *'s* (some writers omit the apostrophe):

k, *k's*; 3, *3's*; ¶, *¶'s*; if, *if's*; I O U, *I O U'S*.

36. Collective nouns. Some nouns, called collective nouns, denote in the singular number a group of persons or things (for the agreement of the verb, see § 197); in the plural they denote two or more groups :

Class, *classes* ; crowd, *crowds* ; flock, *flocks* ; group, *groups* ; jury, *juries* ; kind, *kinds* (§§ 72, 197); people, *peoples* ; sort, *sorts* (§§ 72, 197); swarm, *swarms*.

37. Proper names. Proper names form their plural regularly, by adding *s* or *es* to the singular (§ 24) :

Adam, *Adams* ; Adams, *Adamses* ; Burroughs, *Burroughses* ; Charles, *Charleses* ; Davies, *Davieses* ; Davis, *Davises* ; George, *Georges* ; Jones, *Joneses* ; Knox, *Knoxes* ; Lewis, *Lewises* ; Marx, *Marxes* ; Moses, *Moseses* ; Woods, *Woodses*.

NOTE. French surnames usually remain unchanged in French, the plural being indicated by the definite article or the like ; in English they take a final *s*, unless they end in *s*, *x*, or *z*, and they are usually pronounced with a final *s*-sound : *les Didot* (lā dē'do'), *the Didots* (dē-dōz') ; *les deux Louis* (lā dû lōō'ē'), *the two Louis* (lōō'ĭz).

38. Proper names with titles. When proper names are used with titles, sometimes the names and sometimes the titles are made plural (for titles, see §§ 529, 544, 545) :

1. *Mr.* Thomson, the *Messrs.* Thomson ; *Messrs.* Thomson ; *Messrs.* Thomson and French. (For *Messrs.*, see §§ 423, 529.)

2. *Master* Thomson, the *Masters* Thomson. (A title prefixed to the name of a boy who is not considered old enough to be called *Mr.*)

3. *Doctor* Thomson, the Doctor *Thomsons* ; but, *Doctors* Thomson and Wadsworth (titles like *Captain*, *Doctor*, and *Professor* are made plural when used with more than one proper name).

4. *Mrs.* Thomson, the *Mrs.* Thomsons (*Mrs.* has no plural, and the name must be made plural ; compare *Madam* and *Mesdames*, § 544, II, III).

5. *Miss* Thomson, the *Misses* Thomson (formal style, as in addressing a letter, § 544, II); the Miss *Thomsons* (informal style, as in conversation).

39. Foreign nouns. Foreign nouns usually retain their
foreign plurals, especially in scientific works. The following
are examples of French, Italian, Latin, Greek, and Hebrew
nouns which have kept their own plurals or have adopted
English forms with *s* or *es* (for the pronunciation of Latin and
Greek words, see § 402 ; a key to the English sounds is given
in §423 ; for the endings of Latin and Greek nouns, see §605):

SINGULAR	PLURAL	SINGULAR	PLURAL
addendum	addenda	caput	capita
alumna (fem.)	alumnæ	census	censuses
alumnus (masc.)	alumni	cherub	cherubim
analysis	analyses		cherubs
animalculum	animalcula [1]	corps [2]	corps [3]
antithesis	antitheses	crisis	crises
apparatus	apparatus	criterion	criteria
	(not '-ti ')	crux	cruces [4], cruxes
	apparatuses	curriculum	curricula
appendix	appendices		curriculums
	appendixes	datum	data [5]
automaton	automata	ellipsis	ellipses
	automatons	erratum	errata
bacillus	bacilli	formula	formulæ
bacterium	bacteria		formulas
bandit	banditti	fungus	fungi [6]
	bandits		funguses
beau	beaux, beaus	genus	genera
candelabrum	candelabra	gymnasium	gymnasia
	candelabrums		gymnasiums

[1] The singular form now commonly used is the English word *animal-
cule* (ăn-ĭ-măl′kūl), with a plural in *-s* ; the singular form 'animalcula'
and the plural 'animalculæ' are incorrect ; the Latin plural, *animalcula*, is frequent in scientific use.   [2] Pronounced kōr.
[3] Pronounced kōrz.   [4] Pronounced kroō′sēz (§ 402).
[5] *Data* is plural ; do not use it as singular : 'I have not a *datum*' ;
'*These data are* sufficient'.   [6] Pronounced fŭn′jī (§ 402).

SINGULAR	PLURAL	SINGULAR	PLURAL
hippopotamus	hippopotami	parenthesis	parentheses
	hippopotamuses	phenomenon	phenomena
hypothesis	hypotheses	radius	radii
index	indices [1]	seraph	seraphim
	indexes		seraphs
larva	larvæ	series	series
louis [2]	louis [2]	stamen	stamina [3]
madam	mesdames		stamens
maximum	maxima		
	maximums	stratum	strata, stratums
memorandum	memoranda	synopsis	synopses
	memorandums	tableau	tableaux
miasma	miasmata	thesis	theses
	miasmas	trousseau	trousseaux
minimum	minima	vertebra	vertebræ
minutia	minutiæ	vertex	vertices
nebula	nebulæ		vertexes
oasis	oases	virtuoso	virtuosi
			virtuosos

(Exercise VI, § 551.)

40. Case. Nouns used as the subject of a sentence (§ 4) are in the nominative case. (For the predicate nominative, see § 158; for the nominative absolute, § 233; for the nominative of address, § 471.) Nouns used as the object of a verb (§ 156) or of a preposition (§ 285) are in the objective case (accusative, §§ 604, 606; for the indirect object, see § 212). Nouns keep the same form in the nominative and the objective case:

1. *Dogs* bark. (Nominative case.)
2. Children love *dogs*. (Objective case.)
3. Dogs play with *children*. (Objective case.)

[1] Exponents in mathematics are called *indices* (ĭn'dĭ-sēz); the tables of subjects at the ends of books are usually called *indexes*.

[2] Pronounced loo'ĭ (see § 37, N.).

[3] *Stamina* in the sense of *vigor, staying power*, is used as a singular: 'His *stamina is* gone'.

41. Possessive case ; rule. The possessive case denotes possession or a similar relation (genitive, §§ 604, 606). In the singular number nouns regularly form their possessive case by adding *'s* ; in the plural, by adding the apostrophe (') when the plural ends in *s*, and by adding *'s* when the plural does not end in *s* (this rule, adopted by the Oxford University Press, is in accordance with the best usage, and prevents confusion of singular and plural forms ; for exceptions, see §§ 42, 43) :

1. Singular : girl, *girl's* ; Davis, *Davis's* ; man, *man's* ; manservant, *manservant's* ; son-in-law, *son-in-law's* ; Knight Templar, *Knight Templar's* ; year, a one *year's* course (§§ 46, 502, N. 1).

2. Plural : girls, *girls'* ; Davises, *Davises'* ; men, *men's* ; menservants, *menservants'* ; sons-in-law, *sons-in-law's* ; Knights Templars, *Knights Templars'* ; years, a four *years'* course.

NOTE. The irregular expression ' *savings* bank ' is owing to confusion ; the original form is ' *saving* bank ' (= a bank *for saving*), in which *saving* is a gerund (§§ 215, 227).

The rule for the formation of the possessive case applies to modern proper names, whether English or foreign, and to ancient names (except as noted in §§ 42, 43) :

1. Burns's, Charles's, Cox's, Fritz's, Hans's, Hicks's, James's, Jones's, Mars's, Marx's, Reuss's, Vaux's, Voss's, Zeus's.

2. Augustus's, Bardoux's, Burroughs's, the Countess's, Cousins's, Darius's, Davis's, Dickens's, the Duchess's, Dumas's (*Dumas* is pronounced dü′mà′, § 423 ; *Dumas's* is pronounced dü′màz′), Edwards's, Francis's, Lewis's, Louis's, Marcus's, Harry Moses's, the Princess's (§ 432), Venus's.

3. Cassius's, Junius's, Pamphilius's, Theophilus's.

42. Exceptions to rule. Ancient proper names ending in *es* usually form their possessive case (genitive, §§ 604, 606) by adding the apostrophe only ; so, also, the name *Jesus*, and a few words like *conscience* in *for conscience' sake* ; it is often better to use a phrase with *of* :

1. *Moses'* law, *Achilles'* friend, *Aristides'* house, *Ceres'* daughter, *Xerxes'* soldiers, *Demosthenes'* orations.

2. *Jesus'* disciples, for *conscience'* (*goodness'*, or *righteousness'*) sake.

3. Phrases with *of*: the law *of Moses*, the friend *of Achilles*, the house *of Aristides*, etc.

43. Freedom in poetry. In poetry the meter often determines the use or the omission of the *s*:

You sway the motion of *Demetrius'* heart. — SHAKESPEARE.

44. Joint ownership. In joint ownership the sign of the possessive case is added to the last name only:

1. Ray and *French's* bookstore; Smith, Nye, and *Elder's* office; Davy and *Davy's* logic; Frank and *Mary's* horse; at the time of father and *mother's* last visit; Soldiers and *Sailors'* Home.

2. But, *Spenser's* and *Milton's* spelling; *Frank's* and *Mary's* studies.

45. Noun omitted after possessive. When the meaning is clear, a noun following a noun in the possessive case (genitive, §§ 604, 606) is often omitted; the third and fourth examples are idiomatic variations of this usage (possession being shown both by the possessive and by *of*):

1. They are visiting at *Mary's* [home].

2. The time came for my leaving Doctor *Strong's* [school]. — DICKENS.

3. I was a pupil of Doctor *Strong's*. — DICKENS. (= I was one of Doctor Strong's pupils.)

4. That tongue of *Bob's* (or *of his*) is ever wagging.

46. Misuse of possessive. Neuter nouns (§ 18) seldom admit of the possessive case (genitive, §§ 604, 606), but use a phrase with *of* instead. The correct use of the possessive of neuters is illustrated by the following examples of well-established idioms; the incorrect use is illustrated below these:

The *moon's* light; the *earth's* shadow; the *world's* progress; the *sun's* rays; *heaven's* gate; the *ship's* wheel; the *water's* edge; for *convenience'* sake; for *honor's* sake; for *pity's* sake; at *swords'* points; their *journey's* end; the *cannon's* roar; the *mind's* eye; to his *heart's* content; the *law's* delay; the *day's* work; *today's* papers; two *years'* time; a *moment's* notice; a *stone's* throw; an *hour's* repose; by a *boat's* length; ten *cents'* worth.

NOTE. Sometimes either the possessive form or the uninflected form of a noun may be used as an adjective, with a difference of meaning; in such cases the uninflected form generalizes or characterizes: the *world's* literature (= the literature existing in the world), *world* literature (= literature touching all mankind, not confined to race, nationality, or creed); *schoolboys'* tales, *schoolboy* tales.

The possessive case should not be substituted for such phrases as the following:

1. The legs *of the table*. (Not ' The table's legs '.)
2. The seat *of the chair*. (Not ' The chair's seat '.)
3. The top *of the desk*. (Not ' The desk's top '.)
4. The veto *of the bill*. (Not ' The bill's veto '; see § 225, 10.)
5. The parts *of the verb*. (Not ' The verb's parts '.)
6. The end *of the chapter*. (Not ' The chapter's end '.)
7. The rules *of the university*. (Not ' The university's rules '.)
8. The products *of Europe*. (Not ' Europe's products '.)
9. The streets *of Lexington*. (Not ' Lexington's streets '.)
10. Essays *in the Atlantic Monthly*. (Not '*Atlantic's* essays '.)
11. The queen *of Scotland*. (Not ' Scotland's queen ' except in poetry.)

47. Appositive; apposition. A noun may be added to another noun or a pronoun to explain it. A noun so used is called an appositive of the noun or pronoun which it explains, or is said to be in apposition with it, and is in the same case (for the punctuation, see § 50):

1. Your brother *Tom* came early. (*Tom* explains *brother* by telling which brother is meant.)
2. Miss Davis, the *secretary*. (*Secretary* explains *Miss Davis*.)

3. In her own home, the *country*, Nature is sweet in all her moods. (*Country* explains *home*.)

4. I, your *father*, ask you. (*Father* explains *I*.)

5. They *each* claim the prize. (*Each* is in apposition with a part of *they*, and is called a partitive appositive.)

NOTE. A phrase or a clause (§§ 6, 7) may be used as an appositive:

1. The owner, *Mr. William Lane*, was away.
2. He had one desire, *that he might sleep*.

48. Appositive in possessive case. A noun in apposition with a possessive (genitive, §§ 604, 606) receives the sign of possession (*'s*), which is omitted from the other noun; when the meaning is clear, the noun following the appositive is often omitted; awkward and obscure possessive phrases should be avoided (for the punctuation, see § 50):

1. My sister *Jane's* pony. (Not ' My sister's Jane's pony '.)
2. The boys were at Uncle *John's* (home, farm, or the like).
3. At dinner at our friend Sir Joshua *Reynolds's*. — BOSWELL.
4. The father of Bartlett the bookseller. (Clearer than ' Bartlett the bookseller's father '.)

NOTE. When an appositive is added by way of explanation, being emphatic and set off by a comma, the first noun receives the sign of possession: Johnson and I passed the evening at Miss *Reynolds's*, Sir Joshua's *sister*. — BOSWELL.

49. Apposition denoted by phrase with *of*. Apposition is often denoted by a phrase with *of*:

The city *of Rome* (= the city *Rome*); the month *of April*.

50. Essential and nonessential appositive. When a word, phrase, or clause used in apposition is needed to define the meaning of the noun or pronoun which it modifies, it is an essential appositive, and is not separated from the rest of the sentence; when it is not so needed, it is a nonessential appositive, and is separated from the rest of the sentence by a comma or commas (see §§ 92, 270, 472, 489):

1. My cousin *Fred* lives here. (Essential.)
   My only cousin, *Fred Brown*, lives here. (Nonessential.)
2. Mary *Queen* of Scots; Mary Stuart, *Queen* of Scots.
3. Doctor Edward Fowler, *Vicar* of Saint Giles's. — MACAULAY.
4. War was therefore at once declared against the two most venerable corporations of the realm, the *Universities* of Oxford and Cambridge. — MACAULAY.
5. The spirit of Francis Bacon was abroad, a *spirit* admirably compounded of audacity and sobriety. — MACAULAY.
6. He offered Rochester a simple choice, *to pronounce* the Bishop guilty, or *to quit* the Treasury. — MACAULAY.
7. The thought *that he might be late* made him uneasy.
   His first thought, *that he might be late*, made him uneasy.

51. Adverbial noun. A noun, or a noun with an adjective, is frequently used adverbially (§ 252):

1. They waited *months*. (Modifies verb *waited*.)
2. She sighed *many times*. (Modifies verb *sighed*.)
3. He began *a week* ago. (Modifies adverb *ago*.)
4. It is worth *a fortune*. (Modifies adjective *worth*.)
5. The pony is *three years* old. (Modifies adjective *old*.)
6. They came *this way*. (Modifies verb *came*.)
7. This pencil cost *five cents*. (Modifies verb *cost*.)
8. We fished *all night* (*day*, *winter*, *July*, etc., of definite portions of time); but, with *the*, *all the morning* (*the afternoon*, *the week*, etc., of indefinite portions of time). (Modifies verb *fished*.)

52. Time when, etc. The time when or within which an event takes place is usually expressed by a prepositional phrase; in particular, a preposition is regularly used with the days of the month (and the days of the week unless modified by *next*, *last*, or the like):

1. *On* this particular morning; *on* the following day.
2. What did you receive *at* Christmas?
3. He was born *on* the tenth of July; *on* Friday, the tenth of July (here the preposition *on* is not repeated with the appositive *tenth*).

But such expressions as *this morning, next Monday, last Friday, last year, next June, any day, every day, some day,* are used adverbially, without a preposition :

1. We shall go home *this afternoon.*
2. *Last Saturday* I saw Julia and her mother.

53. Adverbial noun and object. An adverbial noun should not be confused with the object of the verb :

1. I rested *an hour* (adverb); I rested *my horse* (object).
2. The cloth measures *five yards* (adverb); she measures *the cloth* (object).
3. The coal weighs *a ton* (adverb); they weigh *the coal* (object).

54. Noun as adjective. Nouns are often used as adjectives (§ 383), but care should be taken not to use them inappropriately (§§ 153, 416); the headlines in newspapers are often faulty :

1. A collision of trains in Kentucky. (Not 'A Kentucky train crash'.)
2. Sale of skimmed milk to be permitted. (Not 'Skimmed milk sale', etc.)
3. The order of words. (Not 'The word order'.)
4. The Duchess of Manchester arrives. (Not 'The Manchester Duchess arrives'.)
5. A pronounced foe of Wilson. (Not 'A pronounced Wilson foe'.)
6. Threat of death. (Not 'Death threat'.) The expression 'death threat' is vague in meaning, unlike *deathbed, deathblow, death chamber,* and *death knell,* which are definite and clear. Similar faulty expressions are 'a marriage hope' (for 'a hope of marriage') and 'a bankruptcy fear' (for 'a fear of bankruptcy'). Carelessness in using nouns as adjectives leads to vagueness and obscurity both in expression and in thought. Study § 416.
7. The season has again arrived for discussing capital punishment. (Not 'The season for capital punishment discussion has again arrived'.)

8. Antivice crusade. (Not 'Vice crusade'.) In 'vice crusade' the trouble is not in the order of words, but in the sense, which is just the opposite of what is intended. The meaning of 'vice crusade' is 'a crusade for vice'. The author should have said 'antivice crusade'.

9. Sketches of travel. (Not 'Travel sketches'.)

10. The residence of the governor of New York. (Not 'The governor of New York's residence'.)

11. The elegant interior of the bank of Hawaii. (Not 'The bank of Hawaii's elegant interior'.)

12. He approved the suggestion for the celebration of victory. (Not 'the victory celebration suggestion'.)

In the expressions in parentheses style has apparently been sacrificed to space. The seventh erroneous example has the clumsy adjective 'capital punishment', which should at least be hyphened; by being used as an adjective it loses force, and the emphasis is placed on 'discussion', where it should not be. The sentence may be turned into good English, with the proper emphasis, without the addition of a single letter: 'The season for discussing capital punishment has again arrived'. Still better emphasis may be obtained by placing 'capital punishment', the topic under discussion, at the end, and leading up to it (§ 370): 'The season has again arrived for discussing capital punishment'. (For the passive voice in this paragraph, see § 208, N.) (Exercises VII, VIII, §§ 552, 553.)

THE PRONOUN

55. Pronoun. A pronoun is a word used instead of a noun:

Father wanted Mary; *he* (father) called *her* (Mary).

56. Pronoun or adjective. Some words which are properly pronouns are often used to modify nouns; they are then adjectives (§ 113; see § 383 also):

1. *His* pen had fallen from the table. (*His* modifies *pen*, and is therefore an adjective; see §§ 59, N., 67.)

I have a pen. Dick has lost *his*. (*His* is used instead of *his pen*, and is therefore a pronoun, object of the verb *lost*.)

2. *This* scarf belongs to you. (Adjective.)

This is your scarf. (Pronoun.)

3. *Whose* horse have you? (Adjective.)

Whose have I? (Pronoun.)

57. Classification. According to their uses pronouns are divided into the following classes: personal (§ 58), possessive (§ 67), demonstrative (§ 70), interrogative (§ 75), relative (§ 81), compound relative (§ 98), indefinite (§ 101), intensive and reflexive (§ 109).

The Personal Pronoun

58. Person. A personal pronoun indicates the person speaking, the person or thing spoken to, or the person or thing spoken of. If it indicates the speaker, it is of the first person: *I, me, we.* If it indicates the person or thing spoken to, it is of the second person: *thou, you.* If it indicates the person or thing spoken of, it is of the third person: *he, her, they.*

NOTE. By courtesy the speaker regularly puts the second person first, and himself last, in any combination: *you* and *I*; *you* and *she*; *you*, *they*, and *we*; *he* and *I*. See § 179.

59. Number; case. Personal pronouns have number (§ 23) and case (§ 40); but see the note (page 22):

		FIRST PERSON	SECOND PERSON	THIRD PERSON		
SING.	*Nom.*	I	thou	he	she	it
	Poss.	my, mine	thy, thine	his	her(s)	its
	Obj.	me	thee	him	her	it
PL.	*Nom.*	we	ye, you	they	they	they
	Poss.	our(s)	your(s)	their(s)	their(s)	their(s)
	Obj.	us	you	them	them	them

NOTE. The possessive forms (*my*, *mine*, *thy*, etc.) will be found classified as possessive pronouns (§§ 67, 68) and possessive adjectives (§ 118), according to their present use (§ 383; see § 608). This classification, recommended by the American and British joint committees on grammatical nomenclature, agrees with the treatment given to these words in the grammars of other languages studied in school and college.

Thou, *thee*, and *ye* are now found chiefly in the Bible and in poetry :

Thou shalt love thy neighbor.

You is plural in form, and takes a plural verb. In the older language it was used in addressing two or more persons only, but is now regularly employed in addressing one person as well as more than one :

1. Dear cousins, *you are* (*were*) welcome.
2. Dear brother, *you are* (*were*; not ' was ') welcome.

60. Gender. The forms *he* and *him* are masculine (but see the sixth example); *she* and *her*, feminine; *it*, neuter; the other forms (*I, me, thou, thee, we, us, ye, you, they, them*) are either masculine or feminine :

1. Frank is not here; *he* has gone home.
2. Where is Mary? Is *she* at school?
3. Mother looked for the pen, but did not find *it*.
4. *I* (Frank or Mary) live in Salem.
5. *They* (Frank, Mary, and mother) went to the theater.
6. Give to *him* that asketh thee. (When used in a general sense, as here, the masculine includes the feminine.)

61. Uses of *it*. The pronoun *it* has some peculiar uses (see § 89 also) :

a. It is Jane; *it* is father and mother; *it* is I, we, you, he, she, they. Is *it* I? Was *it* they? (*It* is here an indefinite subject meaning *the person* or *the persons*. For the case of *I*, *we*, etc., see § 158.)

b. It (the air) is warm. *It* (today) is a holiday. *It* (things) went well with him. *It* rains; *it* snows. (*It* is here a vague subject, denoting a person or thing not definitely expressed. In such expressions as *it rains* the verb is called impersonal, that is, a verb not having a personal subject.)

NOTE. In general, when the subject is definite, that subject should be used instead of the indefinite *it* (or *they*, § 366, *B*, 2, *b*) : My *geography* says so (not ' It says so in my geography ') ; *Business* is dull today (not ' It is dull today ').

c. We roughed *it* a whole year. (Colloquial ; see § 380. *It* is here an indefinite object.)

d. *It* is best to wait; *it* is doubtful when she will return; *it* is but seldom that he comes our way. (Here *it* appears to be the subject, but is not. The subjects are the phrase *to wait* and the subordinate clauses *when she will return* and *that he comes our way*. The pronoun *it* is merely an introductory or anticipatory subject, which introduces the sentence and permits the real subject to stand after the verb, in apposition, § 50. *It* is here an expletive, which means a filling out ; an expletive is not necessary to the sense, but is useful for such purposes as clearness, euphony, softened statement, and force.)

62. Editorial *we.* The plural *we* (instead of the singular *I*) is proper for an editor, because he represents the editorial staff ; but the usage is not proper in ordinary speaking or writing :

1. *We* welcome the delegates to *our* city. (Editorial.)
2. *I* must now introduce *my* reader to the interior of the cottage. (Not ' we ', ' our '.)

NOTE. In regal and formal style *we* (and the singular *ourself*, § 110) is used of one person : *We* will *ourself* take time to hear your cause.

63. Mistakes in case. Mistakes in using the proper cases of pronouns are very common. We should be careful not to use the nominative for the objective (accusative, §§ 604, 606), or the objective for the nominative (§ 158). Read aloud the following sentences (see § 361):

1. It is *I* (predicate nominative, § 158; not ' me '). It is *we*. It is *she*. It is *they*. It wasn't *I*. Etc.

Is it *I*? Is it *we*? Is it *he*? Wasn't it *they*? Etc.

2. This is between *you* and *me* (not ' you and I '); between *him* and *me*; between *him* and *her*; between *her* and *me*; between *you* and *her*; between *you* and *them*; between *them* and *me*; between *you* and *him*; between *you* and *us*.

They will not let *you* and *me* go with them.

3. You are as tall as *he* (is; § 347).

He likes her as well as *I* (like her; § 347).

He likes her as well as (he likes) *me* (§ 347).

4. You are taller than *he* (is; § 309).

He likes her better than *I* (like her; § 309).

He likes her better than (he likes) *me* (§ 309).

5. There is nobody else here but *I* (am; § 314).

6. I should like to be *he* (§ 219).

7. She took me to be *him* (§ 219).

NOTE. The sentence ' Fare thee well ' means ' may it fare (go) well for thee ' (see dative, § 606). Among the Quakers (Friends) and some others *thee* is used as a nominative, with its verb in the third person : '*Does thee* want anything, father ? '

64. *Them* for *those*. The word *them* is a personal pronoun, and may not be used as an adjective for *those* in such expressions as *those apples, those chairs, those people* (§ 70). (Exercise IX, § 554.)·

65. Repetition of noun, etc. A pronoun is used for the sake of euphony, to avoid the unpleasant repetition of a noun; but if the pronoun does not suggest at once the noun to which it refers, the noun should be repeated. A noun or a pronoun should be repeated whenever its repetition will add clearness or force. The second and third examples are ambiguous in form only, the sense being brought out by the context; but ambiguity of any kind should be avoided, that the attention of the reader may not be diverted from the thought :

1. Faulty: When his father punished him, he was angry. (Say ' The father was angry when he punished his son ' or ' The boy was angry when his father punished him ', according to the sense.)

2. Faulty: The first formal attempt at an account of Shakespeare's life was made by Nicholas Rowe, ninety-three years after *his* death. (Say *Shakespeare's.*)

3. Faulty: The father of Mithridates was murdered when *he* was a child, and for some years *he* led a wandering life. — FROUDE. (*He* refers to *Mithridates.* Use the noun in both places, or recast the sentence : While Mithridates was still a child, his father was murdered, and for some years the boy led a wandering life.)

4. Observe the unpleasant and faulty repetition of *it* in the following quotation : The Chicago team has not scored a run in the world-series games at the Polo Grounds. *It* will be necessary for *it* to do *it* today to win. (The three *it's* mean different things; say ' It must do so today to win '.)

5. *He* was naturally a man of great sensibility ; *he* had been ill educated ; *his* feelings had been early exposed to sharp trials ; *he* had been crossed in his boyish love ; *he* had been mortified by the failure of his first literary efforts ; *he* was straitened in pecuniary circumstances ; *he* was unfortunate in his domestic relations ; the public treated *him* with cruel injustice ; *his* health and spirits suffered from *his* dissipated habits of life ; *he* was, on the whole, an unhappy man. — MACAULAY (on Moore's life of Lord Byron. This illustrates Macaulay's mastery of the pronoun).

66. Substitute for noun, etc. To avoid unpleasant repetition, it is sometimes necessary to use a substitute for a noun or a pronoun ; but such a substitute should be an appropriate equivalent ; it should not degenerate into a hackneyed epithet (the first seven of the following examples have appropriate equivalents ; the last three are faulty) :

1. Mr. Pickwick paused, and looked steadily on Mr. Winkle, who quailed beneath *his leader's* (= *Pickwick's*) searching glance. — DICKENS.

2. The ancient seat of Lidcote Hall was situated near the village of *the same name*. — SCOTT.

3. The astrologer sat down to his repast, while Varney shut two doors with great precaution, examined the tapestry, lest any listener lurked behind it, and then sitting down opposite to *the sage* (= *the astrologer*), began to question him. — SCOTT.

4. " Now, Joe, knives and forks." The knives and forks were handed in, and the ladies and gentlemen inside, and Mr. Winkle on the box, were each furnished with *those useful instruments*. — DICKENS.

5. According to the manners of the times, the master and his attendant sat at the same table, and *the latter* (= *his attendant*) observed, with regret, how little attention *Tressilian* (= *the master*) paid to his meal. — SCOTT.

6. Lawrence and Lambourne gazed a little while after Wayland, and then turned to go back to their tower, when *the former* (= *Lawrence*) thus addressed *his companion* (= *Lambourne*). — SCOTT.

7. Mr. Weller was standing at the door of the Angel, ready to receive them, and by *that gentleman* they were ushered to the apartment of Mr. Pickwick. — DICKENS. (The epithet *that gentleman* is proper here, being a humorous reference to Mr. Pickwick's man, *Sam Weller.*)

8. Faulty: The ceremony was performed by the Reverend Doctor Thayer. When *the officiating clergyman* (say *he*) addressed the bride, etc.

9. Faulty: Next week we shall attend the lecture of Professor Miller. *This distinguished scientist* (say *He*) will explain, etc.

10. Faulty: *The Old Bay State* (say *Massachusetts*) was well represented. After the games newspaper men of the *Hub* (say *Boston*) gathered at the gymnasium in the *city of elms* (say *Cambridge*) to interview the captain of the Harvard team, and were received *by the famous runner and broad jumper* (say *by him*, or simply omit) most courteously. (Here the multiplicity of epithets is the chief objection.)

THE POSSESSIVE PRONOUN

67. Possessive pronoun. A possessive pronoun denotes ownership, or possession:

1. Polly's hat is in the hall. *Yours* (= *Your hat*) is upstairs. (*Yours* is a pronoun because it is used instead of the phrase *your hat*; it is a possessive pronoun because it tells who owns the hat.)
2. This boat is different from *theirs*.
3. The house next to *mine* is Emily's.
4. He thinks that my friends and *yours* will help him.

68. Possessive pronouns. The possessive pronouns are *mine, ours, thine, yours, his, hers, theirs* (see § 59, N.). They have no variation in form, and do not take an apostrophe. (*It's* means *it is*.)

A possessive pronoun may be preceded by *of* in the same manner as a noun in the possessive case (§ 45):

1. I am a friend *of his*. (= I am one of his friends.)
2. They are reading a story *of yours*.
3. This remark *of mine* rather amused Rose.

69. Possessive adjectives. The possessives *mine, thine*, and *his* often modify nouns (§ 56); they are then possessive adjectives (§ 118; see § 59, N.):

1. Give every man *thine* ear, but few thy voice.
2. *His* letter came this morning.

THE DEMONSTRATIVE PRONOUN

70. Demonstrative pronoun. A demonstrative pronoun points out a person or thing:

1. *This* is the best inn of the neighborhood.
2. *Those* (not 'Them', § 64) were the happy days.

71. Demonstrative pronouns. The demonstrative pronouns are *this* (plural *these*) and *that* (plural *those*). They have no variation in form except for number (§ 23).

72. Demonstrative adjectives; *this kind*, etc. The demonstratives in § 71 often modify nouns (§ 56), and are then demonstrative adjectives (§ 116); the plural form *these* or *those* with the singular *kind* or *sort* is incorrect (do not say 'kind of a' or 'sort of a'; for *kind of = rather*, see *rather*, § 417):

1. *This kind* of apple bears well.
2. People of *that sort* are lovable. (Not 'Those sort of people'.)
3. *Those kinds* of fruit do not thrive here.
4. Fruit of *this kind* does well here.
5. What kind of trees *are* these? (*These* is the subject; § 196.)
6. What *kind of* tree is this? (Not 'kind of a'.)
7. This *sort* of men *are* hard to please. (§ 197.)

73. Peculiar uses. *This* and *that* have some peculiar uses:

1. What has brought you to *this*? (= *this condition*.)
2. We expected him before *this*. (= *this time*.)
3. He has been gone *this* three years. (The *three years* are thought of as a single period of time. We generally say 'these three years', in which *these* is plural, agreeing with *years*.)
4. I will come next week; *that* is, if I can. (Introducing an explanation or modification of a statement.)

74. Misuse of *this*. In beginning an address or a composition, introduce your subject by naming it; do not begin by saying *This* or *This subject* (see § 366, *B*, 2, *b*):

1. The subject of *grammar* is important. (Not 'This is an important subject'; nor 'This subject is important'.)
2. The study of *rhetoric* is important. (Not 'This study is important'.) (Exercise X, § 555.)

THE INTERROGATIVE PRONOUN

75. Interrogative pronoun. An interrogative pronoun is used in asking a question:

1. *Who* was here today? *Whom* did you see?
2. *What* is the matter? *What* does he want?

76. Interrogative pronouns. The interrogative pronouns are *who* (possessive *whose*, objective *whom*), *which*, and *what*. The forms are the same for the singular and the plural.

77. Direct and indirect question. A question expressed in the form used by the person asking it is called a direct question ; a question expressed in the form of a subordinate clause is called an indirect question :

1. Who are you? (Direct question.)
2. He asks, "*Who are you?*" (Direct question. The quoted sentence is the object of the verb *asks*; but it is not a subordinate clause, for it may stand alone as a sentence ; § 8.)
3. He asks *who you are*. (Indirect question. The clause *who you are* is the object of the verb *asks*. It is a subordinate clause, for it may not stand alone as a sentence ; § 8.)

78. Case. The case (§ 40) of an interrogative pronoun in an indirect question depends on how the interrogative pronoun is used in its own clause ·

1. *Who* did it?
   He asked *who* did it. (*Who* is the subject of *did*; *who did it* is the object of *asked*.)
2. *Whom* did he send?
   I asked *whom* he sent. (Object of *sent*.)
3. *Who* went? It depends on *who* went. (Subject of *went*; the entire clause, *who went*, is the object of the preposition *on*.)
4. *Whom* did he send? It depends on *whom* he sent.
5. But *who* say ye that I am? — Matthew, xvi, 15 (Revised Version). (Predicate nominative after *am*; § 158.)
   Who do you suppose it was?

79. Interrogative adjectives. The interrogatives *which* and *what* often modify nouns (§ 56); they are then interrogative adjectives (§ 116):

1. *Which* boys did he choose? I ask *which* boys he chose.
2. *What* man is that? You know *what* man that is.

The interrogative pronoun or adjective *what* is often used in exclamatory sentences:

> *What* tall trees you have!

80. Gender. The interrogative *who* is masculine or feminine; *which* and *what* are masculine, feminine, or neuter.

THE RELATIVE PRONOUN

81. Relative pronoun. A relative pronoun connects a subordinate clause with a noun or a pronoun in a principal clause (§ 8):

1. She adopted the boy *who* had no mother.
2. He *who* perseveres will succeed.

NOTE. In the first sentence *who* is a relative pronoun; it not only is the subject of the subordinate clause *who had no mother*, but connects the clause with the noun *boy* in the principal clause. Similarly, in the second sentence, *who* connects the subordinate clause *who perseveres* with the pronoun *he* in the principal clause.

82. Adjective clause; antecedent. But the subordinate clause *who had no mother* (§ 81) is used like the adjective *motherless*, to modify *boy*; and *who perseveres* is used like the adjective *persevering*, to modify *he* (§ 113). A subordinate clause used like an adjective is called an adjective clause. The noun or pronoun modified by the clause (*boy* or *he*) is called the antecedent of the relative (*who*).

83. Relative pronouns. The relative pronouns are *who* (possessive *whose*, objective *whom*), *which*, *what*, *that*, *as* (for usage, see § 93). *Who* (*whose*, *whom*) and *which* agree in form with the interrogative pronouns (§ 76); *what*, *that*, and *as* have no variation in form:

1. There is the flower girl *whom* Ann liked.
2. Is this the picture *that* (or *which*) you wish?
3. She will lend you such books *as* she can spare.

What, used as a relative pronoun, means *that which* or *those which*, and has the construction of both words :

He took *what* was (or *were*) left. (*What* is here both the object of *took* and the subject of *was* or *were*.)

NOTE. In the older language *that* and *who* were sometimes used similarly to *what* :

I earn *that* (= *that which*) I eat. — SHAKESPEARE. (See the quotation at the beginning of the Preface, page iii.)

Who (= *he who*) steals my purse steals trash. — SHAKESPEARE.

84. Relative adjectives. The relatives *which* and *what* are sometimes used to modify nouns (§ 56); they are then relative adjectives (§ 116) :

1. We stayed here twelve days, during *which* time the natives were very obliging to us. — DEFOE.
2. He almost memorized *what* books he had.

85. *That* as adverb. After a noun denoting a point of space or of time the relative pronoun *that* is often used adverbially, meaning *at which*, *in which*, or *on which* :

1. In the day *that* thou eatest thereof thou shalt surely die. — THE BIBLE.
2. The night *that* he went to the play. — MARIA EDGEWORTH.
3. The next time (*that*) he calls she will not be at home. (*That* is often omitted.)

86. Gender. The relative pronouns *who*, *which*, *that*, and *as* have some peculiarities of gender. *Who* is masculine or feminine, and generally refers to persons ; but it may be used of animals when they are spoken of as intelligent beings :

1. We like the *boys* (or *girls*) *whom* you sent.
2. He has a *dog who* is more than human.

Which is neuter, and generally refers to things ; but it may be used of animals, even when they are spoken of as masculine or feminine :

1. We like the *book which* you sent.
2. We like the *pony which* you sent; he is gentle.

That is masculine, feminine, or neuter (see § 93 also):

1. We like the *book* (or *pony*) *that* you sent.
2. They are the only *boys* (or *girls*) *that* I want.
3. He has a *dog that* is more than human.

As is masculine, feminine, or neuter. It may be used when the antecedent clause has *such, same, as many*, or the like:

1. We like *such boys* (or *girls*, or *books*) *as* you sent.
2. He sent the *same as* (he had sent) before.
3. It acted in the *same* way *as* before.
4. She has *as many* books *as* I have. (§ 269, N.)

87. Whose; caution. *Whose* may always be used as masculine or feminine, in referring to persons or to animals; in poetry (and sometimes in literary prose, for the sake of euphony) it is used of things also, even when they are not personified (§ 22); but in everyday use the sentence is generally improved by being recast:

1. That is the *dog whose* leg was broken.
2. Such is the *city* for *whose* sake these men nobly fought and died. (*Whose* is proper here because of the personal element in the antecedent.)
3. A *religion whose* creed they do not understand, and *whose* precepts they habitually disobey. — MACAULAY. (*Whose* is proper here because of the personal element in the antecedent.)
4. They came to a large lake, the shore *of which* was sandy. (Or, ' lake, with a sandy shore ', the emphasis being slightly different, § 370; better than ' lake, whose shore was sandy '.)
5. You will find words the meaning *of which* (better than 'whose meaning ') you will have to guess at.
6. Two rectangles *having equal altitudes* (better than ' whose altitudes are equal ') are to each other as their bases.
7. There are three numbers, the sum *of which* is eleven. (Better than ' There are three numbers, whose sum is eleven '.)

8. A brick eight inches in height. (Not ' A brick whose height is eight inches '.)

88. Agreement. A relative pronoun agrees with its antecedent in gender, person, and number :

1. Harry boards with the *women who employ* him. (Feminine, third person, plural.)

2. Harry boards with the *man who employs* him. (Masculine, third person, singular.)

3. He is one of the best *boys that have* (not 'has', § 204) ever lived.

89. *It* as antecedent; agreement. In the sentence ' It was John that sent me' the antecedent of *that* is not *John*, but the indefinite subject *it*, meaning *the person*; that is, ' The person who sent me was John'. When a sentence begins with the indefinite subject *it* (§ 61), the relative pronoun does not agree in gender, person, and number with its antecedent, but with the noun or pronoun which follows the principal verb (for the use of *that* after *it*, see § 93):

1. It is *I that* (or *who*) *am* to blame. (But, I am the *one who is* to blame.)

2. It is *I*, the woman, *who suffer*. (Not ' suffers '.)

3. It is *I that* (or *who*) *say* so. (But, I am the *man who says* so.)

4. It was *they that* (or *who*) *were* right.

5. It is *you that* (or *who*) *were* my friend.

6. It is not *riches that make* a man happy.

90. Case. The case (§ 40) of a relative pronoun is not determined by the antecedent of the relative, but by the use of the relative in its own clause (see § 99 also):

1. I saw the boy *who* called. (Subject of *called*.)
   I saw the boy *whom* you sent. (Object of *sent*.)

2. Everybody *whom* she invited to tea came. (Object of *invited*.)
   The man *whom* you wrote to is abroad. (Object of *to*.)
   The man with *whom* he lived was poor. (Object of *with*.)

3. He invited those *who* he knew would come. (Subject of *would come*.)

4. He was not the man *who* she supposed he was. (Predicate nominative after *was*; § 158.)

He was not the man *whom* she supposed him to be. (§ 219.)

91. Omission. Often in the objective case, and sometimes in the nominative, a relative pronoun is omitted:

1. Those are the children (*whom*) we saw in the mill.

2. The letter (*that*) you wrote made her happy.

3. The man (*whom*) he lived with was poor.

4. She is not the singer (*that*) she once was. (Nominative.)

5. He isn't the man (*that*) I thought he was. (Nominative.)

6. It called for the best (*that*) there was in him.

7. In this 'tis God [*who*] directs, in that 'tis man.—POPE. (But this is not to be imitated in ordinary use. Do not say, for example, ' It was the worst thing could happen '.) (Exercise XI, § 556.)

92. Essential and nonessential clause. When an adjective clause (§ 82) is needed to define the meaning of the noun or pronoun which it modifies, it is called an essential clause; when it is merely equivalent to *and he, and she*, or the like, in continuing the thought, it is called a nonessential clause, and is separated from the principal clause by a comma or commas (§§ 50, 270, 472):

1. He visited his sister *who lives in Memphis*. (The clause *who lives in Memphis* is needed to tell which sister is meant, and is therefore an essential clause.)

2. He visited his sister Lucy, *who lives in Memphis*. (Nonessential.)

3. His sister Jane, *who lives in Memphis*, is now in New York. (Nonessential.)

4. He had one son, *whose name was David*. (Nonessential.)

93. Usage. In present usage the relative pronoun *that* is employed in essential clauses (§ 92); *who, which*, and *as*, in essential or nonessential clauses; when the relative refers to a person, *that* is often preferred to *who* if the antecedent is *it* (§ 89), or if the antecedent is modified by a word of exclusive meaning, such as *all, best, every, no, only*:

1. It was the only thing *that* I could do. (Essential.)
2. We respect a man *who* keeps his word. (Essential.)
3. They make such machinery *as* he needs. (Essential.)
4. She found a new novel, *which* she proceeded to read. (Nonessential.)
5. That is the woman *whose* arm was broken. (Essential.)
6. He had but one daughter, *whose* name was Sarah. (Nonessential.)
7. He had but one daughter *whose* age was beyond twenty. (Essential; what would the sentence mean if the clause were punctuated as nonessential?)
8. She is the *happiest* girl *that* lives. (Essential.)
9. There was *nobody that* knew him. (Essential.)
10. *Everybody that* knows him likes him. (Essential.)

94. Antecedent a group of words. When *which* and *as* are used in nonessential clauses (§ 92), their antecedent may be a group of words; but if the sentence contains a noun or pronoun which might be mistaken for the antecedent, the antecedent should be repeated in some form (as in the fifth example):

1. The black prince desired me to come to him, *which* I did. — DEFOE.
2. You are ambitious, *which*, within reasonable bounds, does good rather than harm. — LINCOLN.
3. I am a wise fellow, and, *what* is more, an officer.
4. He was a Frenchman, *as* we could tell by his accent.
5. He always talked about money, a *habit which* I detested.

95. Position. A relative pronoun should be so placed that its antecedent will be recognized unmistakably and immediately; otherwise the antecedent should be repeated (§ 94):

1. *I, who* am your best friend, ask you to wait.

2. We read in our Saxon chronicles of *tyrants, who*, when at the height of greatness, were smitten with remorse, *who* abhorred the *pleasures* and *dignities which* they had purchased by guilt, *who* abdicated their crowns, and *who* sought to atone for their offences by cruel penances and incessant prayers. — MACAULAY.

3. The great ones of the earth, however, *those* on *whom* the prince had relied, *those* to *whom* he had given his heart, dukes, princes, and electors, in this fatal change of his fortunes fell away like water. — MOTLEY.

4. Faulty : There were several large pictures on the walls of his cosy room, *which* he was proud of. (Say ' On the walls of his cosy room there were several large *pictures, which* he was proud of '. If *which* refers to *room*, say ' On the walls of his cosy *room*, of *which* he was proud, there were ', etc.)

96. In coördination and subordination. When two or more clauses in a sentence are coördinate, the pronoun introducing the first clause should be repeated with each of the others (§ 375); but when the clauses are not coördinate, different pronouns should be used, or the sentence should be recast (§ 376):

1. He is a man who stands for justice, and *who* (not ' that ') will continue to stand for it.

2. The one *that* you need, and *that* you can now secure, is, etc.

3. He belonged to a set of men *whom* it is easier to describe collectively than separately, *whose* minds were formed by one system of discipline, *who* belonged to one rank in society, to one university, to one party, to one sect, to one administration, and *who* resembled each other so much in talents, in opinions, in habits, in fortunes, that one character, we had almost said one life, may, to a considerable extent, serve for them all. — MACAULAY.

4. The thing *that* pleased them most was the care *which* (not ' that ', because the clauses are not in the same construction) she took of their children. Or, The thing *that* (or *which*) pleased them most was her care of the children.

5. Those *who* think must govern those *that* toil. — GOLDSMITH.

6. Faulty: It was a room in *which* there were two windows, at one of *which* sat a young girl. (Say ' It was a room *with two windows* ', etc.)

7. Faulty: He enjoyed a lucrative practice, *which* enabled him to maintain and educate a family with all the advantages *which* (omit, or say *that*) money can give in this country. — TROLLOPE.

97. And who, and which, etc. Relative clauses connected by *and, but,* or *or* should be either essential clauses or non-essential clauses (§§ 92, 96); that is, an essential clause and a nonessential clause should not be used together; do not use *and, but,* or *or* to connect words, phrases, or clauses which are not parallel (§ 375):

1. Faulty: The gentleman *who* spoke today, *who* is her guardian, is a Frenchman. (Essential and nonessential; such sentences are clumsy, and should be avoided. Say ' The gentleman who spoke today is her guardian. He is a Frenchman '.)

2. Faulty: The speech *that* was made today, *which* was the first of the series, was well received. (Essential and nonessential. Say ' The speech that was made today was well received. It was the first of the series '.)

3. Faulty: He spoke eloquently, *and which* carried the audience by storm. (Omit *which.*)

4. Faulty: I was reading an old sign, *and which* I had never seen. (Omit *and.*)

5. Faulty: I met a man from Baltimore, *but who* was a Northerner. (Omit *but.*)

6. Faulty: He said what he had to say, *but which* was of no importance. (Omit *but* or change *which* to *it.*)

7. Faulty: He was educated in Saint Louis, *and where* he was born. (Omit *and.*)

8. Faulty: A poor man, *but who* has brains, will succeed. (Omit *but* and the commas; or change *but who* to *if he.*)

9. Faulty: She spoke with a gentle voice, *but which* was easily heard. (Change *which* to *she.*) (Exercise XII, § 557.)

The Compound Relative Pronoun

98. Compound relative pronoun. A compound relative pronoun is formed by uniting *-ever* or *-soever* to the relative pronouns *who* (*whose*, *whom*), *which*, and *what*:

1. *Whatsoever* a man soweth, that shall he also reap.
2. *Whoever* entered found a welcome.

NOTE. Here the antecedent of *whatsoever* is the demonstrative *that.* The antecedent of *whoever*, being unemphatic, is omitted; and *whoever*, which is properly the subject of *entered* (in the subordinate clause), acts also as the subject of *found* (in the principal clause).

99. Antecedent; case. The antecedent of a compound relative pronoun (§ 98) denotes an indefinite person or thing. The antecedent may usually be omitted (but see the eighth example; for the case, see § 90):

1. He greeted *whoever* entered. (Subject of *entered*.)
2. He greeted *whomever* he met. (Object of *met*.)
3. Give it to *whomever* you please (to give it).
4. Food and shelter were given to *whoever* asked for them.
5. She received a warm welcome from *whomever* she visited.
6. Nature has a kindly face for *whoever* seeks her company.
7. *Whomever* he entertained he took to the country.
8. But, *Whosoever* will be chief among you, let *him* be your servant.

100. Compound relative adjectives. *Whichever, whichsoever, whatever,* and *whatsoever* often modify nouns (§ 56); they are then compound relative adjectives (§ 116):

1. I will read you *whichever* story you wish.
2. They employed *whatever* men they could find.

The Indefinite Pronoun

101. Indefinite pronoun. An indefinite pronoun points out a person or thing less definitely than a demonstrative pronoun does:

1. *Each* has his work in the world.
2. We have not done *either* of these things.

Note. In the first sentence *each* means *anybody* (nobody in particular). In the second sentence *either* means *the one* or *the other* (neither in particular).

102. Indefinite pronouns. The common indefinite pronouns are *another* (possessive *another's*), *any*, *both*, *each*, *either*, *neither*, *none* (now usually plural when used as a subject, the singular being expressed by *no one* or *not one*), *one* (possessive *one's*; plural *ones*, *ones'*), *other* (possessive *other's*; plural *others*, *others'*), *some*, *such* :

1. *Each* of us has *his* (not 'their'; § 120) faults. (See § 60.)
2. Let *each* of us try *his* (or *her*, if all are women) own method.
3. *Neither* of them has found *his* mistake. (See § 60.)
4. *None* of the men have come to the mill. (But, *None* of the music *is* new; There *is none* of it left.)

103. Indefinite adjectives. The indefinite words in § 102 often modify nouns; they are then indefinite adjectives (§ 116):

1. *Any* plan is better than no plan.
2. *Some* men can do almost anything.

104. Reciprocal pronouns. The phrases *each other* (possessive *each other's*) and *one another* (possessive *one another's*) denote an exchange of acts or feelings, and are called reciprocal pronouns. These phrases are often used interchangeably, but *each other* is more properly used of two persons or things (or of each two in a group), and *one another* of more than two; where there is no reciprocity (as in the fourth and fifth examples), *one another* must be used (do not use *each other* as a nominative) :

1. Jack and I help *each other*.
2. Mary and Helen visited in *each other's* home.
3. Bear ye *one another's* burdens. — The Bible.

4. Bags of money were piled upon *one another.* — ADDISON.

5. In they all came, *one after another.* — DICKENS.

6. *Each* learned what *the other* was doing. (Not ' They learned what each other was doing '.)

NOTE. *The one . . . the other* properly mean *the former . . . the latter.*

105. *One, one's,* etc. The possessive case of the indefinite pronoun *one* is *one's* (not *his*); the objective case is *one* (not *him*); and the reflexive (§ 109) is *oneself* (not *himself*). Care should be taken not to begin with *one* and change to *he* (*his*, etc.; see § 106):

1. *One* cannot be always studying *one's* works. — MATTHEW ARNOLD.

2. What *one* wishes to have done, *one* (not ' he ') should do *oneself* (not ' himself '). (Compare Benjamin Franklin's " If *you* would have *your* work done, go; if not, send ".)

3. Faulty: If *one* showed *oneself* so to *one's* townsmen, they might deride *him.* (Say ' If a *man* showed *himself* so to his townsmen, they might deride *him* '.)

4. Faulty: She never allowed *one* to eat *his* (not ' their ') supper in peace. (Say ' She never allowed *anybody* to eat *his* supper in peace '.)

106. *One, one's,* etc., overworked. The indefinite pronoun *one* (§ 105) is a colorless, vague, and often clumsy substitute for the passive voice or for *it, you, they* (colloquial, § 380; see § 366, *B,* 2, *b*), *we, I, people, somebody, a man, a woman, a person,* or the like, and should generally be avoided. Its excessive use becomes a mannerism, and often leads to inelegant and ungrammatical sentences. If the information to be imparted offers a desirable opportunity, it may be made a matter of personal interest by using *you, people* (§ 417), *a man, a woman, anybody,* or the like; but if the information contains something disagreeable, it may be made less offensive by using *I* or *we*:

1. It might be imagined that they swam across. (Or, if not used to excess, 'One might imagine that they swam across'.)

2. It is possible to imagine such a condition.

3. It is disagreeable to miss a train. (Not 'One hates to', etc.)

4. It was not known how he fell. (Not 'One did not know', etc.)

5. *They* now make the voyage in five days. (Colloquial.)

6. *We* cannot be too careful.

7. *We* should not praise *ourselves*.

8. O that *I* might read the book of fate!

9. If it were said to *us*, *we* should resent it.

10. As *I* make my bed, so *I* must lie in it.

11. Such a vocabulary will enable *you* to read a newspaper understandingly, although *you* will come across many words the meaning of which *you* will have to guess at, as best *you* can, from the context.

107. The numeral *one*. The indefinite pronoun *one* (§ 105) should not be confused with the numeral adjective *one*. The numeral adjective *one* is used either as an adjective or as a noun. It is not followed by 'one', 'oneself', like the indefinite pronoun, but by *he*, *she*, or *it*, according to the context:

1. *One* man did not wait. *He* rose and seized *his* hat.

2. *One* of them sat sewing. *She* wore spectacles.

3. *One* of the plants had lost *its* leaves.

108. *Any one*, etc. The expressions *any one*, *every one*, *no one*, and *some one* are written as separate words when *one* is the numeral, and should be used when needed (as in '*any one* of us'; '*every one* of them'); but to avoid mannerism (§ 106) in the use of the indefinite pronouns 'any one' (or 'anyone'), 'every one' (or 'everyone'), 'no one', and 'some one' (or 'someone'), which often lack clearness and smoothness (§ 374), we may use *anybody*, *everybody*, *nobody*, *somebody*:

1. *Any one* (*every one*, *no one*, *some one*) of us has *his* faults. (Use this form of men, or of men and women together.)

2. *Any one* (*every one*, etc.) of us would be willing to sacrifice *her* personal comfort. (Use this of women.)

3. *Anybody* (*everybody*, *nobody*, *somebody*) is discontented with *his* (not 'their'; see §§ 118, N., 120, 60, Ex. 6) lot in life.

The Intensive and Reflexive Pronouns

109. Intensive and reflexive pronoun. An intensive pronoun emphasizes a noun or another pronoun; a reflexive pronoun is used only as an object, to denote the same person or thing as the subject:

1. Polly *herself* amused the children. (Intensive.)
2. She amused the children *herself*. (Intensive.)
3. She amused *herself* with the children. (Reflexive.)

110. Intensive and reflexive pronouns. The intensive and reflexive pronouns are alike in form:

	Singular	Plural
First person (masc. or fem.):	myself	ourselves (§ 62, N.)
Second person (masc. or fem.):	thyself	yourselves
	yourself	yourselves
Third person (masc. or fem.):	himself	themselves
(feminine):	herself	themselves
(neuter):	itself	themselves

Yourself is ordinarily used for *thyself*, just as *you* is used for *thou* (§ 59); but *yourself*, unlike *you*, is never used in addressing more than one person:

1. Harry, are you *yourself* sure of it?
2. Boys, are you *yourselves* sure of it?

111. Intensive pronoun used alone. An intensive pronoun is sometimes used in the predicate without a noun or another pronoun:

1. Richard is *himself* again.
2. The stranger was *myself*.

112. Personal pronoun as reflexive. After a preposition a personal pronoun is often used as a reflexive:

1. The woman took the boy *with her*.
2. The speaker disregarded those *about him*. (Exercise XIII, § 558.)

THE ADJECTIVE

113. Adjective. An adjective is a word used to modify a noun or a pronoun:

1. *Blue* sky; *red* roof; *tall* tree; O *poor* me! (§ 318.)
2. *This* lamp; *every* town; *five* children; *a* (= *any*) ship.

NOTE. When an adjective modifies a noun directly (as, *blue* sky), it is called an attributive (or adherent) adjective; it usually precedes the noun. An attributive adjective may follow the noun and be separated from it by a comma, like a nonessential appositive (§ 50); it is then sometimes called an appositive adjective: 'An old house, *dark* and *gloomy*, rose before him'. A predicate adjective forms a part of the predicate (§ 158).

114. Adjective phrase and clause. A phrase or a clause (§§ 6, 7) may be used as an adjective; such a phrase is called an adjective phrase, and such a clause an adjective clause (§ 82):

1. She likes the *red-haired* boy. (Adjective.)
2. She likes the boy *with the red hair*. (Adjective phrase; § 282.)
3. She likes the boy *who has the red hair*. (Adjective clause.)

115. Essential and nonessential clause. The adjective clause is essential or nonessential, and is treated accordingly (§ 92).

116. Classification. Adjectives are of the following kinds:

1. Descriptive: *Blue* eyes; *falling* stars; *African* lions.
2. Possessive: *His* hat; *Jane's* pony (*Jane's* = *of Jane*, an adjective phrase denoting possession). (§ 69.)
3. Demonstrative: *This* picture is for you. (§ 72.)
4. Interrogative: *What* book have you? (§ 79.)

5. Relative: We stayed here twelve days, during *which* time the natives were very obliging to us. — DEFOE. (§ 84.)

6. Compound relative: He used *whatever* means he had. (§ 100.)

7. Indefinite: *Any* plan is better than no plan. (§ 103.)

8. Numeral: *Ten* men; a *third* part; a *threefold* cord; a *half* cup of tea. (§ 121.)

117. Descriptive and proper adjective. A descriptive adjective describes, or denotes a quality. Among the descriptive adjectives are those formed from proper names; such adjectives are called proper adjectives. Proper adjectives, unless they have lost their primary meaning, begin with a capital letter (§ 438):

1. The *English* alphabet; *Indian* baskets; *American* cotton.

2. An *Alpine* village (= a village *in the Alps*); but, *alpine* plants (= plants *such as grow in the Alps*).

3. The *Italic* languages; but, *italic* type.

118. Possessive adjectives. The possessive adjectives are *my, mine, our, thy, thine, your, his, her, its, their* (see § 59, N.). When *mine, thine,* and *his* do not modify nouns, they are possessive pronouns (§ 68). *Mine* and *thine* are found chiefly in the Bible and in poetry.

NOTE. *His* is masculine, but includes the feminine (see § 60, Ex. 6); for examples, see §§ 108, 120. In the older language *his* was neuter also (in Shakespeare's day *its* was just coming into use): "the fruit tree yielding fruit after *his* kind". — THE BIBLE.

Do not use an apostrophe with *his* and *its* (§ 68).

Our, ours, your, yours, etc. Distinguish the possessive adjectives *our, your, her,* and *their,* which modify nouns, from the possessive pronouns *ours, yours, hers,* and *theirs,* which do not modify anything (§ 68):

1. He thinks that *your* friends and mine will help him.

2. He thinks that my friends and *yours* will help him.

119. Indefinite adjectives. The indefinite adjectives include those given as indefinite pronouns in § 102 and such words as *a, an* (§ 139), *all* (§ 143), *every, no, few, many, numerous, several, various.*

120. Verb with *each, every,* etc. Do not use a plural verb, a plural pronoun, or a possessive adjective referring to a plural, with such indefinite adjectives as *each, every, either, neither* (see *he, him,* § 60; *his,* § 118, N.; § 200):

1. *Each* of them looks out for *himself.* (Not ' for themselves '.)
2. *Each* (or *Every*) class has *its* president.
3. *Everybody* has *his* troubles. (Not ' their troubles '.)
4. *Neither* of us *has his* umbrella. (Not ' have our umbrellas '.)
5. *Every* boy was busy at *his* bench.
6. *Every* girl was busy in *her* garden.
7. *Every* student brought specimens of *his* work. (§ 118, N.)
8. *All* the students brought specimens of *their* work.
9. Exception : *Each* (or *Every*) ten girls *elect their* leader.

121. Numeral adjectives. Numeral adjectives express number. They are of three kinds, cardinal, ordinal, and multiplicative :

	CARDINAL	ORDINAL	MULTIPLICATIVE
1	one	first	onefold, single, simple
2	two	second	twofold, double
3	three	third	threefold, treble, triple
4	four	fourth	fourfold, quadruple
5	five	fifth	fivefold, quintuple
6	six	sixth	sixfold, sextuple
7	seven	seventh	sevenfold
12	twelve	twelfth	twelvefold
20	twenty	twentieth	twentyfold
21	twenty-one	twenty-first	twenty-onefold
100	one hundred	one hundredth	one hundredfold
101	one hundred and one	one hundred and first	one hundred and onefold

For the use of the hyphen in the writing of the numeral adjectives, see §§ 506, 507.

Cardinal numeral adjectives tell how many; ordinal numeral adjectives tell where in a series; multiplicative numeral adjectives tell how many times taken, or of how many similar parts made up:

1. *Three* fishers went sailing out into the West.
2. He rested on the *seventh* day from all his work.
3. They gave us a *double* measure of corn.
4. The reasons for the delay were *threefold*.

122. *Hundred, thousand, million.* When used as nouns, such words as *hundred*, *thousand*, and *million* either have plurals ending in *s* or are treated as collective nouns (§ 36), but they always take a plural verb (§ 197):

1. *Thousands* of cattle graze on this plain.
2. Several *thousand* of his cattle *graze* on this plain.

123. Concrete and abstract numbers. When a cardinal numeral modifies a noun (that is, a concrete object), it is called a concrete number; when it does not modify a noun, expressed or understood, it is called an abstract number:

1. *Two* boys; *five* oranges; *ten* pennies. (Concrete.)
2. *Five* and *five* are *ten*. (Abstract; see §§ 199, 200.)

124. *And* in numbers. In the reading and writing of numbers *and* is retained before tens, units, and fractions, just as before the last term in any other series (§ 299); the parts of written numbers are not separated by commas (see § 481):

1. A thousand *and* one nights.
2. One hundred *and* one thousand one hundred *and* one.
3. Five thousand three hundred *and* forty-two.
4. Seven hundred *and* ten *and* three tenths.
5. Eight *and* a half; a pound *and* three quarters.

NOTE. The omission of *and* before the last term of a series is so unusual as to be a rhetorical figure, called *asyndeton* ('not bound together'; see *an-* and *syn-*, § 408), as in 'I came, I saw, I conquered'. In the writing of numbers *and* has been used since early times. The various schoolroom devices now employed in the reading and writing of whole or mixed numbers are not for general use, and students should be cautioned against them. In ordinary practice it is no more proper to say 'I counted a thousand one' than 'I saw Frank, Mary'.

125. Time-table style. Colloquially (§ 380) it is usual to announce the time of the arrival and departure of trains, boats, and the like in a short (time-table) style without *and* :

1. Our train starts at *two p.m.* (at *two fifteen*, at *two thirty*, at *two forty*). (Colloquial.)

2. Our train started at *two o'clock in the afternoon* (at *a quarter past two*, at *half past two*, at *twenty minutes to three*). (Literary.)

126. Year of event. The year of an event may sometimes be read in two different ways, the one formal, the other colloquial :

In 1914 the war began. 'In nineteen hundred and fourteen the war began' (formal; see also § 128, *a*, 4–6); 'In nineteen fourteen the war began' (colloquial).

127. Written numbers. In the writing of numbers the literary style should be distinguished from the technical style. In the literary style numbers are generally written out. In the technical style (the style for works of a scientific and technical nature) numbers are generally expressed by figures.

128. Literary style. The literary style for writing numbers is of two kinds, the more formal and the less formal :

a. In the more formal literary style (as in Shakespeare and the Bible, and in proclamations) all numbers are written out (see § 124) :

1. And all the days that Adam lived were *nine hundred and thirty* years. — THE BIBLE.

2. And it came to pass in the *six hundred and first* year, in the *first* month, the *first* day of the month, the waters were dried up from off the earth. — THE BIBLE (Revised Version).

3. The remaining *nine* cohorts consisted each of *five hundred and fifty-five*; and the whole body of legionary infantry amounted to *six thousand one hundred* men. — GIBBON.

4. It was on the *twenty-seventh* of July, in the year *twelve hundred and ninety-nine* of the Christian Era, that Othman first invaded the territory of Nicomedia. — GIBBON.

5. It was in the year of Our Lord *one thousand seven hundred and seventy-five*. — DICKENS.

6. Done in the District of Columbia this *tenth* day of November, in the year of Our Lord *one thousand nine hundred and nineteen*, and of the independence of the United States the *one hundred and forty-fourth*.

b. In the less formal literary style, which is the style for ordinary use, numbers are treated as follows :

(1) In general, most numbers are written out (see § 130):

1. A square chapel, *twenty-four* cubits long, *twenty-three* broad, and *twenty-seven* high. — GIBBON.

2. The year has *three hundred and sixty-five* days.

3. Last Friday was the *eighteenth* of October.

4. At *eight* o'clock on June *the twenty-third*. (Used in formal notes; § 532.)

5. He describes this in the *second* volume of his history.

6. Page *a hundred and nine*, Mr. Boffin. — DICKENS.

7. We waited until *one* o'clock at night. (Not ' one a.m.'; § 125.)

8. The experiment cost him *one hundred and nine* dollars and *thirty-seven* cents in money, and *twenty-three* days and a *half* in time.

9. He had lost *two thirds* or *three fourths* of his property.

10. This ship had *three twenty-four*-pound guns.

11. He had engaged room *two hundred and five*.

(2) Years are generally expressed in figures; days are expressed in figures or are written out:

1. February 2, 1907. (The regular style for the headings of letters; § 520.)

2. Washington was born on (§ 52) the *twenty-second* of February, 1732. (Or, ' on February 22, 1732 '; the former is the better style for connected writing.)

3. Your letter of the *seventeenth* of December (or, of December 17th) made us all happy. (This is better than ' Your letter of December 17', unless the year is expressed: 'Your letter of December 17, 1918, made us all happy'.)

4. In the *first* (*tenth, ninety-ninth*) year of the Christian Era. (Years containing but one or two figures look better written out than put in such form as 'in the year 1 of the Christian Era'; for the use of *A.D.* and *B.C.*, see *A.D.*, § 417.)

5. The conduct of Hastings in 1780 and 1781. — MACAULAY.

6. In the session of 1846–1847. — MARK PATTISON. (§ 131.)

7. The winter of 1868–1869 was spent in London.

(3) In addresses the street numbers of houses, and room numbers, are expressed in figures; but the names of streets are usually written out (see § 529):

1. 349 Lexington Road.

2. 205 West Twenty-first Street. (In ordinary correspondence the names of streets consisting of long numbers are usually expressed in figures: 205 West 169th Street.)

3. 133 Old South Building; Room 205; Suite 21.

For figures referring to pages and the like, see § 131.

129. Technical style. In works of a technical nature, such as mathematics, physics, and chemistry, numbers are generally expressed by figures, except at the beginning of a sentence:

1. If 25 tons of coal cost $187.50, what would be the cost of 99 tons?

2. *Twenty-five* tons of coal cost $187.50. Find the cost of 99 tons.

. **130. Mixed styles.** In works of a literary nature, such as history, and in social and business correspondence, it is frequently desirable or essential to introduce numbers. In doing so we should take care not to mix the technical style with the literary style. Rhetorically, round numbers are more effective than exact figures, and should be used when possible. In books of a general nature figures and tabulated matter may be put at the bottom of the page (in footnotes) or at the end of the volume; references to other books, and to volumes, pages, chapters, and so forth, should be treated similarly. In works of a more or less technical nature, in which cross references are helpful to an understanding of the text, the references may be placed in parentheses, as is done in this textbook :

1. The spoils of this fortunate expedition amounted to *six thousand* captives, *twenty-four thousand* camels, *forty thousand* sheep, and *four thousand* ounces of silver. — GIBBON.

2. The audience, consisting of about *two hundred* persons of moderate means, contributed more than *twelve thousand* dollars. (Not ' An audience of 197 people contributed $12,347 '.)

3. The furnishings of the building cost nearly *two million* dollars. (See Vol. IX, p. 714.)

4. I inclose a dollar ($1) for the book, and twenty cents ($0.20) for the magazine.

5. The revenues amounted to $3,144,789.22.

6. I am happy in my work, and have means enough to remain here the rest of the year. My expenses for the past week have been as follows :

Room and board	$12.50
Tuition and books	4.80
Laundry	.78
Incidentals	1.30

7. Any student in regular standing may apply for one of these scholarships. The application must conform to the rules laid down on page 345.

131. Figures connected by dashes. When figures denoting pages, chapters, dates, and the like are connected by dashes, the figures following the dashes are usually given in full, especially in connected writing, § 128, *b*, (2); in dates before the Christian Era they must be given in full:

1. Pages 200–210, 209–210, 234–240. (If a subject is not continued on consecutive pages, but merely referred to, write 209, 210, etc.)

2. Chapters I–XI, XVI–XIX, XXI–XXIV, XXV–XXX.

3. Years 1893–1895, 1900–1910; 410–409 B.C. Say 'From 1893 to 1895' (not 'From 1893–1895').

132. Comparison. There are three degrees of comparison, the positive, the comparative, and the superlative:

POSITIVE	COMPARATIVE	SUPERLATIVE
wise	wiser	wisest
sweet	sweeter	sweetest
gay	gayer	gayest
pretty	prettier	prettiest
tender	tenderer	tenderest
glad	gladder	gladdest

Adjectives regularly form the comparative degree by adding *r* or *er* to the positive; the superlative, by adding *st* or *est*. Final *y*, when preceded by a consonant, is changed to *i* (as, *prettier*). A single final consonant, when preceded by a single accented vowel, is doubled (as, *gladder*; § 393).

133. Comparison with *more* and *most*. Adjectives may be compared by prefixing the adverbs *more* and *most* to the positive. Many adjectives of two syllables, and almost all adjectives of three or more syllables, are compared in this way only:

1. Fair, fairer (or, *more* fair), fairest (or, *most* fair).
2. Upright, *more* upright, *most* upright.

134. Irregular comparison. A few adjectives have irregular comparison :

POSITIVE	COMPARATIVE	SUPERLATIVE
bad, evil, ill	worse	worst
far	farther	farthest
	further	furthest
good, well	better	best
hind	hinder	hindmost
late	later, latter	latest, last (§ 417)
little	less, lesser	least
	smaller	smallest
much, many	more	most
nigh	nigher	nighest, next
old	older, elder	oldest, eldest

Farther and *farthest* are now generally used of distance (literal or figurative) ; *further* and *furthest,* of something additional :

   1. They sailed to the *farther* shore.
   2. He gave no *further* reason for his absence.
   3. Let us pursue the subject no *farther.* (§ 265.)
   4. What was there to be said *further*? (§ 265.)

Latter and *lesser* modify nouns, but may not be used as predicate adjectives (§ 158) :

   1. His *latter* years. God made the *lesser* light to rule by night.
   2. This amount is *less* than we need. (Not ' lesser '.)

Little has for its comparative and superlative *smaller* and *smallest* (instead of ' littler ' and ' littlest ', which are dialectal and illiterate) ; *little* is often used of persons ; *small* more frequently refers to number, quantity, and the like :

   1. The *little* boy (' the *small* boy ', suggesting greater activity and independence, is used colloquially ; § 380) ; a *little* child.
   2. The *smallest* boy in school. (Not ' littlest '.)
   3. A *small* family ; a *small* loaf ; two *small* fishes.

Older and *oldest* are the more general words; *elder* and *eldest* apply to members of the same family or of the same group, but may not be used as predicate adjectives (§ 158); *elder* is often used as a noun:

1. Jane is much *older* than her sister. (Not ' elder '.)
2. My father's *elder* brother is the oldest man in town.
3. The *elder* officer received the news calmly.
4. The child was wont to listen to his *elders*.

135. Use of comparison. We use the positive degree when we make no particular comparison; we use the comparative when we compare one object or group with another; we use the superlative when we compare one object or group with two or more:

1. This melon is *ripe*; it is *riper* than the apples are.
2. These trees are the *largest* in this region.

136. Emphatic superlative. For emphasis we may use the superlative absolutely, that is, without comparison:

1. *Dearest* mother, I miss you every day.
2. The voyage was a *most agreeable* one.

137. Misuse of superlative. In illiterate and careless speech the superlative is frequently used incorrectly for the comparative (§ 135):

1. John is the *poorer* of the two. (Not ' poorest '.)
2. They soon got the *better* of us. (Not ' best '.)
3. I sold the *more* fertile half of the estate. (Not ' most '.)

NOTE. In a few old expressions the superlative is still in good use for the comparative:

1. She would die *first*. (= *sooner* or *rather*.)
2. I had the *worst* of the bargain. (= *the worse half*.)
3. He was evidently putting his *best* foot *foremost*.

138. Two qualities compared. When two qualities of the same object are compared with each other, the comparison with *more* is generally used (§ 133):

1. He is *more* witty than he is wise.
2. He is *more* witty than wise. (Exercise XIV, § 559.)

139. *The, an*. The demonstrative adjective *the* is usually called the definite article; it is generally less emphatic than *this* or *that*. The indefinite adjective *an*, or *a*, is usually called the indefinite article; it means *one* or *any*, without special emphasis.

The form *an* is used before words beginning with a vowel sound; *a* is used before words beginning with a consonant sound; but before words beginning with *h*, if not accented on the first syllable, *an* is sometimes preferred, especially before *habitual* and *historical*:

1. *An* apple, *an* egg, *an* hour, *an* umbrella, *an* x.
2. *A* boat, *a* history, *a* one-horse carriage, *a* union, *a* year.
3. *A* (or *An*) historian, hypothesis; *an* (or *a*) habitual, historical.
4. Four dollars *a* year; ten cents *an* ounce. (Thus regularly used to denote rate or price; see § 289.)

NOTE. The article *the* is sometimes printed in the form *y*ᵉ (as, 'Yᵉ Red Horse Tavern'), in which *y* stands for an old character representing the letters *th*. This form is pronounced *thē* (§ 423; not *yē*).

140. *The* with generic noun. A noun, singular or plural, is often used in a general sense, to denote a class of objects as a whole; it usually takes *the*:

1. *The lion* is the king of beasts.
2. *The ants* are an industrious people.
3. *Man* is mortal. *Cats* are domestic.

141. Many a, such a. *An* and *a* are often used after *many* and *such* (*such* or *such a*, as a mere intensive, is colloquial; § 380):

1. *Many an* opportunity; *many a* sailor.
2. There had never before been *such a* crowd in the church.
3. We had *such a* narrow escape. (Colloquial.)

142. Adjective repeated. Sense, clearness, or emphasis often requires that an adjective should be repeated; the repetition of the adjective may require a change in the number of the noun which it modifies (see § 200):

a. Adjective repeated; noun unchanged:

1. *Some* bread and milk *was* on the table. (One dish.)
   Some bread and *some* milk *were* on the table. (Two dishes.)
   Some paper, pens, and ink. (No confusion; repetition of adjective unnecessary except for emphasis: *Some* paper, *some* pens, and *some* ink.)
2. *A* red and white cow *was* at the gate. (One cow.)
   A red and *a* white cow *were* at the gate. (Two cows.)
   He was *a* sadder and *a* wiser man. (Emphasis.)
3. *Our* secretary and treasurer *is* here. (One person.)
   Our secretary and treasurer *have* been delayed by the storm. (Two persons, in a group.)
   Our secretary and *our* treasurer *have* been delayed by the storm. (Two persons, distinct.)
4. *Five* girls and boys. (Five in all.)
   Five girls and *five* boys. (Ten in all.)
5. *His* wife and children. (One family.)
   His wife and *his* children. (Two parts of a family.)
6. *The* men and boys (= the defenders) fought; *the* women and children (= the defenceless) stayed in the cellar.
7. *His* aunt and uncle (one group) were there; *his* aunt and *his* uncle (distinct persons) were both there.
   I saw *his* aunt and uncle (one group), and *his* grandfather (another person).
8. Among *the* Greeks and Romans. (One group.)
   Between *the* Greeks and *the* Romans. (Two groups.)
9. *The* president and board of trustees.
   The president and *the* board of trustees.

b. Adjective repeated; noun made singular:

1. *The* Old and New Testaments. (Two, in a group.)

The Old and *the* New Testament. (Two, distinct. Do not say 'Testaments', for there is no such thing as 'the New Testaments'; but '*my* old and *my* new *shoes*', since there are two or more of each kind.)

2. *His* eldest and youngest sons.

His eldest and *his* youngest *son*.

3. *The* fifteenth and sixteenth centuries. (One period.)

The fifteenth and *the* sixteenth *century*. (Two periods.)

4. Through *the* third and fourth centuries.

Through *the* third and *the* fourth *century*.

5. Between *the* first and *the* fourth *century*. (Not 'Between the first and fourth centuries', since *between* indicates two periods.)

In *the* third or *the* fourth *century*.

Both *the* Old and *the* New Testament.

6. *The* first, third, and fifth verses.

The first, *the* third, and *the* fifth *verse*.

7. Moral and social science *lacks* the same kind of, etc. (The singular verb shows that one composite thing is meant, namely, science that deals with moral and social problems.)

8. *The* Ohio and Mississippi *rivers*. (See § 441.)

The Ohio and *the* Mississippi *River*.

9. Primary and secondary education *are* not of the same kind. (The plural verb shows that two distinct things are meant. It would be an improvement to repeat the noun: Primary education and secondary education are not of the same kind.)

143. *All, both.* *All* (§§ 119, 207) and *both* generally stand before any other modifier of the noun which they modify; they generally follow the pronoun which they modify, but precede it if it is governed by *of*; they may also follow an auxiliary verb (§ 157):

1. *All* the boys (better than 'all of the boys'; *of* is rare in literary use except before pronouns, as in *all of them*); *both* our hats ('*both of* our hats' is colloquial, § 380); *all* day, *all* that day, *all* the next day, *all* the following night; *all* these are yours.

  2. You shall see us *all* (or *both*); *all* (or *both*) *of* us.

  3. They had *all* (or *both*) gone away.

144. *Else*, *else's*. The adjective *else* follows the word which it modifies; with such a word as *anybody* or *everybody* it forms a kind of phrase, and in the possessive case takes the sign *'s* (which is then omitted from the other word):

  1. I forgot all *else*; she had nothing *else* to do.

  2. It is his business, and *nobody else's*. (Not 'nobody's else'.)

145. *Else* and *other* omitted. *Else* and *other* are often carelessly omitted; this omission not infrequently changes the meaning of the sentence:

  1. Above all (*else*), don't fail to come. (Here commonly omitted, without particular harm.)

  2. I like the chair better than anything *else* that John has made. (Here necessary if John made the chair.)

  3. Turner knows more about it than any *other* architect in this country. (Here necessary if Turner is an architect and is in this country.)

146. *First two*, *second two*, etc. There is doubt in the minds of some whether to say the *first two* or the 'two first', the *second two* or the 'two second', and so forth. The former is the correct style. For example, in taking apples out of a basket, we may take them out one at a time, two at a time, and so on. If we take them out one at a time, the first apple we take out is the *first one*, the next the *second one*; if two at a time, the two that we take out first are the *first two*, the next the *second two*; but there cannot be 'two firsts'.

Similarly, we may assign lessons in a book, a page at a time, two pages at a time, and so on, and we tell the students to take the *first* page, the *second* page, or, if two at a time, the *first two*, the *second two*, the *next two*. The same would hold true if there were only three pages in the book, and the lesson would be the *first two* or the *last two*.

And thus we say 'every four years', 'these four books', 'the last six weeks', 'the next two years', 'the other two boys', 'the first hundred years of our history', and so on, placing the cardinal numeral before the noun with which it forms a group.

147. Half. *Half* may stand before the noun which it modifies, or before another modifier of the noun; as a noun (§ 207), it may stand before a pronoun governed by *of*; if it is modified by an adjective, it may stand before a noun governed by *of*:

1. A *half* length; a *half* portion; a *half* sheet of paper.
2. *Half* the men (not 'half of'); *half* a pound; *half* his fortune; *half* a dozen eggs; "*half* a dozen of my select friends" (ADDISON).
3. *Half of* them remained for the concert. (Noun.)
4. The better *half of* his estate was lost. (Noun.)

148. Less, fewer. Do not use *less* for *fewer*. *Less* refers to degree, value, or amount; *fewer* refers to number:

1. There is *less* noise today.
2. I have *less* than ten dollars. (An amount.)
3. She has *fewer* (not 'less') flowers this year.
4. No *fewer* (not 'less') than twenty boys and girls came.
5. No *less* than fifty bushels of wheat was needed. (An amount.)
6. No *fewer* than fifty dozens of eggs were broken.
7. No *fewer* than a score of applications came in.
8. The reward is *less* than he deserves.
9. The rewards are *less* (in amount) than last year.
10. The rewards are *fewer* (in number) than last year.
11. Towns of *fewer* than three thousand inhabitants.

149. Male, female. The adjectives *male* and *female* are now not generally used to indicate gender unless the idea of sex is to be made prominent (as in legal or other technical phraseology, shown in the first list below), but are avoided by employing the terms *man* (*men*), *woman* (*women*), *boy*, *girl*, which were originally used appositively (§ 47):

1. *Male* (or *female*) ancestor, attendant, attire, child, citizen, choir, chorus, costume, descendant, dress, garb, heir, inhabitant, issue, line, members of a society, quartette, suffrage (or 'woman's suffrage', § 151; 'woman suffrage', which is sometimes seen, is no better than 'woman dress', 'woman society', 'woman party', 'woman rights', or 'woman curiosity' would be), voice, vote, voter; deer, dog, dove, fish, insect, tiger; fern, plant, tree.

NOTE. Such terms as 'Female Seminary', 'Female College', are now replaced by 'Seminary for Young Women', 'College for Women'.

2. *Man* (or *woman*) acquaintance, chairman, clerk, cook, cousin, critic, doctor, farmer, friend, guest, instructor, lawyer, merchant, musician, nurse, president, professor, reader, saint, secretary, singer, superintendent, surgeon, teacher, treasurer.

Men (or *women*) acquaintances, chairmen, clerks, cooks, cousins, etc.

But, manservant, menservants; maidservant, maidservants; salesman, salesmen; saleswoman, saleswomen.

3. *Boy* (or *girl*) acquaintance, actor, baby, chairman, choir, chorus, clerk, cook, cousin, critic, doctor, farmer, friend, graduate, guest, lawyer, merchant, musician, nurse, page, playmate, president, quartette, reader, saint, schoolmate, scout, secretary, singer, superintendent, treasurer.

Boy (or *girl*) aquaintances, actors, babies, chairmen, choirs, choruses, clerks, etc.

150. Gentleman, lady. Do not use 'gentleman' and 'lady' to indicate gender (§ 149):

1. His *men* friends (not 'gentlemen friends'); a *man* friend; a *man* cousin; a *boy* cousin of mine.

2. My *women* friends (not 'lady friends'); a *woman* friend (not 'a lady friend'); a *woman* cousin; a *girl* cousin.

151. Woman's, women's. Either *woman's* or *women's* may be used as an adjective to indicate gender. The singular refers to women collectively or in the abstract; the plural refers to them as individuals:

1. *Woman's* (or *women's*) rights; *woman's* suffrage (see § 149); *women's* shoes (not 'ladies', § 150).

2. The *Woman's* Christian Temperance Union.

3. The Young *Women's* Christian Association.

152. Lady, madam, mesdames. The word *lady* should not be used in the nominative of address (§ 471) for *madam* except in the plural, and in oral address only (Oxford English Dictionary). In letters *Madam* is the proper formal salutation to a woman, whether she is married or single; the plural now used is *Mesdames* (§ 544, II, III):

Madam (not 'Lady'), here is a seat; *ladies*, here are seats.

153. Makeshifts for adjectives. Care should be taken not to use words indiscriminately as adjectives (§§ 54, 383, 416):

1. They came to a *desert* place. (This is correct.)
   A journey *in* (*into*, or *through*) *the desert*. (Not 'A desert journey'.)

2. Their plan *of colonization*. (Not 'Their colonizing plan' or 'Their colonization plan'.)

3. The south *of France*. (Not 'The French south'.)

4. Look at the page *on athletics*. (Not 'the athletic page'.) (Exercises XV, XVI, §§ 560, 561.)

THE VERB

154. Verb. A verb is a word used to say something about a person or thing:

   The boys *made* a boat.

155. Verb phrase. A phrase (§ 6) may be used as a verb; such a phrase is called a verb phrase:

   The boys *were making* a boat.

156. Transitive; intransitive. When a verb takes an object, it is said to be transitive or to be used transitively (expressing an action that *passes over* to an object; see *trans-*, § 405); when it does not take an object, it is said to be intransitive or to be used intransitively:

1. Father *built* our barn. (Transitive.)
2. The older children *walked*. (Intransitive.)

In English most verbs may be used either transitively or intransitively, often with different meanings:

1. We *rested* the horses. We *rested*.
2. I *broke* my arm. The ship *broke* from her moorings.
3. He *moved* his house. He *moved* to the country.
4. The farmers *grow* grass. The grass *grows*.

NOTE. A verb used intransitively generally has the active voice only (§ 211). A verb used transitively has both the active and the passive voice. When a transitive verb is changed from the active to the passive voice, the direct object becomes the subject or the retained object (§ 213).

157. Auxiliary. In forming verb phrases, a verb receives the help of one or more other verbs, called auxiliaries. The more usual auxiliaries are *am, is, are, was, were, have, has, had, do, does, did, can, could, may, might, must, shall, should, will, would*:

1. I *am* reading. The boys *were* singing.
2. Mother *has* finished her work.
3. What *did* you see at the museum?
4. He *could have* found his way to the post office.
5. We *shall* not go home until next week.
6. They *would have* liked to drive by the river.

158. Linking; predicate adjective, etc. An intransitive verb may be used in two ways. It may stand alone in the predicate, and is then called a complete verb; or it may be

followed by an adjective, noun, or pronoun to tell what the
subject is declared to be, and is then called a linking verb;
the adjective, noun, or pronoun completes the meaning of
the verb, but modifies the subject; an adjective so used is
called a predicate adjective (§ 113, N.); a noun or pronoun
so used is in the nominative case, and is called a predicate
nominative (§ 40):

1. The tree *grew*. (Complete verb.)
2. The tree grew *green*. (Predicate adjective.)
3. Henry became an *engineer*. (Predicate nominative.)
4. That was *he*. (Predicate nominative; § 63.)

The common linking verbs are *is* (*am, are, was, were, has
been, will be*, etc.; §§ 629, 630), *become, feel, get, grow, look,
prove, smell, taste, turn, sound*, and the like (see §§ 238, 239):

1. At last I *got* clear of all debts.
2. The timid boy *became* a great leader.
3. The supplies *proved* insufficient.
4. The tinkling of the bells *sounds* sweet.

159. *There is,* etc. A sentence often begins with *There is,
There were, There will be*, and so forth, in which *there* has lost
its force as an adverb. This order of words adds emphasis to
the subject (§ 370), but its excessive use becomes a mannerism.
Study the following sentences, observing the agreement of the
verb:

1. *There was* not a man to till the ground. — THE BIBLE.
2. *There was* a little city, and [there were, § 347] few men
within it. — THE BIBLE. (Observe the comma before *and*, which
separates the two clauses; § 466.)

There was a very cold winter, and a long frost. — DEFOE.

He took me into his box, where *there was* a fire, a desk, a
telegraphic instrument, and the little bell of which he had spoken.
— DICKENS.

3. *There were* giants in the earth in those days. — THE BIBLE.

SUBJUNCTIVE MOOD   63

4. *There were*, besides, the cottager and his wife. — DICKENS. (The group of two requires the plural *were*. Compare ' And *there was* Mary Magdalene, and the other Mary '; here are two distinct persons, named in two different clauses.)

There were together Simon Peter, and Thomas called Didymus, and Nathanael of Cana in Galilee. — THE BIBLE. (*Together* requires the plural *were*.)

5. *There are* notes and a vocabulary. (Say, rather, ' The editor has added notes and a vocabulary '; or, ' The book is provided with ', etc.)

6. *There are* one or two other matters to be considered. (*One or two = an indefinite small number of*. Compare *two or three* ; *three or four*.)

7. He is one of the best men *there are* in the world (§ 91 ; but the omission of *there are* will improve the sentence).

8. Once upon a time *there lived* in a dark forest a little old man and a little old woman. (Not ' there were '.)

160. Mood. To denote the manner in which its action or state is expressed, the verb has three different groups of forms, called moods : the indicative, the subjunctive, and the imperative. The indicative and the subjunctive are now often alike in form, but their uses are as distinct as ever.

161. Indicative mood. The essential use of the indicative mood is to denote that the action or state expressed by the verb is a fact, or is thought of as a fact (see §§ 334–345 also):

1. He *has* leisure. *Has* he leisure?
2. How warm it *is* today !
3. She *learned* where the poor woman *lived*.
4. If he *is sleeping*, he *is getting* better.

162. Subjunctive mood. The essential use of the subjunctive mood is to denote that the action or state expressed by the verb is not thought of as a fact, but as something possible or desired (see §§ 163, 334–346 also):

1. He *could* go if he *wished*. (Possibility.)
2. The boys insist that Miss Davis *lead* (or, *shall* lead) them. (The subjunctive mood *lead* (or, *shall* lead) shows that the action of leading is the will, or volition, of the boys.)
3. Somebody *run* for help. (Volition, command. *Somebody* is in the third person; for the second person, see § 164.)

    Everybody *rise* and *sing*. *Deny* it who can.

4. Heaven *bless* you for your kindness. (Wish.)

    So *help* me Heaven.

    I wish that she *were* here.

5. *Be* that as it may. (Possibility, concession.)
6. *Come* what may; *come* weal, *come* woe.
7. We *should speak* the truth. (Obligation, propriety.)
8. You *had* better go. (See § 244.)

NOTE. In verbs of blessing and cursing, when used in the subjunctive of wish, the subject (*God, Heaven*, or the like) is commonly omitted to avoid using a name of the Deity:

1. "*Bless* my life", said Mr. Pecksniff, looking up.
2. Well, *hang* it all, I've done more than old J., anyhow.

163. Subjunctive of softened statement. For the sake of politeness, modesty, or caution, the subjunctive is often used to soften a statement or question:

INDICATIVE	SUBJUNCTIVE
1. I *think* so.	I *should think* so.
2. *Can* she go tomorrow?	*Could* she go tomorrow?
3. It *is* your duty to go.	You *should* go.
4. He *wants* you to stay.	He *would like* to have you stay.
5. *Is* it your wish to go?	*Would* it *be* your wish to go?
6. This *seems* to be true.	This *would seem* to be true.

NOTE. *It should seem* (= *it would naturally seem*), an old and somewhat archaic form, is used in guarded statements: *It should seem that the ancients thought in this way.*

164. Imperative mood. The imperative mood is used, in the second person, to express a command, request, or entreaty; the subject (*thou, ye, you*), unless emphatic, is omitted:

1. (You) *Go* to your homes. (Compare § 162, 3.)

2. (You) *Tell* me a good story. *Do* not (you) *leave* me alone.

165. Infinitive. The infinitive is a verbal noun (§ 215), usually with the preposition *to* before it (§§ 282, 614, 616); when required by clearness or emphasis, *to* should be used before each infinitive in a series :

1. *To cross* was dangerous. (Subject of *was*.)

2. He wished *to cross* the river. (Object of *wished*.)

3. Suffer me first *to go* and *bury* my father. — THE BIBLE.

4. He instantly began *to collect* provisions, *to* throw up works, and *to make* preparations for sustaining a siege. — MACAULAY.

5. They instantly begin *to collect* provisions, *to* throw up works, and *to make*, etc. (If *to* were not repeated, the infinitives might be mistaken for indicatives, coördinate with *begin*.)

166. Participle. The participle is a verbal adjective (§ 230):

A *barking* dog ; an *educated* man.

167. Tense. The verb has different forms (called tenses) to indicate the time of its action or state (see §§ 623–653):

1. She *writes* a letter. (Present tense.)

2. She *wrote* a letter. (Past tense.)

3. She *will write* a letter. (Future tense.)

NOTE. Care should be taken not to use the past tense for the present perfect(§§ 623–652); an action or state begun in the past, but completed at the time of speaking, is expressed by the present perfect :

1. I never *saw* him when I lived in Boston. (The past tense *saw* is correct here, because the modifying clause *when I lived in Boston* refers to a period of time now past.)

2. I *have never seen* him. (Not 'I never saw him', because the word *never*, used without some other modifier, includes all my life at the time of speaking.)

3. They are now paid the highest wages they *have ever received*.

4. Many of those men (now dead) *never had* an education.

Many of these men (still living) *have never* had, etc. (Exercise XVII, § 562.)

168. Person ; number. The verb, like the personal pronoun, has person and number (§§ 58, 59). The verb agrees with its subject in person and number (§ 196) :

1. Thou *hast* done well.
2. The boy *sleeps*; the children *sleep*.

NOTE. When pronouns of different persons are joined, the verb is put in the first person instead of the second or the third, and in the second person instead of the third. See § 179.

169. Regular ; irregular. A verb is called regular or irregular according to the formation of its past tense. If the past tense is formed by adding *d* or *ed* to the present, the verb is regular; otherwise it is called irregular :

1. Live, *lived*; play, *played*; walk, *walked*. (Regular.)
2. Fall, *fell*; give, *gave*; lay, *laid*; lie, *lay*. (Irregular.)

170. Principal parts. By knowing certain forms of a verb, called its principal parts, we are able to give all its forms, or conjugate it. The principal parts of a verb are the present indicative (first person singular), the past indicative (first person singular), and the past participle. The past participle of a regular verb is like its past indicative (§ 169). The past participle of an irregular verb is irregular, and must be learned (§ 654). The following are examples of the principal parts :

PRESENT INDICATIVE	PAST INDICATIVE	PAST PARTICIPLE
live	lived	lived
call	called	called
break	broke	broken
go	went	gone

171. Conjugation. The conjugation of the regular verb *call* will be found in §§ 635–640; of the irregular verb *know*, in §§ 641–646.

172. Irregular verbs. The principal parts of irregular verbs are given in § 654. The easiest and best way to learn the parts is to read them aloud in simple sentences; put *have* or *had* before the past participle, and pay particular attention to the confusing and difficult forms; read aloud the following examples (see § 361):

I am	I was	I have been
I beat	I beat	I have beaten (not ' beat ')
I begin	I began (not ' begun ')	I have begun
I break	I broke	I have broken (not ' broke ')
I bring	I brought (not ' brung ')	I have brought (not ' brung ')
I catch	I caught	I have caught
I come	I came (not ' come ')	I have come (not ' came ')
I do	I did (not ' done ')	I have done (not ' did ')
I draw	I drew (not ' drawed ')	I have drawn (not ' drawed ')
I drink	I drank (not ' drunk ')	I have drunk (not ' drank ')
I eat	I ate (not ' eat ')	I have eaten (not ' eat ')
I forget	I forgot	I have forgotten (not ' forgot ')
I get	I got	I have got (not ' gotten ')
I give	I gave (not ' give ')	I have given
I go	I went	I have gone (not ' went ')
I know	I knew (not ' knowed ')	I have known (not ' knowed ')
I lay	I laid	I have laid
I lie	I lay (not ' laid ')	I have lain (not ' laid ')
I ride	I rode	I have ridden (not ' rode ')
I ring	I rang (not ' rung ')	I have rung
I run	I ran (not ' run ')	I have run (not ' ran ')
I see	I saw (not ' seen ')	I have seen
I set	I set	I have set
I shake	I shook	I have shaken (not ' shook ')
I sing	I sang (not ' sung ')	I have sung (not ' sang ')
I sit	I sat (not ' set ')	I have sat
I speak	I spoke	I have spoken
I swim	I swam (not ' swum ')	I have swum (not ' swam ')
I take	I took	I have taken (not ' took ')
I throw	I threw (not ' throwed ')	I have thrown (not ' throwed ')

173. ***Lay, lie; set, sit.*** Distinguish *lay* from *lie*, and *set* from *sit* (see *sit*, § 417):

1. I lie down, I am lying down, I lay down, I was lying down, I had lain down, I had been lying down; I lay (am laying) the clothes away, I laid (was laying) the clothes away, I had laid (had been laying) the clothes away.

2. I sit (am sitting), I sat (was sitting), I had sat (had been sitting); I set (am setting) the clock, I set (had set, had been setting) the clock, she set the hen, the stars set (are setting, were setting; this is a reflexive use of *set*, the object, *themselves*, being omitted); the hen sits (not 'sets'), a sitting hen, the coat sits well, this food does not sit well on the stomach.

174. Emphatic phrases with *do*. In the present and the past tense the verb *do* is used with the infinitive (without *to*) to make emphatic verb phrases:

1. I do see.	We do see.	I did see.	We did see.
2. Thou dost see.	You do see.	Thou didst see.	You did see.
3. He does see.	They do see.	He did see.	They did see.

In negative and interrogative sentences, and often in the Bible and in poetry, *do* is not emphatic (in modern poetry unemphatic *do* is avoided by good writers):

1. Tom *does* not play. *Does* Mary play?
2. I *did* mourn as a dove. — THE BIBLE.

NOTE. *Do* is often used to avoid the repetition of another verb; but, especially in formal writing, it is better to repeat the verb:

1. She sings better than he *does* (= than he *sings*).
2. He tells the story more dramatically than I *told* it.

175. Progressive verb phrases. Some verb phrases, called progressive, denote an action or state not simply as occurring, but as continuing, and are used in picturing scenes and events. They are formed by using the auxiliary verb *be* with the present participle (the simple form of a verb with the ending *ing*; § 230):

1. She *was sitting* before the fire and *dreaming* dreams.

2. They *will be wondering* what has become of us. (Exercise XVIII, § 563.)

176. Direct and indirect quotation. When a person's language or thought is repeated without change, the repetition is called a direct quotation; when it is expressed in a *that*-clause, depending on a verb of saying, thinking, knowing, perceiving, or the like, it is called an indirect quotation:

1. I have a position.
2. Anna says, "I have a position." (Direct quotation.)
3. Anna says *that she has a position.* (Indirect quotation.)
4. It is said *that Anna has a position.* (Indirect quotation.)

NOTE 1. The *that* introducing a clause in indirect quotation may be omitted without affecting the construction; it is by origin the demonstrative pronoun (§§ 70, 71), with a clause in apposition (§ 47, N.): 'Anna says *that* she has a position' = 'Anna says *that*: she has a position'. *That* is called a subordinating conjunction (§ 303, 9).

NOTE 2. In the fourth example the personal subject (*Anna*) may be made the subject of the verb of saying: '*Anna* is said to have a position'. This is called the personal construction in indirect quotation.

177. Sequence of tenses. When the principal verb (the verb of saying, etc.) is in the past or the past perfect tense, the present tense in a direct quotation or direct question (§ 77) is changed to the past in the indirect, and the present perfect is changed to the past perfect; except that if the quotation expresses a general truth, the tense is not changed:

1. "He sings." They *said* that he *sang.*
   "Fire burns." They *said* that fire *burns.* (General truth.)
2. "I can use more books than I own." She *said* that she *could* use more books than she *owned.*
3. When is he coming?
   If I *know* when he *is* coming, I will meet him.
   If I *knew* when he *was* coming, I would meet him.
4. You act as if you *thought* it *was* cold.

NOTE. In 3 and 4 *was* does not agree in tense with *knew* and *thought*; for *knew* and *thought* are in the past subjunctive, and refer to present time (§§ 335, 346). This seeming agreement is called attraction of tense. It occurs frequently.

178. Shall, will, of simple futurity. In the conjugation of the future and the future perfect the verbs *shall* and *will* are used (without emphasis) merely as auxiliaries, to denote that the action or state expressed by the verb will take place in future time. Read aloud the future and the future perfect in §§ 623, 629, 635, 641, 647, but do not ordinarily emphasize *shall* or *will*.

To express simple futurity, therefore, in a declarative sentence, use *shall* in the first person (*I, we*), and *will* in the second and third; in an interrogative sentence use *shall* in the first and second persons (*I, we, thou, you*), and *will* in the third. Read aloud and learn by heart the following forms, but do not ordinarily emphasize *shall* or *will*:

DECLARATIVE	INTERROGATIVE WITH ANSWER
1. I *shall* be glad.	*Shall* I be glad? Yes, you *will*.
2. Thou *wilt* be glad.	*Shalt* thou be glad? Yes, I *shall*.
3. He *will* be glad.	*Will* he be glad? Yes, he *will*.
1. We *shall* be glad.	*Shall* we be glad? Yes, you *will*.
2. You *will* be glad.	*Shall* you be glad? Yes, I (we) *shall*.
3. They *will* be glad.	*Will* they be glad? Yes, they *will*.

NOTE. *I'll* and *we'll* are contractions of *I will* and *we will* (§ 180), and are not to be used for *I shall* and *we shall*; see *isn't*, § 417.

179. Person of verb. When pronouns of different persons are joined (§ 58, N.), the verb is put in the first person instead of the second or the third, and in the second person instead of the third; that is, *you* (or *he*) + *I* = *we*, and *you* + *he* = *you*; this rule is important in determining the use of *shall, will, should,* and *would* (§§ 178, 180, 181, 187–195):

1. *You* (or *He*) and *I shall* be glad to be in the country; *shall you* (or *he*) and *I* be able to catch the train?

2. *You* and *he* are glad; *shall you* and *he* be glad?

Read aloud the following sentences (see § 361):

1. I *shall* walk to town. *Shall* you walk, or drive? ('I *will* walk to town' expresses a promise or determination, §§ 180, 191; 'I *will* be drowned' means 'I wish to be drowned', § 191.)

2. Tomorrow *will* be Saturday. I *shan't* be sorry. *Shall* you?

3. I'm afraid *you'll* miss your train. *Shan't* you?

4. *Will* he be happy there? No, he *will* not.

5. *Shall* we be late? No, we *shall* be early.

6. *Shan't* you and he be at home this evening? No, we *shan't*.

7. By Friday you (or, he) and I *shall* have seen everything.

8. *Shall* you be happy there? Yes, I *shall*.

Is it a place where you *will* be happy? (Here *will* is not changed to 'shall', because it is in a subordinate clause and is not affected by the question. The answer, of course, has *shall*: 'Yes, it is a place where I *shall* be very happy'. See § 187, 8, and § 195, 15.)

180. Shall, will, of obligation, etc. The primary meaning of *shall* is to owe or be under obligation (denoting what is bound to happen); the primary meaning of *will* is willingness (denoting what is willed or desired). To express such obligation and willingness (as seen in prophecy, command, intention, desire, promise, and the like) in declarative sentences, use *will* in the first person, and *shall* in the second and third; in interrogative sentences use *will* in the first and second persons, and *shall* in the third:

DECLARATIVE	INTERROGATIVE WITH ANSWER
1. I *will* go.	**1.** *Will* I go? Of course I *will*.
2. Thou *shalt* go.	**2.** *Wilt* thou go? Yes, I *will*.
3. He *shall* go.	**3.** *Shall* he go? Yes, he *shall*.
1. We *will* go.	**1.** *Will* we go? Of course we *will*.
2. You *shall* go.	**2.** *Will* you go? Yes, I (we) *will*.
3. They *shall* go.	**3.** *Shall* they go? Yes, they *shall*.

NOTE. In the interrogative form, in the first person, *will* is improper unless the question merely repeats in substance a question addressed to the speaker (the repetition may be made for the sake of emphasis or clearness): (question) "*Will* you go?" (answer) "*Will* I go? Indeed I *will*."

Read aloud the following sentences (see § 361):

1. The sun *shall* be darkened. (Prophecy.)
2. Thou *shalt* love thy neighbor as thyself. (Command.)
3. You *shall* meet him soon. (Promise.)
4. He *shall* go in spite of the storm. (Intention.)
5. He intends that you *shall* see him. (Intention.)
6. I *will* have you be a gentleman. (Desire.)
7. Tomorrow *shall* be our holiday in the country.
8. Well, you *shan't* say I do things by halves.
9. *Will* you and he meet me there? We *will* wait near the door.
10. *Will* you be kind enough to direct me to his house?
11. He *shall* go with us. I *will* see to that.
12. Surely goodness and mercy *shall* follow me all the days of my life: and I *will* dwell in the house of the Lord for ever. — PSALMS. (King James Bible, 1611; Revised Version, 1881.) (Here *shall* denotes prophecy or promise; *will* denotes determination. The American Standard Version changes *will* to *shall*, which changes the determination to simple futurity; this may or may not be closer to the meaning of the original Hebrew.) (Exercise XIX, *a*, § 564.)

181. *Shall* or *will*. In the following sentences either *shall* or *will* is correct, according to the sense intended (whether simple futurity or willingness, etc.); explain the meanings:

1. You *shall* (*will*) never get such a secret from me.
2. She *shall* (*will*) have a two weeks' vacation.
3. *Shan't* (*Won't*) you be at your office tomorrow?
4. Where *shall* (*will*) he entertain his friends?
5. I *shall* (*will*) be in town next Friday.
6. *Shall* (*Will*) you write to him? *Shall* (*Will*) you meet him?
7. We *shan't* (*won't*) see him. He *shall* (*will*) hear from us. (Exercise XX, *a*, § 565.)

182. *Will* in commands. By courtesy *will* is commonly used in commands and in requests :

    1. You *will* proceed at once to headquarters.
    2. The audience *will* remain seated.

183. Defective verbs, *can*, etc. A defective verb lacks one or more of the usual forms of conjugation. The defective auxiliary verbs *can*, *could*, *may*, *might*, *must*, *ought*, *should*, and *would* are used in verb phrases denoting ability, permission, necessity, or the like (the subjunctive has become like the indicative in form, § 653 ; all these verbs except *ought* take the infinitive without *to*) :

    1. I *must* (*can*, *could*, *may*, *might*, *ought to*, *should*, or *would*) go.
    2. Thou *must* (*canst*, *couldest* or *couldst*, *mayest*, etc.) go.
    3. He *must* (*can*, *could*, *may*, *might*, etc.) go.
    4. We (You, They) *must* (*can*, *could*, *may*, *might*, etc.) go.
    5. I *must* (*can*, *could*, *may*, *might*, etc.) have gone.
    6. Thou *must* (*canst*, *couldest* or *couldst*, etc.) have gone.

184. *Can*, *could*; *may*, *might*. *Can* and *could* denote ability ; *cannot* is the usual form of *can* with the negative ; when the *not* is emphatic, as in Lincoln's address at Gettysburg, the words are separated, *can not* ; *may* and *might* denote permission or possibility :

    1. Brown *can not* (or *could not*) lift three hundred pounds.
    2. This story *may* (or *might*) have been told.
    3. *May* (or *Might*) she go with you? Yes, she *may* (or *might*).
    4. *Mayn't* we go? You *may* go soon, but you *mayn't* go now.
    5. It *can't* be true. Such a thing *can't* be done.

185. *Must*. *Must* denotes necessity or obligation. The past tense is now regularly expressed by *must* with the perfect infinitive (§ 220), or by *was obliged to* or *had to* with the present infinitive ; but in indirect quotation (§ 177), and in expressions like the fifth example, *must* is used as a past tense :

1. He *must* go home today ; he *must have gone* yesterday.
2. He was *obliged* (or, He *had*) *to go* yesterday.
3. He *said* yesterday that he *must* go home.
4. Those *were* the things that (he said) he *must* do.
5. We were no sooner seated than A—— *must* come in.

186. Ought. *Ought* is used like *should* (§ 190) to denote duty. The past tense is now regularly expressed by *ought* with the perfect infinitive (§ 220), except in indirect quotation (§ 177):

1. He *ought to* (or *should*) go today ; he *ought to* (or *should*) *have gone* yesterday (§ 220).
2. He said yesterday that he *ought* to go. (Not ' *should* go ', which would be ambiguous ; § 195.)
3. *Ought* we not to (or *Should we not*) take off our hats?
4. Our train *ought to* (or *should*) be here now.

NOTE. Do not say ' had ought '. See *ought*, § 417.

187. Should, would, of simple futurity. *Should* and *would* are often used like *shall* and *will* to denote simple futurity (§ 178); read aloud and learn by heart the following forms, but do not ordinarily emphasize *should* or *would*:

DECLARATIVE	INTERROGATIVE WITH ANSWER
1. I *should* like it.	*Should* I like it? Yes, you *would*.
2. Thou *wouldst* like it.	*Shouldst* thou like it? Yes, I *should*.
3. He *would* like it.	*Would* he like it? Yes, he *would*.
1. We *should* like it.	*Should* we like it? Yes, you *would*.
2. You *would* like it.	*Should* you like it? Yes, I (we) *should*.
3. They *would* like it.	*Would* they like it? Yes, they *would*.

Read aloud the following sentences (see § 361):

1. I *should* be glad to see him. *Shouldn't* you?
2. *Should* you be sorry to go? I think you *would*.
3. You and I *should* be happy there, *shouldn't* we?
4. *Should* I find you in if I called tomorrow?

5. I *shouldn't* be surprised if they did not come.

6. *Should* you miss him if you stayed longer?

7. Where *should* you be at ten o'clock if I returned?

8. Is it a book that you *would* like to own? (Here *would* is not changed to ' should ', because it is in a subordinate clause and is not affected by the question. The answer, of course, has *should*: ' Yes, it is a book that I *should* like very much to own '. See § 179, 8, and § 195, 15.)

188. *Should like, should have liked.* The difference between such forms as ' I should like to have gone ' and ' I should have liked to go ' is that the former expresses a choice still present in the mind of the speaker, whereas the latter denotes that the choice once present has ceased to exist. Do not say ' I should have liked to have gone ' or ' He would not have liked to have gone ' (see § 220).

189. *Should, would,* of obligation, etc. *Should* and *would* are often used like *shall* and *will* in § 180, to denote possible obligation and willingness. To express such possible obligation and willingness in declarative sentences, use *would* in the first person, and *should* in the second and third; in interrogative sentences use *would* in the first and second persons, and *should* in the third:

DECLARATIVE	INTERROGATIVE WITH ANSWER
1. I *would* go.	*Would* I go? Yes, I *would*.
2. Thou *shouldst* go.	*Wouldst* thou go? Yes, I *would*.
3. He *should* go.	*Should* he go? Yes, he *should*.
1. We *would* go.	*Would* we go? Yes, we *would*.
2. You *should* go.	*Would* you go? Yes, I (we) *would*.
3. They *should* go.	*Should* they go? Yes, they *should*.

NOTE. The interrogative form in the first person (*Would* I go? *Would* we go?) is not proper except in a repeated question, as stated in § 180, N.

Read aloud the following sentences (see § 361):

1. If he were my boy, he *should* have an education.
2. *Would* you be kind enough to assist him? Yes, I *would*.
3. If I were you, they *should* have the opportunity.
4. You *should* have the books at once if I could get them.
5. He intended that it *should* be a garden.
   He changed his plans, that there *should* be no delay.
6. They *should* never be in want if I could help them.
7. I *would* advise you to wait. (*Would* shows friendly interest.)
   I *should* (§ 187) advise you to wait. (*Should* is simply future.)
8. Master, we *would* that thou *shouldest* do for us whatsoever we *shall* desire. — THE BIBLE. (Exercise XIX, *b*, § 564; XX, *b*, § 565; XXI, § 566.)

190. Shall, should, of duty, etc. In questions of duty or propriety *shall* and *should* (with emphasis) are used in the first person as well as in the second and the third; this use should be distinguished from that of simple futurity (§§ 178, 187):

1. What *shall* I do to inherit eternal life? Thou *shalt* love the Lord thy God, etc. (Duty; compare a question and answer of simple futurity, in which *shall* has no emphasis: How *shall* I recognize him? You *will* know him by his dress.)
2. *Should* we not take off our hats? (Propriety.)
3. *Should* you (he) not have helped in this work? (Duty.)
4. *Shall* I go home now, sir? (Not 'Will'; § 180, N.)
5. *Shouldn't* they have gone to school yesterday?

191. Will, would, of determination, etc. *Will* or *would* is used in all three persons to denote determination (with emphasis) or customary action (sometimes with emphasis, as in Ex. 3):

1. I (You, He) *will* go in spite of everything. (Determination.)
2. I (You, He) *would* sit and read for hours. (Customary action.)
3. Cats *will* steal. (Customary action.)
4. They *will* eat almost to bursting.

192. *Shall*, etc., with *glad*, etc. When *shall, should, will*, and *would* are used to express simple futurity (§§ 178, 187), they may be followed by *like, prefer, be inclined, be glad, be sorry*, and so on (whether adjectives, verbs, or adverbs), to denote willingness (but see § 193):

1. I *shall* be *willing* to go. He and I *shall* be *glad* to go. I *shall* go *gladly*. I *should like* to go. ('I would like to go' is incorrect; it means 'I should like to like to go', a repetition similar to 'audible to the ear'. So, also, 'I will be glad to go' is incorrect; § 413.)

2. *Shall* you and he be *glad* to go? *Should* you go *gladly*? *Should* you *prefer* to go? ('Would you prefer to go?' is incorrect; it means 'Should you like to like to go?' So, also, 'Will you be glad to go?' is incorrect.)

3. She *will* be *eager* to go. She *would* go *eagerly*.

4. *Shall* you be *disappointed* if I do not go? I *shall* indeed.

5. *Shall* you be *happy* there? Yes, I *shall*.

6. We *should prefer* this, and she *would prefer* it too.

193. *Will, would*, with *gladly*, etc. *Will* and *would*, when used to express willingness, promise, and the like (not simple futurity, as in § 192), may not be followed by adjectives or verbs of liking and so on (§ 192), but by adverbs only, to show the degree of willingness (but do not say *will . . . willingly*; § 413):

1. I *shall* (not 'will') be *glad* to go. I *will* go most *gladly*.

2. *Shall* you be *willing* to go? *Will* you go *gladly*?

3. If I (you, he) *should* be *willing* to go; if I (you, he) *would* go *gladly*; I *would sooner* starve (see § 244 and N.).

194. *Shall*, etc., in condition. In a conditional clause (introduced by *if, whoever*, etc., §§ 333, 342) *shall* or *should* is used in all three persons to denote simple futurity (§§ 178, 187); and *will* or *would* to denote willingness (§§ 180, 189):

1. If I (you, he) *shall* fail, the curse may come. See §§ 338, 339.
   Even if I (you, he) *should* help them, they might not succeed.
   Whoever *shall* try may succeed.
   Wherever I (you, he) *should* go, they could follow.
   She intended to wait until I (you, he) *should* return.
2. If I (you, he) *will* only try, nothing is impossible.
   If I (you, he) *would* only help her, she might succeed.
   Whoever *will* try may succeed.

195. Shall, etc., in indirect quotation, etc. In indirect
quotation or indirect question (§§ 176, 177, 77), when the
verb of saying or asking is in the past or the past perfect
tense, *shall* in a direct quotation is changed to the past *should*
in the indirect quotation, and *will* is changed to the past *would*
(*shall* is not changed to *will*, nor *should* to *would*):

DIRECT QUOTATION	INDIRECT QUOTATION
1. " I *shall* go."	I say that I *shall* go.
	I said that I *should* go.
	You say that you *shall* go?
	John said that he (John) *should* go.
2. " Will you go? "	I ask whether you *will* go.
	I asked whether you *would* go.
3. " He shall go."	We say that he *shall* go.
	They said that he *should* go.

This rule holds good for all uses of *shall*, *should*, *will*, and
would, except that when, in expressions denoting simple futurity, the second or the third person in the direct form becomes
the first person in the indirect form, *will* is changed to *shall*,
and *would* to *should* (since the first person requires *shall* or
should to denote simple futurity):

1. " I (John) *shall* fall."	I (John) say that I *shall* fall.
	I said that I *should* fall.
	You (John) said that you *should* fall.
	He (John) said that he *should* fall.

2. " You (John) *will* fall."   She says that you (John) *will* fall.

  She said that I (John) *should* (not ' would ') fall.

3. " He (John) *will* fall."   She says that he (John) *will* fall.

  She said that I (John) *should* (not ' would ') fall.

4. " *Will* he (John) fall? "   She asks me if he (John) *will* fall.

  She asked me if you (John) *would* fall.

  She asked you if I (John) *should* (not ' would ') fall.

NOTE. When an indirect quotation or an indirect question depends on a verb in past time, we cannot always tell whether the direct form had *shall* or *should*, *will* or *would* :

1. He *said* that he *would* go. (Direct, ' I *will* go ' or ' I *would* go '.)

2. They *asked* if he *would* be happy there. (Direct, ' *Will* he be happy there ? ' or ' *Would* he be happy there ? ')

Read aloud each of the following sentences (§ 361); then turn the subordinate clause into the direct form, and read that aloud (the proper auxiliary of the direct form is given in parentheses) :

1. Polly said that she *should* go home to-morrow. (I *shall*.)

  He said that he *should* arrive early, and *would* wait for us. (I *shall . . . will*.)

2. He promised that he *would* walk with us. (I *will*.)

3. I asked you if you *should* like to travel with us. (*Should* you?) I asked her if you (John) *would* like to travel. (*Would* John?)

4. He feared that we *should* get lost. (They *will*; or, You *will*.) He feared that he *should* get lost. (I *shall*.)

5. She often told him that she *should* be glad to help him. (I *shall* or *should*.)

6. I promised him that he *should* not regret what he had done. (You *shall*.)

7. They declared that I (Dick) *should* be happy anywhere. (Dick *will* or *would*.)

8. They asked me why I (John) *should* like to go to Europe. (Why *should* you?)

They asked her why I (John) *should* like to go to Europe. (Why *would* John?)

Give some reasons why you *should* like to go to Europe. (Why *should* you?)

9. They asked me when I *would* call for the letters. (When *will* you?)

10. They told him that I (Jane) *should* have it. (She *shall*.)

11. Let her say what *shall* be done with it. (What *shall*?)

They told her that she *should* have the reward. (You *shall*.)

12. It is a subject which we *shall* be justified in omitting.

They considered (that) it (was) a subject which they *should* be justified in omitting. (We *shall*.)

13. They are going where they *will* have to build houses.

He knew that they (not including himself; § 179) were going ... *would* have ... (They *will*.)

He knew that they (including himself; § 179) were going ... *should* have ... (We *shall*.)

14. If you had had a brother like me, do you think you *should* have loved him as well as Tom? — GEORGE ELIOT. (*Should* you?)

15. Is it a place where you think you *shall* be happy? (Here *shall* is in indirect quotation after *think*, and is not affected by the question. If *you think* is omitted, *shall* must be changed to *will*, as in § 179, 8, and § 187, 8.) (Exercise XXII, § 567.)

196. Agreement of verb.

A verb agrees with its subject in person and number (§ 168):

1. This *field was* yellow with wheat.
    These *fields were* yellow with wheat.
2. Hawthorne's *romances are* interesting.
    Hawthorne's " Twice-told Tales " *is* interesting. (A title is singular, and takes a singular verb.)
3. What *avail* all your *tears*? Of what use *are* such *things*?
4. To these four questions *was* added a *fifth*.
5. *Has either* of you read this book? (Not ' Have '.)

6. Why *doesn't one* of you try it? (Not ' don't '.)

7. *You were* not there at the time. (Not ' was '.)

8. What kind of trees *are these*? (*These* is the subject.)

197. Verb with collective noun. A collective noun (§ 36) in the singular number is grammatically singular, and regularly takes a singular verb ; but if the persons or things denoted by the noun are thought of as separate individuals, the verb is made plural (except that a collective noun should not be singular and plural in the same sentence ; see Ex. 8) :

1. *Congress is* in session.

2. The *committee adheres* to *its* decision.

3. The *family is* at home. The *family are not all* at home (the negative with *all* makes two groups of the family).

4. The *public is* alive to *its* wants. The *public are* admitted.

5. Every *people has* its rights. The *people wish* to be free.

6. The *majority rules*. The *majority* of them *are* happy.

7. The *crowd were* pushing, quarreling, joking. — DICKENS.

8. The *jury is* now agreed ; but an hour ago *it was* (do not shift to ' they were ') not agreed.

9. A *corporation* which *declares* that *its* liabilities, etc.

10. A *series* of experiments *was* made.

11. What *sort* (or *kind*) of tales *were* told? (§ 72.)

12. The better *sort do* not ask for money.

198. Verb with noun of weight, etc. A plural noun denoting weight or measure in a collective sense takes a singular verb :

1. *Ten pounds* of flour *is* sufficient. (An amount ; but, ' Ten bags of flour now *cost* forty dollars '.)

2. *Fifty dollars was* collected (or *were*, if collected at different times ; see Ex. 5). (But, ' The fifty dollars *are* new bills '.)

   Sixty cents of it *was* in pennies. (An amount.)

3. *Three quarters* of the money *was* wasted. (An amount.)

4. *Five per cent* of the proceeds *was* profit. (An amount.)

5. Ten *inches* of rain *have* fallen during the month. See Ex. 2.

199. Verb with numeral. In the reading and writing of numbers care should be taken not to confuse the concrete with the abstract (§ 123). Concrete numbers require a verb in the singular or the plural according as the nouns are singular or plural (for nouns of weight and measure, see § 198). Abstract numbers are treated as collective singulars; if not connected by *and* (§ 200), they take a singular verb (§197; see § 207 also):

1. One *pencil* plus three pencils *is* four pencils. (Concrete.)
   Four *pencils* minus one pencil *are* three pencils.
   Three times three *pencils are* nine pencils. (*Three times* is used adverbially, meaning ' taken three times '.)
   How many *are* seven *pencils* less three pencils?
   Three *pencils are* one third of nine pencils; one third of nine pencils *are* three pencils.
2. *Two* plus two *is* (or *equals*) four. (Abstract; but see 3, below.)
   Three from seven *leaves* four.
   Once *one is* one. Twice *three is* six.
   Eight divided by four *is* two.
   Two *thirds* of nine *is* six.
   Fifteen is one fifth of seventy-five.
3. The principle that two *and* two *are* four. — DICKENS.
   How much *are* three *and* five? (The subject is ' three *and* five'.)

200. Verb with compound subject; *each*, etc. A compound subject with *and* (sometimes omitted) takes a plural verb; but if the parts of the subject refer to one person or thing, or express one idea, or are modified by such words as *each*, *every*, *many a*, *no*, and *such a*, the verb is singular (see §§ 120, 142, 159):

1. The secretary and the treasurer *were* absent.
   The secretary and treasurer *was* absent. (One person.)
2. To read and to write *are* two different things.
   To read, to write, to cipher, *are* fundamental.

3. Bread and milk *is* a feast. (One dish.)
   A horse and carriage *was* approaching.
   There *was* such pressing and crowding to get passes. — DEFOE.
4. *Every* cat and dog of the neighborhood *was* there.
   Every day and *every* hour *has* its opportunity.
5. The wear and tear of life *was* too much for her.
   To see, to understand, and to remember *is* to know.
6. *Many a* soldier and sailor *was* lost in that war.
   No money and *no* employment *was* awaiting him.

201. Verb with *and not*, *not*, etc. When there are two subjects, and one of them is introduced by *and not*, *not*, *not only*, *as well as*, *no more than*, or the like, the verb agrees with the other subject; words joined to a subject by *with*, *along with*, *together with*, *in addition to*, *accompanied by*, and so forth, do not change the number of the verb:

1. *Brains*, and not brawn, *count* most.
2. Not brawn, but *brains count* most.
3. *Brawn*, not brains, *counts* most.
4. Not only the saddles, but the *horse was* stolen.
5. The *grain*, as well as the buildings, *was* lost.
6. The *farm*, with all its belongings, *was* sold.

202. Verb with nearest subject; *or*, *nor*. The verb frequently agrees with its nearest subject, especially when *or* or *nor* is used; but clumsiness should be avoided:

1. No money and no *friends were* awaiting me.
2. One or more *pictures were* on the floor.
3. There *was* no *lack* of men or of money. (Not ' Neither men nor money *was* lacking '.)
4. Mary or Jane *has* lost *her* book. (Not ' their book '.)
5. He *is* to go, or I *am*. (Not ' He or I am to go '.)
6. *Is* he to go, or *am* I ? (Not ' Is he or I to go ? ')
7. Neither of us *has* time. (Not ' Neither she nor I **have time** '.)

8. If this interests you or your father. (Not 'If you or your father is interested in this'.)

9. My brother or sister will lend a horse. (Not 'their horse', which would be incorrect; 'his horse' or 'her horse' would be misleading. 'His or her' is usually better avoided; similarly, 'his' in such sentences as 'Neither my brother nor my sister knew *his* own mind'; say 'My brother and sister did not know their own mind' or 'Neither of them knew his own mind'.)

203. Verb separated from subject. When a noun or a pronoun stands between a subject and its verb, the verb is often made to agree (erroneously) with the nearer word:

1. *Neither* of the boys *was* (not 'were') to blame.
2. Every *one* of them *deserves* (not 'deserve') credit.
3. Two dollars' *worth* of nuts *is* (not 'are') sufficient.
4. The new *series* of experiments *was* (not 'were') begun.
5. A *court* of fifty-six judges *was* (not 'were') appointed.
6. The *amount* of the day's sales *is* (not 'are') not large.
7. A large *supply* of provisions *was* (not 'were') taken on board.
8. A *company* of soldiers *was* posted at the entrance. (See § 197.)

204. Verb with relative pronoun. Since a relative pronoun has the same form for both singular and plural (§ 83), its number is determined by its antecedent; a verb agreeing with a relative pronoun is often put in the wrong number by being made to agree with the wrong antecedent:

1. He is one of the best *men that have* (not 'has') ever lived. (The antecedent is *men*, not 'one'.)
2. This is the only *one* of my children *that likes* (not 'like') to read. (The antecedent is *one*, not 'children'.)
3. This is the worst mistake of *all that were* (not 'was') made.

205. Verb with *athletics*, etc. The following are examples of the uses of the forms *athletics*, *contents*, and similar subjects:

1. *Athletics* (= *athletic training*) *has* helped him greatly.
   The *athletics* (= *sports*) of the school *are* excellent.
2. The *contents* of the bottle (book, house, etc.) *were* known.
3. The *enemy were* repulsed. (Now regularly plural, unless personified as a force: ' They strike at the enemy in *his* weakest spot'; § 22.)
4. The *ethics* of dining *is* a neglected branch of morals. (Now usually singular.)
5. The *Links* themselves for a walk *are* now most enjoyable. (Regularly and properly plural.)
6. *Niagara Falls* (the falls) *are* in North America.
   Niagara Falls (the city) *is* a manufacturing center.
7. Where *are* his *headquarters*? (Now regularly plural.)
8. *Mathematics* (*physics*, etc., § 32) *is* my hardest study.
9. Every *means was* tried.
   Other *means were* tried. His *means* (= *wealth*) *were* large.
10. *Measles has* broken out in school.
11. The *news was* good. (Now regularly singular.)
12. What 's the *odds* (= *difference*) to you? (Colloquial; § 380.)
    The *odds* (= the *chances*) *are* a hundred to one against you.
13. The *oat is* a hardy cereal plant. The *oats are* ripe.
14. We took *every pains*. No *pains were* spared. (A singular verb with *pains* is now rare. The usual expression is *take pains*.)
15. What *percentage* (or *proportion*) of them *are* foreigners? A large *percentage* of them *are* foreigners. *Fifty* per cent of them *are* foreigners. (Do not say ' what per cent ' for *what percentage*; *what* is an interrogative adjective, modifying the noun *percentage*; *per cent* is not a noun, but an adjective phrase, and must modify a noun; *fifty per cent* is correct, because *fifty* is a cardinal number used as a noun; *fifty per cent* means *fifty in a hundred*. See *per cent*, § 417.)
    What *percentage* (not ' per cent ') of it *is* wasted? A very small *percentage* of it *is* wasted. *Three* per cent of it *is* wasted.
16. *Politics* (collectively) *is* a science and an art.
    Oh, what *are* all your *politics* (= *political affairs*)?
17. The *Stars and Stripes was* floating above us.
18. *Statistics is* a most important science.
    There *are* as yet no *statistics* of the wasted material.

19. A *summons was* issued; *summonses were* issued.

20. Their *tactics* by sea *was* a sort of land engagement on deck (tactics as an art). New *tactics were* employed in this battle (tactics as put in practice).

21. Further *tidings were* anxiously awaited.

22. The old landmarks of politics within the *United States themselves* seemed, meanwhile, submerged. (Here the individual states are meant.)

The *United States* hereby *disclaims*, etc. (Here the states are thought of as a unit.)

23. His *wages were* neither high nor low.

24. His *whereabouts is* unknown.

206. Verb with *number*. The word *number* takes a singular or a plural verb according to the sense:

1. *A number* of accidents (= *some* accidents) *occur* now.

2. *A large number* of accidents (= *many* accidents) *occur* now.

3. *The number* (= *the total*) of accidents *is* not large.

4. *The largest number* (= *the maximum*) of accidents occurring (or *that occur*) in the summer *is* inconsiderable.

5. *The largest number* of accidents (= *most* accidents) *occur* (not ' occurs ') in the summer.

207. Verb with *all, half*, etc. The pronoun *all* (§§ 119, 143) and the nouns *half* (§ 147), two *thirds* (and similarly all fractions, § 199), *part, remainder*, and *rest* are singular or plural according to the sense (for *none*, see § 102; for *pair*, § 417):

1. *Half* of this *is* blue; *half* of these *are* blue.

2. Two *thirds* of the wheat *was* bad. Two *thirds* of them *were* lost.

3. The *rest* of the day *was* fair; the *rest* of us *were* tired. (Exercise XXIII, § 568.)

208. Voice. The change of form in verbs which indicates whether the subject acts or is acted on is called voice. There are two voices, the active and the passive. The active voice represents the subject as acting; the passive voice represents the subject as being acted on. As a rule, the active voice is more effective, and hence more desirable, than the passive; do not needlessly mix the two voices (§ 355, *B*, 2):

1. The blacksmith *strikes* the anvil. (Active.)

2. The anvil *is struck* by the blacksmith. (Passive.)

3. We *heard* the tinkling of bells. (Rather than 'The tinkling of bells *was heard*'.)

4. At last he *saw* a light, and *heard* voices. (Not 'and voices were heard'.)

NOTE. The passive voice is useful in avoiding the pronoun *I* and other personal subjects. For example, see the last paragraph of § 54; the passive voice fixes the attention on the faults rather than on the author of them.

209. Passive voice. The passive voice of a verb is formed by the addition of its past participle to the desired form of the verb *be* (§§ 629–634, 647–652):

PRESENT INDICATIVE	PRESENT SUBJUNCTIVE
1. I *am advised*.	If I *be advised*.
2. Thou *art advised*.	If thou *be advised*.
3. He *is advised*.	If he *be advised*.

The passive voice of progressive verb phrases (§ 175) is used in the present and the past tense; these tenses are formed by the addition of *being* and the past participle (§ 170) to the desired forms of the verb *be*:

The water *is being heated*; the town *was being taken*.

210. Adverb or preposition with verb. Some adverbs and prepositions are alike in form, but they may be distinguished by their use:

1. The horse soon got *up*. (Adverb.)

2. They got *up* an entertainment. (Adverb.)

3. We finally got *up* the hill. (Preposition.)

211. Preposition and voice. An intransitive verb is generally used in the active voice only; but when it is followed by a preposition, it may frequently be used in the passive voice. The object of the preposition becomes the subject of the verb, and the preposition becomes an adverb:

1. We *sent for* him; he *was sent for*.
2. She *laughed at* me; I *was laughed at*.

NOTE. In such expressions as 'I sent the boy *for* the doctor', 'The boy was sent *for* the doctor', the word *for* is clearly a preposition; in 'I sent *for* the doctor', 'The doctor was sent *for*', the word *for* is so closely attached to the verb as to form a transitive compound verb, with *doctor* for its object or subject. But oftentimes a distinction between the prepositional and the adverbial use is difficult to make.

Certain expressions containing transitive verbs may also be used in the passive voice:

1. She *took good care of* you; you *were well taken care of*.
2. They *made fun of* him; he *was made fun of*.
3. The summer house *was* now seldom *made use of*.

212. Indirect object. The indirect object denotes the person or thing *to whom* or *to which* something is given or refused; it is in the objective case (§ 40; dative, §§ 604, 606):

1. I gave *him* (= *to him*) my *dog*. (*Him* is the indirect object; *dog* is the direct object.)
2. I promised *my dog* (= *to my dog*) a good supper.

213. Indirect and retained object. When the active voice is changed to the passive, either the direct or the indirect object may be made the subject. If the direct object is made the subject, the indirect object remains as an indirect object; if the indirect object is made the subject, the direct object is retained in the objective case (accusative, §§ 604, 606) and is called the retained object:

1. I promised *him* (= *to him*) a good *supper*. (Active.)

A good *supper* was promised *him*. (Passive.)

He was promised a good *supper*. (Passive.)

2. We told *her* (= *to her*) *that we were hungry*. (Active; the direct object is the clause *that we were hungry*.)

She was told *that we were hungry*. (Passive.)

NOTE. Do not use the passive voice in such clumsy expressions as ' She was told by our guide that we were hungry '; say ' Our guide told her that we were hungry '.

214. Predicate objective, etc. A noun, pronoun, or adjective may be used in the predicate to complete the meaning of the verb and modify its direct object; such a modifier is called a predicate objective (or adjunct accusative, § 606); in the passive voice the direct object becomes the subject, and the predicate objective remains in the predicate as a predicate adjective or predicate nominative, modifying the subject (§ 158):

1. They *made* him *captain*. (= They *made captain* him.)

He was made *captain*. (Predicate nominative.)

2. *What* did you name her? She was named *what*? (Predicate nominative.)

3. He painted his house *gray*. (= He *painted gray* his house.)

His house was painted *gray*. (Predicate adjective.) (Exercise XXIV, § 569.)

215. Verbal nouns. There are two kinds of nouns formed from the verb, called the infinitive (§ 165) and the gerund (§§ 223–229). These verbal nouns are used in the nominative or the objective case, like ordinary nouns; but, unlike ordinary nouns, they have tense and voice, and may take the same constructions (object, modifier, predicate noun, etc.) as the verb from which they are formed (§§ 626, 627, 632, 633, etc.):

1. *To see* is *to believe*; *seeing* is *believing*.

2. *To see her* was *to love her*; *seeing her* was *loving her*.

3. She likes *to read aloud*; she enjoys *reading aloud*.
4. *To be poor* is no disgrace; *being poor* is no disgrace.
5. Houses *to let*, water *to drink*; houses *for letting*, etc.
6. A new way *to make bread*; a new way *of making bread*.

NOTE. The infinitive was formerly classed as a mood. It was called infinitive (= *unlimited*) because of its not being limited by having person and number. The indicative, subjunctive, and imperative, which have person and number, were called finite moods.

216. Infinitive as second object. The infinitive is often used as the second of two objects:

a. Without *to* in the active voice:

1. I saw *her fall*. (Passively, ' She was seen *to fall* '.)
2. We made (or let) *him help* us with our work.
3. He felt his *heart throb*.

b. With *to*, the two objects being equivalent to a clause (often called the infinitive clause, the first object being spoken of as the subject of the infinitive):

1. She believed *him to be* honest (= *that he was* honest).
2. We felt (found, knew, saw, thought, etc.) *him to be* our friend.

217. Infinitive as object of preposition. The infinitive and its subject may be used as the object of the preposition *for*; the infinitive alone may be used as the object of the prepositions *about, but, except, excepting,* and *save* (but no longer of *for*, as in Matthew, xi, 8 : " But what went ye out *for to see* ? ") :

1. *For him to come* would be impossible. (*Him to come* is the object of *for*; *for him to come* is the subject of the sentence, being equivalent to *his coming*. In ' It would be impossible for him to come ' *for him to come* is again the subject of the sentence, *it* being an expletive, with *for him to come* in apposition, § 61, *d*.)
2. They were *about to start* to town.
3. He could do nothing *but laugh* at the whole affair.

218. Infinitive or subject omitted. The infinitive, when used with a subject, is often omitted; colloquially (§ 380) the infinitive after *to* is often omitted; when the infinitive depends on the verb *hear*, the subject of the infinitive is sometimes omitted (colloquial):

1. He ordered the boys (*to go*) to bed.
2. I could go if I cared *to*. (Colloquial.)
3. I have never *heard* (anybody) *say*. (Colloquial.)

219. *To be* with predicate pronoun. When the infinitive *to be* has a subject (in the objective case, § 216), a predicate pronoun following *to be* is in the objective case, to agree with the subject; but when *to be* has no subject, the predicate pronoun is in the nominative case; when the infinitive is followed by a clause (as in the sixth example), the case of the pronoun is determined by the rule in § 78:

1. She took *him* to be *me*. *Whom* did you take *her* to be?
2. He was thought to be *I*. Should you like to be *he*?
3. *Who* were they supposed to be?
4. She thought *him me*. (*To be* is omitted.)
5. Let *him* be *whom*?
6. Let *him* be *who* he may be. Let *him* be *whom* you wish.

220. Wrong tense of infinitive. Do not use the perfect infinitive (§§ 626, 632, 638, 644, 650) except to express time earlier than that expressed by the principal verb:

1. I intended *to see* you. (Not 'to have seen'.)
2. He would have liked *to go*. (Not 'to have gone'. See § 188.)
3. It was not possible *to do* so. (Not 'to have done'.)
4. She ought *to have waited*. (Correct; to refer to past time, the past tense is necessary, since *ought* refers to present time; § 186.)

221. Split infinitive. An adverb may stand in different parts of the sentence, according to the emphasis (§ 370), but should not be placed between *to* and an infinitive. This rule against what is called the split infinitive is supported by the best usage, although violated in rare cases by good writers; at times it is best to recast the sentence (as in the sixth example):

1. To work *quietly* at home was impossible. (Not 'To quietly work'.)

2. They wished to postpone it *indefinitely*. (Not 'to indefinitely postpone'.)

3. It did not *wholly* persuade me. (Not 'It failed to wholly persuade me'.)

4. We had been hoping to achieve our object *quickly*. (Not 'to quickly achieve'.)

5. He asked the members to be kind enough to contribute. (Not 'to kindly contribute'.)

6. The situation forced them to *silent* approval. (Not 'to silently approve'.)

222. Misattached infinitive. The infinitive may be used, without a subject, to denote an action or a state in a general way; but when it is used to denote the action or state of a particular person or thing, that person or thing should be expressed, either in the objective case as the subject of the infinitive, or in the nominative case as the subject of the clause in which the infinitive stands (otherwise the infinitive is faulty, being grammatically attached to the wrong subject; compare § 229):

1. *To see* is *to believe*. (General action.)

2. *He* likes *to read*. (Action of a particular person, *he*.)

3. *She* was too heavy at heart *to watch* her footsteps. (Not 'Her *heart* was too heavy *to watch* her footsteps'; the subject, *heart*, is wrong, for it cannot watch her footsteps. But 'Her heart was too heavy *for her to watch* her footsteps' is correct, because *to watch* has the subject *her*.)

4. *We* were in too critical a situation *to delay*. (Not 'Our *situation* was too critical *to delay*'.)

5. *You* have seen enough with your own eyes not *to need* to be told. (Not 'Your own *eyes* have seen enough not *to need*', etc.)

6. The *fire* was far enough away *for me* not *to be* alarmed. (Do not omit *for me*.)

7. *She* has already endured too much *for us to add* to her burdens. (Do not omit *for us*.)

8. *To judge* from what has been said, *I should think* he meant it. (Do not omit *I should think*.)

9. *To prove* his guilt, *they* brought him to trial. (Not ' he underwent a trial '.)

10. *To carry* on the war, the *people* endured much privation. (Not ' there was great privation '.) (Exercise XXV, *a*, § 570.)

223. Gerund modified by adjective, etc. The gerund may be modified by an adjective (including a noun in the possessive case) or by an adjective phrase with *of* (see § 225 also):

1. *Rapid walking* is good exercise.
2. There is *no believing* old signs. — SHAKESPEARE.
3. Have you heard of *his coming* home? (Not ' him coming '.)
4. Have you heard of *Henry's coming* home? (Not ' Henry coming '; § 225.)
5. *The loading of* the ship delayed them.

224. Gerund as object of *a*. The gerund is often used as the object of the preposition *a* or *a*- (a remnant of the old preposition *on*); after the verb *go* (occasionally after other verbs) the preposition is usually omitted:

1. He set the old clock *a going*. (Or, *a-going*.)
2. We will go (*a*) *hunting*.
3. The children have gone *chestnutting*.

225. Gerund and participle distinguished. The present gerund is identical in form with the present participle (§ 175); but the former is a noun, and the latter an adjective:

1. Then he began, *laughing*. (Participle, modifying *he*.)
2. Then he began *laughing*. (Gerund, object of *began*.)
3. He burst out (*a*) *laughing*. (Gerund, object of the preposition *a*, expressed or understood.)

To distinguish the gerund from the participle, it is sometimes necessary to give the gerund a possessive modifier (§ 223), or to change the form of the sentence :

1. They insisted on *John's being* present ; or, They insisted that John be present. (In ' They insisted on John being present' the word *being* can hardly be classed either as a participle or as a gerund.)

2. That will not hinder *his doing* (or *him from doing*) it. (Not ' him doing '.)

3. You cannot prevent *our believing* it. (Not ' us believing '.)

4. Pardon *my interrupting* you. (Not ' me interrupting '.)

5. I was vexed by *his leaving* us. (Not ' him leaving '.)

6. They insisted that the poor be fed. (Not 'insisted on the poor being fed '.)

7. In case that much rain falls ; or, If much rain falls. (Not ' In case of much rain falling '.)

8. They insist that something be done. (Not 'insist on something being done '.)

9. It prevented the question from being raised. (Do not omit *from*.)

10. He consented to the passage of the bill. (Not 'to the bill passing '; nor ' to the bill's passing ', § 46.)

NOTE. After verbs of seeing and hearing the form in *-ing* is originally a gerund, with the preposition *a* (§ 288) omitted; but it is now usually treated as the present participle modifying the noun or pronoun :

1. I saw Mary (*a*) *coming*.

2. We hear her (*a*) *singing* softly.

3. I could hear their feet (*a*) *rattling* up the old stairs.

226. Gerund for progressive passive. In the older language the gerund with the preposition *a* or *in* was in common use for what is now the progressive passive voice (§ 209 ; the gerund without the preposition is occasionally used so still, but sounds archaic or affected, § 380) :

1. Forty and six years was this temple *in building*.—THE BIBLE.

2. The book *is* now *printing*. (Preferably, *is being printed*.)

227. Gerund in forming nouns. The present gerund is often used as the first part of a noun phrase or compound noun ; it should not be confused with the present participle :

1. A *sleeping* room (= a room *for sleeping*). Compare ' a *sleeping* lion ' (= a lion *that sleeps*), *sleeping* being here a participle ; ' a *living* likeness ' (= a likeness *that lives*), *living* being here a participle.

2. His *working* clothes (= clothes *for working*). Compare ' a *working* man ' (= a man *that works*), *working* being here a participle.

3. A *carving* knife (= a knife *for carving*; the word *carving* is here a gerund, but is easily mistaken for a participle).

4. The *building* trade, *drinking* water, a *stepping*-stone, my *walking* stick, her *writing* lessons. (Gerunds.)

228. *Being* with predicate pronoun. A predicate pronoun used after the gerund *being* is in the nominative case (§ 40); when followed by a predicate adjective, *being* is often omitted:

1. We did not dream of its *being she.*
2. I was surprised at its *being they.*
3. We felt certain of its *being he.*
4. The statement is far from (*being*) clear.

229. Misattached gerund. The gerund, like the infinitive (§ 222), may be used without reference to a subject, to denote action or state in a general way ; but when it is used to denote the action or state of a particular person or thing, that person or thing should be expressed, either as a possessive (possessive adjective, or noun in the possessive case) modifying the gerund, or as the subject of the clause in which the gerund stands (otherwise the gerund is faulty, being grammatically attached to the wrong subject) :

1. *Seeing* is *believing.* (General action.)
2. She was not sure of *his going. She* was not sure of *going.*
3. He went away without *our knowing* it.

4. I lost my way without (*my*) *knowing* it. (Omit *my* ; it repeats the subject *I*. Avoid needless repetition ; § 413.)

5. By *Jane's doing* so his life was saved.

6. On *opening* the door *he* saw a stranger. (Not ' On *opening* the door a stranger appeared '.)

7. After *talking* the matter over, *we* decided on a plan. (Not ' a *plan* was decided on '.)

8. The boat was upset by *my leaning* over. (Do not omit *my*.)

9. In *revising* this book the *author* has added an index. (Not ' In *revising* this book an *index* has been added '.)

10. The *car* was used without *our changing* the tire. (Do not omit *our*.)

11. After *singing* this hymn, *we* shall be addressed by Mr. Thomas. (Not ' Mr. Thomas will address us ' ; for this would mean that Mr. Thomas is to sing the hymn.) (Exercise XXV, *b*, *c*, § 570.)

230. Verbal adjective : participle. From the verb are formed two verbal nouns (§ 215) and a verbal adjective, called the participle. The participle may be used like an ordinary adjective ; but, like the infinitive and the gerund, it has tense and voice also, and may take the same constructions (object, modifier, predicate noun, etc. ; see, also, §§ 175, 209) as the verb from which it is formed (§§ 628, 634, 640, 646, 652). The participle with its modifiers is called a participial phrase :

1. The *babbling* brook ; *faded* flowers.

2. Some gypsies *weaving baskets*.

3. A brook *babbling through the woods*.

4. *Being a boy*, he was frightened.

NOTE. The perfect participle (§§ 628, 634, etc.) denotes time preceding that of the principal verb ; the present participle properly denotes the same time as the principal verb, but is often used with the force of the perfect participle :

1. *Having found* that I was early, I *took* a walk.

2. *Sitting* before the open fire, she *prepared* her evening meal.

3. *Finding* that I was early, I *took* a walk. (= *Having found*.)
   Opening the window, he *looked* down into the street.

231. Misattached participle. The participle, being an adjective, modifies a noun or pronoun (§ 113). Care should be taken to make it modify the proper word (otherwise it is faulty, being grammatically attached to a word to which it does not belong; this is especially true of an introductory participle, which regularly modifies the subject of the sentence; see the fourth example):

1. An *absorbing* story. (Modifier of *story*.)
2. The story was *absorbing*. (Predicate adjective, § 158.)
3. *Being* a boy, he was frightened. (Modifier of the subject *he*.)
4. *Attempting* to get into the canoe, *we* upset it. (Not 'it was upset'. *Attempting* modifies *we*. In the sentence '*Attempting* to get into the canoe, *it* was upset' *attempting* modifies the subject *it*, the canoe; but this makes nonsense.)
5. *Sitting* by the window, *she* heard the watchman. (Not 'the watchman was heard'.)
6. *Judging* by this, *I* think he has talent. (Do not omit *I think*.)
7. *Subtracting* one and *dividing* by five, *we* obtain two for the answer. (Not 'the answer is two'.)
8. My *shoes being* run down at the heel (§ 233), I had them mended. (Not '*Being* run down at the heel, *I* had my shoes mended'.)
9. *Being* a wax doll, *she* immediately forgot her cares. (Not '*Being* a wax doll, her cares were immediately forgotten'.)

232. Exceptions to rule. The participle *speaking* is frequently used independently (without noun or pronoun) with such adverbs as *broadly, correctly, generally, properly, roughly,* and *strictly*, in parenthetic adverb phrases:

1. There are, *strictly speaking*, two classes.
2. *Roughly speaking*, he lives in his shop.

The participles *considering, regarding, saving*, and a few others (§ 283, 3) are sometimes used as prepositions:

1. He did well *considering* (= *in view of*) his youth.
2. What can be done *regarding* all this?

233. Nominative absolute. A noun or pronoun modified by a participle may be used in the nominative case with the force of an adverb clause, without being grammatically connected with the sentence; this construction is called the nominative absolute; the participle *being* is often omitted:

1. *Time permitting* (= *If time permits*), he will return.
2. How can I be happy, *you being* (= *when you are*) absent?
3. All the *rest agreeing*, I was obliged to comply. — DEFOE.
4. *Supper* (*being*) over, they went into the library.

NOTE. The nominative absolute is convenient, but should not be used much; its frequent use tends to mannerism.

234. Punctuation with participle. When a participle is not needed to define the meaning of the noun or pronoun which it modifies, it is nonessential, and is separated from the rest of the sentence by a comma or commas (§§ 50, 92, 477):

1. They found the boat *capsized*. (Essential.)
2. The book *lying* on the table is yours. (Essential.)
3. *Sitting* at the window, she worked late. (Nonessential.)
4. The old man, much *wearied*, ate little. (Nonessential.)

235. Participle compounded. When the participle is used simply as an adjective, it is often compounded:

1. The snow-*capped* summits of the Alps.
2. Such far-*sighted*, sharp-*witted* men.

236. Participle as noun. The participle is often used as a noun:

1. The *loving* are the *daring*.
2. She cared for the *lost* and *forsaken*. (Exercise XXV, *d*, § 570.)

237. Verbs conjugated with *be*. Some intransitive verbs denoting motion are conjugated with *be* (instead of *have*) to express the condition or state attained, rather than the action which leads to it:

1. Babylon *has fallen*. (The act.)
   Babylon *is fallen*. — THE BIBLE. (The condition or state.)
2. We *are met* on a great battle-field of that war. — LINCOLN.
3. The guests *are gone*.
4. The children *are* all *grown* up.

238. Adjective or adverb after verb. After certain verbs (mostly intransitive) it is sometimes puzzling to know whether to use a predicate adjective (§ 158) or an adverb (§ 252). The rule is this : to express quality or state, use the adjective ; to express manner, use the adverb (but see § 239) :

a. Adjective and adverb :

1. The ground felt *soft* ; he felt *softly* about him.
2. He grew *great* ; he grew *greatly* in stature.
3. She looked *shy* ; she looked *shyly* round her.
4. The knife looks *sharp* ; he looked *sharply* at me.
5. I feel *warm* ; I feel *warmly* on that subject.
6. He saw us *safe* across the downs ; you can go *safely*.
7. The flag waved *triumphant* over the old fort ; he waved the flag *triumphantly*.
8. The rule held *good* (adj.) ; the rope held *well* (adv.).
9. The meat kept *good* (adj.) ; meat keeps *well* (adv.) here.
10. He did *well* (adv. ; ' He did *good* ' means he did what was right or helpful, *good* being a noun, § 13).
11. He came (spoke, sang) *first* (*second*, *last* ; adj.) ; he spoke *first* (*secondly*, *lastly* ; adv.) of his hope. See § 275.

b. Adjective :

1. The sky looks *dull* ; the weather looks *unpromising*.
2. The air feels *damp* and *cold* ; the child looks *unhappy*.
3. The cream tastes *sour* ; the egg smells *good* (= *like a good egg*) ; the meat looks *bad* ; the man looks *ill* (do not use *bad* of a person unless you mean a bad person ; Sir James Murray, late Editor of the Oxford English Dictionary, would not use *bad* or *badly* with *look* when speaking of a person's health).

239. *Well* and *badly* after *feel*, *look*, etc. As an exception to the rule set forth in § 238, the adverbs of manner *well* (not the adjective 'good') and *badly* (not the adjective 'bad') follow the intransitive verbs *feel*, *look*, *smell*, *sound*, and *taste* to denote the feeling, look, and so forth, which the subject has or takes on:

1. The garden looks *well* (or *badly*) after the rain.
2. He looks *well* (or *badly*) in this suit. — SIR JAMES MURRAY.
3. I have never felt so *well* (*badly*). (Not 'good', 'bad'.)
4. I can't eat today; everything looks *badly* and tastes *badly*. (Not 'bad'; it is not a question of the quality of the food, but of how the food looks and tastes.)
5. Things began to look *well* (or *badly*) for all concerned.
6. She feels *badly* about the whole affair.
7. The feast smells *well*. — SHAKESPEARE.
8. It [a trout] looks *well*, and tastes *well*. — IZAAK WALTON.
9. Fields of Swedish turnips, all looking extremely *well*.
10. The archbishop and his colleagues *feel* very *strongly* on the subject of the attack upon the Welsh Church. — THE SPEAKER.
11. A moderate party had always *felt kindly* towards the Protestant Dissenters. — MACAULAY. (Exercise XXVI, *b*, *c*, § 571.)

240. *Ask, teach.* The verb *ask* takes two objects, one of the person and the other of the thing; the verb *teach* takes an indirect object of the person and a direct object of the thing (this is made plain in Old English, in which the indirect object and the direct object had different forms; see §§ 604, 606):

1. He asked *me* my *name*.
2. She taught *him* (= *to him*) many *things*.

241. *Bid, forbid.* The verb *bid*, except before a negative or in the passive voice, takes the infinitive without *to*; *forbid* takes the infinitive with *to*:

1. They *bade* me *go* in; they *bade* me *not to go* in.
2. They *forbade* me *to go* in; I was *bidden* (*forbidden*) *to go* in.

242. Come, go. The verbs *come* and *go* are followed by the infinitive (with *to*) to express purpose, or by a coördinate verb (connected by *and*) to express the result of the purpose, but care should be taken not to use a coördinate verb when the infinitive conveys the meaning intended (compare *send, try,* § 251); in the older language *come* and *go* often took the infinitive without *to*, but this is now archaic or dialectal (§ 380):

1. When will you *come to see* me? — DICKENS. (Purpose.)
2. *Come and see* us in our new home. (Result.)
3. She *went to dress* for dinner; she *went and dressed* for dinner.
4. I did not *go to see* him. (Not 'go and see'.)

243. Dare. The verb *dare* may take, as originally, the infinitive without *to*, and in the third person singular of the present indicative may have the form *dare* (instead of *dares*; § 622); when *dare* takes the infinitive with *to*, the form of the third person singular of the present indicative is *dares*:

1. I (You, He) *dare* not go. *Dare* I (you, he) go?
2. If he *dares to* go, I don't *dare to* follow.

244. Had better, etc. The past subjunctive *had* is used with the comparative, superlative, or positive of certain adjectives and adverbs (such as *better, sooner, rather, best, as lief, as soon, as well*) to express preference or choice. For example, 'he had better go' means 'he would have or hold it better to go'; *better* is an adjective, and *go* an infinitive. This idiom has had the sanction of good usage for centuries:

1. You *had better leave* your folly. — MARLOWE.
2. I *had as lief be* hanged. — SHAKESPEARE.
3. I *had rather be* a doorkeeper in the house of my God, than to dwell in the tents of wickedness. — THE BIBLE.

NOTE. *Would rather* and *would sooner* may be used like *had rather* (see § 193): 'I (You, He) *would rather* comfort them'. But 'would better' is not sanctioned by good usage, and should be avoided.

245. *Have been to*, etc. The verb phrase *have been* or *had been* may be followed by the preposition *to*, or a noun denoting motion, to express motion to and from a person or place (this idiom has been in good use for nearly three hundred years):

1. We *have been to* Paris (*to* dinner, *to* mother's).
2. I *had been to* see Irving that night.
3. He *has been* the *rounds*.

246. *Help to*. An infinitive used as the object of the verb *help* has the preposition *to* (the omission of *to* is now dialectal or vulgar, says the Oxford English Dictionary):

1. They *helped to plant* the trees. (Do not omit *to*.)
2. She will *help* you *to secure* employment.
3. He wished *to help* me *to plant* the trees.
4. The hereditary enemies of his house had *helped* him *to* mount a throne. — MACAULAY.

247. *It may be*. The sentence *it may be*, meaning *possibly*, is often shortened to *may be* or (adverbially) *maybe*; but these uses are now archaic or dialectal (§ 380):

This, *it may be*, was the reason for the change.

248. *Need*. The verb *need* takes the infinitive with *to* unless the sentence is (actually or virtually) negative or interrogative; when the infinitive does not have *to*, the third person singular of the present indicative is *need* (instead of 'needs'; § 622):

1. He says *he needs to find* more men. (In 'Does he *need to go*?' *need* is an infinitive, object of *does*; § 174.)
2. I (You, He) *need not ask*; I (You, He) hardly *need ask*. *Need he do* this? Why *need she say* so?

249. *Please*. In such expressions as '*please* to open the door' the verb *please* is for 'please it you' (that is, 'may it please you'), a subjunctive of wish (§ 162):

1. *Please* to stop the carriage. — DICKENS. (*To* is often omitted.)
2. *Please* not to forget that we want you.
3. *Please* your honor, there 's a man at the door.
4. *Please*, may I come in? Give me my hat, *please*.
5. Will you, *please*, take a message for me?

250. Pray, prithee. In such expressions as 'pray do so' the verb *pray* is for 'I pray you' (§ 350); *prithee* is an archaic colloquialism (§ 380) for 'I pray thee':

1. *Pray* tell me what I shall do.
2. *Prithee*, friend, exhibit thy wisdom.

251. Send, try. The verb *send* is followed by *and* with a coördinate verb, or by an infinitive with *to* (like *come* and *go*, § 242); *try* is properly followed by the infinitive with *to*:

1. *Send and find* him; *send* somebody *to find* him.
2. *Try to get* a little rest. (Not 'try and get'.) (Exercise XXV, *d–g*, § 570.)

THE ADVERB

252. Adverb. An adverb is a word used to modify a verb, an adjective, or another adverb (see § 255 also):

1. He walked *slowly*; she sings *well*.
2. *Rather* cheerful; *unusually* kind; *broiling* hot.
3. *More* slowly; *almost* never; *hardly* ever.

253. Adverb phrase and clause. A phrase or a clause (§§ 6, 7) may be used as an adverb; such a phrase is called an adverb phrase, and such a clause an adverb clause (§§ 268–270):

1. The animal leaped *blindly*. (Adverb.)
2. He leaped *without looking*. (Adverb phrase; § 282, 2.)
3. He leaped *before he looked*. (Adverb clause.)

254. Adverb modifying phrase or clause. An adverb may modify an adverb phrase or an adverb clause:

1. The chestnuts lay *all* over the ground. (The adverb *all* modifies the entire phrase, or unit, 'over the ground'. This is more logical than to say that *all* modifies the preposition *over*, as is stated in some grammars.)

2. She found her purse *exactly* where she had dropped it. (*Exactly* modifies 'where she had dropped it'.)

255. Adverb modifying noun. An adverb sometimes modifies a noun (especially a noun implying action), and thus has the force of an adjective (§ 383):

1. The *down* grade; the *up* train; her arrival *here*.
2. The trees *there* (elliptical for *which are there*, § 347) are green.

256. Formation. In formation a good many adverbs are old forms of nouns, pronouns, or adjectives, with or without a preposition; some adverbs are formed from different parts of speech by the addition of *-wards*, *-ward*, *-ways*, *-way*, and *-wise*:

1. Home, aboard, anew, forever, indeed, sometime.
2. Always (= all the way), backward(s), downward(s), endwise, homeward(s), upward(s).

257. Adverb from adjective. Many adverbs are formed from adjectives, by the addition of *-ly* (but there are also a few adjectives ending in *ly*, such as *early*, *friendly*, *kindly*):

Bright, *brightly*; playful, *playfully*; wise, *wisely*.

258. Adverb and adjective alike. Some adverbs have the same form as adjectives; in poetry they are often alike (§ 504):

Best, better, cheap, clean, close, deep, direct (§ 417), early, fair, far, fast, full, hard, high, ill, just, late, long, loud, low, near, pretty, quick, right, sharp, short, slow, soft, straight, well, wide, wrong.

NOTE. The adverbs *quickly*, *slowly*, and *softly* are now more frequently used than the adverbs *quick*, *slow*, and *soft*.

259. Adverb and adjective distinguished. When adjectives and adverbs are alike in form, they are to be distinguished by their use. If they modify nouns or pronouns, they are adjectives; if they modify verbs, adjectives, or adverbs, they are adverbs (§ 383; but see §§ 238, 239, 504):

1. The sun is *bright* (adjective); it shines *bright* (adverb).
2. He is *late* (adjective); he works *late* (adverb).
3. Her voice became *low* (adjective); she spoke *low* (adverb).
4. I heard him breathe *quick* and *deep*. (Adverbs.)

260. Adjective misused for adverb. Care should be taken not to use adjectives for adverbs (see §§ 238, 239):

1. He sings *badly*. (Not 'bad'.)
2. She paints *finely*. (Not 'fine'.)
3. She reads *well*; that sounds *well*. (Not 'good'; § 238.)
4. You row *excellently*. (Not 'excellent'.)
5. *Surely* I will meet you. (Not 'Sure'.)

261. Adverb after *be*. An adverb is frequently used in the predicate after the verb *be*:

1. School is *over*. (Not 'out'; see *out, over*, § 417.)
2. The great secret was at last *out*.

262. Classification. Adverbs may be divided into different classes, according to their meaning:

1. Time, denoting *when*: afterwards, again, daily, never, now, often, sometime, sometimes, soon, etc.
2. Place, denoting *where*: above, anywhere, forward, here, in, out, somewhere, there, thither, up, yonder, etc.
3. Manner, denoting *how*: fast, likewise, quick, quickly, slowly, thus, truly, well, wisely, etc.
4. Degree, denoting *how much*: abundantly, all, almost, also, besides, but (= only), enough, half, hardly, merely, more, most, much, quite, rather, scarcely, so, too, very, etc.

5. Number, denoting, *how many times* or *where in a series*: once, twice, three times, tenfold; first, secondly, fifthly, etc.

6. Cause, denoting *why*: consequently, hence, so, therefore, etc.

7. Opposition, denoting *contrast*: however, still, yet, etc.

8. Assertion, denoting *affirmation* or *denial* (some of which, such as *yes* and *no*, do not modify other words, and may stand alone as complete sentences): apparently, aye, certainly, indeed, really, surely, yea, yes, etc.; by no means, no, not at all, etc.; likely, perhaps, possibly, probably, etc.

263. Interrogative adverb. An interrogative adverb is used in asking a question:

1. *When* did you see him? *Where* does he live?
2. *How* did you find him? *Why* don't you speak?

264. Comparison. The comparison of adverbs is similar to that of adjectives (§ 132):

POSITIVE	COMPARATIVE	SUPERLATIVE
close	clos*er*	clos*est*
soon	soon*er*	soon*est*
early	earl*ier*	earl*iest*
often	often*er*	often*est*
	more often	most often
gladly	more gladly	most gladly

265. Irregular comparison. A few adverbs have irregular comparison; some forms are like irregular adjectives (§ 134):

1. far	farther	farthest (§ 134)
	further	furthest (§ 134)
2. ill, badly	worse	worst
3. late	later	latest, last
4. little	less	least
5. much	more	most
6. nigh	nigher	nighest, next
7. well (not 'good'; § 239)	better	best
	rather	

266. Comparative and superlative. The use of the comparative and the superlative of adverbs is similar to that of the comparative and the superlative of adjectives (compare §§ 135, 136):

1. Jack ran *faster* than my brother.
2. Your brother ran *fastest* of all.
3. Mary played *most skillfully*. (= 'most skillfully of all who played'; or, 'in a most skillful manner', without comparison.)

267. Numeral adverbs. The numeral adverbs are of two classes, ordinal and multiplicative; the word *times* used in adverb phrases is adverbial (for the use of *first, secondly*, etc., see § 275):

ORDINAL	MULTIPLICATIVE
first (not ' firstly ')	once, singly
secondly (not ' second ')	twice, doubly, twofold
thirdly (not ' third ')	threefold, triply, three times
tenthly (not ' tenth ')	tenfold, ten times

268. Adverb clause. An adverb clause is introduced by a subordinating conjunction, such as *after, although, as, because, before, if, since, than, that, though, till, unless, until, when, where, while, why* (§ 304); § 303.

269. Classification. Adverb clauses are of the following kinds:

1. Time, denoting *when*: He reads *when others sleep*.
2. Place, denoting *where*: You may sit *where you wish*.
3. Cause, denoting *why*: The girl ran *because the boy ran*.
4. Purpose, denoting *intention*: He works *that we may eat*.
5. Result, denoting *consequence*: I was so tired *that I soon fell asleep*.
6. Condition, denoting *on what terms*: We will go skating *if it freezes tonight*.
7. Concession, denoting an *admission*: He would try hard *though* (= *even if*) *he should fail*.

8. Comparison, denoting *similarity* or *dissimilarity* :

Manner : We do *as they do*.

Degree : You are taller *than I am*.

You are as tall *as I am*.

Go as soon *as you can*.

NOTE. In the last two sentences the first *as* is an adverb meaning *to that extent* (modifying the adjective *tall* and the adverb *soon*) ; the second *as* is a subordinating conjunction meaning *to which extent*.

270. Essential and nonessential clause. The adverb clause, like the adjective clause, is essential or nonessential, and is punctuated accordingly (§§ 50, 92, 472) :

1. I want you *when you are free*. (Essential.)
2. I want you next week, *when you will be free*. (Nonessential.)
3. Go yonder, *where* you see the tent. (Nonessential.)

271. Position. An adverb is made emphatic by being placed at the beginning or the end of the sentence (§ 370) ; otherwise it may stand between the subject and the verb, or separate a verb phrase (but not *to* and the infinitive ; § 221) :

1. *Yesterday* I was reprimanded *severely*.
2. The dog *now* saw his opportunity.
3. He is *always* being praised.
4. They had *hardly* begun their long voyage.

Whether the adverb or the verb shall stand at the end of the sentence is a matter of meaning or of emphasis :

1. This must be gradually *rewritten*. (That is, this must be *rewritten*, and it may be done gradually.)

This must be rewritten *gradually*. (That is, the rewriting of this must be done *gradually*.)

2. These obstacles must immediately *be overcome*.

These obstacles must be overcome *immediately*.

3. In that part of the western division of this kingdom which is commonly called Somersetshire, there lately *lived*, and perhaps lives *still*, a gentleman . . . — FIELDING.

272. Two or more negatives. In the older language a negation was strengthened by using two or more negatives; this is now improper:

1. Old style:

He *nevere* yet *no* vileynye (= discourtesy) *ne* sayde
In al his lyf (= life) unto *no* maner wight (= manner of person).
CHAUCER (about 1386).

2. Old style: *Nor* this is *not* my nose *neither*. — SHAKESPEARE.

3. Faulty: I *didn't* say *nothing*. (Say 'I said *nothing*'; or, 'I did not say *anything*'.)

4. Faulty: There were*n't* *no* pies equal to hers. (Omit *n't*.)

5. Faulty: She *won't* go, I *don't* think. (Omit *don't*.)

6. Faulty: I have*n't* *no* time now. (Omit *no*.)

In present usage two negatives in the same clause make an affirmative (but see the third example):

1. *Nor* did they *not* perceive their evil plight. (= They *did* perceive their evil plight.)

2. His language, though inelegant, is *not ungrammatical*.

3. He will *never* consent, *not* he, *no*, *never*. (Here every negative has a negative force; the last three are added repetitions, § 474.)

NOTE. Do not use a negative with such words as *hardly, barely, scarcely, only* (§ 276):

1. I could*n't* *hardly* tell what he meant. (Omit *n't*.)
2. He had*n't* *only* (or *but*) one horse. (Omit *n't*.)

273. *Also, too.* The adverbs *also* and *too* both mean 'in addition', but *too* is less formal than *also*, and hence commoner in the spoken language. Be careful to place them where they will unmistakably modify the proper word (see § 276). If they ought to stand at the end of the sentence or clause, do not hesitate to put them there, but without a comma before them (§ 480); when you use them in the middle of a sentence to refer to a preceding sentence, set them off from the rest of the sentence by commas (*also* is not a conjunction; see § 298, N.):

1. She *too* (or *also*) must see Rome; she must *also* see Rome; she must see Rome *too* (or *also*).

2. You must sell the heirlooms *too*.

3. There was *also* a strife among them.

4. For where your treasure is, there will your heart be *also*.

5. I found that he was at home. I found, *also* (or *too*), that he was at leisure.

6. The increased cost of supplies, the delays in service, *and* (not 'also') the decreasing profits make the business uncertain.

274. *Enough.* The adverb *enough* stands after the word it modifies :

1. The weather is warm *enough*.

2. We did not go slowly *enough*.

275. *First, secondly,* etc. One of the commonest errors is the use of the adjectives 'first, second', for the adverbs *first* (not 'firstly', § 267), *secondly*, and so forth; anybody who says 'first, second', for *first, secondly*, should also say 'final' (or 'last') for *finally* (or *lastly*), but nobody does that.

The adverbs are *first* (= *in the first place*), *secondly* (= *in the second place*), *thirdly*, . . . *tenthly* (or *finally*, or *lastly*), § 267 ; the adjectives are *first, second, third*, . . . *tenth* (or *final*, or *last*), § 121 ; but the adjectives should be accompanied by *the, my, his*, or the like (but see § 238, *a*, 11) :

a. Adverbs :

1. His three reasons were, *first*, that he was busy; *secondly*, that he was without sufficient means ; and *thirdly* (or *finally*, or *lastly*), that he was not interested in the matter.

2. His three reasons were these (or *as follows*): *first*, . . .; *secondly*, . . .; *thirdly* (or *finally*, or *lastly*), . . .

3. She had several objects in view. *First*, . . . *Secondly*, . . . *Thirdly*, . . . *Tenthly* (or *Finally*, or *Lastly*), . . . (When necessary, these adverbs are placed at the beginning of paragraphs, as shown at the bottom of page 150.)

4. This action should have three qualifications in it. *First*, it should be but one action. *Secondly*, it should be an entire action; and *thirdly*, it should be a great action. — ADDISON.

b. Adjectives :

1. He had three reasons : *the first* was, that he was busy ; *the second*, that he was without sufficient means ; *the third*, that he was not interested in the matter.

2. He had three reasons. *The first* was, ... *The second* was, ... *The third* was, ...

3. There are also two kinds of thoughts which are carefully to be avoided. *The first* are, such as are affected and unnatural ; *the second*, such as are mean and vulgar. — ADDISON.

276. Only. The adverb *only* may stand before or after the word or words which it modifies ; but, like other modifiers, it should be so placed that the meaning is unmistakable (§ 366) ; do not hesitate to place it at the end of a sentence or clause if it ought to stand there :

1. There was *only* one day left.

2. He asked them for lodging for one night *only*. — DEFOE.

3. *Only* take heed to thyself ; take heed to thyself *only*.

4. Talking in the rear room *only*. (' Talking *only* in the rear room ' means either that the rear room is not to be used except for talking, or that talking is not permitted except in the rear room.)

277. Quite. Primarily, the adverb *quite* means *completely*, *wholly* (see § 414, N.) :

1. The room was not *quite* without ornament.

2. A man should be *quite* certain of what he knows.

Secondarily, *quite* means *actually*, *really*, *positively* (implying that the case or circumstances are such as justify the use of the word or phrase qualified ; but even this is objectionable) :

1. It is *quite* a comfortable dwelling. (Omit *quite*.)

2. She was *quite* charmed with her new lodger. (Omit *quite*.)

But *quite* should not be used in the loose or erroneous sense of ' to a considerable extent ', ' noticeably' (avoid ambiguity) :

1. This room is *rather* warm. (Not ' quite warm '.)
2. He is *a pretty fair* artist. (Not ' quite an artist '.)
3. He is *fairly well*. (Not ' quite well ', which properly means *entirely well*, but, as generally misused, ' not entirely well '.)

278. Right. The adverb *right* usually means *straight* ; be careful not to misuse it (see *immediately*, § 417) :

1. The airship flew *right* over the town.
2. She works *without stopping*. (Not ' right along '.)
3. The train starts *immediately*. (Not ' right off '.)
4. There is a *considerable* crop this year. (Not ' right smart '.)

279. The . . . the. In expressions like ' the sooner you go, the better it will be ', or ' the sooner the better ', the first *the* is a subordinating conjunction meaning ' by how much '; the second *the* is an adverb of degree meaning ' by so much '. The first expression means ' by how much sooner you go, by so much will it be better '. The second clause with *the*, being a principal clause (§ 8), may be used independently, and *the* is then frequently modified by *all* : ' He will work *the* busier '; ' He goes *all the* more '.

280. Very, too. Do not use *very* (or *too*) with past participles that are felt to be more than mere adjectives. *Very* is generally too handy, and its use not only robs words of their proper meaning, but robs the speaker's vocabulary of synonyms (§ 385 ; see *bad*, § 417); in the spoken language the intonation or emphasis of the speaker indicates his meaning of *very*, but in the written language these aids are absent (§ 363) :

1. I was made *very tired* (adjective) by the journey.
2. I was *too much exhausted* (participle) by the journey.
3. He is *well educated*. (Not ' very educated '.)
4. She was *greatly pleased* to go. (Not ' very pleased '.)

281. *What*. *What* is sometimes an adverb, meaning *partly*:

What with pride, projects, and knavery, poor Peter was grown distracted. — SWIFT. (Exercise XXVI, § 571.)

THE PREPOSITION

282. Preposition. A preposition is a word used to connect a noun or a pronoun with some other part of the sentence. The noun or pronoun is called the object of the preposition. The preposition with its object is called a prepositional phrase (for its use, see §§ 114, 165, 253). Some prepositions were originally adverbs (see § 383):

1. The meeting broke *up*. (Adverb.)
2. He rode *up* the hill. (Preposition, connecting *hill* with *rode*; *up the hill* is an adverb phrase, § 253.)

283. List of prepositions. The most common prepositions are as follows:

1. A (§ 288), after, at, but (= except), by, down, for, from, in, of, off, on, out, over, past, round, save, since, through, till, to, under, up, with.

2. Aboard, about, above, across, along, alongside, amid, amidst, among, around, before, behind, below, beneath, beside, besides, between, beyond, into, outside, throughout, toward (or towards), underneath, until, upon, within, without.

3. Barring, concerning, considering, during, except, excepting, notwithstanding, past, pending, regarding, respecting, saving, touching. See § 232.

284. Compound prepositions. Certain idiomatic phrases may be conveniently classed as compound prepositions:

According to, as for, as to, because of, by means of, by reason of, by way of, for the sake of, in keeping with, in regard to, in spite of, instead of, on account of, out of, outside of, with reference to, with regard to, with respect to.

285. Object of preposition. The object of a preposition may be a word, a phrase, or a clause :

1. Near *him*; between *you* and *me*; by *whom*; to *them*.
2. They were about *to start* (object of *about*); the horse ran from *in front of the house* (object of *from*).
3. It depends on *who wishes to go* (object of *on*; §§ 78, 90).
4. A pretty, plump woman of *from forty to fifty*. — DICKENS. See *from four to ten*, § 417.

286. Position of preposition; object omitted. A preposition often stands after its object; it always does so when its object is the relative pronoun *that* (§ 83; see § 370); the object of the preposition is sometimes omitted (§ 91) :

1. *Whom* did you write *to*? (or, *To* whom did you write?)
2. There is the carriage *that* they came *in*.
3. Odd and uncommon characters are the game *that* I look *for*, and most delight *in*. — ADDISON.

Read aloud the following sentences (see §§ 78, 90, 361) :

1. Will you tell me whom you walked with yesterday?
2. A question arose as to who was to do the cooking.
3. My going will depend on whom he wishes to take.
4. Can you tell me to whom I shall apply for a ticket?
5. There is the boy whom I ran the race with last week.
6. The policeman whom we saw in the park told us.
7. At last they found a guide whom they could depend on.
8. At last they found a guide who could be depended on.

287. Idioms. The following examples illustrate difficult prepositional and adverbial idioms :

abound : **in**, of inherent qualities (English *abounds in* figurative expressions); **with**, of unessential or accidental properties (the house *abounds with* rats).

accommodate : **to** (circumstance); **with** (a coat, a light, a loan).

accompanied : **by** (a person, a dog); **with** (a smile, a remark).

accordance : **with** (*in* accordance *with* his convictions).

acquiesce : in (an opinion, an arrangement, the propriety or necessity).

acquit : of (a person *of* a crime); **with** (he acquitted himself *with* credit).

advantage : of (have *the* advantage *of* a person); **over** (gain *an* advantage *over* a person, unbelief has no advantage *over* belief).

afflicted : by (persecution, death); **with** (a chronic disease).

agree : on (a plan); **to** (a proposal); **to** (tell a thing); **with** (a person).

amuse : by (telling a story); **with** (an anecdote). **Amuse yourself : with** (a toy, a puzzle); **with, by, in** (sketching). **Be amused : at** (an incident, a person's simplicity); **by** (a story).

angry : at (a thing); **with** (a person).

apply : for (a position); **to** (a person); **to** (study).

arrive : at (a village or town, knowledge, a conclusion, manhood); **in** (town, a large city or a country); **upon** (the scene).

ask : about, for (a person or thing); **after** (a person).

authority : on (a subject).

averse : to (a thing).

aversion : to (sometimes **for** or **toward**) (a person or thing).

blush : at (a mishap); **for** (a person); **to** (tell a thing); **with** (pleasure).

bring : down to (*down to* the present; see ' up to date ', § 417).

buy : for (a person or thing); **of** or **from** (a person); **with** (blood).

call : at (a house); **by** (name); **for** (a person or thing); **on** (a person); **to** (a person *to* account); **to** (a person).

change : for (the better); **with** (the season; places *with* a person). But, **exchange** one thing **for** another.

charge : against (a person or an account); **to** (an account); **with** (a person *with* a responsibility or a crime).

circumstances: in (he found himself *in* easy circumstances); **under** (*under* such circumstances he became indolent).

come : across (an expression); honestly **by** (a fortune); **into** (fashion, a fortune); **of** (a good family); **off** (with honor); **on** or **upon** (an army *on* a town ; a plague *on* a people; come *upon* each other); **to** (grief, the point, an understanding); **up to** (expectation).

communicate : **to** (a thing *to* a person); **with** (a person).

compare : **to** (a person *to* a lion); **with** (a person or thing *with* another, Grant *with* Lee). **In comparison with** (of persons or things : He is a weakling *in comparison with* her).

competitor : **for** (a position, a prize); **with** (a person).

concur : **in** (an opinion or action); **with** (a person).

conform : **to** (**conformable to**; but, **in conformity with**) (reason, circumstances, custom, justice, nature, a pattern).

connect : **with** (a person or thing *with* another).

consist : **in** (doing something, being obedient to the law); **of** (iron and wood, five pieces).

contend : **about** (a thing); **against** (misfortune); **for** (a prize); **with** (fate).

contrast' (verb): **with** (a person or thing *with* another). **Con'trast** (noun): **between** (persons or things); **to** (he presented a strong *contrast to* his brother). **In contrast with** (place this *in contrast with* that).

correspond : **to** (actions *to* words, one part *to* another); **with** (one person *with* another by letter).

cry : **for** (a person or thing); **with** (pain).

cut : **in** (two; § 290, N.); **off with** (a shilling); **to** (pieces).

depart : **at** (sunrise); **for** (a destination); **from** (a place); **in** (season). See *prompt*, § 417.

depend : **on** (assistance, circumstances, friends).

die : **by** (violence, the sword); **for** (a cause, your native land); **from** (a wound, inattention); **in** (battle); **of** (a disease, the plague, hunger, old age, grief); **through** (neglect); **with** (laughter).

differ : **from** (iron differs *from* lead); **with** (a person in opinion). See *different from*, § 417.

disappointed : **in** (a person, the result, my hope of meeting you); **to** (hear a thing); **with** (a thing).

displeased : **at** (a thing); **with** (a person).

distinguished : **by** (looks, a plume); **for** (loyalty); **from** (one person or thing *from* another).

draw : **on** (a bank, the imagination).

enter : **at** (a door, a gate); **for** (a race); **into** (business, a friend's amusements, society, a treaty); **on** (duties, a career).

essential : **in** (the first essential *in* speaking is to have something to say); **of** (essentials *of* penmanship, arithmetic); **to** (the first essential *to* his recovery is sleep; a knowledge of grammar is essential *to* the understanding of a language).

excuse : **for** (an action); **from** (attendance).

fall : **among** (thieves); **by** (the sword); **in** (love with); **in with** (a person); **on** (an enemy); **out with** (a person); **short of** (expectation); **under** (my observation).

get : **along with** (a person or thing); **at** (the truth); **into** (good graces, society); **in with** (a person); **on with** (a person or thing); **over** (a difficulty, an illness); **round** (a person or thing).

go : **about** (work); **against** (wishes); **for** (nothing); **to** (pieces); **with** (the stream).

identical : **with** (a thing *with* a thing).

immigration : **into** (a country, a state).

incorporate : **into** (doctrines *into* teaching).

initiate : **into** (a society, ways of doing something).

inquire : **about, after, concerning, for** (a person or thing); **into** (a thing); **of** (a person).

insensible : **of** (cold, danger); **to** (fear, love).

insight : **into** (man, Spanish life, character).

interfere : **in** (a thing); **with** (a person).

introduce : **into** (a place, a family, society); **to** (a person).

intrust or **entrust :** **to** (a thing *to* a person); **with** (a person *with* a thing).

join : **to** (a shed *to* a house; one letter *to* another; shoulder *to* shoulder); **with** (his wishes *with* mine; *with* me in reading; learning *with* experience).

listen : **to** (a person or thing).

live : **at** (Newport); **by** (his wits); **in** (New York, Virginia, Washington Street, § 293); **on** (a friend, an income, milk); **up to** (promises); **within** (means).

look : **about** (you); **after** (a person or thing); **at** (the consequences); **down on** (a person or thing); **for** (news); **into** (a thing); **on with** (pity, amusement); **out for** (bad weather); **over** (an account); **through** (a book, records); **to** (a person for assistance); **up to** (a person).

monopoly : **of** (wheat, manufactures, the carrying trade, right and wrong). (Not ' monopoly on '.)

moved : **at** (the sight, the thought); **by** (pity, prayer); **to** (laughter, tears); **with** (compassion).

name : **after** (a person); **from** (a person or event). See *named after*, § 417.

necessary : **for** (a journey, comfort); **to** (life, progress).

oblivious : **of** (not ' to '). See *oblivious*, § 417.

offended : **at** (a thing); **with** (a person).

opportunity : **of** (doing something); **to** (do something).

originate : **from** (an unknown cause); **in** (his own head); **with** (a person).

part : **from** (a person); **with** (a thing).

postpone : **for** (a thing *for* a time, a month); **to** (a thing *to* the afternoon, *to* a more suitable time).

practice : (medicine, your music, singing); **on** (the piano, a person, a person's credulity or feelings).

present′ : **to** (a person or thing *to* a person); **with** (a person *with* a thing).

prevail : **against** (a person or thing); **on** (a person to do something); **over** (a person or thing).

preventive : **of** (disease, trouble).

reconcile : **to** (a person *to* a thing); **to, with** (one person *to* or *with* another); **with** (one thing *with* another).

reference : **to** (*a* reference *to* a person or thing; *with* reference *to* a person or thing).

regard : **to** (*in* or *with* regard *to* a person or thing). Do not say ' in (with) regards to '.

rely : **on** (a person or thing).

respect : **to** (*with* respect *to* a person or thing).

search : **after** (truth, wisdom); **for** (a person or thing); **into** (a thing, the root of the matter). **In my search after, for** ; but, **in search of** (I am in search of a house).

see : **about** (a person or thing); **after** (a person or thing); **into** (a thing); **through** (a person or thing); **to** (a person or thing).

sick : **at** (heart); **for** (a person or thing); **of** (a person or thing, a fever); **with** (influenza, fear).

similar : **to** (one thing *to* another); **similarly to** (one thing situated, used, etc., *to* another).

stand : **by** (a person); **for** (a thing); **in** (your own light); **to** (your oars); **up for** (a person or thing); **up to** (obligation).

suffer : **from** (headache, a breakdown); **under** (a king).

suitable : **for** (a purpose); **to** (an occasion).

sympathy : **for, with** (a person in his distress). **In sympathy with** (nature, a thing; *with* a person *in* a thing).

take : **after** (a person); **at** (his word); **for** (a friend); **in** (subscriptions, lodgers, new notions, the meaning of a thing); **into** (his head); **on** (extra men, an appearance); **on** or **upon** (yourself); **to** (heart, task); **up** (a matter); **up with** (a person); **taken up with** (sorrow, reflections).

talk : **about** or **of** (a person or thing); **over** (a person or thing); **to** or **with** (a person).

thirst : **after** or **for** (a thing); **to** (do something).

tinker : **at** (a thing). (Not 'with'; but, He tinkered *at* the lock *with* a file.)

tired : **from** (waiting); **of** (delay, waiting); **with** (exertions).

transplant : **into** (a person or thing *into* a new place, country).

treat : **for** (peace); **of** (different subjects); **to** (a person *to* a thing, *to* tea and cake); **with** (electricity, a nation). A **treatise on** (botany, ethics).

unite : **to** (him *to* your cause); **with** (us in the song).

vexed : **at** (a thing); **with** (a person).

view : **of** (*in* view *of* the past, the facts); **to** (*with* a view *to* doing something).

wait : **for** (a person or thing); **on** (a person).

---

288. *A, an.* The preposition *a* (*an*) is used in certain idiomatic expressions and in compound words :

1. Twice *a* day, five miles *an* hour. (Here *a, an,* is now commonly regarded as the indefinite article; § 139.)

2. Set the clock *a* going (or *a*-going). (§ 224.)

3. *A*board, *a*bove, *a*breast, *a*fire, *a*float, *a*foot, *a*head, *a*live, *a*shore, *a*side, *a*sleep, *a*sunder.

289. Per. Except in a few phrases like *per annum, per cent* (perhaps from *per centum*), and *per se* (= *by itself, by themselves*) the preposition *per* is confined to scientific and commercial language, in expressions denoting rate (see *a, an,* § 139, 4):

1. He has an income of five hundred dollars *per annum.*
2. What rate *per cent* is paid? (See *per cent,* § 417.)
3. Five *per cent* of the material *is* enough. (§ 205, 15.)
4. Fifty *per cent* of the population *were* uneducated. (§ 205.)
5. The thing is (things are) worth nothing *per se.*
6. The pendulum makes sixty vibrations *per* minute. (Physics.)
7. Flour at twenty dollars *per* barrel. (Commerce.)

290. In, into. The preposition *into* (not ' in ') should be used to denote motion to a point within :

1. You may walk *in* the garden.
2. You may walk *into* the garden.

NOTE. In Anglo-Saxon (§ 601) the preposition *in* meant ' in ' when used with the dative case, and ' into ' when used with the accusative case (§§ 604, 606). The two cases became alike in form, and *into* was substituted for *in* when used with the accusative. Remnants of the early use of *in* meaning ' into ' still survive in certain long-established idioms with verbs like *break, cut, fall, lay, put* : ' break *in* two ', ' cut *in* pieces', 'fall *in* love' (compare 'fall *in* the street', 'fall *into* the street').

291. Of. The form *o'* occurs in some phrases like *o'clock* (= *of the clock*) and *will-o'-the-wisp*, and in dialectal and colloquial use (§ 380); but *O'* in Irish names means ' descendant' :

At the turn *o'* the tide (dialect).   John Boyle *O'*Reilly.

292. On to. The preposition ' onto' for *on, to, into,* and the like, is not established by good usage ; it is easily avoided :

1. We walked *on to* the next town.
2. Do not step *on* the grass. (Not ' onto '.)
3. The bird fell *to* the ground. (Not ' onto '.)
4. He tumbled *into* a chair. (Not ' onto '.)
5. He climbed up and got *on* the roof. (Not ' onto '.)

293. At, in, on. In expressions of locality *at* is used of towns, small cities, and small islands; *in* is used of large cities; *in* is used of streets and squares (this has been the usage for centuries; *on* is an American colloquialism; see § 417, N.):

1. He lives *at* Bradford; *at* Newton; *at* Malta.
2. My friends are *in* Chicago; *in* New Orleans; *in* Omaha.
3. She uttereth her voice *in* the streets. — THE BIBLE.
4. A shopkeeper *in* Whitecross Street. — DEFOE.
5. At Mrs. Bardell's, *in* Goswell Street. — DICKENS.
6. When he is in town, he lives *in* Soho Square. — ADDISON.
7. My lot of ground *in* Arch Street. — FRANKLIN.
8. I shall think you mean to keep me *in* Grub Street.— LOWELL.
9. An office *in* Lombard Street. — LEONARD MERRICK.
10. But, The house *fronts on* Ware Street, *on* Adams Square.

NOTE. The preposition corresponding to *in* is used with streets and squares in French, German, Spanish, and various other modern languages. The expression 'They were *on* the streets' means that they were dependent on the streets for a living.

294. On, round. Do not use *upon* and *around* to the exclusion of *on* and *round*. The use of 'around' (or 'round'), which means *on all sides*, as an adverb for *about* in the sense of *here and there*, *near*, is an American colloquialism (§ 380); so, also, the use of 'around' as an adverb for *round*:

1. Agree *on*; based *on*; call *on*; depend *on*; enter *on*; fall back *on*; insist *on*; look *on*; march *on*; rely *on*; *on* his return.
2. She did not stop to look *round* her.
3. We gathered *round* the fire.
4. They live *round* the next corner.
5. He travels *about* the country. (Not 'around'.)
6. Sit (Stand, Hang, Fool) *about*. (Not 'around'.)
7. There are just enough oranges to go *round*. (Not 'around'.)
8. A hall, hung *round* with many old portraits. (Not 'around'.)
9. They wake up the neighbors for a mile *round*. (Not 'around'.)
10. He's an *all-round* man. (Not 'all-around'.)

295. *Aware that,* etc. Adjectives like *aware, certain, uncertain, positive,* and *sure* may be modified by a prepositional phrase or by a clause :

    1. We were *aware of his coming.*
    2. We were *aware that he came.*
    3. They were *uncertain how he escaped.*

296. *Have been to.* For this idiom with *to,* see § 245. (Exercise XXVII, § 572.)

THE CONJUNCTION

297. Conjunction. A conjunction is a word used to connect words, phrases, or clauses. Conjunctions are coördinating or subordinating.

298. Coördinating conjunctions. The coördinating conjunctions are *and, but, for, nor, or ; both . . . and ; either . . . or ; neither . . . nor.* They connect words, phrases, or clauses of the same kind, or order ; *and, but, for, nor, or,* connect sentences also (see Ex. 9, 10) :

    1. Father *and* mother will go with us.
    2. They live in a small *but* beautiful house. (§ 476.)
    3. He works at Wilmington *or* at Dover.
    4. His youngest son, whom he most loved, *and* to whom he had given everything, had gone away.
    5. We searched, *but* we could not find anything.
    6. He is not only bright, *but* studious. (§ 476.)
    7. I stayed at home ; *for* I had work to do. (§ 476.)
    8. We did not wait, *nor* did we wish to do so.
    9. They refused. *But* they will not always refuse.
    10. He could not return. *Or* did he not wish to return?
    11. He is *both* bright *and* studious.
    12. He is *either* bright *or* studious.
    13. He is *neither* bright *nor* studious.

NOTE. This list includes all the coördinating conjunctions, according to the report of the English joint committee. The words in pairs, *both . . . and, either . . . or, neither . . . nor*, are sometimes called correlative conjunctions. Such words as *also* (§ 273), *consequently, hence, so, therefore* (§ 262, 6), *still*, and *yet* (§ 262, 7) are not conjunctions, but adverbs (§ 252); they are preceded by a semicolon (§ 483) or a period, unless accompanied by *and* (*and so, and therefore, and yet*, etc. Of course *and so*, etc., may also be preceded by a semicolon or period). See *so*, § 417.

299. Conjunction omitted or repeated. When several words, phrases, or clauses are connected by *and, but, nor*, or *or*, the conjunction is usually omitted except with the last; but for emphasis it may be repeated:

   1. The oranges were good, bad, *and* indifferent.
   2. They had music *and* song *and* athletic contests.

300. Punctuation. For the punctuation with *and, or*, or *nor* in a series, see § 467; for *but* and *for*, see § 476. Study the following examples of *or* and *nor* in negative sentences; *or* is used to connect words or phrases, and *nor* to connect clauses; *nor* is preceded by a comma or semicolon:

   1. They have *no* trade *or* commerce.
      They have *no* ships, *nor* have they wood to make them.
   2. It was *not* kind *or* just.
      It was *not* kind, *nor* was it just.
   3. He heeded *not* me *or* my sorrow.
   4. We had *no* revolutions to fear, *nor* [did we have; § 347] fatigues to undergo. — GOLDSMITH.
   5. He did *not* wish to be unkind *or* to seem so. (Here *or* may have a comma before it to set the phrase off rhetorically, as an added thought; § 474.)
      He did *not* wish to be unkind; *nor* [did he wish] to seem so.

301. Verb with *or, nor*. For the agreement of the verb in sentences containing *or* or *nor*, see § 202.

302. Subordinating conjunctions. A subordinating conjunction connects a subordinate clause with a principal clause (§§ 7, 8). Some subordinating conjunctions, like some prepositions, were originally adverbs (see § 383):

1. I never saw him *before*. (Adverb.)

2. I saw him *before* he returned. (Subordinating conjunction, connecting the clause *he returned* with the verb *saw*.)

303. Classification. Subordinating conjunctions are classified according to the kind of subordinate clause which they introduce (compare § 269); phrases used as conjunctions are called compound conjunctions:

1. Clause of time: after, as (= while), as soon as, before, ere, since, till, until, when, whenever, whensoever, while. He trembled *as he spoke.*

2. Clause of place: where, wherever. I will go *where you go.*

3. Clause of cause: as (= since), because, inasmuch as, in that (= since), since, that (= because), whereas. I did not wait *because I was alone.* He did right *in that he stayed away.* I am sorry *that you waited.*

4. Clause of purpose (with the present or the past subjunctive): lest (= *that . . . not, for fear that,* with the subjunctive), so that, that. She went at once, *lest she should be late.* He has come *that he may help us.*

5. Clause of result: so that, that. It rained in such torrents *that we stayed at home.* See *so,* § 417.

6. Clause of condition: if, in case that, in case, unless (= if . . . not), whether (= if). *In case you succeed,* build a fire. We shall not go *unless you do.* He will go *whether we do or not.*

7. Clause of concession or contrast: although, even if, though, whereas (= while on the contrary, although). *Although it is cheap,* I do not want it. He was there, *whereas we were not.*

8. Clause of comparison (of manner or degree):

Manner: as, as if (§ 346), however. We do *as he does.* He acted *as if he were frightened. However it happened,* I was to blame (see § 470, 2).

Degree: according as, in proportion as, in so far as, as well as, however, much as, than. He is as tall *as I am* (see § 347). He is taller *than I am.* They thought it flimsy *as well as* (they thought it) *expensive.* She accepted no favors, *however small they were. Much as he dislikes to do so,* he will wait.

9. Noun clause: if (= whether), that, whether. I asked him *if* (or *whether*) *he lived near.* It is uncertain *whether his brother returned.* (The noun clause includes indirect questions; see §§ 77, 78.)

304. Relative adverbs. A clause introduced by a subordinating conjunction is often used to modify a noun; such a clause is therefore not an adverb clause, but an adjective clause (§ 114), and the subordinating conjunction so used is called a relative adverb (being used similarly to a relative pronoun, § 81). Such subordinating conjunctions as *after, before, since* (expressing time), *when, where, while,* and *why* may be relative adverbs:

1. We saw him the day *before he went away.* (Modifies *day.*)
2. There is the house *where we lived.* (Modifies *house.*)
3. That is the reason *why he returned.* (Modifies *reason.*)

For subordinating conjunctions of time, place, and the like in conditional sentences, see § 342.

305. *As . . . as, so . . . as.* Use *as . . . as* in affirmative declarative sentences; use *so . . . as* in negative and other sentences implying a fixed limit or a comparison in which there is felt to be a marked contrast:

1. She is *as* tall *as* he (is ; § 347).
2. She is not *so* tall *as* he (is; § 347).
3. Who could be *so* helpful *as* she?
4. *So* far *as* I know, he deserves assistance.
5. Do *as* much *as* you can.
6. Do only *so* much *as* you can conveniently. (= Don't do more than you can conveniently.)

306. *As* overworked. The conjunction *as* is overworked, often being made to take the place of *because, since, when,* or *while*:

1. *Since* he could not come, he wrote a letter. (Not 'As'.)
2. *While* she was reading, she fell asleep. (Not 'As'.)

307. *As follows*. In the expression *as follows* the *as* is a subordinating conjunction denoting manner; the impersonal subject (*it*) is omitted:

He wrote a letter of apology, *as* (it) follows.

308. *Because, since*, etc. In causal clauses *because* gives the real reason; *since, as, inasmuch as*, or *for* (not a subordinating conjunction; § 298), gives the logical reason:

1. The thermometer is rising *because* the air is warmer.
2. *Since* the thermometer is rising, (I infer that) the air is warmer.

309. *Than*. In the older language *than* was frequently followed by the objective case instead of the nominative; although now grammatically incorrect, *than whom* is still used occasionally, but it is clumsy, and sounds pedantic. In present usage the case after *than* depends on the construction:

1. He is older *than she* (is).
2. He likes her better *than* (he likes) *me*.

310. *That, to*. In clauses of purpose we are sinking into a mannerism in using the heavy phrase 'in order that' for the old and simple *that*, a habit formed at school and college in the translation of foreign languages. The same thing is true of 'in order' placed before the infinitive with *to*. Omit 'in order', and observe how much smoother the language is; or read the Bible and Shakespeare aloud and hear how the language would sound with 'in order' inserted:

1. *That* we may accomplish these things, we need time.

To obtain the books, we need time.

For the purpose of accomplishing these things (or, If we are to accomplish these things), we need time.

2. Fools, who came *to* scoff, remained *to* pray. — GOLDSMITH.

3. But all this was done, [in order] *that* the scriptures of the prophets might be fulfilled. — THE BIBLE.

4. And when he had sent the multitudes away, he went up into a mountain apart [in order] *to* pray. — THE BIBLE.

5. [In order] *To* save your life in this extremity,

This favor will I do you for his sake. — SHAKESPEARE.

6. *To* justify this assertion, I shall put my reader in mind of Horace, the greatest wit and critic in the Augustan age. — ADDISON.

311. Confusion of relatives, etc. In the analysis of subordinate clauses relative pronouns, relative adverbs, or subordinating conjunctions are often confused with interrogative pronouns, interrogative adverbs, or interrogative subordinating conjunctions introducing indirect questions (§§ 77, 263, 330):

1. I met the man *whom* they elected. (Relative pronoun.)

I asked *whom* they elected. (Interrogative pronoun.)

2. He had gone *when* you came. (Subordinating conjunction.)

He wondered *when* you came. (Interrogative adverb.)

3. He will go *if* I do. (Subordinating conjunction.)

It is doubtful *if* I can go. (Interrogative subordinating conjunction; § 303, 9.)

4. I see the house *where* you live. (Relative adverb.)

Tell me *where* you live. (Interrogative adverb.)

5. He gave *what* I wanted. (Relative pronoun; § 83.)

He learned *what* I wanted. (Interrogative pronoun.)

312. *But*, etc., subordinating. The prepositions *but* (§ 314), *considering*, *notwithstanding* (§ 283), and *seeing* may take a *that*-clause as object; but *that* may be omitted, and these words then have the force of subordinating conjunctions (do not say 'but what' for *but that* or *but*; see *but that*, *but* *what*, § 417); a few other words, such as *now* and *provided*, with or without *that*, are used as subordinating conjunctions; the subordinating conjunction *but* does not have a comma or other mark of punctuation before it (§§ 476, 477):

1. Nothing would please him *but that* I must go too.
2. It never rains *but* it pours (= *that* it does *not* pour).
3. *Now that* (= *Seeing that*) you have it, keep it.

313. *But* as relative pronoun. After a negative the subject or the object in a subordinate clause introduced by *but* is frequently omitted, and *but* has the force of a negative relative pronoun meaning *who . . . not* or *that . . . not* (do not say ' but what' for *but*; see *but that, but what*, § 417):

1. There was not a boy *but* (= *who . . . not*) was grateful.
2. Nobody knew her *but* loved her.
3. There is no task *but* (= *that . . . not*) he will undertake.

314. *But* as preposition. In elliptical sentences (§ 347) the coördinating conjunction *but* often has the force of a preposition. In colloquial speech (§ 380) it is commonly followed by the objective form of the pronouns (*me, us, him*, etc.) instead of the nominative (*I, we, he*, etc.) ; but careful speakers or writers either use the nominative form or recast the sentence :

1. Nobody is at home *but* Polly [is at home].
2. Nobody is at home *but she*. (Colloquially, *her*. Recast : ' She is the only one at home'. If *but* precedes the verb, as in ' Nobody *but she is* at home ', ' but her ' would be awkward, and should be avoided.)
3. The boy stood on the burning deck,
       Whence all *but he* had fled. — Mrs. Hemans.
(Sometimes erroneously printed ' him '.)
4. I saw nobody *but* [I saw] *him*. (*Him* is correct here, being the object of the verb *saw*, understood.)
5. Nobody *but she* sympathized with her dear daughter's sufferings. —Dickens.

315. *Can but, cannot but,* etc. In expressions like *can but, could but,* and *dare but* the word *but* is an adverb, meaning *only*; in *cannot but, could not but,* and *dare not but* (or, in an interrogative sentence, *dare but*) it is a coördinating conjunction (§ 347):

1. I *could but* smile. (= I could only smile.)
2. I *could not but* smile. (= I *could not* [choose,] *but* [I could] smile = I could not help smiling.)
   We *cannot but* be gratified.
3. He *dares not but* obey.
4. What man *dares but* sanction it?

NOTE. It is correct to say 'I *cannot help* thinking so'; but 'I cannot but help thinking so' is contradictory and incorrect. See *help*, § 417. (Exercise XXVIII, § 573.)

THE INTERJECTION

316. Interjection. An interjection is a word used to express feeling or emotion. Interjections may have a variety of meanings according to the manner of utterance (for the punctuation, see § 319):

1. Ah, O, oh. (In sorrow, regret, appeal, remonstrance.)
2. Aha. (In triumph, mingled with surprise or derision.)
3. Alas. (In sorrow, pity, or concern.)
4. Bah, faugh, huh, pah, pish, poh, pshaw. (In contempt.)
5. Ha. (In surprise, joy, grief, suspicion, indignation.)
6. Hem. (In doubt, hesitation, warning.)
7. Ho. (In surprise, exultation, triumph, taunting.)
8. Hurrah. (In approbation, encouragement, exultation.)
9. Tush, tut. (In rebuke.)

NOTE. Some interjections are imitations of sounds, or are cries used to attract attention:

1. Baa, bang, bowwow, caw, ding-dong, mew, splash.
2. Ahem, hist (a signal for silence), hollo, hullo.

317. Exclamations. Nouns, pronouns, adjectives, adverbs, and short phrases are often used in exclamation, like interjections, but they are not to be classed as interjections (for the punctuation, see § 319):

1. Stuff and nonsense; what; what ho; good; well; why.
2. Dear me; bless me; good gracious.

318. *O, oh.* The words *O* and *oh* are both used as interjections. Formerly *oh* was often used in all positions where *O* is now more common. The words are still sometimes interchangeable, but their several uses have become more distinct:

The interjection *O* is the word now used before the nominative of address (§ 471):

1. Bless me, even me also, *O* my father.
2. Praise the Lord, *O* Jerusalem; praise thy God, *O* Zion.

In other connections, or without construction, *O* expresses, according to the intonation, various emotions, as of appeal, entreaty, surprise, pain, or lament:

1. *O* take me back again.
2. *O* would I were there.
3. *O* the pity of it! *O* dear me! *O* me!
4. *O* no; *O* yes; *O* indeed; *O* really.
5. *O*, but we all live beyond our incomes.

The interjection *oh* was probably intended to express a longer or stronger sound than *O*. It is now chiefly used when the exclamation is detached from what follows. It expresses emotion of various kinds, but is used especially as a cry of pain, terror, shame, derisive astonishment, or disapprobation, and is often repeated:

1. *Oh!* I thought you were going to leave me.
2. "*Oh*, the river!" she cried passionately.
3. Here's the smell of the blood still: all the perfumes of Arabia will not sweeten this little hand. *Oh, oh, oh!* — SHAKESPEARE.

319. Punctuation. Interjections and interjectional words and phrases may be followed by the comma or the exclamation mark (§ 464; see the examples in § 318 also):

1. *Fie, fie,* he'll never come. — SHAKESPEARE.
2. *What,* could ye not watch with me one hour? — THE BIBLE.
3. I have still, *alas!* much to do. — SIR JAMES MURRAY.
4. *Bless you!* how can I serve you?

THE SENTENCE

320. Classification. Sentences may be classified as declarative, interrogative, or exclamatory; affirmative or negative; simple, compound, or complex.

NOTE. Sentences containing an imperative were formerly called imperative sentences; in the Report of the Joint Committee on Grammatical Nomenclature they are classed as declarative.

321. Declarative. A sentence that tells or declares something is called declarative. A declarative sentence may tell a thing as a fact, or it may express the will or wish of the speaker:

1. We *had* good skating this year. (Indicative; § 161.)
2. Heaven *bless* you for your kindness. (Subjunctive; § 162.)
3. *Read* me your favorite poem. (Imperative; § 164.)

322. Interrogative. A sentence that asks a question is called interrogative; it is followed by the interrogation mark (§ 463):

1. Did you have good skating this year?
2. You had good skating this year?

323. Exclamatory. A sentence beginning with the exclamatory word *how* or *what* is called exclamatory; it is followed by the exclamation mark (§ 464):

1. *How* the sun shines! *What* a beautiful day it is!
2. *What* beautiful flowers and vines those are!

NOTE. A writer may use the exclamation mark after a declarative sentence to express surprise, incredulity, disgust, ridicule, or other emotion at what somebody else has said; such a sentence is exclamatory in character. See §§ 464 and 465.

324. Affirmative or negative. A sentence may be classed as affirmative or negative according to the absence or presence of a negative modifier of the verb:

1. Geography is an interesting study. (Affirmative.)
2. Has he *never* let you hear from him? (Negative.)

325. Simple or compound. A simple sentence has one subject and one predicate (either or both of which may be compound, § 328); the joining of two or more simple sentences makes a compound sentence:

1. We visited the old sawmill. (Simple.)
2. Men worked, women watched, children slept. (Compound.)
3. Who are you, and what do you want? (Compound.)
4. Alice, you sing; and Mary, you play. (Compound.)

326. Complex. The joining of one or more subordinate clauses (§ 8) to a simple sentence makes a complex sentence:

1. The light *that you have* is excellent.
2. The room *where I sleep* has two windows.
3. He had gone *before we reached the landing*.
4. *When he is to begin* is not yet decided.

327. Compound complex. The joining of one or more subordinate clauses (§ 8) to a compound sentence makes a compound complex sentence:

1. The pictures *that you sent* have arrived, and I am pleased.
2. *If you fail*, try again; and we will help you.
3. He asked *what you wanted*, but I did not tell him.

328. Compound subject, etc. Two or more simple subjects may be united to form one compound subject, and two or more simple predicates to form one compound predicate (§ 325):

1. *Tom* and *Anna* sing. (Compound subject.)
2. Tom *sings* and *plays*. (Compound predicate.)
3. *Tom* and *Anna* sing and *play*. (Compound subject and compound predicate.)

329. Subordinate clause. Subordinate clauses (§ 8) are of three kinds, noun clauses, adjective clauses, and adverb clauses (§§ 330–332).

330. Noun clause. A noun clause is a clause used as a noun, in the nominative or the objective case. It may be introduced by an interrogative pronoun or interrogative adjective (§§ 76–79), by an interrogative adverb (§ 263), or by the subordinating conjunction *if* (= *whether*), *that*, or *whether* (§§ 303, 311):

1. *Which way is best* is uncertain.
2. *How he entered the house* was a mystery.
3. All depends on *how you do it*.
4. I asked *if you were at home*.
5. Our expectation is *that mother will return today*.
6. I waited with one hope, *that he was safe*.
7. It is said *that his dog is an Irish setter*.

331. Adjective clause. An adjective clause is a clause used as an adjective (§ 114). It may be introduced by a relative pronoun (§ 83), a relative adjective (§ 84), or a relative adverb (§ 304):

1. The old man *whom he met* is my grandfather.
2. Is that a field *where sugar cane grows*?

332. Adverb clause. An adverb clause is a clause used as an adverb. It may be introduced by a subordinating conjunction (§§ 302, 303), or by a compound relative pronoun or adjective (§ 342):

1. I arrived *after the boat had started*.
2. *Whatever you do*, he will be dissatisfied.

333. Conditional sentence. A sentence containing an *if*-clause (or an equivalent) is called a conditional sentence. Conditional sentences refer to the present, past, or future; they are neutral (capable of fulfillment) or contrary to fact (incapable of fulfillment).

NOTE. Sections 334–340 are intended chiefly for reference. They are too difficult to be assigned in a single lesson.

334. Present neutral condition. A present neutral condition takes the present indicative in both clauses; in the condition the present subjunctive is sometimes used:

If this *is* (or *be*) so, he *deserves* praise.

335. Present condition contrary to fact. A present condition contrary to fact takes a past subjunctive in the condition, and the past subjunctive *could, might, should,* or *would* in the conclusion:

1. If she *were* here (but she isn't), we *should be* happy.
2. If he *had* money (now), he *would throw* it away.

336. Past neutral condition. A past neutral condition takes the past or the present perfect indicative in either or both clauses; in the condition the past perfect is sometimes used:

1. If he *was* there, I *did* not know it.
2. If he *saw* them, he *has told* them everything.
3. If he *had been* happy before, he *was* doubly so now.

337. Past condition contrary to fact. A past condition contrary to fact takes the past perfect subjunctive in both clauses, the conclusion usually having *could, might, should,* or *would*:

1. If he *had sent* them word (but he hadn't), they *would have come*.
2. If she *could have seen* us, we *might have waited*.

338. More vivid future condition. A future condition that is thought of as more likely to be fulfilled is called a more vivid future condition. A more vivid future condition takes the present indicative or present subjunctive in the condition, and a future indicative, or a verb expressing futurity, in the conclusion ; in formal language expressing simple futurity the subjunctive *shall* is used in the condition in all three persons :

1. If he *goes* (or *go*) now, he *will succeed.*
2. If I (you, he) *shall promise* this, what *can* they *do*?

339. Less vivid future condition. A future condition that is thought of as less likely to be fulfilled is called a less vivid future condition. A less vivid future condition takes the past subjunctive in both clauses ; in formal language expressing simple futurity the subjunctive *should* is used in the condition in all three persons :

1. If he *went* (or *were to go*) today, I *could go* with him.
2. If I (you, he) *should go* today, they *might go* too.

340. Mixed form of conditional sentence. In conditional sentences, when the thought requires it, the condition and the conclusion may be of different kinds. The condition may be contrary to fact in past time, and the conclusion contrary to fact in present time ; or the condition may be more vivid future, and the conclusion less vivid ; and so on :

1. If we *had* not *missed* the boat, we *should be* at home.
2. If your brother *comes* soon, I *should like* to see him.
3. If Mary *is* here, she *drove* in great haste.

341. Condition expressed by subjunctive. The condition is sometimes introduced by the subjunctive, without *if* :

1. *Had* I time, I would see him. (= If I had time, etc.)
2. *Had* he *wanted* to stay, he could have done so.
3. *Were* he *invited* soon, would he go?
4. She will be sixteen, *come* Sunday. (= if Sunday comes.)

342. Conditional relative sentence. A compound relative pronoun or adjective (§§ 98, 100), or a subordinating conjunction such as *when, whenever, wherever, however* (§§ 302, 303), may take the place of *if* in any conditional sentence (§ 333); the sentence is then called a conditional relative sentence. In structure the conditional sentence and the conditional relative sentence are the same. We use one kind or the other according as we wish to emphasize the idea of condition, or that of time, place, or the like:

1. *If* he went to school, he was always late. (§ 336.)
   When he went to school, he was always late.
2. *If* anybody had come, he would have been welcome. (§ 337.)
   Whoever might have come would have been welcome.
3. *If* we go anywhere, let us stick together. (§ 338.)
   Wherever we go, let us stick together.
4. *If* a person had means, he could do this. (§ 339.)
   A person *who* had means could do this.

343. Condition expressed variously. The condition may be expressed in other ways:

1. He would succeed *here*. (= if he came here.)
2. *To tell the story* would take hours. (= If I told, etc.)
3. *By doing so* we might cross. (= If we did so, etc.)
4. *You drive*, and I will walk. (= If you drive, I will walk.)

344. Conditional sentence quoted. Conditional sentences in indirect quotation follow the rules already given (§§ 176, 177, 195):

1. If you *go* back, I *shall* go back.
   He *said* that if you *went* back, he *should* go back.
2. If you *could* wait, I *would* wait.
   He *said* that if I *could* wait, he *would* wait.
3. If he *has* arrived, he *has* done well.
   You *said* that if he *had* arrived, he *had* done well.
4. If he *was* there, he *was* invited.
   I *presume* that if he *was* there, he *was* invited.

345. Mood in subordinate clause. In the subordinate clause the verb may be indicative or subjunctive (§§ 160–163). The indicative is used to denote that the action or state expressed by the verb is a fact, or is thought of as a fact; the subjunctive is used to denote that the action or state is not thought of as a fact, but as something possible, expected, or desired (wish or volition):

1. He stays because he *likes* the climate. (Indicative.)
   He stays because he *would* not like traveling. (Subjunctive.)
2. It is said that he *is* here. (Indicative.)
   It is necessary that he *be* here. (Subjunctive.)
3. It was so warm that ice *melted*. (Indicative.)
   It was so warm that ice *would* have melted. (Subjunctive.)
4. We shall not go if it *is* raining. (Indicative.)
   We *should* not go if it *rained*. (Subjunctive.)
   We *should* not have gone if it *had* rained. (Subjunctive.)
5. They were glad that he *asked* for it. (Indicative.)
   They were pleased that he *should* wish it. (Subjunctive.)
6. We waited until the dawn *came*. (Indicative.)
   We were waiting until the dawn *should* come. (Subjunctive of expectation.)
7. He was sorry that he *stayed* at home. (Indicative.)
   He wished that he *had* stayed at home. (Subjunctive of wish.)
8. They command that the gates *shall* be closed. (Subjunctive of volition.)
9. Suppose this *is* (now), *was* (yesterday), true. (Indicative.)
   Suppose this *were* (now), *had been* (yesterday), true. (Subjunctive, contrary to fact, §§ 335, 337.)
10. She *may* come here today. (Indicative.)
    She is coming that she *may* see you. (Subjunctive of purpose; § 303.)

NOTE. Verbs like *take care, mind,* and *see* are now usually followed by the indicative with the meaning of the subjunctive: See that he *does* it.

346. *As if*. *As if* (or *as though*, with some notion of opposition; see § 347, 15) takes the subjunctive (§§ 335, 337, 339) or the infinitive :

1. You laugh *as if* (or *as though*) you *enjoyed* it. (§ 347, 15.)
2. They ran *as if* they *had seen* a ghost.
3. He sat down and opened a book *as if* to read.

347. Ellipsis. When the meaning is made clear by the context, a portion of a sentence is often omitted. Such an omission is called an ellipsis, and the sentence is said to be elliptical. In analysis the ellipsis should be supplied ; the ability to supply it indicates a more thorough knowledge of the meaning of the sentence (§ 3) :

1. [I] Thank you, sir ; I am alone, but [I am] not unhappy.
2. What [shall we do] if our kites blow away?
3. What [do you say]? [You say that] You have no hat?
4. [It is] Impossible. Who are you? [You are] Mr. Brown?
5. While [we were] waiting, we unpacked the baskets and set the table.
6. O [I long] for a day in the woods !
7. He thought [that] you had gone across the lake.
8. [I bid you] Good morning, sir.
9. Why [are you] afraid? You are safe here.
10. [Do I] Remember thàt ride? I shall never forget it.
11. If [we were] tired, we took a drive.
12. I can hear quite as well where I am [as I could hear if I went elsewhere].
13. Although [he was] out of work, he was too proud to ask.
14. I am neither glad nor [am I] sorry.
15. He acts as [he would act] if he were ill.
    He acts as though he were ill = He acts as [he would act] were he ill, though [he is not]. § 346.
16. Be so good as [you would be good] to come.
17. He likes her better than [he likes] me.
18. He likes her better than I [like her].

19. She is taller than he [is tall].

20. He is not so tall as she [is tall].

21. They will need such men as he [is]. (Not ' him '.)

22. Nobody is at home but I [am at home]. (See § 314.)

23. He received more [votes] than a thousand votes [are].

24. She accepted no favors, however small [they were].

25. Why did I stay? [I stayed] Because I was needed.

26. Where did he go? [He went] Wherever he was sent.

27. What are you reading? [I am reading] The Doll in the Pink Silk Dress.

348. Erroneous elliptical sentence. An elliptical sentence is erroneous or faulty if the omitted form of a verb is different from the form used in the sentence, or if the ellipsis causes obscurity :

1. I have *been* and shall always *be* sorry. (Do not omit *been*.)

2. He wishes us to *study* the same things that he has *studied*. (Do not omit *studied*.)

3. The guests *were* seated, and the dinner *was* served. (Do not omit *was*.)

4. One man *was* killed, and several *were* hurt. (Do not omit *were*.)

5. Faulty: He had succeeded, failed, and began again. (Say 'He had succeeded, had failed, and had begun again'; or 'He had succeeded and failed, and had begun again'; or 'He had succeeded and failed, and began again'; or 'He succeeded, failed, and began again'.)

349. Misattached clause. A subordinate clause may be elliptical if its subject is the same as the subject of the principal verb (if its subject is not the same, the elliptical clause is faulty, being grammatically attached to the wrong subject) :

1. While [*she* was] sitting at the window, *she* saw a parade go by. (' *She* was ' may be omitted.)

While *she* was sitting at the window, a *parade* went by. (Do not omit ' *she* was '.)

2. *He* died when [*he* was] a child. ('*He* was' may be omitted.)

His *grandmother* died when *he* was a child. (Do not omit '*he* was'.)

3. Don't [*you*] eat the cream until *it* is frozen. (Do not omit '*it* is'.)

350. Ellipsis in telegrams. In the expressions *thank you* and *pray* (§ 250), and before *would* in such expressions as *would thou wert as I am*, the subject (*I, we*) may be omitted; but the omission of the subject of verbs in general is not proper except in telegrams, where various ellipses are used to save expense; the use or repetition of *I* or *we* in letters is easily avoided:

1. [We] *Thank* you for writing to us. Tell us what to do, *pray*.

2. Your letter amuses me. (Rather than 'I am amused by', etc.)

3. No apology is necessary. (Rather than 'I do not ask', etc.)

4. Telegram: Letter received. Starting home immediately. Meet you Friday. Invite friends. (= 'Your letter has been received. I am starting', etc.) (Exercise XXIX, § 574.)

CHAPTER IV

RHETORIC: STYLE

Do not neglect your style, whatever language you speak in, or whomsoever you speak to, were it your footman. Seek always for the best words and the happiest expressions you can find. Do not content yourself with being barely understood; but adorn your thoughts, and dress them as you would your person.

LORD CHESTERFIELD.

Obscurity and affectation are the two greatest faults of style.

MACAULAY.

351. Having something to say. The first essential in speaking or writing is to have something to say. If you are full of your subject, you will usually be able to express yourself. The more clearly you think out what you wish to say, the more clearly you will express it. To write interestingly, you must not only tell the truth, but tell it with a simplicity, directness, and charm that will delight the eye and ear, and captivate the mind and heart. Success or failure lies chiefly in the telling. By persistent study and practice you will form good habits of thinking, and attain effective methods of expression, or good style.

352. Clearness, force, smoothness; unity. The qualities of good style are clearness, force, and smoothness. These qualities should be found in every sentence. Every sentence should be clear; otherwise the thought is not fully understood. Every sentence should be forcible; otherwise the thought loses a part of its power. Every sentence should be smooth, that it may give pleasure; otherwise the thought may not awaken interest and hold the attention.

But underlying the qualities of clearness, force, and smoothness is the fundamental quality of unity, or oneness. Every
sentence should have unity; that is, it should contain one
thought, and one only, and should present this thought from
but one point of view. Without this quality of unity a sentence
may fail to be clear, or forcible, or smooth.

353. Unity. We cannot attain unity in expression until
we have attained unity in thought; and unless we attain unity
in both, we shall never achieve any high measure of success
either in speaking or in writing.

Unity should extend to all parts of spoken or written matter.
For example, the subject of a book should be a unit. Every
sentence in the book should be a unit. Every group of sentences, or paragraph, should be a unit. Every chapter should
be a unit. The entire book should be a unit.

354. Unity in title. The title David Copperfield, used by
Charles Dickens for one of his stories, has unity, since the two
words form the name of one person who is the central character in the story. But if the title were David Copperfield and
Peggotty, the unity of subject and story would be destroyed;
for the interest would be divided, and the story would be more
or less unsatisfactory. On the other hand, a compound subject
(§ 328) which presents a contrast attracts and holds the attention; for example, Mammon and the Archer, and The Cop
and the Anthem, by O. Henry, are good titles.

A title should be short, original, interesting, and suggestive.
It should not tell too much, but it should not be general or
obscure. The following are examples of good titles: Treasure
Island (Stevenson), By Courier (O. Henry), The Light that
Failed (Kipling), The Mystery of Marie Rogêt (Poe), The
Cask of Amontillado (Poe), The Tragedy of a Comic Song
(Leonard Merrick). See § 587.

Note. Do not waste time at the outset by trying to determine the exact form of a title. Let the title develop with the story. See § 359, Outline, note. Use your imagination, and improve it; and when you write fiction, write it so truthfully that it will sound like history.

355. Unity in sentence. Every sentence should contain but one thought, and should present that thought from but one point of view. Test unity by the following outline:

A. Unity in thought.
    1. More than one thought; incorrect use of *and*.
        a. If the sentence consists of a long series of related thoughts connected by *and*, it should be broken up into several sentences, any or all of which may be complex to indicate the proper subordination. See the examples below, *A,* 1, *a.* (Exercise XXX, § 575.)
        b. If the sentence consists of unrelated thoughts (likewise connected by *and*), it should be broken up into independent sentences, to express the unrelated thoughts independently. See the examples below, *A,* 1, *b.* (Exercise XXXI, § 576.)
    2. Less than one thought. (Exercise XXXII, § 577.)
        a. If what is considered to be a sentence is only a subordinate clause, it should be completed by the addition of a principal clause (§ 8). See the examples below, *A,* 2, *a.*
        b. If the thought is divided by being expressed in independent sentences, it should be united in one complex sentence having the proper subordination. See the examples below, *A,* 2, *b.*
B. Unity in point of view. (Exercise XXXIII, § 578.)
    1. If the sentence does not keep the same subject throughout, it should be made to do so unless a change of subject is necessary. See the examples below, *B,* 1.
    2. If the sentence does not keep the same mood, voice, tense, gender, person, and number throughout, it should be made to do so unless a change is necessary. See the examples below, *B,* 2.

A, 1, *a.* **Joining related thoughts.** Perhaps the most common violation of unity is the long, loose sentence of related thoughts without subordination:

1. Faulty: Some white-winged sea gulls are skimming over the water, and others circle round a lighthouse standing on a small island and having a quaint little window at the top, and from this window a light streams out to warn approaching vessels of the dangerous rocks along the shore. (Say 'Some white-winged sea gulls skim over the water; others circle round a lighthouse standing on a small island. At the top of the lighthouse is a quaint little window, from which a light . . . shore'.) (Exercise XXX, § 575.)

2. Faulty: I came home, and I found that my cousin had arrived. (Say 'When I came home, I found', etc.)

NOTE. On the other hand, the sentence 'In the evening my mother sews, and my father reads aloud' is a unit, because the two thoughts are united to form the larger single thought of 'how my parents spend the evening'.

A, 1, *b.* **Joining unrelated thoughts.** Such a sentence as 'Harry was born in Europe, and he has one sister' is not a unit, because it contains two principal thoughts which have no logical connection with each other; Harry's being born in Europe has nothing to do with his having one sister. Similarly, 'Harry is five years old, and lives in Pennsylvania' lacks unity, because it has a predicate of two parts which are not logically connected. But the sentence 'Harry is five years old, and has begun going to school' has unity, because it makes a connection between the boy's age and his going to school.

In the following sentences observe the lack of unity caused by joining unrelated thoughts:

1. Faulty: Miss Warner was the daughter of Mr. and Mrs. John W. Warner, and had spent all her life in North Hampton. (Say 'Miss Warner was the daughter of Mr. and Mrs. John W. Warner. She had spent all her life in North Hampton'; or 'Miss Warner, the daughter . . . Warner, had spent', etc.)

2. Faulty: The prisoners had a roast-pork dinner, and spent the afternoon in their cells. (It looks as if the eating of pork caused them to go to their cells. Say 'The prisoners . . . dinner in the dining room. They spent . . . cells'.) (Exercise XXXI, § 576.)

A, 2, *a*. Using subordinate clauses for sentences:

1. Faulty: He likes to read. Because it increases his vocabulary and broadens his sympathies. (Say 'to read, because', etc.)

2. Faulty: She said that she lived in a wild country. Where she was free to do as she pleased. (Say 'country, where', etc.) (Exercise XXXII, § 577.)

A, 2, *b*. Using detached sentences. To expand closely related thoughts into detached, abrupt sentences is no less a violation of unity than to crowd unrelated thoughts into one sentence; pick out the principal thought, and then make the others subordinate to it (for an example of the proper use of short sentences, see § 375, 6; read § 372):

Faulty: The observer watched from an airplane. He saw patches of woods. The villages were ruined. There were trenches. The most important things he saw were the enemy's batteries. (Say 'The observer, watching from an airplane, saw patches of woods, ruined villages, trenches, and, most important of all, the enemy's batteries'.) (Exercise XXXII, § 577.)

B, 1. Changing subject. Every sentence should present its thought from but one point of view. This means, for example, that there should not be any unnecessary shifting from one subject to another; for the reader, even if he is able to follow such mental gymnastics on the part of the writer, grows weary, loses the impression of unity of action, and becomes perplexed and displeased. "As in an instrument," says Ben Jonson, "so in style, there must be harmony and consent."

The sentence 'When he opened the window, he heard a moaning' is a unit, because the two clauses have the same subject (*he*), and hence keep to one point of view; but the

sentence ' When *he* opened the window, a *moaning* was heard '
lacks unity, because the shifting from *he* to *moaning* changes
the point of view.

In the following sentences observe the violation of unity
caused by a change of subject :

1. Faulty : When *I* went to your office, the *clerk* informed me
that you were out of town. (Say '*I* learned that you ', etc.)

2. Faulty : The *highway* was now left, and *we* entered the woods.
(Say '*We* now left the highway, and entered the woods '.)

3. Faulty : If *he* did not talk so much, *it* would be better for
him. (Say '*he* would be better off '.)

4. Faulty : Immediately after eating *our* breakfast, the *horses*
were saddled. (This sentence states that the horses ate our breakfast. Say ' *we* saddled the horses ' ; § 229.)

5. Faulty : *Rising* suddenly, the *canoe* upset. (The *canoe* did
not rise. Say '*I* upset the canoe' ; § 231.) (Exercise XXXIII,
§ 578 ; Exercise XXV, *c, d,* § 570.)

B, 2. Changing mood, voice, tense, etc.

In the follow-
ing sentences observe the violation of unity caused by a change
in mood, voice, tense, person, or number ; in narration the
past tense is generally better than the so-called historical present (the present is common in the headlines of newspapers,
to bring the narrative vividly before the reader) :

1. Faulty : Strangers *are* always welcome, and *would* not be
asked to contribute anything. (Say ' *are* not asked ', etc. ; § 340.)

2. Faulty : When he *dashed* from the room, he *was caught* by
a policeman. (Say ' he *found* himself in the arms of a policeman '.
The active voice is preferable to the passive ; § 208.)

3. Faulty : When he *opened* the window, he *hears* a moaning.
(Say ' he *heard*', etc. Do not say ' When he *opens* the window, he
hears a moaning ' ; see § 370, *C.*)

4. Faulty : *Strangers* are welcome, and *you* do not have to contribute anything. (Say ' and *they* do not ', etc.)

5. Faulty : *Everybody* did *their* best. (Say '*his* best' ; § 120.)

6. Faulty : *Students* should rewrite their work, again and again. Thus the *student* learns the value of revision and enjoys the satisfaction of having accomplished something. (Say ' Thus *they* learn ', etc.) (Exercise XXXIII, § 578.)

356. Unity in paragraph. Paragraphing, used as a mere mechanical device, aids the reader by furnishing resting places for the eye. But paragraphing is much more than a mechanical device ; it indicates the transition in the thought from one part of the subject to another, and by thus marking the divisions and subdivisions of the whole composition leads the reader step by step in the development of the entire subject.

A paragraph may contain a single sentence (as it often does in dialogue) or a group of sentences. It should be short enough to afford a resting place for the eye and the voice. The transition from one paragraph to another is often indicated by a transitional word or phrase, such as *also, too, but, however, so, thus, therefore, first, (secondly,* etc., § 275), *for example, on the other hand.* Read aloud (§ 361) such books as the teacher may name, and study the sentences and the paragraphs. Study the paragraphs in § 1 of this book.

357. Topic sentence. Every paragraph, whether short or long, should have the qualities of the sentence, namely, clearness, force, smoothness, unity. When a paragraph is composed of several sentences, one of the sentences (usually the first) often sets forth, in brief form, the particular point (or topic) of the entire paragraph. Such a sentence is called the topic sentence of the paragraph. The other sentences in the paragraph develop the thought expressed by the topic sentence (§ 579).

358. Coherence. If a paragraph is to have unity, it must, like the sentence, have coherence (§ 366); that is, it must be developed in such a way that the sentences composing it will not merely touch each other, like marbles in a bag, but will hang together like links in a chain (§ 577).

In the following paragraphs observe the topic sentence and the unity of the paragraphs as a whole:

1. You might wear natural flowers. At this season of the year they are particularly stylish. For ten francs you can get two or three magnificent roses. — DE MAUPASSANT.

2. When I came to my castle, for so I think I called it ever after this, I fled into it like one pursued. Whether I went over by the ladder, as first contrived, or went in at the hole in the rock, which I called a door, I cannot remember; no, nor could I remember the next morning, for never frightened hare fled to cover, or fox to earth, with more terror of mind than I to this retreat. — DEFOE.

3. I am not the last boy in the school. I have risen, in a few months, over several heads. But the first boy seems to me a mighty creature, dwelling afar off, whose giddy height is unattainable. Agnes says " No ", but I say " Yes ", and tell her that she little thinks what stores of knowledge have been mastered by the wonderful Being, at whose place she thinks I, even I, weak aspirant, may arrive in time. He is not my private friend and public patron, as Steerforth was; but I hold him in a reverential respect. I chiefly wonder what he'll be, when he leaves Doctor Strong's, and what mankind will do to maintain any place against him. — DICKENS.

4. The life of Johnson is assuredly a great, a very great work. Homer is not more decidedly the first of heroic poets, Shakespeare is not more decidedly the first of dramatists, Demosthenes is not more decidedly the first of orators, than Boswell is the first of biographers. He has no second. He has distanced all his competitors so decidedly that it is not worth while to place them. Eclipse is first, and the rest nowhere. — MACAULAY.

5. It has been remarked that Mr. Pecksniff was a moral man. So he was. Perhaps there never was a more moral man than Mr. Pecksniff: especially in his conversation and correspondence. It was once said of him by a homely admirer, that he had a Fortunatus's purse of good sentiments in his inside. In this particular he was like the girl in the fairy tale, except that if they were not actual diamonds which fell from his lips, they were the very brightest paste, and shone prodigiously. He was a most exemplary man:

fuller of virtuous precept than a copy-book. Some people likened
him to a direction-post, which is always telling the way to a place,
and never goes there: but these were his enemies; the shadows
cast by his brightness; that was all. His very throat was moral.
You saw a good deal of it. You looked over a very low fence of
white cravat (whereof no man had ever beheld the tie, for he fas-
tened it behind), and there it lay, a valley between two jutting
heights of collar, serene and whiskerless before you. It seemed to
say, on the part of Mr. Pecksniff, "There is no deception, ladies
and gentlemen, all is peace, a holy calm pervades me." So did his
hair, just grizzled with an iron-grey, which was all brushed off his
forehead, and stood bolt upright, or slightly drooped in kindred
action with his heavy eyelids. So did his person, which was sleek
though free from corpulency. So did his manner, which was soft
and oily. In a word, even his plain black suit, and state of widower,
and dangling double eyeglass, all tended to the same purpose, and
cried aloud, "Behold the moral Pecksniff!" — DICKENS. (Exercise XXXIV, § 579.)

359. Unity throughout ; paraphrase ; outline. The entire composition, no less than the sentence and the paragraph,
should have unity. The easiest as well as the surest way to
attain this is by means of paraphrase and outline. The student should begin, not by trying to produce original work, but
by studying the work of good authors, and by paraphrasing
that work into simple and familiar English.

Paraphrase. Paraphrasing teaches clear and close thinking, which not only is the first and most direct step toward
original composition, but is fundamental to all education.
The student who approaches composition through paraphrasing is not bewildered and made unhappy by having to hunt
about for something to say, but finds himself engaged in
the problem of analyzing and reproducing what somebody else
has said. He studies the meaning of the words and phrases,
and then expresses the thought in his own language.

After a considerable amount of practice of this kind, his next step is to take topic sentences (§§ 357, 579) and develop them by the same method by which he has learned to develop the thought in making paraphrases. Having formed the habit of studying words, he now applies his skill to his own original work, and finds himself able to produce something creditable.

Paraphrasing should begin with prose, and should continue with prose until the student becomes familiar with the process, and acquires facility. The transition to poetry may then be made without loss of power, and with increasing interest. The passages chosen for paraphrasing should be inviting and stimulating, and should be so carefully graded that the student's mind runs ahead, instead of being painfully driven through an exercise which is too difficult. The teacher should not be satisfied with paraphrases which are inaccurate or crude, but should teach the student to be discriminating in the choice of words (§ 382) and in the style, that he may catch not only the thought but the spirit of the original work. Sometimes the language of the original should be condensed, and sometimes expanded. This kind of study may give the student a glimpse of the beauty of poetry, and induce him to read the poets.

In paraphrasing poetry, observe the following points :

First, write the paraphrase in the form of prose, disregarding the division of the poetry into lines with capital letters.

Secondly, avoid poetic expressions, however simple : *methinks, doth, hath, findeth, o'er, ne'er, sooth, swain.*

Thirdly, expand the language (use a larger number of words) when necessary ; the poet may have been obliged to compress his thought into the fewest words possible.

Fourthly, in a selection of some length it may be advisable to pick out a thought for a topic sentence (§ 357), regardless of where the thought occurs in the original.

ORIGINAL

But now, at this early age, he quits the paternal roof; goes forth into looser, louder, more exciting society; and becomes initiated in those dissipations, those vices, which a certain class of philosophers have asserted to be a natural preparative for entering on active life; a kind of mud-bath, in which the youth is, as it were, necessitated to steep, and, we suppose, cleanse himself, before the real toga of Manhood can be laid on him. — CARLYLE.

PARAPHRASE

But early in life Burns leaves home, to enter into the more inviting companionship of the world, with all its bustle and excitement. He forms those wasteful and injurious habits which certain persons maintain to be the usual experiences for every youth to pass through in preparing for his future. These misguided persons think that this saturation with filth has a cleansing effect on him, and fits him to be called a man.

ORIGINAL[1]

Only the prism's obstruction shows aright
The secret of a sunbeam, breaks its light
Into the jeweled bow from blankest white;
  So may a glory from defect arise:
Only by Deafness may the vexed Love wreak
Its insuppressive sense on brow and cheek,
Only by Dumbness adequately speak
  As favored mouth could never, through the eyes.

PARAPHRASE

Perfection is sometimes attained only through imperfection. It is only when broken by the prism that a ray of light reveals the brilliant colors of the rainbow. So it is only when hindered by deafness that unconquerable love impresses itself on brow and cheek, and only when hindered by dumbness that it speaks, through the eyes, more eloquently than gifted tongue could speak.

(Exercise XXXV, § 580.)

[1] Browning wrote this poem after seeing Woolner's sculptured group of Sir Thomas Fairburn's deaf and dumb children.

Outline; composition. When the student has acquired skill in paraphrasing and in developing topic sentences, his next step toward original work is to plan and develop his intended composition by means of an outline. The outline indicates the divisions and subdivisions of the subject, and thus teaches how to arrange the subject matter in logical order, and how to group those points which are related, without repetition. An outline bears the same relation to an entire composition that the topic sentence bears to the paragraph (or that a table of contents bears to a book; see Contents, and the outlines in §§ 355, 366). Study § 587.

A simple outline, sufficient for ordinary purposes, may be made by answering the questions *Who?* (= any subject) *When? Where? What? How? Why?* Group your material under these headings, and develop it in whatever order seems desirable.

NOTE. The beginning is perhaps the most difficult part to write. Do not waste time at the outset by trying to decide what form it shall take, but let it develop with the rest of the composition. See § 354, note.

OUTLINE

Who?   (Benjamin Franklin)
When?   (colonial times)
Where?   (at home and abroad)
What?   (from candle-maker's assistant to scientist, statesman, and diplomat)
How?   (by study, economy, perseverance, integrity)
Why?   (because of his love for his fellow men; he never sought office)

OUTLINE

Who?   (a crop of oranges)
When?   (this year)
Where?   (in Florida or California)
What?   (unusual in amount and quality)
Why?   (good conditions, better care)

Who? (I)	*What?* (fishing)
When? (last summer)	*How?* (in a sailboat)
Where? (in Buck's Harbor)	*Why?* (food for the camp)

COMPOSITION

Observe the paragraphing and unity in the following letter (postscripts, as a rule, should be avoided; they violate the principle of unity, § 353):

Buck's Harbor, Maine,
August 16, 1922.

Dear Jack,

A week of my outing with my cousins is already gone. Nothing in particular has happened except my adventure of yesterday, out in the harbor. I was fishing alone in a small sailboat, and had caught some haddock and hake, when I looked out to sea. Noticing a thin belt of fog along Pickering's Island, I pulled up anchor and set sail.

The fog grew thicker, and the wind almost died away. I was soon shut in by the mist, and couldn't keep the right direction, but I took my fog horn and blew every minute.

For a long time I sailed about in the bay, and wondered where I could be. It was nearly dark, and I was cold and hungry. At last I blew two or three times, louder than ever. Then I listened. A faint shout answered. I sailed in the direction of the sound, listening and watching. A light finally shone through the fog. It was the camp fire which the boys were building. They were heaping up the faggots to guide me to the shore.

I was soon beside the blazing fire, and a big haddock was spluttering over the coals.

The boys ask when you are coming. We shall have more fun when you are here. You will come soon, won't you?

With love from us all I am, as ever,

Your old pal,
Dick.

PS. Don't trouble to bring fishing tackle; we have everything you need. Just pack up some old clothes, and come as soon as you can.

360. Clearness; good usage. To attain clearness in speaking or in writing, we should choose the words which best express our thought, and arrange them in such a way that those which are grammatically related stand together. In our choice of words we should be guided by good usage; that is, we should choose such words as are used by our best speakers and writers of the present day. (For the study of words and the use of the dictionary, see §§ 378–402.)

361. Reading good authors aloud. To know good usage, we should live with those who speak and write our language correctly. If we cannot have this environment, we should create such an atmosphere by reading good authors aloud; for by constantly seeing, pronouncing, and hearing proper words and phrases we unconsciously make them a part of ourselves.

If the pupil in the elementary school should spend one hour a day in reading aloud, whether to his teacher, to his classmates, to a member of his family, or to himself, he would be astonished at the result, not only in his acquirement of language, but in his other studies. He would understand his lessons better, and learn them more easily; impropriety in his speech would give way to propriety; and his difficulties of expression, both in speaking and in writing, would gradually be smoothed away. Furthermore, reading aloud would train his voice, and make it more agreeable.

362. Language an imitation. Language is, at the beginning, purely imitation. Just as the carpenter's apprentice imitates his master in learning the ordinary uses of chisel and plane before he employs them in his own way, so, in learning the mechanism of speaking and writing, the apprentice begins by imitating others. Individuality of expression, like the invention of new patterns of chisel or plane, does not begin until the early apprenticeship is over.

363. Speaking; writing. The attainment of clearness is easier in speaking than in writing; hence the necessity of practice in writing. When we speak, we choose and arrange our words with a good deal of freedom, and by means of pause, modulation of the voice, phrasing, and emphasis make them mean to our hearers what they mean to us; but when we write, we must, without having any of these external aids to assist us, put our thoughts on paper for others to read; and if we would be understood, we must so choose and arrange our words that they will mean what we intend, and nothing else. We should not break the unity of our sentences by introducing foreign and heterogeneous matter, or cover up the main points by a mass of subordinate and unimportant details.

364. Reading aloud; rewriting. The importance of reading aloud, and of rewriting again and again, can hardly be overestimated. Newman once wrote in a letter, "When I have read over a passage which I had written a few days before, I have found it so obscure to myself that I have either put it altogether aside or fiercely corrected it."

Rousseau said, "Nor can I express my thoughts on the most trivial subjects save at the cost of hours of fatigue. If I write immediately what strikes me, my letter is without beginning or end, a long, confused string of expressions, which, when read, can hardly be understood."

Tennyson corrected his work with infinite pains, and often read his poems aloud, first to his family and afterwards to visitors. When his poems were in type, he usually kept them by him for a long time, months or even years, reconsidering and perfecting every part.

Balzac, perhaps the greatest novelist of the world, showed no cleverness at school, and possessed no literary gift. When he began to write, he sometimes despaired of ever being able to put his thought on paper. He spent countless nights in composing books which he never acknowledged. A man of less dauntless will would have been vanquished; but Balzac, happily, had unshaken faith in his genius, which others ignored. He usually began writing at midnight, and continued till almost any hour of the following day. Sometimes he would spend a whole night on a single sentence, weighing it, twisting it, kneading it, hammering it, lengthening it, shortening it, writing it in a hundred different ways, until he found the proper form. Oftentimes, with a single stroke of his pen, he would courageously destroy the result of four or five nights of toil.

365. Fair speaking ; faulty writing. The writer of the following letter was a man thirty years old. He was a successful manager. He owned three automobiles, dressed well, had good manners, and was agreeable in conversation. Observe in his letter the violation of good usage in regard to arrangement (§ 535), abbreviations (§ 543), punctuation (§§ 535, 542, 460), capitalization (§ 424), spelling, and grammar :

                                                            Nov. 21 19—.

——W. 34 st
      New York City
          N. Y.

      M^r —— —— Bostin Mass

      Dear Sir. I write You again in reference to representing You with the —— Carbuerator. I have resigned with the —— and would like to here from You before I close up with some one elce, which I have had several offers, but I am willing to wait to here from You. I would rather represent the —— then any Carbuerator I know about. I want to represent You in My usual work. to appoint Dealers. and to install & Teach the Dealer all about Carbuerators I am well known all over the U. S. A. and My acquaintence is Valuable to You, I knowe of You being with the —— Regester, My Home is in Dayton. Right oppisit No —— Building and what I knowe I will feel honord to Sell the —— Carbuerators with You.

as I stated before in My last letter M^r —— knows Me and also M^r —— and I am sure they will be able to tell You of My System of Selling. I am so well known as a Carbuerator Man that the People believe Me when talking Carbuerators. M^r —— made me an Offer, but I can not talk with *him*. I was anxious to speak a word with You, when You was in his Office. but we only had a Chance to say *howdoue*. You promised him to be back at 5 Pm which I was their at that time hoping I could see You I hope to here from You. I remain Your

Resp J— ——.

366. Coherence in sentence. *Cohere* means *stick together* (see *hes-*, § 407). A sentence should be so arranged that those parts which are related stand next to each other, or that they otherwise show clearly their grammatical relation to each other (§ 358). To test the coherence of a sentence, use the following outline (some faulty examples are given after the outline):

A. Position of words, phrases, and clauses.

If the words, phrases, and clauses do not stand next to those which they modify, they should be made to do so. See the examples below, *A.* (Exercise XXXVI, *a*, § 581.)

B. Reference.

1. Of infinitive, gerund, and participle.

If an infinitive, gerund, or participle does not refer to the proper word, it should be made to do so. See §§ 222, 229, 231, 570.

2. Of pronoun.

a. If a pronoun does not suggest at once the antecedent to which it refers, the antecedent should be repeated. See §§ 65, 66, 94–97. (Exercise X, § 555.)

b. If a pronoun has no definite and clearly expressed antecedent, it should receive one. See §§ 61, *b*, N., 65, 74, 94, 95. See the examples below, *B*, 2, *b*. (Exercise XXXVI, *b*, § 581.)

   C. Coördination and subordination.
      1. In sentence.
         If the ideas in a compound sentence are not of equal value,
           the sentence should be made complex, with the proper
           subordination. Compare § 355, *A*, 1, *a*.
      2. Of word, phrase, and clause.
         If ideas of equal value are not expressed in parallel con-
           struction, that is, in parallel words, phrases, or clauses,
           the construction should be made parallel. See §§ 96,
           97, 375, 376.

A. Misplacing words, phrases, and clauses:

   1. Faulty: George L. Dunn died in his seventeenth year of
blood poisoning and typhoid fever. (Say ' George L. Dunn died
of blood poisoning and typhoid fever. He was in his seventeenth
year '.)

   2. Faulty: I am requested to announce next Wednesday evening that there will be a second meeting held in this room. (Put the
that after *announce.*)

   3. Faulty: The explosive was discovered by a private detective
concealed under a settee in the women's parlor. (The explosive was
concealed, not the detective; furthermore, the word *discovered*
makes the word *concealed* tautological (§ 413).) (Say ' A detective
discovered the explosive under a settee in the women's parlor '.)

   4. Faulty: Good should have told the teacher that Bad broke
the window when she asked him. (Say ' When asked by the teacher,
Good should have said that Bad broke the window '.)

   5. Faulty: It is regretted that Mr. Gardner was forced to retire
by the alumni and students. (The alumni and students had nothing
to do with the matter; nor did anybody force Mr. Gardner to retire.
Say ' The alumni and students regret that Mr. Gardner felt obliged
to retire '.)

   6. Faulty: A special train will convey the remains of B. Sanders
Walker, the banker who died early this morning as a result of taking
bichloride of mercury to his boyhood home, at Monroe, Georgia.
(Say ' A special train will convey to his boyhood home, at Monroe,
Georgia, the remains of ', etc.)

7. Faulty: They will spend the vacation in travel through Italy, where they meet Mrs. Benton's mother, Switzerland, and France. (Say 'They will . . . Italy, Switzerland, and France. In Italy they will meet Mrs. Benton's mother'; but perhaps 'meet' should be 'be joined by'.)

8. Faulty: Kneeling by the bedside, she was covering a hand fast growing cold with kisses and tears. (Say 'Kneeling by the bedside, she was covering with kisses and tears a hand', etc.) (Exercise XXXVI, *a*, § 581.)

B, 2, *b*. **Indefinite antecedent.** The use of pronouns with an indefinite antecedent should generally be avoided:

1. Faulty: Such customs are usual in countries where *they have* no large communities. (Say 'where *there are*', etc.)

2. Faulty: *They* don't have trees like this in our town. (Say '*We* don't have', etc.)

3. Faulty: She explained coloration in animals, of *which* I knew nothing. (Say 'animals, a *subject* of *which*', etc.) (Exercise XXXVI, *b*, § 581.)

367. For other points of clearness, see *Clearness* in the Index.

368. Clearness through figures of speech. The difference between the literal and the figurative use of words is explained in § 379. Figures of speech are word pictures. They should not be used unless they illustrate the thought or express it more clearly and more forcibly. They should not be mixed; for this produces, not a picture, but a blur. For example, we may say 'his *burning* words *inflamed* his hearers' or 'his *cold* words *chilled* his hearers'; but we may not say 'his *burning* words *chilled* his hearers'.

In the following sentences observe the figures of speech:

1. The camel is the *ship* of the desert.

2. This novel is said to be *founded* on fact.

3. I have gone astray *like a lost sheep.* — THE BIBLE.

4. A poor man that oppresseth the poor is *like a sweeping rain* which leaveth no food. —THE BIBLE.

5. The love of money is the *root* of all evil. — THE BIBLE.

6. The earth shall wax old *like a garment*. — THE BIBLE.

7. Some books are to be *tasted*, others to be *swallowed*, and some few to be *chewed* and *digested*. — LORD BACON.

8. They have sown the wind, and they shall reap the whirlwind. — THE BIBLE.

9. As the mountains are round about Jerusalem, so the Lord is round about his people from henceforth even for ever. — THE BIBLE.

10. She speaks *poniards*, and every word *stabs*. — SHAKESPEARE.

11. Silently, one by one, in the infinite *meadows* of heaven,
　　Blossomed the lovely stars, the *forget-me-nots* of the angels.

369. Mixed figures. Avoid mixing figures of speech (§ 368). In the following sentences observe the mixed figures :

1. Faulty: The trouble was not *rooted out*, and soon *blazed* forth again with renewed vigor. (Say ' and soon *sprang* up '.)

2. Faulty: Like a *sheep* without a shepherd, he became the plaything of the winds and sea. (Say ' Like a *ship* without a rudder, he ', etc.)

3. Faulty: The dog *handled* him roughly. (A dog has no hands ; say ' *treated* '.)

4. Faulty: He wished to *eradicate* all *obstacles*. (*Eradicate* means to pull up by the roots ; we speak of *eradicating evil* or *disease*, but of *removing* or of *overcoming* obstacles.)

5. Faulty: By *watching* your *steps* you will avoid the *reefs* and *sandbanks*. (Say ' avoid the *snares* and *pitfalls* '.)

6. Faulty: The *backbone* of the *cold wave is broken*. (Say ' The backbone of winter is broken '. Winter is here personified ; a wave does not have a backbone.)

7. Faulty: The *ship* of state has a rough *road* to travel. (Say ' is starting on a rough *voyage* '.)

8. Faulty: Columbus sailed across the Sea of Darkness, and *stumbled* on America. (Say ' and by chance found America '.)

9. Faulty: We *shipped* the goods by *rail*. (Say ' We *sent* ', etc.) This misuse of *ship* is an Americanism. A company that sends goods otherwise than by ship should use the term ' *transportation* department ' (not ' *shipping* '). See *ship*, § 417.

370. Force in sentence. To make language forcible, it is necessary not only to choose the right words to express the thought, but to put the most emphatic words in the most emphatic places. The most emphatic places in the sentence are at the beginning and the end. Care should be taken not to smother emphatic words by putting them in the middle of the sentence (or of a clause), and not to close the sentence with a weak ending; an unemphatic preposition at the end of the sentence does not violate this principle, since the emphasis falls on the word before the preposition (see § 286).

To test the force in a sentence, use the following outline (some examples are given below the outline):

A. Position of words. (Exercise XXXVII, *a*, § 582.)

   1. In ordinary sentence.

      If the emphatic words are not at the beginning and the end, they should be put there; a change in the usual order of the words produces unusual emphasis. See the examples below, *A*, 1.

   2. In climactic sentence.

      If the emphatic words are not arranged in an ascending series, growing in interest and power, they should be rearranged. See the examples below, *A*, 2.

B. Faulty repetition.

   1. Of words. (Exercise XXXVII, *b*, § 582.)

     a. Redundancy.

       If there are words, phrases, or clauses which do not help to express the thought, they should be omitted. See § 413. See *Redundancy* in the Index.

     b. Tautology.

       If there is a needless repetition of ideas, the repetition should be omitted (for the correct use of repetition, see § 371). See §§ 192, 413.

   2. Of sound.

      If there is an unpleasant repetition of sound, it should be avoided. See the examples below, *B*, 2.

C. Voice and tense. (Exercise XXXVII, *c*, § 582.)

    If the verb is in the passive voice, it should, if possible, be changed to the active; if the present tense is used to denote past action, it should preferably be changed to the past tense. See §§ 208, 213, N., 355, *B*, 2 (examples).

D. Force in repetition. See § 371.

E. Periodic and loose sentence; variety.

    If the sentences are monotonous in length and form, they should be varied. See § 372.

A, 1. Arranging words in ordinary sentence :

1. A great *dog* sat at the *door.* (Normal emphasis.)

    At the *door* sat a great *dog.* (Unusual emphasis.)

2. *Starvation* was the only thing left to him if he *delayed.*

    If he *delayed,* the only thing left to him was *starvation.* (Do not say 'If he delayed, starvation was the only thing left to him'; for the ending is weak.)

3. The West-India *trade*; the trade with *West India.* § 416.

4. They have eyes, but they do not see.

    Eyes have they, but they see not. — THE BIBLE.

5. Thou didst not anoint my head with oil.

    My *head* with *oil* thou didst not *anoint.* — THE BIBLE.

6. Towards this *spot* they directed their *weary steps.* — DICKENS.

7. In the thicket two eyes *watched,* and two ears *listened.*

8. Faulty: There was no alternative, however. (Say 'However, there was', etc.; or, with less emphasis on *however,* and with more formality, 'There was, however, no alternative'.) (Exercise XXXVII, § 582.)

A, 2. Arranging words in climactic sentence (see *climax,* § 417):

1. Tribulation worketh *patience*; and patience, *experience*; and experience, *hope.* — THE BIBLE.

2. He was an object of admiration to his *subjects,* his *allies,* and his *enemies.*

3. Onward he journeyed to a happier shore,

    Where *danger, death,* and *shame* assault no more.

4.   Last scene of all,
That ends this strange eventful history,
Is second *childishness*, and mere *oblivion*,
Sans *teeth*, sans *eyes*, sans *taste*, sans *everything*.

SHAKESPEARE.

NOTE. Anticlimax is used to produce a humorous effect: 'I have left at your house my heart and my toothbrush' (A. S. HILL). (Exercise XXXVII, § 582.)

B, 2. Avoiding unpleasant repetition of sound:

1. Faulty: I *know* of *no* other. (Say 'I do not know of any other'.)

2. Faulty: Every *one* will want *one*. (Say 'Everybody will want one'; § 108.)

3. Faulty: He *ordered* that the *orders* should be *forwarded* immediately. (Say 'He commanded that the orders should be sent immediately'.)

4. Faulty: They wished the *uniforms* to be *uniform* in size. (Say 'They wished the uniforms to be of one size'.)

5. Faulty: This *means* that he will succeed by *means* of his *own* efforts *only*. (Say 'will not succeed except through his own efforts' or the like; care should be taken not to use a word in two ways in the same sentence.)

6. Faulty: This has been recently abundantly and conclusively demonstrated. (Say 'This has, in recent times, been abundantly', etc.)

7. Faulty: This number is *probably considerably* too high. (Say 'It is probable that this number is', etc.)

8. Faulty: This gave *rise* to an *uprising*. (Say 'This caused an uprising'.)

9. Faulty: I was *unaware* of his *whereabouts*. (Say 'I was ignorant', etc.)

10. Faulty: She described the *proceedings preceding* the dinner. (Say 'She described what took place before the dinner'.)

11. Faulty: He *charged* them to send for a doctor, while he bent over his beautiful *charge* and tried to restore her. (Say 'He bade them send', etc.)

12. Faulty: They were *really constantly thinking* about the remodeling of their house. (Say 'Their minds were constantly on the remodeling of their house'; or, 'They thought of nothing else but the remodeling of their house'.)

371. Force in repetition. Another means of securing force is repetition:

1. And a scornful *laugh laughed* he. — LONGFELLOW.

2. *She* was the most arch and at the same time the most artless creature, was the youngest *Miss Pecksniff*. — DICKENS.

3. He *followed* out of the room, *followed* down the stairs, *followed* down the court, *followed* out into the streets. — DICKENS.

4. This edition is *ill* compiled, *ill* arranged, *ill* written, and *ill* printed. — MACAULAY.

5. He was truly a *spoiled child*, not merely the *spoiled child* of his parent, but the *spoiled child* of nature, the *spoiled child* of fortune, the *spoiled child* of fame, the *spoiled child* of society. — MACAULAY.

NOTE 1. A subject sometimes begins a sentence and is left without a predicate; a new sentence is introduced which contains the first subject in a different form (this is not for ordinary use): *He* that hath, to *him* shall be given. — THE BIBLE.

NOTE 2. A noun or pronoun in a subordinate clause is sometimes made emphatic by being carried forward into the principal clause (this is not for ordinary use): Consider the *lilies* how *they* grow. — THE BIBLE.

372. Periodic or loose sentence; variety. A sentence may be so composed that it is not grammatically complete until the end is reached. Such a sentence is called periodic. A sentence that is grammatically complete elsewhere than at the end is called loose. Latin is characteristically a periodic language. In the sixteenth and seventeenth centuries English was largely modeled after Latin; but today there is greater freedom, and the good writer obtains variety and emphasis by mingling his sentences, making them long or short, periodic or loose, at his pleasure. The periodic sentence is particularly useful in arousing and maintaining attention and interest. The loose sentence is particularly useful in conversation, letter writing (which is conversation on paper), and narrative; but care should be taken not to let it ramble into a mere collection of clauses connected by *and* (§ 355, *A*, 1). The following are examples of periodic and loose sentences:

1. He not only wished to go, but he went. (Periodic.)
   He wished to go, | and he went. (Loose.)
2. Yesterday, at this very hour, we were in Westminster Abbey. (Periodic.)
   We were in Westminster Abbey | yesterday, | at this very hour. (Loose.)
   He did not give up, | although he was tired. (Loose.)
3. Finally, after wandering far out of our way and meeting with many mishaps, we reached the river. (Periodic.)
   We finally reached the river, | after, etc. (Loose.)
4. How much of this morbid feeling sprang from an original disease of the mind, how much from real misfortune, how much from the nervousness of dissipation, how much was fanciful, how much was merely affected, it is impossible for us, and would probably have been impossible for the most intimate friends of Lord Byron, to decide. — MACAULAY. (Periodic.)

373. Smoothness. Lord Chesterfield frequently urged his son to seek elegance of diction. On one occasion he wrote, " I need not, I am sure, tell you what you must often have felt, how much the elegancy of diction adorns the best thoughts, and palliates the worst." In another letter he said, " It is not every understanding that can judge of matter ; but every ear can and does judge, more or less, of style : and were I either to speak or write to the public, I should prefer moderate matter, adorned with all the beauties and elegancies of style, to the strongest matter in the world, ill worded and ill delivered."

374. Aids to smoothness. If we cannot learn to write and speak with elegance, we can at least attain a certain smoothness by avoiding unpleasant repetition (§§ 65, 66, 370, *B*, 2), harsh words, and clumsy and obscure methods of expression (§ 375). And just as we can improve our style by reading good authors aloud, so we can correct many of our own mistakes by reading our own work aloud for the ear to pass judgment on (§ 364).

375. Parallelism. Irregularity in the form of a sentence does harm by diverting the reader from the thought. Clearness, force, and smoothness are all gained by expressing a series of parallel ideas in a series of parallel words, phrases, or clauses (a series of three is usually most effective, having a beginning, a middle, and an end):

A. Parallel words.
  1. Nouns: He enjoys *reading*, *writing*, and *ciphering*.
  2. Adjectives: She was *young*, *beautiful*, and *intelligent*.
  3. Adverbs: He spoke *simply*, *directly*, and *forcibly*.

B. Parallel phrases.
  1. Nouns: He likes *to read*, *to write*, and *to cipher*.
  2. Adjectives: She had the gift *of youth*, *of beauty*, and *of intelligence*.
  3. Adverbs: He spoke *with simplicity*, *with directness*, and *with force*.

C. Parallel clauses.
  1. Nouns: *That* his poetry will undergo a severe sifting, *that* much of what has been admired by his contemporaries will be rejected as worthless, we have little doubt.
  2. Adjectives: All his books are written in a learned language, in a language *which* nobody hears from his mother or nurse, in a language in *which* nobody ever quarrels, or drives bargains, or makes love, in a language in *which* nobody ever thinks. — MACAULAY.

3. Adverbs: He likes to read *because* it increases his vocabulary and broadens his sympathies; he likes to write *because* it makes him exact and improves his self-expression; he likes to cipher *because* it teaches him to analyze and to reason.

Study the following examples of parallelism:

1. He [Addison] owed his elevation *to* his popularity, *to* his stainless probity, and *to* his literary fame. — MACAULAY.

2. When I was a child, I spake as a child, I understood as a child, I thought as a child: but when I became a man, I put away childish things. — THE BIBLE (1 Corinthians, xiii, 11).

3. Though I speak . . . And though I have . . . And though I bestow all my goods . . . — THE BIBLE (1 Corinthians, xiii, 1–3. Study the entire chapter; see Matthew, v, 3–9, and vii, 24–27).

4. The way was through the dense forest, encumbered with rocks and logs, tangled with roots and underbrush, damp with perpetual shade, and redolent of decayed leaves and mouldering wood. — PARKMAN.

5. If the flights of Dryden therefore are higher, Pope continues longer on the wing. If of Dryden's fire the blaze is brighter, of Pope's the heat is more regular and more constant. Dryden often surpasses expectation, and Pope never falls below it. Dryden is read with frequent astonishment, and Pope with perpetual delight. — SAMUEL JOHNSON.

6. The spirits of Milton are unlike those of almost all other writers. His fiends, in particular, are wonderful creations. *They* are not metaphysical abstractions. *They* are not wicked men. *They* are not ugly beasts. *They* have no horns, no tails, none of the fee-faw-fum of Tasso and Klopstock. *They* have just enough in common with human nature to be intelligible to human beings. — MACAULAY. (See the last quotation in § 65.)

7. This work [a new edition of Boswell's Life of Johnson] has greatly disappointed us. Whatever faults we may have been prepared to find in it, we fully expected *that* it would be a valuable addition to English literature; *that* it would contain many curious facts, and many judicious remarks; *that* the style of the notes

would be neat, clear, and precise; and *that* the typographical exe-
cution would be, as in new editions of classical works it ought to
be, almost faultless. — MACAULAY. (Exercise XXXVIII, § 583.)

376. Coördination; caution. In using relative pronouns
and conjunctions we should be careful not to violate the principle of coördination in parallelism by connecting words,
phrases, or clauses which are not coördinate (for relative
clauses in parallel arrangement, see §§ 96, 97):

1. She could *neither play nor sing*. (Not ' She neither could
play nor sing'; nor ' She could neither play or sing'; nor ' She
neither could play or sing'.)

She neither asked to go nor wished to go. (Not ' She asked
neither to go nor wished to go '.)

2. She could *not only play, but sing*. (Not ' She not only could
play, but sing'.)

She *not only could play*, but *wished* to play. (Not ' She
could not only play, but wished to play '.)

3. I am afraid *that* he will be too busy to see me. (Not ' I am
afraid *that* he will be so busy *that* he can't see me '.)

He said it rained so hard the day he was starting back that
he hesitated to undertake the trip. (Not ' He said *that* it rained so
hard the day *that* he was starting back *that* he ', etc.)

4. It was a small room with one window, at which a young girl
sat. (Not ' It was a small room, in *which* there was but one window,
at *which* ', etc.; see the quotation from Trollope in § 96.)

5. A committee was appointed, consisting of Messieurs Brown
and Jones, *who* represented capital, and Messieurs Lee and Thomas,
who represented labor. (Not ' A committee was appointed, *consisting* of Messieurs Brown and Jones, *representing* capital, and
Messieurs Lee and Thomas, *representing* labor'.) (Exercise
XXXVIII, § 583.)

377. Lincoln's style. As for style, Lincoln has left examples of purity of speech that will be as enduring as the language in which they were written. His model was the Bible.

" Our English Bible ", it has been well said, " is a wonderful specimen of the strength and music of the English language." Along with the Bible, Lincoln studied Æsop's Fables and Bunyan's Pilgrim's Progress. We are told that he read and digested these books until they were his own. " Better books he could not have found in all the universities of Europe, and we begin to understand where he got his moral vision, his precision of English style, and his shrewd humor." These books are no less serviceable as models today than they were in Lincoln's time, and they will probably remain so for generations to come.

Read aloud and study the following selections (the passages from the Old Testament are translated from Hebrew; observe how *and* is used in the first selection to connect sentences, a style not to be imitated); compare the thought in the first selection with that in the fourth:

1. And Abram went up out of Egypt, he, and his wife, and all that he had, and Lot with him, into the south. And Abram was very rich in cattle, in silver, and in gold. And he went on his journeys from the south even to Beth-el, unto the place where his tent had been at the beginning, between Beth-el and Hai; unto the place of the altar, which he had made there at the first: and there Abram called on the name of the Lord. And Lot also, which went with Abram, had flocks, and herds, and tents. And the land was not able to bear them, that they might dwell together: for their substance was great, so that they could not dwell together. And there was a strife between the herdmen of Abram's cattle and the herdmen of Lot's cattle: and the Canaanite and the Perizzite dwelled then in the land. And Abram said unto Lot, Let there be no strife, I pray thee, between me and thee, and between my herdmen and thy herdmen; for we be brethren. Is not the whole land before thee? separate thyself, I pray thee, from me: if thou wilt take the left hand, then I will go to the right; or if thou depart to the right hand, then I will go to the left. — THE BIBLE.

2. Happy is the man that findeth wisdom,
And the man that getteth understanding.
For the merchandise of it is better than the merchandise
of silver,
And the gain thereof than fine gold.
She is more precious than rubies:
And all the things thou canst desire are not to be compared
unto her.
Length of days is in her right hand;
And in her left hand riches and honour.
Her ways are ways of pleasantness,
And all her paths are peace.
She is a tree of life to them that lay hold upon her:
And happy is every one that retaineth her. — THE BIBLE.

3. For I was an hungred, and ye gave me no meat: I was thirsty, and ye gave me no drink: I was a stranger, and ye took me not in: naked, and ye clothed me not: sick, and in prison, and ye visited me not. — THE BIBLE.

4. Quarrel not at all. No man resolved to make the most of himself can spare time for personal contention. Still less can he afford to take all the consequences, including the vitiating of his temper and the loss of self-control. Yield larger things to which you can show no more than equal right; and yield lesser ones, though clearly your own.

Better give your path to a dog than be bitten by him in contesting for the right. Even killing the dog would not cure the bite. — LINCOLN.

5. With malice toward none; with charity for all; with firmness in the right, as God gives us to see the right, let us strive on to finish the work we are in; to bind up the nation's wounds; to care for him who shall have borne the battle, and for his widow and his orphan — to do all which may achieve and cherish a just and lasting peace among ourselves, and with all nations. — LINCOLN.

CHAPTER V

THE DERIVATION OF WORDS

Whenever you doubt of the propriety or elegancy of any word, search the dictionary, or some good author, for it, or inquire of somebody who is master of that language; and in a little time propriety and elegancy of diction will become so habitual to you, that they will cost you no more trouble. — LORD CHESTERFIELD.

Neither is a dictionary a bad book to read. — EMERSON.

378. Acquiring a vocabulary. An excellent way to acquire a vocabulary is to read good authors aloud (§ 361) and look up the new words in a dictionary. The dictionary should be large enough to contain etymologies. An unabridged dictionary will be found the most instructive and the most entertaining. For directions about using the dictionary, see Exercise XXXIX, § 584. For the development of English, see Chapter XII.

379. Literal and figurative meaning. In studying words in the dictionary, learn first their pronunciation, derivation, and original, literal meaning, since from this meaning arise their figurative meanings. For example, the word *sharp* is used literally in the expression *sharp knife*, and figuratively in *sharp words*; the word *dry* is used literally in *dry wood* and *dry air*, and figuratively in *dry speech* and *dry wit*.

380. Slang, etc. Do not use, ordinarily, in speaking or in writing, any of the meanings marked *Archaic* ('old-fashioned'), *Cant*, *Dialectal* (*Dial.*), *Local*, *Obsolete* (*Obs.*), *Provincial*, *Rare* (*R.*), *Slang*, or *Vulgar* (*Vulg.*). Those marked *Colloquial* (*Colloq.*) are suitable for ordinary conversation, familiar letters, and the like, but should not be used in formal writing. Slang is objectionable not only because it is in bad taste, but because it narrows the vocabulary. For example, *to be up against it* means to be in any kind of discomfort or trouble, from a mishap to a disaster; and when the boy who has grown up on such phrases is required, in school, in college, or in business, to translate them into language suited to the occasion, he finds himself more bewildered than if he were translating from a foreign tongue.

In choosing words we should heed the advice of Pope:

> In words, as fashions, the same rule will hold;
> Alike fantastic, if too new, or old:
> Be not the first by whom the new are try'd,
> Nor yet the last to lay the old aside.

As a rule, an Anglo-Saxon word (§ 388) is preferable to a Romance word (§ 595), a familiar word to an unfamiliar word, a short word to a long word, a specific word to a general word, a single word to a phrase (see *pet expressions*, § 417), a usual meaning of a word to an unusual meaning.

381. Etymology. Many etymologies explain ancient customs and manners:

Anemone (§ 423), from Greek, means *daughter of the wind.*

Arrive, from Latin, means *come to the shore*, showing that the word originated where traveling was done by water.

Bankrupt, from the Italian *banca rotta*, means *bench-broken*; it is said that at Florence, when a money changer became insolvent, his bench (or money table) was broken.

Bonfire, originally *bonefire*, a fire for burning bones, which were collected and saved for the annual summer burning.

Canary, a bird from the Canary Islands. But the name of the islands is Latin, and means *Dog Islands*, from the large dogs which the Romans found there.

Canopy, from the Greek word for *mosquito*, was originally an Egyptian bed or couch with gauze curtains to keep out mosquitoes.

Companion, from Latin, means *bread-sharer, messmate*.

Cynosure (§ 423), from Greek (meaning *dog's tail*), is the Greek name of the constellation Ursa Minor (Little Bear), containing the North Star, to which ancient mariners and travelers turned their eyes; hence, a center of attraction: as, She was the *cynosure* of all eyes.

Digit, from the Latin word for *finger*, so named because counting was done on the fingers. Decimal numeration ('numeration by tens'), common in all ages, is owing to our having ten fingers.

Doll, a pet form of *Dorothy*. Compare *Hal* for *Harry*.

Esteem, estimate, to *set a value on*, from the Latin word for copper or bronze, which was used as money.

Govern, from Greek, means *steer a ship*.

Library, from the Latin word for book (*liber*), which originally was the inner bark of a tree, used for writing material. The English word *book* is an old Teutonic word meaning *writing tablet*, and is perhaps connected with the name of the beech tree (*boc*), the suggestion being that the ancient Saxons and Germans used boards from this tree to write on. The word *paper* (Latin *papyrus*) is from the Greek name of a plant used by the Egyptians for making writing material. From another Greek name of the same plant (*biblos*) came the Greek word for book; from this we get the word *Bible*, which properly means, as it is often called, the *Book*, or the *Book of Books*.

Neighbor ('near boor'), from Anglo-Saxon, means *farmer who lives near*.

Pecuniary is from the Latin word for *cattle, sheep*, and the like, which constituted the wealth of the early Romans.

Pedagogue, from Greek (meaning *boy-leader*), was originally the slave who led his master's boy to and from school and had general charge of him.

Persuade, from Latin, means *sweeten through* (compare *suavity*), and hence to make attractive.

Rival, from Latin, means *of the same brook*. Rivals contended for the water.

Salary, from Latin, means *salt money*, the money allowed Roman soldiers to buy salt.

Squirrel, from Greek, means *shadow-tail*.

Volcano is from *Vulcan*, the name of the Roman god of fire. Vulcan was the blacksmith of the gods; he had his forge under Mount Ætna and other volcanoes.

Window is another form of *wind eye*, originally an opening in the wall to admit air. (Exercise XL, *a*, § 585.)

382. Denotation; connotation. Words, like people, acquire good or bad reputations according to their associations. The word *mansion*, for example, now means *stately house*, whereas originally it meant simply *dwelling* or *dwelling place*. The word *accident* now usually means *unfortunate event*, but its original meaning was simply *event*, as in Shakespeare. In the sentence ' Even the name of *lemon pie* makes Jack sick ' the words *lemon pie*, which to most people recall merely a kind of dessert, have for Jack the added suggestion of something disagreeable. A person's name may be agreeable or disagreeable because of the associations which it recalls. *Grand* and *wonderful* are schoolgirls' words.

Thus all words have denotation, and may have connotation. The denotation of a word is its actual meaning. The connotation of a word is the meaning which the word suggests or implies in addition to its actual meaning. To use words effectively, therefore, we need to know both their denotation and their connotation.

383. Use determines classification. In ancient English there were many inflections (see §§ 601, 604, 611, 612, 619, 620), and words could usually be classified by their looks; but since these inflections are now mostly lost, words must often be classified according to their use:

1. He lives on a *farm*. (Noun; § 10.)
   She enjoys *farm* life. (Adjective; § 113.)
   They *farm* for pleasure. (Verb; § 154.)

2. We shall not see his *like* again. (Noun; § 10.)
   She is *like* her father. (Adjective; § 113.)
   They *like* to live by the sea. (Verb; § 154.)
   He ran *like* a deer. (Adverb; § 252.)
3. She has not played *since*. (Adverb; § 252.)
   She has not played *since* last year. (Preposition; § 282.)
   She has not played *since* you went away. (Subordinating conjunction; § 302.) (Exercise XL, *b*, *c*, § 585.)

384. Homonym. A homonym is one of two or more words which have the same sound, but different meanings:

1. We *ate* early. The play began at *eight*.
2. These trees *bear* fruit. The *bear* walked away.
3. They are *beech* trees. We play on the *beach*.
4. The cloth was *coarse*. Follow the *course* of the river.
5. *Rite, right, write, wright*.

385. Synonym. A synonym is one of two or more words which have the same general meaning (see *bad*, § 417):

1. The air was *hot* (broiling, parching, scorching, sultry, torrid, stifling, suffocating).
2. The air was *cold* (chilly, bleak, frigid, frosty, icy, raw, bitter, biting, cutting, nipping, piercing).
3. The story was *amusing* (entertaining, funny, humorous, laughable).
4. The woman was *courteous* (mannerly, polite, civil, refined, respectful, well-bred).
5. The boy was *rude* (boorish, disrespectful, gruff, impolite, rustic, saucy, surly).
6. The girl *chuckled* (giggled, laughed, snickered, tittered).
7. The name was *told* (announced, declared, mentioned, proclaimed, published, recited, rehearsed, repeated, reported, uttered).
8. A bevy, cluster, company, drove, flock, group, herd, pack, shoal.
9. To make, to accomplish, to achieve, to build, to complete, to compose, to construct, to contrive, to organize.

386. Antonym. An antonym is one of two words which have opposite meanings:

1. The pencil is *good*, but the pen is *bad*.
2. The grapes are *sweet*, the apples *sour*.
3. Some words are *short*, and some are *long*.
4. The lion is *large*, the monkey *small*.
5. The ocean is *deep*, the brooks are *shallow*.
6. The pictures were *dear*, the book *cheap*.

387. Living and dead languages.

A language, like a tree, comes into existence, lives and grows, and passes away. The changes in it are so slow and imperceptible, however, that to any generation of people it virtually remains fixed. When a language ceases to be spoken, it is called dead. Egyptian, for example, is a dead language. Greek is not dead; it continues to be the language of Greece, the islands of the Ægean Sea, and the coast of Asia Minor. Ancient Latin is no longer a spoken language, but it lives in the languages spoken in Italy, France, Spain, Portugal, Roumania, Mexico, South America, and other Romance countries, and in English. About ninety per cent of the words in Italian, Spanish, and French are of Latin origin. About sixty per cent of the words in English come from the same source.

388. Vocabulary of Modern English.

Only about a fourth or a fifth of the words in the vocabulary of Modern English are of Anglo-Saxon origin; the other words are borrowed from foreign languages, chiefly from Latin and Greek. But although the borrowed words in English are much more numerous than the native Anglo-Saxon, many of these native words are used in our daily speech far oftener than the borrowed words, for they mean more to us, and better express our feelings. Compare, for example, the refined Latin word *decayed* with the strong but uncouth Anglo-Saxon word *rotten*; or the calm and dignified Latin word *depart* with the impetuous Anglo-Saxon *get out.* Of all our books the Bible has the purest English, only about one word in ten being borrowed. In ordinary modern prose, however, about half the words are Latin or Greek ; in scientific books the percentage of borrowed words is higher.

389. Anglo-Saxon. From the Anglo-Saxon have come down to us most of the pronouns, irregular verbs, prepositions, and conjunctions, and such nouns, adjectives, and adverbs as are daily in our mouths :

1. I, me, we, us, thou, thee, he, his, who, which.
2. Go, come, see, sing, find, shall, should, can.
3. In, at, on, up, down, ever, under, before, after, out.
4. And, or, neither, whether, as, if, while, since.
5. Man, woman, child, mother, father, sister, brother, daughter, son, house, home, yard, door, roof, thatch, fire, hearth, bed, clothes, knife, ax, hammer, saw, shoe, foot, arm, hand, finger, eye, heart, hair, head, hat, mouth, tooth, tongue, food, hunger, thirst, sleep, bread, butter, fodder, sheep, dog, deer, goose, ox, cow, milk, mouse, fox, tree, leaf, sea, land, earth, heaven, sun, moon, star, wind, rain, storm, hill, dale, light, day, night, week, month, year, winter, summer, spring, harvest, Sunday, Monday.
6. Hot, cold, warm, wet, dry, sweet, sour, bitter, wise, bright, sharp, weak, strong, good, white, green, red, high, little, wild, tame, raw.
7. Soon, early, ever, never, now, then, there, here, where, when, why, so, thus, almost, gladly, kindly.

390. Latin and Greek. The lists in §§ 405-410 contain important roots and stems of Latin and Greek, with examples of words derived from these languages. The mastery of these lists, with the occasional aid of the dictionary, will be an important step in the learning of English. Many words already familiar will appear in a new light when studied etymologically, and many new words met in reading will be understood at first sight.

In addition to the thousands of words in common use the scientific terms in medicine, theology, physics, chemistry, zoölogy, botany, astronomy, engineering, and other sciences are chiefly from Latin and Greek. The rapid advancement in arts and sciences has created such a demand for new words that a dictionary may be incomplete before it is printed. But these new scientific terms are usually formed from Latin and Greek roots, so that even a slight knowledge of these languages makes the meanings of the new words easy to understand and to acquire.

In the study of words from Latin and Greek (§§ 405–410) do not become discouraged if your progress at first seems slow. Learn and review a few words every day, and you will soon find enjoyment and reward; language will take on a new face, and in literature new vistas will open before you. Observe how the meanings of Latin and Greek roots and stems underlie the meanings of the English words borrowed from them. When you look in the dictionary for a word, study words near it that have the same derivation. Occasionally browse about in the dictionary to become acquainted with other interesting and useful words.

The similarity of Italian, Spanish, Portuguese, Roumanian, French, and English to Latin is readily seen in many words:

Latin	Ital.	Spanish	Port.	Roum.	French	English
aurum	oro	oro	ouro	aur	or	auric
fatalis	fatale	fatal	fatal	fatal	fatal	fatal
ferrum	ferro	hierro	ferro	fer	fer	ferric
flos	fiore	flor	flor	floare	fleur	flower
fructus	frutto	fruta	fru(c)to	fruct	fruit	fruit
gloria	gloria	gloria	gloria	glorie	gloire	glory
infans	infante	infante	infante	infante	enfant	infant
piscis	pesce	pez	peixe	pesce	poisson	fish
rosa	rosa	rosa	rosa	rosa	rose	rose
septem	sette	siete	sete	septe	sept	seven

391. Prefixes. When the English words in the lists of Latin and Greek roots and stems have prefixes, study these prefixes in their proper lists (§§ 405, 408). See how many other prefixes you can attach to the same roots and stems to form English words. For example, from the Latin root *duc-*, *lead* (§ 407), and its compounds are derived such English words as *ab-duct*, *ad-duce*, *con-duce*, *con-duct*, *con-ductivity*, *con-ductor*, *deduct*, *e-duce*, *in-duce*, *intro-duce*, *pro-duce*, *pro-duct*, *pro-duction*, *re-duce*, *se-duce*, *se-ductive*, *tra-duce*; the root *fac-* (§ 407) is used in forming several hundred words; the prefix *com-* (§ 405) occurs thousands of times. When you do not understand fully the meaning of a word, consult the dictionary.

392. Spelling. The spelling of many English words must be learned from the dictionary. Words borrowed from Latin and Greek usually follow the original spelling, so that a knowledge of Latin and Greek roots and stems is of assistance in spelling thousands of words borrowed from these languages. The Greek diphthong *ei* in proper names is an exception, being represented by *ei*, *e*, or *i*; as, Pos*ei*don, Med*e*a, Ch*i*ron.

393. Final consonant doubled. Before a suffix beginning with a vowel, if a single final consonant (except *h* or *x*) is preceded by a single accented vowel, the single final consonant is doubled, usually to preserve the short sound of the single accented vowel preceding it (but *contrōl*, *contrōlled*, and a few others have a long vowel); otherwise the final consonant need not be doubled, since the vowel before it is not affected:

Bag, *baggage*; beg, *begged*, *begging*; bus, *busses* (but, om′nibus, om′nibuses*); god, *goddess*; hot, *hotter*, *hottest*; stop, *stopped*, *stopping*.

Acquit, *acquitted*, *acquitting*; admit, *admitted*, *admitting*; begin, *beginner*; compel, *compelled*, *compelling*; confer, *conferred*, *conferring*; occur, *occurrence*; permit, *permitted*, *permitting*; regret, *regretted*, *regretting*; transfer, *transferred*, *transferring*.

But, act, *actor, acted*; brief, *briefer*; daub, *daubed, daubing*; moan, *moaned, moaning*; need, *needed, needing*; perform, *performance*; prefer', *pref'erence* (see exceptions, below); travel, *traveled, traveling* (see note, below).

EXCEPTIONS. The most important exceptions are *infer, inferable*; *transfer, transferable*; and derivatives in which the accent is thrown back to another syllable, such as *preference* (from *prefer'*). *Humbugged* and *humbugging* (from *humbug*) have *gg* to preserve the hard sound of *g*. The words *chancellor, tranquillity*, and derivatives of *crystal* and *metal* (for example, *crystallize, metallurgy*) are from Latin and Greek words having *ll*, and hence are not exceptions; but *tranquilize* is better with one *l*, being a derivative of *tranquil*.

NOTE. Some words having a single final consonant not preceded by a single accented vowel (chiefly verbs ending in *l*) are frequently, but needlessly, written with the final consonant doubled before a suffix beginning with a vowel:

Cancel (*cancelled, cancelling*), counsel, empanel, enamel, equal, imperil, kidnap (*kid'nap'*, having a secondary accent on the ultima, commonly has *kidnapped*), label, level, libel, marshal, marvel, model, parallel, parcel, pencil, quarrel, ravel, revel, rival, shovel, shrivel, snivel, travel, unravel, worship.

394. Silent final *e* retained.

Silent final *e* is generally retained before a suffix beginning with a consonant:

Hope, *hopeful, hopeless*; false, *falsehood*; move, *movement*; name, *namely*.

EXCEPTION. In many words ending in silent *e* preceded by another vowel except *e*, the silent *e* is omitted before a suffix beginning with a consonant:

Due, *duly*; true, *truly*; awe, *awful* (*w* is silent). But, flee, *fleeing*; see, *seeing*.

The following important words are exceptions also (*e* is properly retained after *g* to show the soft sound of *g*; see *c* and *g*, § 402): abridge, *abridgment* (or *abridgement*); acknowledge, *acknowledgment* (or *acknowledgement*); judge, *judgment* (or *judgement*); whole, *wholly*; wise, *wisdom*.

395. Silent final *e* omitted. Silent final *e* is generally omitted before a suffix beginning with a vowel:

Hope, *hoping*; move, *movable*; name, *naming*.

EXCEPTION. To prevent mispronunciation, or confusion of words, silent final *e* is sometimes retained before a suffix beginning with a vowel; it is also retained in words ending in *ce* and *ge*, to preserve the soft sound of *c* and *g* (see *c* and *g*, § 402):

Hoe, *hoeing*; shoe, *shoeing*; toe, *toeing*; dye, *dyeing* (compare *die, dying*); singe, *singeing* (compare *sing, singing*).

Notice, *noticeable* (but, *noticing*, *c* being soft before *i*, § 402); manage, *management*. The word *mortgagor* (mor-ga-jor′) from *mortgage* is an exception.

NOTE. In words formed with the suffix *able* usage varies:
Use, *usable* (or *useable*); sale, *salable* (or *saleable*).

396. Final *ie* before *ing*. When *ing* is to be added to a word ending in *ie*, *e* is generally dropped, and *i* is changed to *y*:

Die, *dying*; lie, *lying*; tie, *tying*; vie, *vying*.

397. Final *y*. Final *y* preceded by a vowel is generally retained before a suffix; final *y* preceded by a consonant is generally changed to *i* (unless the suffix begins with *i*: *pity, pitying*):

Delay, *delays, delayed, delaying*; gay, *gayly* (or *gaily*), *gayety* (or *gaiety*); stay, *stayed* (or *staid*). The words *daily* (from *day*), *laid, paid, said*, and *staid* are exceptions.

Pity, *pitiful, pitiless* (but, *pitying*); edify, *edifies, edified* (but, *edifying*); happy, *happiness*; lovely, *loveliness*.

398. Compounds of *all, full, well*. Observe the following compounds of *all, full*, and *well*:

All-pervading, *all*-wise; but *al*mighty, *al*most (§ 417), *al*ready (§ 417), *al*though, *al*together (§ 417), *al*ways. (See *all right*, § 417.)

Full-grown, *full*-length, *full*-rigged; but, *ful*fill (or *ful*fil), aw*ful*, cheer*ful*, teaspoon*ful*.

Well-being, *well*-doer, *well*-nigh, fare*well*; but, *wel*come, *wel*fare.

399. Words with *cei* and *lie*. To spell words containing *cei* and *lie*, remember that *c* is followed by *e* (the vowel which rimes with it), and *l* by the other vowel (*i*), as in *Celia*:

conceit	deceive	belief	relief
conceited	perceive	believe	relieve
conceive	receipt	believed	relieved
deceit	receive	believing	relieving

400. Words ending in *el* and *le*. A good many common words end in *el*; many others end in *le* (a *mantel* is a shelf, and a *mantle* is a garment):

bevel	hovel	ravel	ample	dazzle	people
bushel	kernel	revel	apple	double	prattle
camel	label	satchel	axle	eagle	puzzle
channel	level	sentinel	baffle	fable	quibble
chapel	libel	shovel	battle	feeble	riddle
chisel	lintel	shrivel	bottle	fickle	rifle
cudgel	marvel	sorrel	bridle	fiddle	sample
dishevel	model	tinsel	buckle	handle	sickle
easel	nickel	towel	cable	kettle	spindle
enamel	novel	trammel	candle	maple	stable
flannel	panel	travel	castle	marble	table
funnel	parcel	trowel	cattle	middle	trestle
gospel	pommel	tunnel	cradle	muzzle	whistle
gravel	quarrel	vessel	crumble	noble	wrinkle

401. Words frequently misspelled. Master the spelling and the meaning of the following words; mark those that you do not know, and consult the dictionary:

ac-cept', ex-cept'	af-fect', ef-fect'
ac-cuse', ac-com'mo-date	a-gree', ag-gres'sion
a-cross', a-rouse'	al'ley, al-ly'
ac'tu-al, ac'tu-al-ly	al-read'y, all right
ad-vice', ad-vise'	al'tar, al'ter
Æ-ne'as, Æ-ne'id	an'gel, an'gle

a-nom′a-lous, a-non′y-mous
ant-arc′tic, arc′tic
A-pol′lo, Il′i-ad
ap-pear′, ap-par′ent
ar-rive′, ar-riv′al
as-cent′, as-sent′
ath′lete, ath-let′ics
at-tend′ant, de-pend′ent
au′di-ble, au′di-ence
a while, a-while′
bach′e-lor, bound′a-ry
born, borne
breath, breathe
bus′y, busi′ness
cal′en-dar, cal′en-der
cap′i-tal, cap′i-tol
cas′u-al, cas′u-al-ties
change′a-ble, chang′ing
choose, chose
coarse, course
com-mand′, com-mend′
com′ple-ment, com′pli-ment
con-cede′, con-ces′sion
con′science, con-sci-en′tious
con-ven′ience, con-ven′ient
coun′cil, coun′sel
de-cease′, dis-ease′
de′cent, de-scent′
depth, height
de-scribe′, de-scrip′tion
des′ert, des-sert′
de-spair′, des′per-ate
de-vel′op, en′ve-lope
de-vice′, de-vise′
dif′fer-ence, dif′fi-dence
dis-ap-pear′, dis-ap-point′
dis-ap-prove′, dis-pel′

dis-ci′ple, fas′ci-nate
dis′si-pate, di-vide′
dye′ing, dy′ing
ec′sta-sy, ec-stat′ic
el′i-gi-ble, el-lip′sis
em-bar′rass, em′bas-sy
ex-ag′ger-ate, ex-hil′a-rate
ex-ist′ence, ex-ist′ent
ex-plain′, ex-pla-na′tion
fa-mil′iar, sim′i-lar
fare-well′, wel′fare
Feb′ru-a-ry, Wednes′day
fi-an-cé′, fi-an-cée′
fi′nal-ly, fi-na′le
fir, fur
for′ci-ble, for′ci-bly
for′mal-ly, for′mer-ly
forth, fourth
ge-ol′o-gy, gen-e-al′o-gy
gov′ern, gov′ern-ment
grieve, sieve
guard, guard′i-an
im-pas′sa-ble, im-pos′si-ble
in-gen′ious, in-gen′u-ous
in′tel-lect, in-tel′li-gent
in-ter-cede′, in-ter-rupt′
in-trigue′, in-tri′guing
ir-rel′e-vant, ir-rep′a-ra-ble
its, it 's (= it is)
knowl′edge, priv′i-lege
la′bor, lab′o-ra-to-ry
la′ter, lat′ter
lead, led
les′sen, les′son
light′en-ing, light′ning
loose, lose
Ma-cau′lay, Ni-ag′a-ra

main-tain´, main´te-nance

man´tel, man´tle

meant, mean´ness

mys´ter-y, mys´ti-fy

nec´es-sa-ry, ne-ces´si-ty

o-blige´, o-blig´ing

oc-ca´sion, oc´cu-py

oc-cur´rence, op-por-tune´

op´er-ate, op´po-site

par´al-lel, par´a-mount

part´ner, par-tic´i-pate

passed, past

planed, planned

pose, pos-ses´sion

pre-cede´, pro-ceed´

pre-pare´, prep-a-ra´tion

prin´ci-pal, prin´ci-ple

priv´i-lege, sac´ri-lege

pro-fes´sion, pro-fes´sor

pro-nounce´, pro-nun-ci-a´tion

proph´e-cy, proph´e-sy

pur-sue´, pur-suit´

rap, wrap

re-cede´, re-cep´ta-cle

rec-ol-lect´, rec-om-mend´

re-pair´, rep-a-ra´tion

re-peat´, rep-e-ti´tion

rhythm, rid´i-cule

sac-ri-le´gious (§ 423)

se-crete´, sec´re-ta-ry

seize, siege

sen´tence, sen´ti-ment

sep´a-rate, sep´a-ra-ble

shone, shown

speak´er, speech´less

sta´tion-a-ry, sta´tion-er-y

stat´ue, stat´ute, stat´ure

strat´e-gy, su-per-in-tend´ent

suc-ceed´, su-per-sede´

sym´me-try, syn´o-nym

tem´per-ate, tem´po-ra-ry

than, then

their, there, they're (= they are)

thor´ough, through

to-pog´ra-phy, ty-pog´ra-phy

trag´ic, trag´e-dy

veg´e-ta-ble, veg´e-tate

vil´lage, vil´lain, vis´i-ble

weath´er, wheth´er

who's (= who is), whose

wreath, wreathe

your, you're (= you are)

402. Pronunciation of Latin and Greek. In pronouncing words of Latin or Greek origin observe the following rules (for a table of sounds and letters, and for words frequently mispronounced, see § 423; for the effect of the accent on the forms of French and English words, see § 599, N.):

A at the end of an accented syllable has the sound of *a* in *fāce* (not the sound of *a* in *ask*):

Apparatus (ap-a-rā´tus), candelabra (can-de-lā´bra), gratis (grā´tĭs), verbatim (ver-bā´tĭm).

Æ and *œ* have the sound that *e* would have in the same position :

Cæsar (sē'zar), Ætna (ĕt'na), alumnæ (a-lŭm'nē), Crœsus (krē'sus).

C and *g* (or *gg*) have the soft sound (*c* = *s*; *g* or *gg* = *j*) before *e, i, y, æ, œ, eu*; they have the hard sound (*c* or *cc* = *k*; *g* or *gg* = *g* in *go* or *get*) before *a, o, u*, and elsewhere :

Cicero (sĭs'er-o), Cyrus (sī'rus), Cæsar (sē'zar), Ægeus (ē'jūs), receive (re-sēv'), agitate (ăj'ĭ-tāt), exaggerate (ĕg-zăj'er-āt), fungi (fŭn'jī).

Captive (kăp'tĭv), conduct (kŏn'dŭkt), cure (kūr), account (a-kount'), accretion (a-krē'shŭn), gastric (găs'trĭk), mimic (mĭm'ĭk), mimicking (*k* is added to preserve the hard sound of *c*), govern (gŭv'ern), disgust (dis-gŭst'), aggregate (ăg're-gāt).

NOTE. In words like *accept* (ăk-sĕpt'), *access* (ăk'sĕs), and *accident* (ăk'sĭ-dent) the second *c* is soft and the first *c* hard, according to the rule.

Words like *get*, *begin*, *gift*, *give*, and *girdle*, in which *g* has the hard sound, are not of Latin or Greek origin.

Ch has the sound of *k* (a few exceptions, such as *chapter*, *chart*, *church*, although derived from Latin and Greek, do not come directly from these languages ; see the dictionary) :

Achilles (a-kĭl'ēz), character (kăr'ak-ter), charta (kär'ta), chorus (kō'rus), chrysalis (krĭs'a-lĭs), orchestra (ôr'kĕs-tra).

E at the end of an accented syllable has the sound of *e* in *bē*; *es* at the end of a word has the sound of *ēz* :

Hysteria (hĭs-tē'rĭ-a), ellipses (ĕ-lĭp'sēz).

I at the end of an accented syllable or of a word has the sound of *i* in *pīne* :

Appendicitis (a-pĕn-dĭ-sī'tĭs), alumni (a-lŭm'nī).

Y at the end of an accented syllable has the sound of *y* in *bȳ* (but words beginning with *hypo-* vary, and should be looked up in the dictionary) :

Hydra (hī'dra), Cyrus (sī'rus), hypercritical (hī'pēr-krĭt'ĭ-kăl).

403. Anglo-Saxon prefixes. A knowledge of Anglo-Saxon prefixes will give a better understanding of many common English words:

a- (a remnant of *on*), *on, in, at*: aboard, asleep, alive, aloft, across.

be-, *about, all about, all round, over*: beset, besiege, bedaub, besmear, besmudge, bespatter, bechalk, beguile, befriend (act the friend of), bespeak ('speak round or over, discuss', a meaning now obsolete; it now usually means 'speak for ahead, engage').

for-, *forth, away, gone, thoroughly* (often with the idea of risk, disadvantage, or loss): forbid, forget, forgive, forgo, forsake.

fore-, *before*: foretell, forebode, forecastle, forenoon.

in-, *in*: inlet, insight, income, inlay, inbred, indeed, inroad.

mis-, *ill, wrongly*: misbehavior, mislead, miscount, misspent, mislay, mishap, mistake, misdeed, misdemeanor.

out-, *out, outer, outside, beyond*: outflow, output, outfield, outdistrict, outdoor, outhouse, outrun, outdo, outlast.

over-, *over, beyond, in excess*: overthrow, overcoat, oversight, overload, overdo, overheat, overgrown, overfed.

un-, *not* (with verbs it denotes the opposite action or intensifies): unkind, untrue, unmoral, un-Homeric; unlock, unloose.

under-, *under, insufficient*: underground, underhand, underline, underdose, underload, underfed.

404. Anglo-Saxon suffixes. A knowledge of Anglo-Saxon suffixes will also give a better understanding of many common English words:

-dom, *dominion, state*: kingdom, dukedom, Christendom, freedom, serfdom, thraldom, wisdom.

-er (**-ier, -yer**), *agent* (compare **-or** and **-tor**, § 406), *person connected with*, and the like: player, maker, hatter, glazier, lawyer.

-ful (from *full*), *full of, quantity that would fill*: beautiful, graceful, awful, mournful, cupful, teaspoonful, handful.

-hood, *state, condition*: manhood, boyhood, girlhood, childhood, knighthood, neighborhood, falsehood, likelihood.

-ie (-y), *little* (of endearment or playfulness): Bessie, Charlie, kitty, dearie, doggie, Johnny, pussy, Tommy.

-ish, *belonging to, like* (often denoting an undesirable quality): Scottish, bluish, bookish, boyish, childish, mannish.

-kin, *little*: lambkin, manikin, napkin, Wilkinson (= William, -kin, son), Watkins (Wat = Walter).

-less, *without,* *unable to* : friendless, spotless, fearless, witless.
-like, *resembling* : childlike, dovelike, bell-like, Apollo-like.
-ling, *little, contemptuous* : gosling, nestling, sapling, darling (little dear), hireling, underling, worldling.
-ness, *quality* : goodness, greatness, kindness, greenness, darkness, weakness, sweetness.
-ship, *state, office, skill* : friendship, clerkship, authorship, scholarship, marksmanship, horsemanship.
-ster, *person* : songster, spinster, huckster, dabster, youngster.
-ward (-wards), *direction to* : eastward, homeward, downward.
-ways (-wise), *way, manner* : endways, lengthwise, otherwise.

405. Latin prefixes. The study of Latin prefixes is best undertaken with the study of Latin roots and stems (§ 407 ; see §§ 390, 391):

abs- (ab-, a-), *away from* : abstain (see **ten-,** § 407), abduct, abstract, abuse, abdicate, abrupt, avert, aversion, avocation, abhor, abscess.
ad- (ac-, af-, ag-, al-, an-, ap-, ar-, as-, at-, a-), *to* : adhere, adjective, adverb, advent, accede, accept, accessory, affix, affinity, affiliate, aggregate, aggressor, allure, ally, allusion, annex, announce, appendage, apply, appeal, arrive, assist (stand by), assent, assign, assume (take to yourself, undertake, suppose), attach, attract, attain, ascend (climb to), ascribe.
ambi- (amb-, am-), *on both sides, about, round* : ambient, ambidextrous, ambiguous, ambiguity, ambition, amble, ambulatory, somnambulist, perambulate, preamble, amputate.
ante- (anti-), *before* : anteroom, antecedent, anterior, antediluvian, antiquity, anticipate (seize beforehand, prevent), ante-Norman.
bis- (bi-), *two, twice* : biped, bimonthly, biennial, biweekly (see *weekly,* § 417), biconvex, bilabial, bilateral, bicycle, bilingual, bisect, bivalve, biscuit (twice baked), bisulphide (compare **dis-,** *disulphide,* § 408).
circum-, *round* : circumnavigate, circumlocution, circumvent, circumstance, circumference, circumscribe.
com- (col-, con-, cor-, co-), *with, together* : compound, collect, collision, colloquy, connect, consonant, contact, contagious, contend, conduct, correspond, correlative, corrupt, coöperate, coequal, coeducation, congregation, coincidence.
contra- (contro-, counter-), *against* : contradict, contrary, controversy, counteract, counterbalance, counterfeit, countersign, country (the land over against you, the landscape confronting you).

de-, *from, down from* : decay, deciduous, depend, defend, descend, describe, depart, devious, deposit, decapitate, dethrone, decolorize, denaturalize, delocalize, deform.

dis- (dif-, di-), *asunder, apart* : disjoin, dismiss, discuss, distrust, disaster, differ, diffuse, difficulty, diffident, dispute, dissect, indigestion, disease, disgrace, dissuade, disgust, disappoint, disappear, dispose (put at intervals, arrange).

ex- (ef-, e- ; compare Greek **ex-,** § 408), *out of* : evade, except, extend, extort, express, efface, effect, effluvium, effluence, emigrant, event, elect, eject, elude, eradicate, exclude, exhume, exaggerate, exonerate, ex-president (out of office of president), ex-captain.

extra-, *outside of* : extravagant, extrahistoric, extra-European.

in- (il-, im-, ir-, em-, en-), *into* : inject, indent, invade, inaugurate, income, inundate, incite, induce, illuminate (throw light on), imbibe, immigrant, import, impose (place on), impel, impede (entangle the feet), irruption, embody, embroil, embrace, envelop, encourage.

in- (ig-, i-, il-, im-, ir-), *not* : incurable, inability, inaccurate, insecure, intact, ignoble, ignore, ignorant, ignoramus, illegal, illiterate, illegible, immortal, improper, impecunious, impurity, irregular, innocent, infant.

inter-, *between, among* : interpose, intercede, interrupt, interfere, intercourse, interjection, intermission, intervene, inter-Celtic.

intro- (intra-), *within* : introduce, introductory, introspection, introactive, intramarginal, intramural, intramolecular, intramundane.

non-, *not* : nonsense, nonexistent, nonproductive, non-Greek.

ob- (oc-, of-, op-, os-), *before, facing, against* : obstacle, obstruct, obtrude, object (something thrown before you), obvious, obviate, occur, offend, offer, oppose, opponent, opportune (before the harbor, timely), opposite, ostensible, ostentatious, obtain (secure possession of in the face of opposition, as in ' He obtained the prize '; see **ten-,** § 407).

pen-, *almost* : penult, antepenult, peninsula, penumbra.

per- (pel-), *through, thoroughly* : perennial, perforce, perhaps, perceive, percussion, perdition, perfect, perforated, perfume, perish, perpetual, persecute, person (mask through which an actor spoke), pervious, perplexed (thoroughly entangled), pertinacious, perturb, pellucid.

post-, *after* : postscript, postpone, posthumous, p.m.(post meridiem), postern, posterity, post-Augustan.

præ-(pre-), *before* : prænomen, precede, predict, premature, preface (say beforehand), prevent (come before, anticipate), precipice (headforemost, headlong), preclude (close beforehand), prefer, previous, pretext (woven before or in front, a cloak that covers the real reason), pretend, pretense, prevail, preposition, preposterous, preside, president, present, presence, prescription, presentiment, previous, pre-Roman.

pro- (**pur-**; compare Greek **pro-**, § 408), *forward, before, in place of, for*: promote, pronounce, prominent, protect, provide, provident, promise, proceed, progress, propose, purpose, pursue, profane, proficient, pronoun, procure, pro-Russian.

re- (**red-**), *back, again*: recede, retreat, retract, reduce, reflect, repulse, regard, rejoin, recur, renew, redeem (buy back), redolent, redound (flow back), redundant, rejoin, reread, recuperate, recruit, recumbent, recrudescent, reënter.

se- (**sed-**), *by itself, apart*: secede, sedition, seduce, seductive, select, seclude, secrete, secret, secretary, secretion, secure (apart from care), segregate, separate.

semi- (compare Greek **hemi-**, § 408), *half*: semicircle, semiannual, semicolon, semiofficial, semicivilized, semi-Spanish.

sub- (**suc-, suf-, sug-, sup-, sus-, su-**), *under*: subterranean, subscribe, suburb (below the city; cities were anciently built on hills), subject, subtract, succeed, succor (run to support, run to assist), suffer, suffuse, suggest (carry under, offer indirectly), suppress, suppose, supplant, support, suspect (look at secretly, mistrust), suspicion, suspend, suspense.

super- (**supr-, sur-**; see § 599, N.), *above, over, beyond*: superstructure, superfluous, superfine, superhuman, superintend, supernatural, superlative, supreme, supercilious, supervise, surplus, surname, surcharge, survive, surfeit, surface (upper face), surrender, survey, supersede.

trans- (**tra-, tres-**), *across*: transport, transatlantic, transmarine, transfer, transition, translate, transit, transitive, transform, transgress, transient, tradition (going across the space of time), transept, transpose, transparent (appearing through), translucent, trespass, trestle (little crossbeam), traduce.

ultra-, *beyond, extreme*: ultramarine, ultramontane, ultraviolet, ultratropical, ultramundane, ultraconservative, ultrademocratic, ultradespotic, ultraliberal, ultra-Spartan.

406. Latin suffixes. The study of Latin suffixes is best undertaken with the study of Latin roots and stems (§ 407; see §§ 390, 391):

-able (-ible), *capable of being, worthy to be, capable of*: lovable, desirable, indestructible, peaceable.

-ac, *inclined to*: loquacity, tenacity, vivacity, veracity.

-acious (= **-ac-** + **-ous**), *full of inclination to, abounding in*: pugnacious, loquacious, vivacious, tenacious, voracious, veracious, audacious.

-age, *act, condition*: passage, voyage, breakage, bondage, tillage, courage, marriage.

-eer (-ier), *agent*: charioteer, muleteer, auctioneer, gondolier, cashier, financier, premier.

-ess, *female agent*: actress, governess, patroness, princess, duchess.

-fy (-fic), *make*: magnify, amplify, verify, nullify, edify, vilify, terrify, Frenchify, terrific, pacific, soporific.

-or, *action, agent* (compare **-tor**, below, and **-er**, § 404): clamor, error, pallor; donor, mortgagor (§ 395).

-ous (-ose, -os), *full of*: joyous, piteous, dangerous, poisonous, curious, gracious, verbose, verbosity, grandiose, sententious.

-tion (-sion, -ion), *act*: construction, narration, information, subjection, emotion, decision, extension, session, dominion.

-tor (-sor), *doer, agent* (compare **-or**, above, and **-er**, § 404): actor, doctor, impostor, successor, aggressor.

-tude, -ty, *state, condition*: servitude, fortitude, magnitude, gratitude, multitude, liberty, beauty, piety, poverty, vanity, charity, amiability, prosperity.

407. Latin roots and stems.

The Latin roots and stems in compound English words (as, *in-animate*) are best studied with the Latin prefixes (§ 405; see §§ 390, 391):

ac-, *sharp*: acute, acid, acrimony, acrid, eager (from Latin *acer*).

ag- (ac-), *drive, lead*: agile, agitate, agent, act, active, actor, action, react, transaction.

ama- (am-), *love*: amiable, amity, amicable, amorous, enamored, inimical (= *in* and *amicus*, unfriendly, hostile), amateur.

anima (anim-), *breath, life, soul, mind*: animal, animation, animated, inanimate, magnanimous, pusillanimous, equanimity.

ang-, *squeeze, choke*: anger, anguish, anxious (= ang-sious), anxiety.

aqua (aque-), *water*: aquarium, aquatic, aqueduct, aqueous.

ar-, *burn*: arid, ardent, ardor, arson.

aud-, *hear*: audible, auditor, inaudible, audience, auditorium, auditory.

aug- (auc-), *grow, increase*: augment, auction, auctioneer, auxiliary (= aug-siliary ; increasing, helping).

avi-, *bird*: aviary, aviation, aviator.

bene-, *well*: benevolent, benefactor, benefit, beneficent, benediction, benedict.

cad- (cid-, ca-), *fall*: cadence, decadent, decay, deciduous, accident, coincidence, incident, occident, casual, occasion.

cand- (cend-), *glow, shine*: candle, candid, candidate, incandescent, incendiary.

cap- (cep-, cip-), *take, hold*: capable, capacity (ability to hold), captive, captivating, accept, reception, anticipate, receptacle, recipient, incipient, principal, participate, deception, deceive, precept, perception.

capit-, *head*: decapitate, precipitate, capital, capitulate.

carn-, *flesh*: carnal, carnivorous, incarnate, carnival.

ced- (ces-), *give way, yield*: recede, recess, proceed, procedure, procession, access, exceed, excess, intercede, intercession, precede, cede, cessation, incessant, concede, accede, antecedent, succeed, succession.

cid- (cæ-, ci-), *cut, slay*: decide, decision, incision, cæsura, germicide, regicide, homicide, precise, precision.

cit-, *rouse*: cite, excite, incite, recite, recitation.

clin- (compare Greek **clin-,** § 410), *slope, lean*: incline, recline, decline.

clud- (clu-), *shut*: exclude, exclusion, include, seclude, seclusion, conclude, conclusion, cloister.

cord- (compare Greek **card-,** § 410), *heart*: cordial, concord, discord, accord, courage, encourage, discourage.

corpus (corpor-, corp-), *body*: corpuscle, corps, corpse, corporal, corporeal, incorporate, corporation, corpulent.

cred-, *believe*: credit, credential, creed, credibility, incredible, discredit, credulous, incredulous.

culpa-, *fault*: culpable, exculpable, inculpate, inculpable, culprit.

cur-, *care*: cure, incurable, secure, insecure, sinecure, curate, accurate, curious, curiosity.

curr- (cur-), *run*: current, currency, cursory, course, excursion, incursion, concur, occur, recur, precursor, discursive.

da- (di-), *give*: date, datum, data, dative (case of giving, case of indirect object), addition, edit, edition, tradition.

dent-, *tooth*: dentist, dental, indent, indenture, trident.

dic-, *say*: predicate, predict, edict, dictation, diction, dictionary prediction, contradict, benediction.

doc-, *teach* : docile, doctor, document, doctrine.

dom-, *tame, master* : dominate, dominant, dominion, domineer, predominate, indomitable.

dorm-, *sleep* : dormant, dormitory, dormer, dormancy.

duc-, *lead* : duke, viaduct, aqueduct, abduction, induce, produce, conductor, conducive, reduction, ductile, educate (lead forth), deduct, deduction.

fa-, *speak* : preface, infant, infantry, fate, fatal, fame, defame, infamy, fable, fabulous.

fac- (fec-, fic-), *make, do* : facile, fact, benefactor, beneficent, perfect, imperfect, fiction, manufacture, affection, effect, defect, deficient, efficient, proficient, malefactor, satisfaction.

fer-, *bear, carry, bring* : transfer, confer, prefer, suffer (bear up under), difference, refer, reference, infer.

fid-, *trust* : fidelity, diffident, confident, confidential, perfidy (through pretense of faith), infidel, infidelity.

flec-, *bend, turn* : deflect, deflection, reflect, reflection, inflect, flexible (= flec-sible).

flic-, *strike, dash* : •conflict, afflict, affliction, inflict.

flu-, *flow* : fluid, fluent, influence, confluence, influx, superfluity, superfluous, effluvium, effluence.

frang- (fring-, frag-, frac-), *break* : frangible, fragile, fraction, fracture, fragment, fragrance, infraction, fractious, infringe, irrefrangible, irrefragable.

fug-, *flee* : fugitive, refuge, subterfuge.

fund- (fu-), *pour* : foundry, fusion, fusible, confound (pour together, defeat, ruin), confusion, infusion, transfusion, effusion, diffuse, refund, refuse (pour back, give back, reject).

gen- (compare Greek gen-, § 410), *produce* : generation, Gentiles (nations, as distinguished from the Jews), gentle (of good or noble birth ; frequently so in Shakespeare), genus, congenial, general (applicable to all persons), generous, generic, regenerate, gender (kind, class).

ger- (ges-), *carry* : belligerent, indigestion, congestion, gesture (manner of carrying yourself), gesticulation, suggest (carry under, offer indirectly), suggestion.

grad- (gres-), *step* : grade, gradual, graduated, degrade, degradation, retrograde, progress, digression, transgress, congress, egress, ingress, aggressive.

grav-, *heavy* : gravity, gravitate, aggravate (add weight to, increase, as in ' She aggravated her cold by exposure '. This word does not mean ' provoke ', ' annoy ').

greg-, *flock* : congregate, congregation, segregate, aggregate (flocking to, sum total), gregarious, egregious.

hes- (**her-**), *stick, cling*: adhesion, adhere, cohere, coherent, incoherently, cohesion, inherent, hesitate.

hom- (**hum-**), *human being*: homicide, human, inhuman, humanity, humanities, humanitarian, humane, homage.

hum-, *ground* : exhume, posthumous, humble, humility, humiliate.

insula (= in the salt sea), *island*: insular, peninsula, insulate.

jac- (**jec-**), *throw*: ejaculate, reject, object, injection, project, dejected, abject, conjecture, interjection, subject, adjective.

jug- (**junc-**), *yoke, join*: conjugate, conjugal, conjunction, disjunctive, adjunct, subjunctive (subjoined, usually a subordinate clause), subjugate (put under the yoke, as a sign of submission), jugular, juncture.

jus (**jur-**), *right, law*: just, justice, justify, jurisdiction, jury, perjury (through pretense of right), injustice, unjust.

leg- (**lig-, lec-**), *pick, gather, read* (pick out letters) : elect, election, college, lecture, legible, illegible, eligible (suitable to be picked out).

liber-, *free* : liberate, illiberal, liberty, liberality.

linqu- (**lic-**), *leave* : delinquent, relinquish, derelict, relic.

litera (**littera**), *letter*: literal, letter, literary, literature, alliteration, obliterate.

loc-, *place, put* : location, locality, local, localism, localize, collocate, dislocate, locomotive, locate (§ 417), locus.

loqu- (**locu-**), *talk* : loquacious, eloquent, elocution, colloquy, colloquial, grandiloquence, circumlocution.

luc- (**lu-**), *light* : lucid, translucent, pellucid, luminous, illuminate, elucidate.

lud- (**lu-**), *play* : prelude, postlude, elude, delude, delusion, allusion, illusion, allude (§ 417), collusion.

magn-, *great* : magnify, magnificent, magniloquent, magnanimous, magnate, Charlemagne (Charles the Great).

mal-, *bad* : malice, maltreat, malady, malediction, malevolence, malefactor.

man-, *stay, abide* : manor, manse, mansion, permanent, remain, remnant.

manu- (**man-**), *hand*: manuscript, manufacture, manual, amanuensis, emancipate.

mar-, *sea* : marine, submarine, mariner, maritime, transmarine.

mit- (**mis-**), *send*: remittance, remit, admit, admissible, emit, dismiss, commit, committee, mission, missile, missive, missionary, transmit, permit.

mod-, *measure* : moderate, modify, modesty, accommodate.

mon-, *remind* : monument, monitor, admonition, premonition.

mov- (**mo-**), *move* : movable, motion, emotion, commotion, motor, locomotive, promote, motive, mobile.

mut-, *change* : mutable, immutability, transmute, permutation.

nav-, *ship* : navy, naval, navigate, navigable.

noc-, *injure* : innocent, innocence, innocuous.

nov-, *new* : novel, innovation, novice, novitiate.

ocul-, *eye* : ocular, oculist, inoculate.

omni-, *all* : omnipotent, omniscient, omnibus.

pan-, *bread* : pantry, pannier, companion, company.

pat- (**pas-** ; compare Greek **path-**, § 410), *bear, suffer* : patient, impatient, passion, compassion, compatible, passive, impassive, dispassionate.

pecu-, *cattle* : pecuniary, peculiar (belonging to your own herd), impecunious, peculate.

ped- (compare Greek **pod-**, § 410), *foot* : pedal, biped, quadruped, impede, expedite, pedestal, pedestrian.

pel- (**pul-**), *beat, drive* : repel, impel, expel, propel, dispel, compel, pulse, impulse, expulsion, repulse.

pend- (**pond-**, **pen-**), *weigh, hang* : expend, expense, pendulum, pendant, depend, independent, dependence, suspend, suspense, propensity, recompense, append, appendix, stipend, compendium, compensation, ponderous, ponder (weigh in the mind).

pet-, *strive for, seek* : impetuous, impetus, petition, competition, petulant.

plaud- (**plau-**, **plod-**, **plo-**), *beat, clap the hands* (usually in approval): plaudit, plausible, applaud, explode (clap noisily off the stage), explosion.

plec- (**plic-**), *weave, fold* : complex (= complec + s), complicate, complicity, implicate, explicit, implicit, inexplicable, supplicate.

plus (**plur-**), *more* : plus, surplus, plural, plurality.

pon- (**pos-**, partly Latin and partly French), *put, place* : component, deponent, postpone, compose, depose, expose, impose, repose, repository, position, composition, proposition, preposition, dispose, transpose, deposit, suppose, apposition, disposition, imposition, exposition, exponent.

port-, *carry* : porter, port, export, import, report, transport, purport, deport, support, supportable, insupportable.

pot- (**pos-**), *able* : potent, potentate, omnipotent, possible.

prehend- (**prehen-**), *seize* : apprehend, apprehension, comprehend, comprehension, apprentice.

prim- (**prin-**), *first*: primer, primary, prime, primitive, primrose, prince, principle (taking first place).

pugn- (**pug-**), *fight* (with the fists): pugnacious, pugilist, repugnant, impugn.

put-, *reckon, think*: compute, dispute, repute, reputation, impute, imputation, computation.

rap- (**rep-**), *snatch*: rapacious, rapine, rapture, surreptitious.

reg- (**rec-**), *keep straight, guide, rule*: regulate, regular, rector, regent, regal, correct, rectitude, direction (straightening out), direct.

rid- (**ri-**), *laugh*: ridicule, deride, derision, risibility.

riv-, *brook*: rivulet, derive, derivation, derivative, rival (neighbor on the same brook, competitor for water).

rod- (**ro-**), *gnaw*: rodent, erosion, corrode, corrosive.

rup-, *break*: eruption, abrupt, corrupt (break together, break to pieces), incorruptible, rupture, disrupt, irruption, interrupt, bankrupt (§ 381).

scend- (**scen-, scan-**), *climb*: ascend, ascension, descend, condescend, transcend, scan (go through step by step, examine point by point).

sci-, *know*: science, scientific, conscious (knowing with yourself), conscience, omniscient.

scrib- (**scrip-**), *write*: scribe, scripture, manuscript, inscribe, description, transcribe (make a copy of), postscript, subscribe.

sec- (**seg-**), *cut*: dissect, section, segment, insect (cut into, cut in segments), bisect, trisect.

sed- (**sid-, ses-**), *sit*: sedentary, sediment, sedate, subside, reside, residence, assiduous, insidious, preside, session, supersede.

sent- (**sen-**), *perceive, think*: sensation, sensitive, presentiment, assent, consent, dissent, dissension, resent, sentence, sense.

sequ- (**secu-**), *follow*: sequel, sequence, consequence, subsequent, consecutive, persecute, prosecute, obsequies.

sol-, *alone*: solitary, solitude, sole, soliloquy, solo.

solv- (**solu-**), *loosen*: dissolve, absolve, solution, solve, absolute.

son-, *sound*: sonant, assonant, dissonant, consonant, resonant, sonorous, unison, person (originally the mask, Latin *perso'na*, through which an actor spoke), sonnet (sound or song).

spec- (**spic-**), *look*: spectator, spectacle, spectacles, inspect, prospect, prospective, respect, respective, aspect, circumspect, retrospect, spectator, conspectus, suspect (look secretly at), suspicion, specimen.

spir-, *breathe*: spirit, inspire, expire, aspire, aspirate, conspiracy, perspire, transpire (see *happen*, § 417).

sta-, *stand*: obstacle, station, statue, stable, unstable, establish, state, distant, extant, constant, constantly, circumstance, substance.

sum- (sump-), *take*: resume, assume, assumption, consume.

tac-, *be silent* (of speech): taciturn, tacit, tacitly.

tang- (ting-, tag-, teg-, tig-, tac-), *touch*: tangible, tangent, contact, contagious, contiguous, contiguity, contingency, intangible, integer, integrity, tact, disintegrate.

teg- (tec-), *cover*: integument, protect, detect, detective.

tempor-, *time*: temporary, temporal, contemporary, contemporaneous, tense (of a verb; from the Latin word *tempus*).

ten-, *hold*: tenacious, tenable, tenant, tenement, retain, retentive, contain, sustain, contentment, detain, detention, sustenance, tenure.

tend-(ten-), *stretch*: extend, tension, intend, contend, distend, intense, tense (adjective), tent, extent.

tim-, *fear*: timid, timorous, intimidate, intimidation.

trah-(trac-), *draw*: subtrahend, traction, attraction, detract, contract, retract, extract, subtract, protract, distraction, intractable.

tribu-, *bestow, grant, give*: tribute, attribute, contribute, contribution, retribution.

trud- (tru-), *thrust, push*: intrude, intrusion, protrude, protrusion.

umbra, *shade, shadow*: umbrella (little shade), umbrage, penumbra, adumbration.

und-, *wave*: inundation, undulate, abundance, superabundance, abound, redound (flow back, return).

uni- (un-), *one*: union, unity, unite, unify, uniform, universe, universal, university, unanimous, unanimity.

urb-, *city*: urban, urbanity, suburb (below the city; cities were anciently built on hills), suburban.

ut- (us-), *use*: utensil, usual, unusual, usury, abuse, utility, peruse (use up, go through, read thoroughly).

vad- (va-), *go*: invade, invasion, evade, pervade, vade mecum.

val-, *be strong*: valor, valiant, prevalent, valid, value, in'valid, inval'id, invalidate, validity, valedictory.

ven-, *come*: convene, convention, convenient, invent (come upon, find), invention, prevent, advent, convent, adventure, venture, intervene, circumvent, intervention, event, uneventful, adventitious, inventory, revenue.

verb-, *word*: verbal, verbose, verbosity, verbiage, verbatim, verb, proverb (expression put forth).

vert- (ver-), *turn*: divert, diversion, diverse, invert, vertical, conversion, revert, verse, version, transverse, perverse (thoroughly turned, turned to the bad), pervert.

via (vi-), *way, road*: viaduct, deviate, devious, obviate (meet, pre-vent), pervious, previous (going before).

vid- (vi-), *see*: provident, provide, provision, revision, visage, visor, visible, invisible, visual, vision, visionary, visit (go to see), prudent (= provident), prudence, providence, improvise, imprudent, supervise, vista, evident.

vinc- (vic-), *conquer*: invincible, victor, victory, convince, evince (prove beyond doubt, show forth).

vir, *man*: virile, virility, virtue (strength of manhood), virtuous, triumvir, triumvirate, decemvir.

viv- (vig-, vi-), *alive, living*: revive, survive, vivid, vivify, vital, vitality, vitalize, devitalize, convivial, victuals (= vig-tuals).

voc-, *call*: convocation, convoke (*k* is substituted for *c*; *c* would be soft before *e*; § 402), invoke, vocation, avocation, revoke, vociferate, vociferous.

vol-, *wish*: benevolent, malevolent, benevolence, voluntary, involuntary, volunteer, volition, volitive.

volv- (vol-), *roll*: revolve, involve, evolve, evolution, involution, revolution, volume, voluminous, voluble.

vulg-, *multitude*: vulgar, divulge, Vulgate.

vulner-, *wound*: vulnerable, invulnerable.

408. Greek prefixes.

The study of Greek prefixes is best undertaken with the study of Greek roots and stems (§ 410; see §§ 390, 391):

an- (a-), *not*: atheist, anarchist, anomaly, anonymous, anæmia, anæsthetic, anodyne, apathy, atom, asyndeton, anhydrous.

ana-, *up*: analysis, analyze, anatomy, anabasis, anachronism (mixing up of time), anachronistic.

anti- (ant-), *against*: antithesis, antipathy, antipodes, antiphonal, antidote, antiseptic, antitoxin, anticlimax, anti-imperialist, antarctic, antagonist, anti-Bohemian.

apo- (aph-), *off, away*: apoplexy, apostle, apogee, apology, apostrophe, aphelion, aphorism, apocope, apocalypse.

cata- (cath-), *down*: cataract, catastrophe, cathedral (sitting down, seat of a bishop), catalogue, catarrh, catalepsy.

dia-, *through*: diameter, diametrically, diagonal, dialogue, diaphragm, diaphanous, diagnosis.

dis- (di-), *twice*: dissyllable, diphthong, dilemma, diploma (folded paper), dihedron, dihexagonal, dihydric, dioxide, disulphide (compare **bis-,** *bisulphide*, § 405).

epi- (eph-), *on*: epitaph, epilogue, epidemic, epilepsy, epigram, epidermis, epiglottis, ephemeral (for a day).

ex-(ec-; compare Latin **ex-**, § 405), *out of, from*: exodus, exogenous, exotic, exegesis, eccentric, eclectic, eclipse, ecstasy.

hemi- (compare Latin **semi-**, § 405), *half*: hemisphere, hemicycle.

hyper-, *over, beyond*: hypercritical, hyperbola, hyperbole, hyperphysical, Hyperborean, hyperthermic.

hypo-, *under, less than*: hypothesis, hypothetical, hypotenuse, hypodermic, hypochondria, hyposulphite.

para-(par-), *beside*: parallel, paraphrase, parable, parhelion, paralysis, parasite, parody, paradox.

peri-, *round*: period, periodic, perimeter, periphrastic, periphrasis, peristyle, peripatetic, periscope.

pro-(compare Latin **pro-**, § 405), *before*: prologue, program, problem, prophet, prolepsis.

syn- (syl-, sym-, sy-), *with, together*: syntax, synagogue, syllable, symphony, sympathy, symbol, system, syllogism, synchronous, symmetry, symptom, synthesis.

409. Greek suffixes. The study of Greek suffixes is best undertaken with the study of Greek roots and stems (§ 410; see §§ 390, 391):

-ism, *act, state, character*: baptism, criticism, hypnotism, despotism, heroism, barbarism, realism, Gallicism.

-ist, *agent*: monopolist, theorist, artist, botanist, physicist, humorist, florist, oculist, atheist, Buddhist.

-itis, *inflammation of*: arthritis, appendicitis, tonsillitis (§ 423).

-ma (-m), -sis, *action, result, state*: drama, system, genesis, thesis.

410. Greek roots and stems. The Greek roots and stems in compound English words (as, *ant-agonist*) are best studied with the Greek prefixes (§ 408; see §§ 390, 391):

ag- (agog-, eg-), *drive, lead*: pedagogue, synagogue, pedagogy, demagogue, stratagem, strategy, strategist.

agon-, *contest*: antagonist, agony, agonize.

alg-, *pain*: neuralgia, neuralgic, cephalalgia, nostalgia.

angel-, *announce*: angel, evangelist, evangelize, evangelical.

anthrop-, *man*: philanthropy, philanthropist, misanthropic, anthropology, anthropography, anthropometric.

arch-, *begin, be first, rule*: archaic, archæology, monarch, monarchy, patriarch (ruler of a family), hierarchy, archangel, arch (chief), archbishop, anarchy, archon, archetype.

arct-, *bear* (animal): arctic, antarctic, Arcturus.

aristo-, *best*: aristocrat, aristocracy.

aster (astr-), *star*: asteroid, asterisk, disaster, astronomy, astrology, astronomic, astrophotometry.

auto-, *self*: autograph, autobiography, autocrat, automatic, automaton, automobile, autonomy, autopsy.

bar-, *heavy*: barometer, barometric, barytone.

biblio-, *book*: Bible, bibliomania, bibliography. See *Library*, § 381.

bio-, *life*: biography, biology, biograph, amphibious.

bol- (bl-), *throw*: symbol, hyperbola, hyperbole, parabola, diabolic, problem, parable, emblem.

card- (compare Latin **cord-**, § 407), *heart*: cardiac, cardiometer, cardiograph, carditis, endocarditis.

chron-, *time*: chronology, chronometer, chronicle, chronic, anachronism, anachronistic.

clin- (**cli-**; compare Latin **clin-**, § 407), *slope, incline, lean*: clinical, incline, climate, climax, anticlimax.

cosmo- (cosm-), *order, world*: cosmogony, cosmography, cosmopolitan, cosmopolite, cosmic, cosmetic.

crat- (-cracy), *power, rule*: democrat, democracy, democratic, aristocrat, aristocracy, autocrat, plutocrat, plutocracy.

cri-, *separate, judge*: critic, critical, criticism, criterion, diacritical, crisis.

cycl-, *circle*: cycle, cycloid, cyclone, bicycle, cyclometer.

cyn-, *dog*: cynic, cynical, cynicism, cynosure (§ 381).

deca, *ten*: decagon, Decalogue, Decameron, hendecagon.

dem-, *people*: democrat, democratic, democracy, epidemic, demagogue, Demosthenes (strength of the people).

derm-, *skin*: epidermis, hypodermic, dermatology, dermatitis, taxidermy, taxidermist, pachyderm.

doc- (dog-), *think*: doxology (= doc-sology), orthodox, orthodoxy, heterodox, paradox, dogma, dogmatic.

dyna-, *power*: dynamite, dynamo, dynamics, dynasty, dynastic, dynamograph, electrodynamics, hydrodynamics.

eco-, *house*: economy, economics, economize.

erg-, *work*: energy, erg, ergometer, ergon.

eu- (ev-), *well*: euphony, eulogy, Eucharist, evangelist, euphemism, euphuism, eugenics.

gam-, *marry*: bigamy, monogamy, polygamy, bigamist, monogamous, cryptogam.

ge-, *earth*: geography, geology, geometry, George (earth worker, farmer), apogee, perigee.

gen- (**gon-**; compare Latin **gen-**, § 407), *produce*: genesis, Genesis, genealogy, eugenics, hydrogen, biogenesis, cosmogony, endogenous, exogenous.

graph- (**gram-**), *write*: graphite, graphic, telegraph, telegram, biography, geography, diagram, epigram, program, grammar, cryptogram.

helio-, *sun*: heliotrope, heliograph, heliotype, helioscope, heliometer, heliotherapy.

hippo-(**-ip-**), *horse*: hippodrome, hippopotamus, Hippocrene(horse's fountain), Philip (lover of horses).

homo-, *same*: homogeneous, homologous, homonym.

hydr-, *water*: hydrant, hydrophobia, hydraulic, hydraulics, hydroplane, hydrogen, hydrostatics, hydrodynamics, hydroelectric, hydrographic, hydrometer, hydrolysis, anhydrous.

icon, *image*: icon, iconoclast, iconoclasm, iconography, iconometer, iconometry, iconoscope.

idio-, *peculiar*: idiotic, idiom, idiosyncrasy.

lith-, *stone*: lithograph, lithography, monolith.

log-, *word, speech*: monologue, dialogue, geology, theology, philology, logic.

lysis, *loosening*: analysis, analyze, paralyze, electrolysis.

meter (**metr-**), *measure*: meter, diameter, perimeter, thermometer, barometer, electrometer, metric, metrically, symmetry.

micro-, *little*: microbe, microcosm, micrometer, microscope.

mon-, *alone, single*: monosyllable, monolith, monastery (minster), monogram, monarch, monologue, monotype, monopoly.

nau-, *ship*: nautical, nautilus, nausea, nauseate, nauseous.

necro-, *dead*: necropolis, necromancy, necromancer, necrology, necrosis, necrophobia.

nom-, *law*: astronomy, astronomer, Deuteronomy, autonomy, anomaly, anomalous, economy.

od-, *way*: exodus, Exodus, period, method, synod, cathode, anode.

onym-, *name*: anonymous, synonym, synonymous, patronymic, pseudonym, homonym.

op-, *see*: optic, optical, optician, synopsis, optometer, optometry, optometrist, thanatopsis.

ortho-, *straight, right*: orthography, orthodoxy, orthodox, orthoepy, orthopedics.

pan- (**pant-**), *all*: panoply, Pan-American, pantheism, pantomime, pantograph, panorama, pandemonium.

path-, *suffer* (compare Latin **pat-**, § 407): pathos, pathetic, sympathy, sympathetic, antipathy, pathology, homeopathy, allopathy.

ped-, *boy*: pedagogue, pedagogy, pedagogics, encyclopedia (instruction in the circle of arts and sciences).

phe- (phon-), *voice*: prophet, euphony, euphemism, phonetics, phonograph, telephone, megaphone, symphony.

phil-, *love*: philter, philology, philosophy, Philadelphia, Philip (lover of horses), philanthropy, bibliophile.

phos (phot-), *light*: phosphorus. photography, photometer.

physi-, *nature*: physics, physical, physiology, physiography, physician, physiognomy.

pod- (compare Latin **ped-**, § 407), *foot*: tripod, antipodes, podagra.

poli-, *city*: polity, politics, political, police, metropolis, acropolis, necropolis, cosmopolitan.

pseudo- (pseud-), *false*: pseudoprophet, pseudonym, pseudoclassic, pseudo-Gothic.

rheu- (-rrh), *flow*: rheum, rheumatic, catarrh.

scop- (skep-), *see, look*: microscope, telescope, spectroscope, skeptic, skeptical.

soph-, *wise*: philosophy, sophism, sophist, sophistry.

sta-, *stand*: apostate, ecstasy, hydrostatics.

strat-, *army*: strategy, strategic, stratagem, strategist.

tag- (tac-), *arrange*: taxidermy (= tag-sidermy), taxidermist, syntax, tactics, tactical.

tele-, *at a distance*: telegraph, telephone, telegram, telescope, telepathy.

theo- (the-), *God*: theology, theological, theist, atheist, atheism, pantheism, pantheon.

therm-, *heat*: thermometer, thermal, isotherm, thermodynamics, thermostat.

thesis (the-), *placing*: hypothesis, synthesis, antithesis, hypothetical, antithetical, parenthesis.

tom-, *cut*: anatomy, atom, entomology, epitome, tome.

trop- (troph-), *turn*: tropic, trophy, trope, heliotrope.

zoö- (zo-), *animal*: zoölogy, zoölogical, zodiac, zodiacal, zooid, zoögeography.

CHAPTER VI

USES AND ABUSES OF WORDS

Zounds, I was never so bethump'd with words,
Since I first called my brother's father dad. — SHAKESPEARE.

He multiplieth words without knowledge. — THE BIBLE.

411. Exaggeration. In this period of our great physical progress we strive to make our language as gigantic as our achievements. We seem to think that our inherited speech (which is indeed a priceless inheritance), although good enough for the centuries of repose of our forefathers, is too feeble for men of our might; and in our ignorance of its power we create slang and heap words on one another, thinking to increase their efficiency thereby, with the result that our language teems with jargon and gross exaggeration. In the eyes of the world we are a people of raw and untutored strength, whose opinion in literary matters is neither trained nor organized. Until we become less satisfied with intellectual shoddy, and seek cultivation and taste, we can hardly expect to attain an exalted position in the leadership of mankind.

412. Slang. Objections to slang have already been mentioned (§ 380).

413. Redundancy, tautology. The needless repetition of ideas (§§ 192, 193) by the multiplication of words not only adds nothing to the thought, but robs words of a part of their meaning, distorts the sense, and by improper emphasis distracts the attention from the main point. Study the following examples of faulty expressions; omit the italicized words:

Successful achievements; *absolute* misunderstanding; *complete* master; *completely* intact; *unfair* distortion; the *real, positive* truth; *deep* passion; *genuine* pity; *delicate* grace; *solid* erudition; *very* perfect; *absolute* perfection; *selfish* vindictiveness; *very careful* investigation; *sincere* uncertainty; *unsuccessful* attempts; *truly* remarkable fact; *perfectly* right; *perfectly all* right; panacea *for all ills* (look up *panacea* in the dictionary); *surrounding* circumstances (see *circum-*, § 405); *joint* partnership; *evidently* seem; *temporary* loan; *respectfully* solicited; Rio Grande *River* ('Rio Grande' means *Great River*); Loch Lomond *Lake* ('Loch' means *lake*); *Mount* Ben Lomond ('Ben' means *mountain*); *divinely* beautiful; *extremely* handsome; *very* elegant; *supremely* brilliant; *perfectly* (or *absolutely*) exquisite; scrutinize *very carefully*; practice *again and again*; decide *fully* (or *very definitely*); *absolutely* necessary; *absolutely* essential; *absolutely* indispensable; *absolutely* requisite; *absolutely* charming; *final* drowning; *final* completion; *actual* explosion; *absolute* scandal; *positively* shameful; *entirely* misleading; *steadfastly* resolved; *really* improved; *utterly* banished; *absolutely* prohibited; *absolutely* unique record; *very much* delighted; *splendidly* ready; *distinctively* new; *convincingly* worthy; *very full* program of events; *very* roughly; *very* rudely; *very* fiercely (§ 414); *absolutely* differing points of view (different points of view, or, widely different points of view); the case was contested with extreme bitterness *on both sides.*

"Vulgarism in language", Lord Chesterfield once wrote to his son, "is the next and distinguishing characteristic of bad company and a bad education. Proverbial expressions and trite sayings are the flowers of the rhetoric of a vulgar man. Would he say that men differ in their tastes, he both supports and adorns that opinion by the good old saying, as he respectfully calls it, that *what is one man's meat is another man's poison.* He has always some favorite word for the time being, which, for the sake of using often, he commonly abuses, such as *vastly* angry, *vastly* kind, *vastly* handsome, and *vastly* ugly." (See *pet expressions*, § 417.)

414. Universal statements. As a rule, universal state-ments should be avoided, especially in writing; for such sweep-ing words as *all, always, none, never, wholly, completely, utterly, entirely, supremely,* and *absolutely* (§ 417) are apt to sound like exaggerations, and may prove to be erroneous (but see the note, below). It is well to omit, also, that too convenient, over-worked, and colorless word *very* (§ 280); instead of saying, for example, *very warm, very hot,* and the like, say *warm, sunny, hot, torrid, tropical, sultry, stifling, suffocating, oppressive,* and so on; instead of *very cold* say *cold, wintry, freezing, frigid, keen, bleak, cutting, raw, inclement, bitter, biting, piercing, icy, glacial, arctic,* and the like; instead of *very tired* say *tired out, faint, worn out, weary, wearied, exhausted, fatigued, jaded, prostrated, fagged, fagged out,* and so forth (§ 385).

NOTE. Universal words are particularly useful in negative sen-tences : ' He is *not entirely* blind '; ' The glen was *not absolutely* void of beauty ' (Scott).

415. Strong words weakened. Try to say just what you mean, and say it in the simplest way. Do not call a thing *adorable, handsome, elegant, exquisite, gorgeous, splendid, grand, magnificent, wonderful, disgusting, detestable, excruciating, hide-ous,* or *ghastly* unless it is so; for these are strong words, and they should not be made commonplace by being applied to trivial matters. And do not give to a *mishap* or *slight accident* the name of *calamity* or *disaster* or *tragedy.* Study such words in the dictionary. In language, as in all things else, seek the truth and moderation.

416. Makeshifts for adjectives. Furthermore, in speak-ing or writing, do not turn all kinds of adjective phrases (which normally stand after the noun) into attributive adjectives (which normally stand before the noun; § 113, N.); this kind of change often shifts the emphasis from words which should be emphatic to words which should be unemphatic (§ 370), and the adjectives are frequently misleading or unintelligible (see §§ 54, 153, 383). For example, a prominent periodical says, " President Eliot is at home again from his *around-the-world* journey", instead of *journey round the world*, which expresses the idea properly, and places the emphasis on *round the world*, where it should be (§ 370). Such an expression as '*precise* instinct' (for '*instinct for precision*') is obscure if not unintelligible; '*romantic* associations' does not mean ' associations *with romanticists*', as the author of it intended, but ' associations of a romantic nature'. In general, therefore, we should avoid expressions like the following :

Learn-by-heart method (say 'method of *learning by heart*'); *typhoid-fever* microbes (microbes *of typhoid fever*); *evolution* theory (theory *of evolution*); *Congress* session (session *of Congress*); *baseball* game (game *of baseball*; compare ' game *of tennis*', ' game *of chess*'); *travel* sketches (sketches *of travel*); *sentence* unity (unity *in the sentence*); *public* attitude (attitude *of the public*); *convention* action (action *of the convention*); *artistic* criticism (criticism *of art*); *giant* stories (stories *of giants*; compare ' giant *strides*', ' giant *might*', ' giant *mountains*', which are correct); *near-by* house (house *close by*; see *near*, *close by*, § 417); *foam* burst (burst *of foam*); *French* south (south *of France*); *merchandise* invoice (invoice *of merchandise*); *jury* trial (trial *by jury*); *degree* requirements (requirements *for a degree*); *sound* table (table *of sounds*); *romantic* associations (associations *with romanticists*); *precise* instinct (instinct *for precision*); *humanity* interest (interest *in humanity*); *pay* increase (increase *in pay*); *Bible* chapter (chapter *in the Bible*); *adult* camp (camp *for adults*); *artist* colony (colony *of artists*); *jury* address (address *to the jury*); *mayoralty* candidate (candidate *for the mayoralty*); *candy-business* outlook (outlook *for the candy business*); his *Spanish* residence (his residence *in Spain*); Washington Irving's *English* sojourn (Washington Irving's sojourn *in England*; compare ' *French* south ', above, and ' death threat ', etc., in § 54, 6); *view*point (point *of view*).

417. Do's and don't's. This section is based on Webster's New International Dictionary and the Oxford English Dictionary. Words and phrases marked *colloquial* (§ 380) are permissible in familiar conversation and the like; those marked *cant, dialectal, local, provincial, slang,* or *vulgar* are usually to be avoided, both in writing and in speaking (§§ 378–383).

NOTE. Some of the expressions given here are common to the United States and England; others, peculiar to the United States (Americanisms), are marked *U. S.* Expressions peculiar to Great Britain (Briticisms) are of course omitted.

abbreviations. In general, do not use abbreviations in letters or in other literary work. See §§ 529 and 541.

abide, abode, abode. The past tense and past participle of *abide* is *abode* (§ 654); do not say ' abided ' for *abode* :

    1. He had *abode* there three days.
    2. They have not *abode* by their agreement.

ability, capacity. *Ability* means the power of doing; *capacity* means the power of receiving or holding :

    1. *Ability* to do work; *ability* to teach; natural *ability*.
    2. The *capacity* of a barrel; electric *capacity*; mental *capacity*; mental *ability*.

about. The adverb *about* means approximately, not many more or less; its use in the sense of *nearly, almost,* is colloquial :

    1. *About* one hundred persons saw the wreck.
    2. I'm *about* tired out; is your work *about* done ? (Colloquial.)

above. *Above*, as an adjective, should be avoided :

    1. The *foregoing* discussion. (Not ' The above discussion '.)
    2. The particulars cited (given, mentioned) *above*. (Adverb.)

absolutely. *Absolutely* is a favorite word nowadays; like *positively, quite, literally,* and some other words, it is much used, but seldom needed. See § 414, N.

accept, except. *Accept* means to receive; *except* means to make an exception of; do not say ' accept of ' for *accept* (the preposition here adds no new idea; but see *admit, admit of*):

>   1. She *accepted* the gifts; the gifts were *accepted*.
>   2. He was *excepted* from the general pardon.

A. D., B. C. The abbreviations *A.D.* and *B.C.* are common in all kinds of writing, especially in histories, encyclopedias, and the like, where dates are frequent. They are seldom written out except in the most formal style.

The abbreviation *A.D.* is for the Latin *anno Domini*, which means *in the year of our Lord*. Properly it should be used in this sense only, and should be placed before (not after) the figures representing the year; the abbreviation *B.C.*, meaning *before Christ*, is used either with figures or with the word *century*, and is generally placed after them:

>   1. Augustus was born in *63 B.C.* He died *A.D. 14.*
>   2. Pericles lived in the *fifth century B.C.*
>   3. Done in the District of Columbia this sixteenth day of November *in the year of our Lord* one thousand nine hundred and eighteen, etc. (Formal style; § 128, *a*.)

At present there is a tendency to treat *A.D.* as if it simply indicated the period after Christ, and use it with or without figures and after prepositions; but the more careful writers avoid this (as in the third example):

>   1. This happened in the third century *A.D.* (Say, rather, 'after Christ', or ' of the Christian Era ', or ' of our era '.)
>   2. '*In* (*About*, etc.) *A. D. 28* (or, *28 A.D.*) he was ', etc. (Say, rather, ' In the twenty-eighth year of the Christian Era ', etc.)
>   3. In the second *century of the Christian Era* the Empire of Rome comprehended the fairest part of the earth, and the most civilized portion of mankind. — GIBBON.

addendum, data, etc. See § 39.

addict. *Addict*, as a noun, is unknown to good usage.

adjectives; adverbs. Do not confuse adjectives and adverbs. See §§ 238, 239, 258–260.

administer, minister to. Do not confuse *administer* and *minister to*; do not use *administer* for *deal* and the like:

    1. He *administered* the remedy (the finances). (Correct.)
    2. She *ministered to* the sick. (Correct.)
    3. He *dealt* him a severe blow. (Not 'administered'.)

admit, admit of. *Admit* means to grant entrance; *admit of* means to be capable of (for other phrases, see § 287):

    1. The gate *admits* carriages; the ticket *admits* the bearer.
    2. His latest letter *admits of* another interpretation.

advance, advanced. Do not confuse *advance* (= *in advance, ahead*) with *advanced* (= *moved forward, far on*):

    1. *Advance* sales (ahead of the regular sales); *advance* copies (of a book).
    2. *Advanced* thinkers; the most *advanced* truths of mathematics.

affect, effect. Do not confuse *affect* and *effect*. *Affect* is a verb (meaning to produce an effect on); *effect* is a noun (usually meaning a result) or a verb (meaning to make):

    1. He was deeply *affected* by the loss of his father.
    2. What *effect* did the loss of his father have on him?
    3. The loss of his father *effected* a great change in him.

aggravate, annoy. *Aggravate* means to add weight to, to increase (see **ad-**, § 405; and **grav-**, § 407); do not use it for *annoy, displease, exasperate, irritate*, and the like:

    1. The treatment *aggravated* the wound.
    2. His words *aggravated* his offense.
    3. Such conduct *irritated* his best friends. (Not 'aggravated'.)

agreeably surprised. Do not use (except humorously) 'agreeably disappointed' for *agreeably surprised*. A disappointment cannot be agreeable.

allow. *Allow* means to permit; do not use it for *say* or *think*:

    1. He *allowed* us to play in the meadow.
    2. He *thought* it would do no harm. (Not 'allowed'.)

all right. *All right*, used in expressing assent and the like, is colloquial. Do not write it 'alright'.

allude, allusion, illusion. Do not use *allude to* (which means to refer to indirectly by a hint or suggestion) for *refer to* or *mention*; do not confuse *allusion* (an indirect reference, or hint) with *illusion* (a harmless and often pleasing deception, or fancy; whereas *delusion* is a harmful deception):

1. He did not *mention* or *allude* to our having met.
2. My *allusion* to his occupation pained him.
3. Optical *illusions*; the happy *illusions* of childhood.
4. Laboring under a *delusion*; a poor *deluded* fool.

almost, nearly. Do not use 'most' for *almost* or *nearly* :

1. It rained the *most* of the time.
2. It rained *almost* all the time. (Not 'most'.)
3. It rained *almost* every day. (Not 'most'.)
4. Our food is *almost* gone. (Not 'most'.)
5. *Almost* everybody's here. (Not 'most'.)

aloud. Do not use 'out loud' for *aloud*:

She was reading the book *aloud*.

already, all ready. Do not confuse *already* and *all ready* :

He is *already* gone; He is *all ready* to go.

alternative. An *alternative* is a necessary choice of one or the other of two things, or of the second of two things :

1. The *alternative* of peace with dishonor, or of war with honor.
2. He must escape; his only *alternative* was to starve.

altogether, all together. *Altogether* means completely, wholly; do not use it for *all together*:

1. The judgments of the Lord are righteous *altogether*.
2. They came separately, but went home *all together*.

among, between, after. *Among* is used of more than two persons or things; *between* is ordinarily used of two objects or two groups of objects, but "is still the only word available to express the relation of a thing to many surrounding things severally and individually, *among* expressing a relation to them collectively and vaguely" (Oxford English Dictionary); do not use *between* for *after*. The following examples are correct:

1. The clothing was divided *among* the (several) children.
2. The clothing was divided *between* the (two) children.
3. Our fruit trees have plenty of space *between* them.
4. A space *between* three points; a treaty *between* five powers.
5. *Between* every two pages; *after* every mouthful (not 'between').

and. Do not omit *and* in numbers. See § 124.

antagonize. *Antagonize* is properly used of two forces of the same kind; do not use it for *alienate* or *oppose*:

1. These forces *antagonize* each other. (Compare 'These forces are *antagonistic*'.)
2. He *alienated* his friends. (Not 'antagonized'.)
3. He openly *opposed* the bill. (Not 'antagonized'.)

anthracite. *Anthracite* means *hard coal*; therefore do not use *coal* with it:

1. Soft (or, Bituminous) coal; hard coal, or *anthracite*.
2. The *anthracite* regions of Pennsylvania.

anxious. *Anxious* means disquieted or solicitous, in painful suspense; then it means eagerly desirous; do not use it as a mere equivalent for *eager*. The following examples are correct:

1. They were *anxious* for their brother's safety.
2. The general was *anxious* to expedite the undertaking.
3. I am not now so *eager* about your coming to town.

anywhere. Do not add *s* to *anywhere, nowhere, somewhere*.

apart, aside. Do not use *aside* for *apart*. To put a thing *aside* is to put it to one side, or out of the way; to put a thing *apart* is to dismiss it from thought:

1. Lay your work *aside* and let us be off.
2. The decision of the court was set *aside*.
3. I stepped *aside*. They sat *apart* from the others.
4. Jesting *apart*, how do you like him? (Not 'aside'.)
5. He took the machine *apart* (= *to pieces*).

appreciate. *Appreciate* means to set a price on (see **ad-**, § 405; compare *appraise*); then, to esteem adequately or highly; therefore do not add *highly* or the like to it; *appreciate* in the sense of increase in value is a misuse of the word (U.S.), but *depreciate*, meaning to lower or fall in value, is proper (see **de-**, § 405):

1. She *appreciates* their kindness to her.
2. Your labors will never be fully known and *appreciated*.
3. Gold had *increased* in value. (Not 'appreciated'.)
   But, Property has *depreciated* here.

approve, approve of. *Approve* means *sanction officially*, then *commend*; *approve of* means *have a favorable opinion of* (for other idioms, see § 287):

1. The colonel *approved* the sentence.
2. He has read all, but *approves of* very few.
3. Your father does not *approve of* your going.

apropos. *Apropos* means to the point or purpose, pertinent; it may be followed by *of* or *to* (see § 287):

1. The story he told was not *apropos*.
2. His question was *apropos of* nothing.
3. Did they say nothing *apropos to* the question?

apt, likely, liable. *Apt*, *likely*, and *liable* express tendency toward something. *Apt* denotes a natural tendency; do not confuse *likely* (denoting probability) and *liable* (denoting exposure):

1. The young mind is *apt* to receive impressions.
2. An impulsive person is *apt* to make mistakes.
3. The frost is *apt* (or *likely*) to kill the fruit.
4. An angry dog is *likely* to bite.
5. We are constantly *liable* to accidents.
6. *Liable* to arrest; *liable* to be broken.

arrival, advent. *Advent* means an important or epoch-making arrival; do not use it for *arrival*:

1. The *advent* of spring; the *arrival* of the train.
2. The *advent* of the Normans.
3. His *arrival* gave them hope. (Not 'advent'.)

as. Do not use *as* for *because, since, when,* or *while* (see § 306). In citing examples, do not use *as* (except with a comma after it) for *such as*; do not use *as* for *that*:

    1. Animals of the cat kind, *such as* the lion and the tiger.
    2. I don't know *that* I can wait. (Not ' as '.)
    3. Did he go? Not *that* I know. (Not ' as '.)

as far as. Do not use ' all the farther ' for *as far as*:

    That 's *as far as* the lesson goes. (Not ' all the farther '.)

as well as or better than. In expressions like *as well as or better than* do not omit the second *as*:

    1. She can write *as well as or better than he.* (Say, rather, ' She can write *as well as he, or better* '.)
    2. She is *as tall as* he, *or taller.* (Not ' She is as tall or taller than he '.)

at. Do not use ' at about' for *about*:

    1. They returned to their quarters *at* three o'clock.
    2. They returned to their quarters *about* three o'clock.

audience, spectators. Use the word *audience* of persons who listen (see **aud-**, § 407); use *spectators* of persons who look on (see **spec-**, § 407):

    1. He lectured to large *audiences* in New York.
    2. She was a silent *spectator* of the fight.

author. In general, avoid such nouns as ' authoress ' and ' poetess '. Use *author* and *poet* as masculine or feminine.

automobile. ' Auto ' for *automobile* is colloquial. Do not use ' auto ' as a verb for *motor*:

    We *motored* through the country.

avocation, vocation. A person's *vocation* is his calling, or regular employment; his *avocation* is his diversion, or secondary occupation, which calls him away from his regular employment (see **abs-**, § 405; and **voc-**, § 407):

    1. His *vocation* is surgery; his *avocation*, photography.
    2. To our *vocation* let us add an *avocation.*

away. The adverb *away* often means at a distance, far (see *way*):

1. You can see the city *away* through the stifling air.
2. They live *away* down the valley.

awful, awfully. *Awful* means frightful, fearful, appalling; as a mere intensive, it is slang:

1. An *awful* disaster; an *awful* sight.
2. An *ugly* hat, *ludicrous* mistakes, *bad* manners. (Not 'awful'.)
3. I was *exceedingly* careful. (Not 'awfully'.)

awhile, a while. Do not confuse the adverb *awhile* with *a while*:

1. They waited *awhile* at the station.
2. For *a while* we heard nothing.

bad, good. Instead of describing everything as *bad* or *good*, be more specific in your meaning by using synonyms (§ 385):

1. *Bad*: dull (day), gloomy (disposition), destructive (storm), clumsy (workman), fatal (accident), insecure (foundation), hazardous (undertaking), filthy (condition), foul (language), coarse (talk), offensive (manners), musty (flour), tainted (meat), unjust (decision), unfair (advantage), improper (conduct), cruel (treatment), harsh (voice), inhuman (act), barbarous (customs), imperfect (copy), unpromising (season), malicious (intent).

2. *Good*: savory (dish), nutritious (food), delicious (fruit), praiseworthy (act), faithful (friend), useful (invention), noble (nature), valuable (advice), cheerful (disposition), courteous (manners), productive (soil), advantageous (offer), beneficial (exercise), profitable (reading), opportune (moment), desirable (opportunity), agreeable (companion), favorable (outlook), excellent (education), brilliant (speaker), healthful (climate), amusing (story), sound (sense), pleasing (concert), just (grounds), fair (weather), graceful (style), refined (society), pleasant, enjoyable, delightful (time; 'a good time' is colloquial, chiefly U. S.).

badly. *Badly* means in a bad manner; with words meaning to want or need, *badly* and *sadly* are often used colloquially for *greatly*:

1. The work was done *badly*; he was *badly* hurt.
2. The house is *badly* (or *sadly*) in need of repairs. (Colloquial.)

balance. Do not use the bookkeeper's term *balance* for *rest* or
remainder:

    1. I cannot bring my accounts to a *balance*. (Correct.)
    2. He has a comfortable *balance* at his banker's. (Correct.)
    3. They spent the *rest* of the day in camp. (Not ' balance '.)
    4. The *remainder* of us went elsewhere. (Not ' balance '.)

because. Do not use as the subject or predicate of a sentence a clause
beginning with *because*:

    1. He was tardy *because* he was ill. (Correct.)
    2. His tardiness was no excuse. (Not ' Because he was tardy
        was no excuse '.)
    3. His reason was *that* he had an appointment. (Not ' because '.)

beg, beg leave. Do not use ' beg pardon ' for *I beg your pardon*
(or *pardon me*); do not use ' beg to ' for *beg leave to*:

    1. *I beg your pardon*; I did not quite catch what you said.
    2. I have received your letter, and *beg leave to* say, etc.

behave. *Behave* is used sometimes with and sometimes (colloquially)
without an adverb:

    1. The children *behaved well* (or *badly*).
    2. Can't you learn to *behave* yourself? (Colloquial.)
    3. He *behaved* like a man of sense and spirit.

behind. Do not use ' in behind ' or ' in back of ' for *behind*:

    The pasture is *behind* the barn.

belong to. Use *to* with *belong*, rather than ' in ' or ' with '
(colloquial, U. S.):

    The house *belongs to* the estate; the yard *belongs to* the house.

beside, besides. Do not confuse *beside* (at the side of) and *besides*
(in addition to):

    1. She sat *beside* her mother.
    2. Did anybody come *besides* (or *except*) him?

besides, indeed, etc. *And* means ' in addition ', and hence should
not be used with such words as *besides, furthermore, indeed,
moreover*, which have a similar meaning (§ 413):

1. He had the means; *besides*, he was popular.
2. She did not go; *indeed*, she had no intention of going.
3. They were homeless. *Indeed*, they were vagabonds.

best of all. Do not say ' the best of any ' for *the best of all* or for *better than any other*:

1. This is *the best of all* our newspapers.
2. This paper is *better than any other* in the city. (But, ' This paper of yours is *better than any* of ours'. See § 145.)
3. He was *the most powerful of all* the kings of history.

big, large, great. *Big* implies mere size or bulk, and is often used colloquially for *large* (a more refined word); do not use ' big ' in formal speech or writing for *great, forcible, vigorous, strong, wise, discreet, gifted, influential, broad-minded*, and the like:

1. *Big* ships; *big* hotels; *big* shops; *big* drums; *big* dinners.
2. *Big* changes and little changes; children, *big* and little.
3. No *bigger* than a glowworm shone the tent. — TENNYSON.
4. He made *large* profits on some articles.
5. An infant and then a few *larger* children appeared.
6. A *great* man; the *great* men of the nation. (Not ' big '.)

blame for. Do not use ' on ' after *blame*:

Don't *blame* me *for* it. (Not ' Don't blame it on me '.)

bring. *Bring* means to convey to the place (real or supposed) of the speaker or the auditor; do not use *bring* for *take*:

1. Will you *bring* somebody to dinner? Yes, I will *bring* Helen.
2. *Take* these letters to the post office. (Not ' bring '.)

bunch. ' Bunch ' applied to a group of people is slang.

but, yet. *Yet* is an adverb (§ 298 and N.), and means *nevertheless*; do not use *yet* for *but*:

1. He was kind, but *yet* I did not trust him.
2. Although he was kind, *yet* I did not trust him.
3. You succeeded, *but* I didn't. (Not ' yet '.)

but that, but what. Do not confuse *but that* with *that* or *but what* (§§ 312, 313); in Examples 2–5 *but that* = *that . . . not*:

1. She would go *but that* (= *except that*) she lacks courage.
2. He was not so brave *but that* he hesitated.

3. It is impossible *but that* storms will arise.
   But, It is *not* impossible *that* (not 'but that') storms will arise.
4. We are *not* sure *but that* he will return.
   Who knows *but that* he will return?
5. There is no *fear but that* my grandfather will recover.
   But, There is no *doubt that* (not 'but that') he will recover.
6. We know nothing *but what* (= *except that which*) you told us.

by, with. *By* is used of a person (or thing personified), to denote the doer, or agent; *with* is used of a thing, to denote the instrument with which the act is done (for similar idioms, see § 287):

1. This house was built *by* my father.
2. The cattle were sheltered *by* the great trees.
3. The farm was well equipped *with* machinery.

calculate. *Calculate* means to determine by mathematical process, to estimate; do not use it for *expect, intend, plan,* or *think*:

1. To *calculate* an eclipse; *calculate* the velocity of light.
2. We did not stop to *calculate* the costs.
3. They *expect* that he will assist them. (Not 'calculate'.)
4. He *intends* to begin next week. (Not 'calculates'.)
5. I *think* they have gone home. (Not 'calculate'.)

cannot but, can but. See § 315.

capital letters. See § 424.

carry on. *Carry on* means to continue or conduct; in the sense of behaving in a rude or boisterous fashion it is colloquial:

1. The conflict was *carried on* with great vigor.
2. He *carried on* like a madman. (Colloquial.)

casualty. Do not say 'casuality'. See § 423.

catch fire. Do not say 'catch on fire' for *catch fire*:

The house (roof, woods, etc.) *caught fire.*

center, middle. The word *center* implies circumference or definite outline, and suggests a point; do not use it for *middle*, which suggests a space rather than a point; do not use 'center round', which is illogical, for *center at, in,* or *on*:

1. The *center* of a circle, of a target, of the earth.
2. The *middle* of the road, forest, room, floor, wall, line.

3. The *middle* door, gate, isle, seat, street. (Not 'center'.)
4. The storm *centered at* Portsmouth; their hopes *centered in* (or *on*) one person. (Not 'round'.)
5. At some future time trade may *center on* the Mississippi.

character, reputation. The *character* of a person (or thing) is what he (or it) really is; his *reputation* is what people think him to be:

    1. His *reputation* was above reproach.
    2. Of his *character* little was ever known.
    3. What is the *character* of this metal?

cheat, fraud, defraud. The use of 'gouge' for *cheat, fraud, defraud,* and the like is slang.

chock-full. Do not use 'chuck-full' for *chock-full*:

    His head was *chock-full* of these impertinences.

claim, maintain. *Claim* means to assert a right to; when there is no question of right, do not use it for *assert* or *maintain*:

    1. This question *claims* our immediate attention. (Correct.)
    2. Both sides *claimed* victory; he *claimed* the land. (Correct.)
    3. It was *asserted* that the story was true. (Not 'claimed'.)

clergy, clergymen. *Clergy* is a collective noun (§ 36); do not use it like the plural *clergymen*:

    1. These are duties belonging to the *clergy*.
    2. The *clergy* were men of enlarged minds and varied culture.
    3. Ten *clergymen* attended the exercises. (Not 'clergy'.)

climax. *Climax* (a Greek word meaning ladder; see **clin-**, § 410) is the name of a rhetorical figure in which a number of words, phrases, or clauses are arranged in an ascending series, beginning with the least important and ending with the most important (§ 370, *A*, 2); the word is often applied, erroneously, to the highest of a series, or to the point of anything, where *acme, culmination, summit, zenith,* or the like should be used:

    1. But now abideth *faith, hope, love.*
    2. He had reached the *acme* (or *zenith*) of fame. (Not 'climax'.)

coincidence, incident. *Coincidence* means the occurrence or existence of two or more events or circumstances at the same time;
incident means the occurrence of a single event or circumstance,
usually of minor importance (see **com-**, § 405, and **cad-**, § 407):

    1. His being there when I arrived was a mere *coincidence*.
    2. The *incidents* of our long journey were few.

college, school. Do not use *school* for *college* or *university*:

    1. From *school* I was dismissed to the *University*.
    2. How long have you been back from *college*?

condign, severe. *Condign* means deserved, appropriate, or merited;
do not use it for *severe*:

    1. He received *condign* punishment. (Correct.)
    2. He deserved *severe* punishment. (To say that a man *deserves*
       condign punishment is a needless repetition, or tautology,
       § 413; it is like saying that he *deserves deserved* punishment.)

complexioned. Do not say ' complected ' for *complexioned*:

    It was a *dark-complexioned* woman.

conduct, manage. Do not use ' run ' for *conduct, manage,* or *have
charge of*:

    1. He *conducts* a hotel at the seashore.
    2. He *manages* a large farm in the West.
    3. In the United States a conductor *has charge of* the train.

confuse. Do not use ' rattle ' for *confuse, disconcert,* or the like:

    1. He became *confused*, and lost his way. (Not ' rattled '.)
    2. The slightest remark from a stranger *disconcerted* her.

considerable. *Considerable* (like *inconsiderable*) is an adjective, and
means deserving of notice, important; do not use it as a noun
for *a large quantity of* or *a good deal of*:

    1. She has read a *considerable* amount of English.
    2. They were men of *considerable* influence.
    3. They were men of *inconsiderable* influence.
    4. *Considerable* trouble; a *considerable* amount of energy; *con-
       siderably* more energy.
    5. *A large amount of* fruit is lost. (Not ' Considerable fruit '.)

consist of, consist in. *Consist of* is used of the material things of which something is composed; *consist in* is used of actions, conditions, qualities, and other nonmaterial things (for similar idioms, see § 287):

1. The fence *consists of* a ditch and a bank.
2. Happiness does not *consist in* having a multitude of friends.

contain, hold. *Contain* means to have something inside; *hold* means to be capable of containing:

1. This barrel *contains* winter apples.
2. That pail *holds* two quarts; it *contains* molasses.

contemptible, contemptuous. *Contemptible* means deserving of contempt; *contemptuous* means showing contempt:

1. I had grown *contemptible* even to myself.
2. It was a *contemptibly* little thing.
3. He assumed an air of *contemptuous* indifference.
4. He behaved *contemptuously* toward us.

continual, continuous. *Continual* usually means of frequent occurrence; *continuous* means without interruption:

1. *Continual* applause; *continuous* applause for ten minutes.
2. I was *continually* choked with laughter.
3. A *continuous* performance; a *continuous* round of gayety.
4. The water flowed *continuously* for eleven hours.

costume, dress, vehicle. 'Rig' for *costume* or *dress* is colloquial; for *vehicle* it is also colloquial (U. S.).

country, native land. 'Fatherland' is not so good as *country* or *native land*:

1. My *country*, 'tis of thee.
2. He never saw his *native land* again.

couple. *Couple* is properly used of two persons or things of the same kind taken together; it is often used loosely for *two* (do not use it for *a few*; see *pair*):

1. Other *couples* joined the procession.
2. A *couple* of as arrant knaves as any in Messina.
3. *Two* hours; *two* letters. (Not 'A couple of'.)

crowd. *Crowd* means a throng or multitude; its use for *set* or *clique* is colloquial:

    1. A *crowd* had gathered in the street.
    2. I don't belong to that *crowd*. (Colloquial.)

cunning. *Cunning* implies skill; its misuse for *small, pretty, attractive, interesting*, and the like should be avoided (colloquial, U.S.):

    1. The desk showed *cunning* workmanship.
    2. They were *cunning* in the use of their weapons.
    3. *Attractive* little shelves for bits of pottery. (Not ' cunning '.)

cut. *Cut* in the sense of ' break off an acquaintance ' or ' absent yourself from ' is colloquial:

    1. He had *cut* me ever since my marriage. (Colloquial.)
    2. I *cut* his lecture this morning at eight. (Colloquial.)

cute. *Cute* (short for *acute*) is used colloquially for *acute, clever, keen-witted, shrewd*; its use for *pretty, dainty, cosy, attractive*, and the like is slang:

    1. A *cute* answer was made him. (Colloquial.)
    2. Isn't she a *dainty* little thing? (Not ' cute '.)
    3. He has a *cosy* study. (Not ' awfully cute '.)

damage. *Damage* means loss, harm, or injury; its use for *charge, cost*, or *expense* is slang:

    1. The storm did the crops great *damage*.
    2. What is the *expense*? (Not ' damage '.)

dangling participle, etc. See § 231; compare §§ 222, 229.
dash. Do not misuse the dash. See §§ 487–489.
date. *Date* means a point or period of time; its use for *appointment* is a vulgar colloquialism (U.S.; see *up to date*):

    1. What was the *date* of the discovery?
    2. Did you keep your *appointment*? (Not ' date '.)

deadly, deathly. *Deadly* means *fatal*; *deathly* means *like death*:

    A *deadly* blow; a *deathly* pallor (or silence).

deal. The noun *deal*, meaning a quantity or amount, is usually modified by *good* or *great*; colloquially, it is used without *good* or *great*; do not use it for *underhand agreement* or *secret arrangement* (U. S. cant):

    1. There is a *great deal* of truth in what you say.
    2. They talked a *deal* of nonsense. (Colloquial.)
    3. The leaders made an *underhand agreement*. (Not 'a deal'.)

decimate. *Decimate* means to take a tenth part of; then simply a large part; do not modify it by 'terribly' or any other adverb:

    1. The regiment was *decimated* for mutiny. (Every tenth man was put to death.)
    2. The population was *decimated* by the plague. (Not 'terribly decimated'.)

degrade. 'Demote' (local, U.S.) for *degrade* is unknown to good usage.

demean. *Demean*, like *demeanor*, has to do with behavior or deportment; do not use it for *degrade, lower, disgrace*, or the like:

    1. He *demeaned* (= *conducted*) himself like a gentleman.
    2. She would *lower* herself by such a marriage. (Not 'demean'.)

depot. A *depot* is properly a place where provisions, clothing, goods, and the like are stored; its use for *station* (a *stopping place* for trains) is not desirable (U.S.):

    1. The *depots* were being rapidly filled.
    2. I will be at the *station* to meet you. (Not 'depot'.)

determined, resolved. Do not use 'bound' for *determined* or *resolved*:

    1. He was *determined* to have his own way.
    2. They had *resolved* to lead an honest life.

develop rapidly. 'Boom' for *develop rapidly* and the like is colloquial (U. S.).

dialectal, dialectic. *Dialectal* refers to dialect (as, *dialectal* variants). *Dialectic* refers to dialectics (as, *dialectic* philosophers).

different from. Do not use 'to' or 'than' after *different* (see *differ*, § 287):

    1. He is *different from* his brother.
    2. He is *different from* what he was a year ago.
    3. He thinks *differently from* me on many points.

dining car. Use *dining car, sleeping car.* (Not 'diner', etc.)

direct, directly. The adverb *direct* usually means *straight, without deviation*; *directly* means *straight* or *immediately*; do not use 'directly' for *pretty soon*; the use of 'directly', 'immediately', or 'once' for *when* or *as soon as* is preferably to be avoided (chiefly colloquial Briticisms):

    1. We are going *direct* to France. Write to him *direct.*
    2. The object advanced *directly* toward them.
    3. *Directly* after this he was taken away.
    4. I will see him *immediately.* (Better than 'directly'.)
    5. We started *as soon as* it stopped raining.

disconcert. Say *disconcert, worry,* or *daunt,* not 'faze', 'fease', 'feaze', 'feeze', or 'phase' (dialectal, and colloquial in U. S.):

    You couldn't *disconcert* him.

disinterested, uninterested. *Disinterested* means uninfluenced by self-interest, free from selfish motive; *uninterested* means not interested:

    1. She acted from *disinterested* motives.
    2. He was an *uninterested* spectator.

dispense, dispense with. *Dispense* means to deal out, distribute; *dispense with* means to give up, do without:

    1. To *dispense* medicine, charity, the truth.
    2. They *dispensed with* medicines and lived outdoors.

distance, way. Do not use 'piece' for *distance* or *way*:

    1. They live a short *distance* down the street.
    2. I will walk a little *way* with him.

dive, dived. Do not use 'dove' for *dived.*

dock, pier. A *dock* is a waterway for ships; a *pier* is the wharf or landing; do not use ' dock ' for *pier* (avoid ambiguity):

1. The ship steamed out of the *dock*.
2. I fell off the *pier* into the *dock*.

doesn't, don't. Do not use ' don't ' (= do not) for *doesn't* (= does not):

1. *Doesn't* she want to see the elephants? (Not ' don't '.)
2. *Don't* you like this kind of performance?

done, did. Do not use ' done ' for *did*. See § 172.

doubt of, doubt that, doubt whether. Use *of* or *that* after *doubt* when you feel that there is no doubt; use *whether* (or *if*) when you feel that there is a doubt, or when you wish to assume that there is a doubt (do not use ' but ' or ' but that ' after *doubt*):

1. I did not *doubt of* his sincerity. (*Of* may be omitted.)
2. I did not *doubt that* he was sincere.
3. I *doubted whether* (or *if*) he was sincere.
4. I *doubted whether* (or *if*) I was alive. (Assumed.)

drive, ride. A person *drives* in a vehicle which for the time is under his control, whether private or hired; he *rides* in a vehicle which somebody else is driving:

1. Fred went *driving*. He took me *riding*.
2. You can *ride* all the way by electric car.
3. You had better take a cab and *drive* by the bridge.

dry. Do not use ' dry ' for *thirsty* :

1. *Dry* wood; *dry* weather; a *dry* throat; a *dry* speech.
2. The dog is *thirsty* ; give him some water.

due to, owing to. Do not confuse *due to* with *owing to*. A thing is *due to* a person when it *is owed to* or *is payable to* him; a thing is *owing to* a person or thing when it *owes its existence to*, *is caused by*, *arises from*, the person or thing; *due* and *owing* are adjectives, and hence they must modify nouns (§ 158), not verbs:

  1. The first place *is due to* (that is, *is owed to*) Milton.
  2. His ill health *was owing to* (that is, *was caused by*) overwork. (Not 'due to'.)
  3. The success of this enterprise *was owing to* you. — DEFOE.
  4. The gardens failed *because of* the heat. (Not 'owing to'; but, The failure of the gardens *was owing to* the heat.)
  5. The train was wrecked *by* a broken rail. (Not 'due to' or 'owing to'.)

dull, heavy. Do not use 'logy' for *dull, heavy, stupid*, and the like: He was feeling rather *dull*.

duty. Do not use 'up to' for *the duty of, incumbent on*, and the like:

  1. It is *our duty* to find a way. (Not 'up to us'.)
  2. It was *incumbent* on him to explain matters.

each, every. *Each* usually refers to the individuals composing a group, and *every* refers to the totality of the group; *every* sometimes loses its distributive sense and means *all possible*; do not use *either* (which means 'one or the other of two things') for *each, every*, or *both*:

  1. *Each* theory (of those enumerated) is open to objection.
  2. *Every* theory (in the whole world) is open to objection.
  3. *Every* student must be here tomorrow, and *each* must have his special work with him.
  4. This deserves *every* (= *all possible*) consideration; I feel *every* respect for him; I have *every* confidence in him.
  5. You may have *either* of the (two) rooms.
  6. *Each* side (or *Both* sides) had windows. (Not 'Either'.)
  7. You may sit on *either* side of the boat.

each other, one another. See § 104.

early, soon. *Early* means *before* a particular or usual point of time; *soon* means within a short time *after* a particular point of time specified or implied:

  1. *Early* to bed and *early* to rise. (Not 'soon'.)
  2. He died too *early*. (Not 'soon'.)
  3. We started *soon* after sunrise. He will come *soon*.
  4. The music has begun; the curtain will rise *soon*.
  5. We are late; the *sooner* we start, the better.

DO'S AND DON'T'S

elegant. *Elegant* implies grace, propriety, refinement, niceties of manner; its use for *excellent, fine,* and the like is vulgar:

1. An *elegant* vase; a woman of *elegant* taste.
2. A *beautiful* day; a *delicious* pie. (Not 'elegant'.)

else but, else than, other than. *Else, other,* and their compounds are now regularly followed by *than*; but sometimes, especially in negative and interrogative sentences, *else* (more rarely *other*) is still followed by *but* (for the erroneous omission of *else* and *other,* see § 145; for *else's,* see § 144):

1. The conduct of any *other* person *than* himself.
2. This occurred *elsewhere than* in Italy.
3. It could not be *other than* pleasant to me.
4. She had no *other* reason *but* (she had) this.
5. It is nothing *else but* laziness. (See *more.*)
6. Who *else* could go *but* he? (See § 314.)

emeritus. *Emeritus* ('having served out his time') may stand before or after a person's title:

1. An *emeritus* Professor of Moral Philosophy. — DE QUINCEY.
2. Chauncey Goodrich, President *Emeritus.*
3. George B. Adams, Professor of History, *Emeritus.*

emigrant, immigrant. An *emigrant* is one who moves out of a country; an *immigrant* is one who moves into it (see **ex-** and **in-**, *into,* § 405):

1. *Emigrants* from Europe; *immigrants* into Asia.
2. They were forced to *emigrate* in a body to America.

emphasize. 'Stress' for *lay stress on, emphasize, bring into prominence,* or the like is a recent use (chiefly U. S.):

1. We *lay* more *stress* on our miseries than on our blessings.
2. This *adds* greater *emphasis* to his argument.
3. The spruces and the pines *emphasize* the nakedness of the other trees.
4. Its importance *comes into* historical *prominence.*

enjoy. Use *enjoy* with the gerund, not with the infinitive (§ 215)·
What do you *enjoy doing*? (Not 'to do'.)

enough to. *Enough* may be followed by the infinitive with *to*, **but** not by a *that*-clause:

> 1. He was wise *enough to* tell the truth.
> 2. The animal was near *enough for me to seize it*. (Not 'near enough that I could seize it'.)

enthusiastic. 'Enthuse' for *be enthusiastic, become enthusiastic,* or *make enthusiastic* is a vulgar colloquialism (U. S.), and should be avoided (see *handwritten*):

> We all *became enthusiastic* at the prospect.

equally with. *Equally* may be followed by *with*, but not by *as* (which would be tautological, *equally* and *as* meaning here the same thing; see § 413):

> 1. The two boats were *equally* swift.
> 2. His boat was *equally* swift with mine.
> 3. His boat and mine were *equally* swift.
> 4. His boat was *as* swift *as* mine. (Not 'equally as swift as'.)

equanimity. *Equanimity* means *evenness of mind* (see **anima,** § 407); therefore do not say 'with equanimity of mind':

> He bore his misfortunes with *equanimity*.

et al. *Et al.* is an abbreviation of the Latin plural *et alii* (ā′lǐ-ī) or *et aliæ* (ā′lǐ-ē), 'and others' (§ 605). Do not write it 'et als.'

etc. Avoid abbreviations in literary style (see §§ 482, 529, 543):

> He put his hat, coat, and gloves on a chair. (Not 'his hat, coat, etc., on a chair'.)

ever so, never so. The original expression is *never so*, meaning 'more than ever before'; but *ever so* is now common, meaning 'to any conceivable degree or extent':

> 1. Ask me *never so* much dowry. — THE BIBLE.
> 2. Her mind was *never so* bright.
> 3. His eyes, though *ever so* perfect, lacked something.
> 4. Thank you *ever so* much for your kindness.

everywhere. Do not say 'everywheres' for *everywhere*:

> The children looked *everywhere* for the dog.

exceptionable, exceptional. *Exceptionable* means that to which exception may be taken, objectionable; *exceptional* means that which is an exception, unusual, rare:

    1. His manner toward you was *exceptionable*.
    2. She had *exceptional* opportunities for travel.

exclamation mark. Study the exclamation mark; §§464, 465.

expect. *Expect* means to look forward to something (in the future); do not use it for *intend*, *suppose*, or *think*:

    1. We *expect* them to arrive next week.
    2. He *expects* to go (futurity); he *intends* to go (purpose).
    3. I *think* (*presume, suspect*) he has gone. (Not ' expect '.)

experiment. The noun *experiment* means a trial; therefore do not say ' try an experiment ' (tautological, § 413):

    1. I wish you would *make* the *experiment*.
    2. He *performed* an *experiment* before his class.
    3. They are *conducting* a series of *experiments*.

explicit, implicit. *Explicit* means clear, definite; *implicit* means implied, unreserved, absolute:

    1. His orders were *explicit*; speak *explicitly* and to the point.
    2. An *implicit* agreement. (Implied.)
    3. I have *implicit* confidence in him; he obeys *implicitly*.

falls, woods. *Falls* and *woods* are plural:

There *are falls* (or *woods*) near the town. See § 205.

farther, further. See § 134.

favor. The verb *favor* means to show favor to; do not use it for *resemble* (avoid ambiguity; see § 360):

    1. He *favored* me by reading my manuscript.
    2. The child *resembles* his mother. (Not ' favors '.)

feature. *Feature* means anything especially prominent or important; do not use it as a verb meaning to make a feature of or give prominence to (see *handwritten*):

    1. A *feature* of the country; a *feature* of their program.
    2. Our newspapers *give prominence* to short stories.

feel inclined. Do not use ' feel like ' for *feel inclined*:

    1. He *felt like* an impostor. (Correct.)
    2. She *felt inclined* to wait. (Not 'felt like waiting'.)

fellow. *Fellow*, qualified by *good, bad, brave, old, poor,* and the like, is used in familiar conversation as a synonym for *man* or *boy*; in careless conversation (especially among young men) it is used without such qualifications as a synonym for *man* or anybody in general:

    1. He looks weak still, *poor fellow.*
    2. Why don't they give a *man* a chance? (Not 'fellow'.)

female. See § 149.

fewer, less. Do not use *less* for *fewer*. See § 148.

fine. *Fine* means not coarse, delicate, sensitive, subtle, refined; then it becomes a general term of admiration meaning good of its kind, excellent (but a more specific word is often to be preferred):

    1. *Fine* sand; *fine* thread; a *fine* comb.
    2. A *fine* taste; *fine* distinction; *fine* manners.
    3. A *fine* day; a *fine* view; a *fine* man; a *fine* opportunity.
    4. *Fine* feathers make *fine* birds.
    5. They thought of the *fine* times coming.
    6. An *enjoyable* place; a *convincing* (*witty*, etc.) speaker.

finished. Do not use ' through ' for *finished, have done,* or the like; *be through with*, meaning *have finished*, is colloquial:

    1. Have the older boys *finished* dinner? (Not 'Are the older boys through dinner?')
    2. She has not yet *finished* writing her letter.
    3. But with Lucretia Tox I *have done.* — DICKENS.
    4. I am *through with* the book. (Colloquial.)

first, secondly, etc. See § 275.

first rate. *First-rate* is proper as an adjective; its use as an adverb for *well* is colloquial:

    1. He is a man of *first-rate* ability.
    2. He's doing *first-rate.* (Colloquial.)

fix. The noun *fix* is used colloquially for *predicament* or *dilemma* ; the verb *fix* means to set, fasten, establish, or determine, and then, colloquially (chiefly U. S.), to arrange, mend, or repair :

    1. We soon found ourselves in a *fix*. (Colloquial.)
    2. *Fix* a post in the ground ; *fix* the hour for meeting.
    3. *Fix* (arrange) the hair ; *fix* (mend) a clock. (Colloquial.)

flee, fly. *Flee* is used of persons ; *fly* is used of birds and the like, but in a figurative sense suggesting rapid motion it may be used of persons :

    1. The people *fled* from their houses.
    2. The birds have *flown* to the south.
    3. My sister *flew* at me ; he *flew* into a passion.

folks. *Folks* is a colloquial word for people, relatives, and the like :

    1. That doesn't help poor *folks* much. (Colloquial.)
    2. He has gone home to see his *folks*. (Colloquial.)

forget. Do not say ' disremember ' for *forget* or *not remember*.

friend. Do not ordinarily use 'friend' as a salutation (§ 521, N. 2).

from four to ten. " Expressions like 'from four to ten' are treated grammatically as simple numerals, and may qualify the subject of a sentence, or the object of a verb or preposition " (Oxford English Dictionary); but *more than*, *less than*, and *fewer than* are usually preferable to phrases with ' over ' and ' under ' :

    1. *From twenty to thirty* members were absent.
    2. *Fewer than* twenty members were absent. (Not ' under '.)
    3. It cost *less than* ten dollars. (Not ' under '.)
    4. There was a group of *from seventy to eighty* women. (§ 285.)

fruition. *Fruition* means enjoyment or possession; it is frequently misused for *realization* or *fulfillment* :

    1. Dainties sweet in hope, but in *fruition* sour.
    2. His ideas were brought to *realization*. (Not ' fruition '.)

function. Avoid the hackneyed word 'function' for *meeting* or *gathering*, or for *act*, *be useful*, or the like (see *pet expressions*):

    1. These machines *act* independently. (Not ' function '.)
    2. This course may *be taken* with any other. (Not ' function '.)

funny. *Funny* means amusing, laughable; do not use it for *odd*, *peculiar*, *strange*, or the like:

> 1. It was a *funny* sight; a *funny* story.
> 2. A *peculiar* man; an *unusual* accident. (Not 'funny'.)
> 3. It 's *strange* that she isn't at home. (Not 'funny'.)

gentleman. The use of 'gent' for *gentleman* is vulgar. Do not say 'gentleman friend'; see § 150.

get, have got. *Get* means to come by, obtain, become, and the like, and is used in many idiomatic expressions; do not use 'have got' unless you mean *have obtained* (do not use 'gotten' for *got* except in expressions like *ill-gotten gains*; see § 172):

> 1. *Get* wisdom; *get* a bad fall; *get* the measles.
> 2. *Get* well; *get* to sleep; *get* to be friends; *get* to town.
> 3. At last I *have got* it; he *has* a cold (not 'has got').
> 4. He succeeded in *getting* it; he *was* punished. (Not 'got'.)
> 5. Anything can be *got* nowadays if you have money. (Not 'gotten'.)
> 6. She *has* to go to meeting tonight. (Not 'has got'.)
> 7. I couldn't *manage to* see your friend. (Not 'get to'.)

get used to. Do not use 'get the hang of' for *get used to*, *understand*, and the like.

go. Colloquially the noun *go* has various uses:

> 1. He has plenty of *go* (spirit, energy) in him. (Colloquial.)
> 2. We'll have another *go* (turn) at it. (Colloquial.)
> 3. You want to trot me out, but it 's *no go* (useless). (Colloquial.)
> 4. That's *all the go* (all the rage) now. (Colloquial.)
> 5. I've been *on the go* (hurrying about) all day. (Colloquial.)

go for. *Go for*, in the sense of *attack*, is colloquial:

> 1. The black cow immediately *went for* me. (Colloquial.)
> 2. The critics will *go for* him all the same. (Colloquial.)

good, well. The adjective *good* is much misused for the adverb *well*; see § 239. For the general word *good*, see *bad*.

goods. Do not use *goods* as a singular:

> 1. *These* dress *goods are* new.
> 2. This *grade of* dress *goods is* cheap. (Do not omit *grade of*.)

graduate. In university phraseology *graduate* as a transitive verb is rare (except in U. S.):

> 1. The thermometer *was graduated* according to the method of Fahrenheit.
> 2. He *graduated* at Leyden. (Better than 'was graduated'.)

grand. *Grand* means *magnificent, imposing* (§ 415); its use as a general term of admiration for *good, excellent, fine,* and the like is a colloquialism which should be avoided (see *wonderful*):

> 1. *Grand* scenery; a *grand* banquet; a *grand* lady. (Correct.)
> 2. He alighted at the *grand* entrance. (Correct.)
> 3. *Good* news; *beautiful* weather; an *interesting* companion. (Not 'grand'.)

guess, think. *Guess* means to judge of at random, to solve by conjecture; do not use it for *believe, suppose,* or *think*; do not use 'think for' for *think*:

> 1. We *guessed* them to be foreigners.
> 2. She *guessed* the riddle; *guess* my thoughts.
> 3. I *believe* he forgot it. (Not 'guess'.)
> 4. I *think* I'll (= I will) go to bed. (Not 'I guess I'll', etc.)
> 5. He likes her more than you *think*. (Not 'think for'.)

Guy. *Guy* (from Guy Fawkes, a grotesque figure of whom was paraded on the anniversary of the Gunpowder Plot) is properly used of a person of strange or fantastic appearance; but as a mere term for *man* or *fellow* it is slang:

> 1. He was such an old *guy* in his dress. — THOMAS HUGHES.
> 2. Oh, he's a good *fellow*. (Not 'guy'.)

had been, had known, etc. Do not say 'had of been' for *had been,* 'haf to' for *have to,* 'could of' for *could have,* and so on:

> 1. If she *had been* away, I would have waited.
> 2. He *could have* come if he *had known* sooner.

had better, had rather. See § 244.

half, all. For *half,* see §§ 147, 207; for *all,* § 143. The use of 'cut in half' for *cut in* (or *into*) *halves* is colloquial (see § 290, N.).

half year. 'Semes'ter', for *half year*, is a term (borrowed from Germany) used by some colleges in the United States.

hand, at hand, etc. Do not use *on hand* (= in a person's possession) for *at hand* (= within easy reach, near, close by); *on* (not 'at') *every hand* means *on every side*:

> 1. We have a large stock of tweeds *on hand*.
> 2. Satan was now *at hand*. — MILTON. (Not 'on hand'.)
> 3. It is seen *on every hand* (*on every side*).

handbag. 'Grip' or 'gripsack' is colloquial (U. S.) for *handbag*.

handwritten. We may say *handwritten*, just as we say *hand-carved* or *machine-carved*; but we should not say 'handwrite' for *write by hand* any more than 'hand-carve' for *carve by hand*; nor 'proofread' for *read the proof*; nor 'feature' for *make a feature of*; nor 'major in' for *make a major subject of*; nor 'referee' for *be the* (or *act as*) *referee*; nor 'umpire' for *be the* (or *act as*) *umpire*; nor 'wire' for *telegraph*, nor 'room' for *have a room* (or *live*). Do not make verbs at random; consult the dictionary.

handy. *Handy* means ready for use, convenient, dexterous; its use for *close by* is vulgar:

> 1. I happen to have the books *handy*.
> 2. This dictionary is delightfully *handy*.
> 3. Jackson was an unusually *handy* man.
> 4. They live *close by*. (Not 'quite handy'.)

hanged, hung. Do not use *hung* for the legal term *hanged*:

> 1. He *hung* his head in shame; a flag was *hung* out.
> 2. He deserves to be *hanged*. (Not 'hung'.)

happen, occur. Do not use 'transpire' (= become known) for *happen, occur, take place*, and the like:

> The whole thing *happened* in one day.

has not, have not. The use of 'hain't' for *has not* or *have not* is vulgar.

have gone. Do not say 'have went' for *have gone* (§ 172).

have something happen to you. *Have* meaning to experience or suffer something has been in good use for centuries :

   1. Another *had* one of his hands burnt. — DEFOE.
   2. He deserves to *have* his biography written.

heading. The legal term ' caption ' is sometimes misused (chiefly U. S.) for *head, heading, title*, or the like :

   How do you like this *heading*?

healthful, healthy. Avoid using *healthy* for *healthful*. A thing is *healthful* that promotes health ; a person or thing is *healthy* that enjoys health :

   1. *Healthful* food ; *healthful* or *unhealthful* environment.
   2. A *healthy* child ; *unhealthy* plants ; *healthful* climate.
   3. Vegetation may be both *healthy* and *healthful*.

heap. The use of *heap* for a great number or quantity is colloquial :

   1. The apples lay in *heaps*.
   2. We had *heaps* of fun. (Colloquial.)

hear of, learn. Do not say ' learn of ' for *hear of* or *learn* :

   1. We had not *heard of* your coming.
   2. We had not *learned* your wishes.

help. Avoid using ' help ' for *domestic servants, maids, farm hands, employees*, and the like (colloquial and local, U. S.) ; *help* may mean *prevention, avoidance, relief*, and the like ; the verb *help* takes the infinitive with *to* (see §§ 246, 315) :

   1. The *servants* were away for the day.
   2. He dispelled my illusion ; there was no *help* for it.
   3. He does no more work than he cannot *help* doing. (The *not* in *cannot* is often erroneously omitted.)

high, lofty, tall. Avoid ambiguity in using *high* and *tall*. *High* is used either of extent (as, a *high* wall) or of *position* (as, a *high* plateau) ; *tall* is used of extent only :

   1. A *high* (or *lofty*) mountain (extent) ; a *high* peak (position).
   2. The *highest* cabin in the Alps. (Position.)
   3. The *tallest* building in the city. (Extent.)

hint, suggestion. The use of 'tip' for *hint* or *suggestion* is slang.

historic, historical. *Historic* means 'forming an important part of history', 'famous in history'; *historical* means 'based on history':

> *Historic* scenes; a *historic* spot; an *historical* novel (§ 139).

home, at home. Do not use the adverb *home* after the verb *be* unless the sentence implies motion; do not say 'to home' for *at home*; do not use *home* for *house*:

> 1. She went *home* yesterday; she is *at home* today.
> 2. She hasn't been *home* for a year. (Here *home* expresses the result of implied motion.)
> 3. He is just *home* from college.
> 4. Carpenters build *houses*; families make *homes*.

honorable, reverend. Use *the* before *honorable* and *reverend*; use these titles and *Sir* before the Christian name or another title, but never before the surname (see §§ 529, 545, VIII–XVII):

> 1. *The Honorable* Peter Sterling. (Never 'The Honorable Sterling'.)
> 2. *The Reverend* Charles Browne. (Never 'The Reverend Browne'. His calling card should also have *The*: *The* Reverend Charles Browne.)
> 3. *The Reverend* Doctor Browne was here yesterday.
> 4. *Sir* Roger de Coverley. *Sir* Roger. (Never 'Sir de Coverley'.)

hope, hopes. Do not use the plural *hopes* for the singular *hope* unless you mean it; the verb *hope* means to look forward to something desired (its use in the sense of desiring that a thing may happen or turn out as stated is colloquial; the proper word is *trust*):

> 1. I was in *hope* you would tell us about it.
> 2. She had been disappointed in almost all her *hopes*.
> 3. I *hope* they have arrived. (Colloquial; say 'I *trust*'.)

how, that, what. Do not use 'how' for *that* or *what*:

> 1. We discovered *how* he escaped. (Correct.)
> 2. I have read *that* no fruit grows there. (Not 'how'.)
> 3. *What*? You don't think he will return? (Not 'How'.)

human beings. ' Humans ' for *human beings*, *men*, *mankind*, or the like is now chiefly humorous or affected.

hyphen. Study the uses of the hyphen, §§ 498–509.

i.e. The abbreviation *i.e.* is for the Latin *id est*, meaning ' that is '. Do not use *i.e.* in literary style (§ 529).

if, whether. Either *if* or *whether* may be used to introduce an indirect question (§ 77); when *if* might be mistaken for the conditional *if* (§ 303, 9), use *whether*:

> 1. I asked him *if* (or *whether*) his father helped him.
> 2. I would ask him *whether* his father helped him. (Not ' if '.)

immediately. Do not use ' right ' (§ 278) for *immediately* (such expressions as ' right away ', ' right off ', ' right now ', ' right here ', ' right back ', ' right down ', are colloquial, U.S.); do not use ' immediately ' for *as soon as* (see *direct*, *directly*); avoid ambiguity:

> We ought to go back *immediately*.

improving. ' Looking up ' for *improving* is commercial slang:

> Business is *improving*. (Not ' looking up '.)

in, into. Do not use *in* for *into*. See § 290 and N.; do not use *on* for *in* or *into*:

> 1. I got *into* the car (train, boat).
> 2. He was *in* a sleeping car.
> 3. They were *in* a somewhat crowded train.

individual. *Individual* means a single or particular person; do not use it for *person* in general:

> 1. We are jealous of the rights of *individuals*.
> 2. *Individual* style; *individual* action; *individual* greatness.
> 3. She beheld a *monstrosity*. (Not ' shapeless individual '.)
> 4. There were a score of *persons* in the room. (Not ' individuals '.)

inferior to, superior to. *Inferior* and *superior* are followed by *to* (not by ' than '; for similar idioms, see § 287):

> 1. This is *inferior* (or *superior*) *to* that.
> 2. I feel myself *inferior to* the task.

instant, proximo, ultimo. The words *instant* (= *of the present month*; commonly abbreviated, *inst.*), *proximo* (*of next month*; *prox.*), and *ultimo* (*of last month*; *ult.*) are adjectives, and do not take a plural:

> Your letters of the tenth and thirteenth *instant*.

intend, mean. The use of 'go' for *intend* or *mean* is vulgar:

> He didn't *mean* to do it. (Not 'go'.)

in time, prompt, punctual. *Prompt* means 'without delay'; *punctual* means 'not late' (the use of 'on time' for *in time*, *prompt*, or *punctual* is an illogical colloquialism, chiefly U.S.):

> 1. Shall we be there *in time*?
> 2. A *prompt* answer; call me *promptly* at seven.
> 3. The play will begin *promptly* after the music.
> 4. He is *punctual* in his engagements.
> 5. You can't expect trains to arrive *punctually* on Christmas eve.

isn't, aren't, hasn't, haven't. Certain contractions are proper in familiar conversation, but not elsewhere. Do not use 'ain't' or 'hain't' for *isn't*, *aren't*, *hasn't*, or *haven't*. *I'll* and *we'll* are contractions of *I will* and *we will*, and should not be used for *I shall* and *we shall*; similarly, *I'd* and *we'd* are for *I would* (or *I had*) and *we would* (or *we had*), and should not be used for *I should* and *we should* (§ 187).

join issue. *Join issue* means properly to accept a disputed point as a basis of argument; it is also used like *take issue*, which means to take up the opposite side of a case:

> 1. I *join issue* with you on that point.
> 2. I *took* (or *joined*) *issue* with him (or his conclusions).

kind, sort. See § 72.

know, have known, etc. *Know* usually takes the infinitive with *to*; *have known* and *had known* often omit *to* in the active voice, but retain it in the passive:

> 1. We never *knew* him *to be* discourteous.
> 2. In other hands I *have known* money *do* good.
> 3. They *have been known to* do so.

lady. For the use of *lady*, see §§ 150, 152.

later. *Later* is usually better than ' later on ':

> *Later* we will go to the theater. (Not 'later on'; § 413.)

latest, last. *Last* means that which follows all others ; *latest* means that which is nearest to the present time ; do not use *last* for *latest* :

> 1. The *last* page of a book ; the *latest* book on the subject.
> 2. Have you read her *latest* book ? Indeed I have.
> 3. I have never read his *last* novel. (He wrote no more.)
> 4. The *latest* news ; his *latest* adventure ; your *latest* letter.
> 5. Take the *latest* train you can. (It may be the *last* train of the day.)

lay, lie. Do not use *lay* for *lie* (§§ 172, 173).

lay, plan. ' Layout ', for *plan* or *display* (meaning the selection and arrangement of type), is colloquial (chiefly U. S.) ; for a banquet or the like (as in ' the dinner was a fine layout ') it is slang :

> 1. We studied the *lay* (less commonly *lie*) of the land. (Correct.)
> 2. The town lies south of the original *plan*.
> 3. The *display* on this page is unusually good.

leave. *Leave* used intransitively (§ 156) for *go, start*, and the like is colloquial ; do not use *leave* for *let* (*leave alone* means to go away from ; do not use it for *let alone*, which means not to interfere with) :

> 1. The train has just *left* the station.
> 2. I shall not *leave* till tomorrow. (Colloquial.)
> 3. She *left* her child *alone* ; don't *leave* me *alone*.
> 4. *Let* him *alone*. (Not ' Leave him alone ', unless you mean it.)
> 5. *Let* go of me. (Not ' Leave go of me'.)

let's. *Let's* is colloquial for *let us*. Do not say ' let's us ' (= let us us) or ' let's we '.

like, love, admire. *Love* is properly used of the affections, and *like* is used of the tastes (the use of *love* for *like* is a frequent vulgarism in U.S., says the Oxford English Dictionary) ; do not use *admire* (for *like*) with an infinitive :

1. To *love* children, parents, books, adventures.
2. I respect the nation, but I do not *like* their manners.
3. To *like* a fine horse, good company. (Not 'love'.)
4. I *like* to study history; I *like* to travel. (Not 'admire'.)
5. To *be fond of* reading, fishing, telling stories. (Not 'love'.)
6. Don't you *like* bread and butter with your tea? (Not 'love'.)
7. He isn't what I should *like* him to be.

like, unlike. *Like* (*unlike*), *near* (*nearer, nearest*), *nigh* (*nigher, next*), and *opposite* are followed by the objective case (dative, §§ 604, 606); do not use *like* for *as* or *as if* to introduce a clause :

1. You are *like* her; old bachelors *like* you and me.
2. He writes *like* me; he writes *as* (not 'like') I do.
3. I feel *as if* I had caught cold. (Not 'like'.)
4. Pies *like* mother's; such *as* mother used to make. (Not 'like mother used to make'.)
5. They sat down *opposite* (or *opposite to*) us.

line, lines. *Line* is used in many ways which should be avoided (see *pet expressions*); 'lines' for *reins* is dialectal and provincial :

1. A *course* of action (or reasoning). (Not 'line'.)
2. Bookkeeping wasn't *to my taste*. (Not 'in my line'.)
3. Have you anything to *eat*? (Not 'in the eating line'.)
4. He is well informed *on that subject*. (Not 'along that line'.)
5. I don't like this *kind* of treatment. (Not 'line'.)
6. Don't hold the *reins* so tight. (Not 'lines'.)

little, smaller, smallest. See § 134, examples.

loan. *Loan* is a noun; do not use it as a verb for *lend* :

1. They quickly repaid the *loan*.
2. Will you *lend* me a magazine? (Not 'loan'.)

local. Do not use 'local' as a noun for 'item of local news'.

locate, settle. *Locate* means to state or discover the locality of; do not use it for *settle* :

1. To *locate* a town on the map; *locate* a fire. (Correct.)
2. He *established* his headquarters near the capital.
3. They *settled* in Pennsylvania. (Not 'located'.) ('Where was he located?' means 'Where was he found?')

look so. Do not say 'look it' for *look so*:

> He may be poor, but he doesn't *look so*.

lot. *Lot* means a separate portion or a number of persons or things; its use for *great deal* is colloquial:

> 1. A miscellaneous *lot* of stationery; goods sold in *lots*.
> 2. He went across the fields. ('Across *lots*' is colloquial.)
> 3. We had a *lot* of bother; *lots* of fun. (Colloquial.)

lovely. *Lovely* means *beautiful*; its use in enthusiastic praise of anything delightful is colloquial:

> 1. A *lovelier* picture was never seen.
> 2. They had a *lovely* time in the country. (Colloquial.)

luxuriant, luxurious. *Luxuriant* means abundant, profuse; *luxurious* means pertaining to luxury:

> 1. *Luxuriant* vegetation; *luxuriant* ornamentation.
> 2. A *luxurious* age; *luxurious* habits.

mad. *Mad* means insane, foolish, unwise; its use for *angry* or *furious* is colloquial:

> 1. He jumped up and ran about like *mad*.
> 2. He was not *mad* enough to risk a quarrel.
> 3. I am *mad* with myself when I think of it. (Colloquial.)

maid, servant. 'Hired girl' for *maid* or *servant* is colloquial (U.S.); similarly, 'hired man'.

major. Do not use *major* as a verb (see *handwritten*):

> My *major* subjects are Greek and philosophy. (Not 'I am majoring in Greek', etc.)

male, female. See § 149.

mean. *Mean* has the sense of ignoble, base; do not use it in the trivial sense of *disobliging*, *ill tempered*, or the like; *mean* for *meanly* is illiterate:

> 1. She always despised *mean* things.
> 2. Now don't be *disobliging* about it. (Not 'mean'.)
> 3. I have never felt so *ashamed* in all my life. (Not 'mean'.)
> 4. Don't think *meanly* of him. (Not 'mean'.)

meant to go. Do not use the perfect infinitive incorrectly for the present (see § 220):

> 1. They meant *to see* you. (Not 'to have seen'.)
> 2. You would have liked *to be* there. (Not 'to have been'.)

middling. The use of 'middling' as an adverb for *fairly, moderately, rather, tolerably,* or the like is colloquial or dialectal:

> 1. It was a town of *middling* size. (Correct.)
> 2. She was thin, light, and *middling* tall. (Colloquial.)
> 3. You're *middlin'* well now, be ye? (Dialectal.)

midst of us. Do not say 'in our (your, their) midst' for *in the midst of us (you, them)*:

> 1. In the *midst of* the forest.
> 2. There am I in the *midst of* them. — THE BIBLE.

mighty. The use of *mighty* in the sense of *very, exceedingly,* or *extremely* is colloquial:

> 1. He is wise in heart, and *mighty* in strength. (Correct.)
> 2. That's a *mighty* funny song. (Colloquial.)

Miss. See §§ 38, 544, II. Do not use *Miss* as a title without a surname or Christian name:

> 1. Can I assist you, *Miss Clarke*? (Do not omit *Clarke*.)
> 2. Please to be seated, *Miss Edith*. (Do not omit *Edith*.)

more, worse. Do not use *worse* for *more*; do not use *more than* for *as much as, as many as,* and the like; *more or less* means 'to a greater or less degree'; *neither more nor less* means 'exactly (that) and nothing else':

> 1. She hates it *more* than poison. (Not 'worse'.)
> 2. They treated him *worse* than before.
> 3. This weighs twice *as much as* that. (Not 'twice more than that'.)
> 4. She has three times *as many* friends *as* he. (Not 'three times more', etc.)
> 5. She was *more or less* offended.
>   It is *neither more nor less* than selfishness.

Mrs. For the use of *Mrs.*, see §§ 38, 544, 111.

mutual, common. *Mutual* means interchanged, reciprocal; *common* means shared equally; when ambiguity in the use of *common* might arise, say *in common* :

    1. *Mutual* love ; *mutual* trust ; a *mutual* promise.
    2. A *common* enemy ; no *common* ground.
    3. They have friends *in common*. (Not '*common* friends'.)
    4. I heard the blessing which to you
       Our *common* Friend and Father sent. — WORDSWORTH.

named after, named from. ' Named for ' is colloquial (U. S.) for *named after* or *named from* (see § 287):

    1. She was *named after* her great-grandmother.
    2. The province was *named* Normandy *from* the Normans.

nasty. *Nasty* means foul, dirty, offensive, disagreeable, indecent ; then it becomes a general epithet expressing dislike or annoyance (chiefly colloquial); do not use it in the sense of *mean, dishonorable,* or *ungenerous* :

    1. The streets are narrow, steep, and exceedingly *nasty*.
    2. There was a *nasty* smell about the premises.
    3. ' A *nasty* night, Mr. Noggs ', said the man.
    4. ' He's a *nasty*, stuck-up monkey ', said Mrs. Squeers.
    5. They were *dishonorable* to him. (Not ' nasty '.)

naught. Call a cipher a *naught* (not an ' aught ').

near, close by. Avoid the faulty expression ' near by ' or ' near-by ' (= ' near near ', § 413 ; chiefly dialectal and U. S.); use *adjacent, close by* (= *closely near, very near*; *close* is similarly used with other adverbs and prepositions, *close beside, close behind, close on, close to*), *near, neighboring,* and the like ; use *adjoining* or *contiguous* of things which are in contact :

    1. They live *near* the village. (Not ' near by '.)
    2. There is a river *close by*, or near. (Not ' near by '.)
    3. He has bought a *neighboring* farm. (Not ' near-by '.)
    4. She has a shop *close to* the post office. (Not ' near by '.)
    5. Rows of *contiguous* houses ; lands *adjoining* the road.

near, nearly. Do not confuse the preposition *near* with the adverb *nearly* :

1. I *nearly* missed my train ; *nearly* exhausted.
2. I came *near* missing my train ; *near* exhaustion.

negotiate. The use of *negotiate* for *surmount*, *clear*, *get over*, and the like is objectionable (avoid the rare and unusual meanings of words) :

1. They *negotiated* a treaty (or a loan). (Correct.)
2. The horse *cleared* the fence. (Not ' negotiated '.)

nice. *Nice* means requiring or involving precision, minute, subtle, discriminative ; its use for *agreeable*, *pleasing*, and the like is colloquial ; do not use ' nicely ' for *well* :

1. A *nice* problem ; a *nice* distinction.
2. We appreciate the *nicer* shades of meaning.
3. He evinces a *nice* sense of elegance and form.
4. She wished to look as *nice* as possible. (Colloquial.)
5. I feel *well* today, thank you. (Not ' nicely '.)

none, not one. Do not use ' not a one ' for *none* or *not one* :

Not one was left ; *none* were left. See *none*, § 102.

no sooner . . . than. *Sooner* is a comparative and requires *than :*

He had *no sooner* arrived *than* (not ' when ') he began work.

not nearly. Do not use ' nothing like ' or ' nowhere near ' for *not nearly* :

This is *not nearly* so good. (Not ' nothing like as good '.)

oblivious of. *Oblivious* (from Latin) means *forgetful*, *unmindful*, and takes *of* (not ' to ' ; for other idioms, see § 287) :

They were *oblivious of* what was going on.

observation, observance. *Observation* means the act or result of looking attentively at an object ; *observance* means the heeding of a custom or duty :

An *observation* of the eclipse ; religious *observances*.

obtain. *Obtain* means to gain possession of; its use for *prevail*, *be established*, and the like is objectionable (avoid the rare and unusual meanings of words):

    1. He *obtained* the desired information.
    2. That custom does not *prevail* here. (Not ' obtain '.)

of, off. Do not use ' off of ' for *of* or *off*; do not use ' off from ' redundantly (§ 413) for *off*:

    1. I tried to buy something *of* him. (Not ' off of '.)
    2. The boys jumped *off* the plank into the water.
    3. He was cut *off from* all help. (Correct.)
    4. The books fell *off* the shelf. (Not ' off from ' or ' off of '.)

on, round. See § 294.

only. See §§ 276, 315, 272, N.

opportunity, chance. Do not use ' show ' for *opportunity* or *chance*:

    1. He will have a fair *chance* here. (Not ' show '.)
    2. They gave him no *opportunity*. (Not ' show '.)

oral English; written English. Do not let oral exercises in English take the place of written exercises. See §§ 363–365.

other. *Other* is often improperly omitted. See § 145.

ought, ought not, oughtn't. Do not say ' had ought ' for *ought*, ' hadn't ought ' for *oughtn't*:

    You *ought* to go, *oughtn't* you?

out, over. Do not use *out* for *over*; do not use ' over with ' for *over*:

    1. The news was not yet *out*.
    2. School is *over*. (*Out* is an American colloquialism.)
    3. Our troubles were at last *over*. (Not ' over with '.)

outside. *Outside* (better than ' outside of ') means on or to the exterior of; do not use ' outside of ' for *besides* or *except*:

    1. They were sitting *outside* the house.
    2. He was sent *outside* the grounds.
    3. There is nobody here *besides* me. (Not ' outside of '.)
    4. Nobody knew him *except* the old man. (Not ' outside of '.)
    5. *Except* this I can think of nothing. (Not ' outside of '.)

over, more than. Do not use *over* to the exclusion of *more than* (see *from*); do not use 'overly' for *over, too much, too, exceedingly,* or *excessively*:

1. The fish was *over* three pounds in weight; the fish weighed *more than* three pounds.
2. This desk cost *more* (or *less*) than fifty dollars.
3. The journey lasted a little *more than* a week.
4. She was *oversensitive.* (Not 'overly sensitive'.)

overshoes, arctic overshoes. The use of 'gums' for *overshoes* is local (U. S.); 'rubbers' is colloquial (U. S.).

pair, pairs. *Pair* is used of two persons or things associated together (do not use it loosely for *two*; see *couple*); do not use *pair* as a plural for *pairs*:

1. This *pair* of spectacles is broken.
2. The newly married *pair* are at home.
3. A *pair* of gloves; two *pairs* of gloves.

pantaloons. The use of 'pants' for *pantaloons* or *trousers* is vulgar.

parallelism. Use parallelism in speaking and in writing. See § 375.

partially, partly. It is better not to use *partially* for *partly* (avoid using a word of doubtful meaning for an equally good word of clear meaning):

1. An *impartial* witness; a *partial* eclipse.
2. He discussed the question *impartially.*
3. The funds were *partly* divided. (Not 'partially'.)

party. Except in a legal sense *party* means a group of persons; do not use it for *person*:

1. Were you invited to the *party*?
2. The two *parties* to the contract. (Legal usage.)
3. The fourth *person* did not come. (Not 'party'.)

past, etc. In speaking of ages and the like, do not use 'going on':

1. He is *past* twenty-one. (Not 'going on' twenty-two.)
2. It is *past* ten o'clock; it is *nearly* eleven o'clock.

people, persons. *People* may be used of men and women indefinitely, but in the sense of individuals *persons* is preferable:

DO'S AND DON'T'S 245

1. All sorts of *people*; literary *people* of all nations.
2. Not three *persons* were conscious of the change.

per cent, percentage. For *per*, see § 289. *Per cent* is an adjective phrase meaning *by* (or *in*) *the hundred*; colloquially, in the designation of bonds, it takes a plural form, *per cents*; do not use it for the noun *percentage* (§ 205):

1. What rate *per cent* did he ask? Six *per cent*.
2. She was investing in *five per cents*. (Colloquial.)
3. What *percentage* goes to waste? (Not 'per cent'.)
4. The pupils study for *percentages*. (Not 'per cents'.)

perspire, sweat. *Sweat* means to perspire excessively; an animal *sweats*; a person *perspires* or *sweats* according to circumstances (but do not use *sweat* of persons when it is of doubtful propriety):

1. We *perspired* even when sitting in the shade.
2. In the *sweat* of thy face shalt thou eat bread.
3. Playing tennis makes you *sweat*; he *sweat* his collar.

pet expressions. Avoid using hackneyed and pet expressions. The individual words in these expressions are as good as they ever were, and some of the expressions themselves are proper under proper circumstances; it is their misapplication, their use in season and out of season, that is objectionable (read the quotation from Lord Chesterfield in § 413):

Downy couch (say *bed*), satisfy the inner man (*eat*), school system (*schools*), seat of learning (*college*), student body (*students*), thanking you in advance (*I shall be grateful*, or the like; 'in advance' sounds as if the writer did not wish to write again), along these lines (see *line, lines*), up to date (see *up to date*), the fact that he did so (*his doing so*; or recast the sentence), in order that (*that*; § 310), pronounced success (*success*), vast concourse (*crowd*), floral tribute (*flowers*), staff of life (*bread*), matrimonial alliance (*marriage*), pay the debt to nature (*die*), voice the sentiments of (*speak for*), put in an appearance (*appear*), get in touch with (*see, write to*, etc.), keep in touch with (*follow, keep informed*, etc.), take your departure (*go*), be the recipient of (*receive*), the yellow metal (*gold*), the devouring element (*fire*), officiating clergyman (*minister*), tie the knot (*perform the ceremony*), blissfully ignorant (*ignorant*), last but not least (*last*), dark as Egypt (*dark*), do full justice to (*do justice to*), as straight as a string (*straight*), the weaker sex (*women*), gown (*dress*), the lords of creation (*men*), rendition (*performance*), decease (*death*), perform (*play*), function (*meeting, gathering, action, activity, duty*; *be useful, have a place, act, serve*, etc.), motivate (*give an incentive to, make useful or practical*, etc.), repast (*dinner, supper*), peruse (*read*), indorse (*approve*), purchase (*buy*), reside (*live*), residence (*house*), your valued favor (*your letter*; see § 535), rise (*get up*), retire (*go to bed*), inaugurate (*begin*), try out (*try*), attire (*dress*), limb (*leg*), limbs (*legs and arms*), lose out (*lose*), sign up (*sign*), donate (*give*), odor (*smell*), words in many cases (*many words*), in case that (*if*).

photograph. The use of 'photo' for *photograph* is colloquial.

pitiable, piteous, pitiful. Study the following examples:

1. A *pitiable* condition; a *piteous* cry. (Arousing pity.)
2. Be *pitiful* (full of pity); a *pitiful* (pathetic) smile.

place. *Place* means a spot or locality; do not say 'any place', 'no place', and 'some place' for *anywhere, nowhere*, and *somewhere*:

1. He did not find any *place* for rent or sale.
2. I couldn't find a house *anywhere*. (Not 'any place'.)
3. You may stay *in* any place you like. (See § 52.)

plead, pleaded, have pleaded. Do not use 'plead' or 'pled' for *pleaded*.

plenty. *Plenty* is a noun; do not use it as an adjective or adverb; do not say 'a plenty':

1. There is *plenty* of work for those who want it.
2. We were in *plenty* of time.
3. The number of rooms was *adequate*. (Not 'plenty'.)
4. Fruit is *plentiful* this year. (Not 'plenty'.)
5. It is *large enough*. (Not 'plenty large enough'.)
6. These pens are *good enough*. (Not 'plenty good enough'.)

porch, veranda. A *porch* is a roofed and partly inclosed entrance to a building; a *veranda* is roofed, but not inclosed (do not use 'piazza', which means a public square, for *veranda*); a porch or veranda resembles a room, and the preposition *in* should be used with it (not ' on '; see § 293):

    1. 'Tis ready, sir, here *in* the porch. — SHAKESPEARE.
    2. They sprawl *in* palm-leaf verandas. — STEVENSON.

possessive case. Observe the proper and improper uses of the possessive case. See §§ 41–48.

post, inform. Do not use *post* for *inform*; do not use the noun *mail* for the verb *post* (see *handwritten*):

    1. To *post* notices; to *post* (not 'mail') a letter.
    2. I had *posted* myself at his door.
    3. He was *well informed* in history. (Not 'posted'.)

postal card, postcard. ' Postal' for *postal card* (U.S.) or *postcard* is colloquial and inelegant.

powerful. *Powerful* means full of power; do not use it as an adverb for *exceedingly*; do not use 'a powerful deal' or 'a powerful sight' for *a great deal, a great many*, and the like:

    1. She was accompanied by a *powerful* dog.
    2. He was *exceedingly* popular in his own town.
    3. There was *a great deal* of dissatisfaction.

practicable, practical. *Practicable* means capable of being done; *practical* means capable of being turned to use, useful:

    1. Electric lighting is both *practicable* and *practical*.
    2. A heater on the roof is *practicable*, but not *practical*.
    3. A telescope to study distant stars would be *practical*.

precēd′ence, prĕc′edent. *Precedence* means 'going before' (often because of a right or privilege); the noun *precedent* means ' something done or said that may serve as an example':

    1. Some people like to have *precedence* on public occasions.
    2. This work is to have *precedence* over everything else.
    3. He promptly followed the *precedent* set by Oxford.
    4. By this act a dangerous *precedent* will be introduced.

prefer to. Use *to* (not ' than ') after *prefer*:

    1. She *prefers* California *to* Florida.
    2. We *preferred* walking *to* riding.

prepositions. For a general treatment of prepositional idioms, see § 287. Prepositions should not be omitted where they are necessary (§ 52); nor should they be used where they are redundant (§ 413):

1. Where are we? (Not 'Where are we at?')
2. Where have they gone? (Not 'gone to'.)
3. I got *off* the horse. (Not 'off of'; see *of, off*.)
4. All my friends. (Not 'all of'; see § 143.)
5. Both the boys. (Not 'both of'; see § 143.)

preventive. Do not say 'preventative' for *preventive*:

1. A *preventive* of smallpox; a *preventive* of evil.
2. Such a federation is a *preventive* of internal wars.

previous, previously. Do not use the adjective *previous* for the adverb *previously*; use *before* rather than 'previous to', 'previously to', or 'prior to'; similarly, use *after* rather than 'subsequent to' or 'subsequently to':

1. Our *previous* arrangements could not be changed.
2. This condition arose *before* (*after*) the Revolution.

project, undertaking, purpose. Do not use *proposition* for *project, undertaking*, or *purpose*:

1. He made us a most fair *proposition*. (Correct.)
2. To cross the river was a difficult *undertaking*.

pronouns. Do not use *me* for *I*, or *them* for *they* (§§ 61, 314); *one* for *we, you*, etc. (§ 106); *who* for *whom* (§§ 78, 90, 99); *whose* for *of which* (§ 87).

proportion to, proportionate. *Proportion* is followed by *to* (not 'with'); do not confuse *proportional* and *proportionate*:

1. The arms are out of *proportion* to the body.
2. The increase in the number of teachers is *proportional* to the increase in the number of students.
3. The number of students has increased, but the number of teachers has been increased *proportionally*.
4. The results are not *proportionate* to the outlay.

propose, purpose. *Propose* means to put forward or present something for consideration, or as an object to be attained; *purpose* means to resolve or determine to do something; do not use *propose* vaguely in the sense of *mean* or *intend*:

1. To *propose* a change of name, plan, treaty, or residence.
2. They had *proposed* to relate his family's history.
3. My friend *purposes* to open an office.
4. I *meant* to begin early today. (Not 'proposed'.)
5. I don't *intend* to be fooled again. (Not 'propose'.)

protest, protest against. Do not confuse *protest* (= *solemnly declare*) and *protest against*:

1. He *protested* his innocence.
2. He *protested against* the changes.

proved. In general, use *proved*; the form *proven* is proper in the legal phrase *not proven*:

1. Multiplication is also naturally *proved* by division.
2. We must accept it as a *proved* fact.
3. It was a custom of *proved* antiquity.
4. The verdict '*not proven*' indicates suspicion.

provided. Do not use 'providing' for *provided* (§ 312):

Provided (= *it being provided*) that all is safe, you may go.

PS. Since *postscript* is one word, the abbreviation *PS.* is better than *P. S.* (similarly *NNE.* for *north-northeast*; etc.); as a rule, postscripts should be avoided; see the letter in § 359.

punctuation. Do not overpunctuate (§ 460); do not use punctuation to cure bad English (§§ 460, 487); do not misuse the exclamation mark (§§ 464, 465) or the dash (§ 489).

quit, leave. *Quit* means to go from without the intention of returning, and thus differs from *leave*:

1. To *quit* school; to *quit* business; to *quit* the stage.
2. He *left* the road and walked by the brook.

quite. *Quite* means *entirely, completely* (§ 277). Do not use 'quite a few' for *a good many*, or 'quite a while' for *some time*:

1. *A good many* people have moved to the country.
2. We lived there for *some time*.

raise, rear, increase. Do not use *raise* for *rear*; do not use *raise* as a noun for *increase*:

1. To *raise* corn, vegetables; to *raise* (or *rear*) cattle.
2. To *rear* children; to *rear* a family. (Not 'raise'.)
3. The price of sheep and cows has been *raised* (or *increased*).
4. They have had an *increase* in wages (or salary). (Not 'raise'.)
5. The rent has been *increased*. (Not 'raised'.)

rare, scarce. *Rare* means *seldom occurring*, or *unusual*; *scarce* is used of things that are useful or necessary. Do not use *scarce* for *rare*:

1. Money, food, and clothing were *scarce*.
2. A *rare* plant; *rare* coins; *rare* paintings.
3. Weeds are *rare* in his garden. (Not 'scarce'.)
4. Flies are *rare* this winter. (Not 'scarce'.)

rarely. Do not use 'rarely ever' for *rarely, seldom,* or *hardly ever*; do not use 'rarely or ever' for *rarely if ever* or *rarely or never*; do not use 'seldom or ever' for *seldom if ever* or *seldom or never*:

1. He goes to town *rarely* nowadays.
2. He goes to town *rarely if ever*.
3. He goes to town *seldom or never*.

rather, somewhat. The use of 'kind of' or 'sort of' for *rather* or *somewhat* is vulgar; do not use 'something' for *somewhat*:

1. I felt *rather* sorry for him. (Not 'kind of'.)
2. *Somewhat* obscure; *somewhat* deeply in debt.
3. Their calendar was *somewhat* like ours.

reading aloud. The reading aloud of good authors will cure many faults of speech. The reading aloud of your own work will enable you to correct many of your faults. See §§ 361, 364.

real, really. Do not use the adjective *real* as an adverb; *really* means *actually, truly*:

1. It was a *real* joy to see her. (Adjective.)
2. He was *unusually* kind to me. (Not 'real'.)
3. Do you *really* like to live by the seashore?

receipt, recipe. *Receipt,* meaning *formula,* applies especially to cookery; *recipe* applies strictly to medicine, but is often used for *receipt*:

> 1. Have you a *receipt* for making apple dumplings?
> 2. He has a *recipe* for every ailment.

reckon. *Reckon* means to count, calculate, estimate; then (colloquially) to consider, think, or suppose, followed by a *that*-clause (but this meaning of the word, like that of *guess,* § 417, is so common in some parts of the United States as to be considered provincial and vulgar); do not use it parenthetically for *suppose*:

> 1. She *reckoned* her savings for the year.
> 2. I *reckon* that nobody could accuse him of insincerity.
> 3. Neither of them wanted to wait, I *suppose.* (Not 'reckon' or 'guess'.)

regard as. *Regard* in the sense of *consider* should be followed by *as*:

> 1. I *regarded* him *as* a friend. (I *considered* him a friend.)
> 2. He was *regarded as* one of the leaders of the uprising.

region, part, section. *Section* means a *part cut off,* a *division* (as of a book or writing); avoid using it as a general term for *region, part, district,* and the like:

> 1. The last *sections* of the chapter; a *section* of the society.
> 2. The farmers of this *region* are prosperous.
> 3. Many *parts* of the country are deserted.

relative, relation. *Relative(s)* is usually clearer than *relation(s)*:

> He has *relatives* in Ohio.

reliable, trustworthy. *Reliable* is usually applied to things, but sometimes to persons (under similar circumstances); *trustworthy* is usually applied to persons (do not use 'dependable' for either of these words):

> 1. *Reliable* information; the data are *reliable.*
> 2. A *trustworthy* man, witness, friend.
> 3. The secretary is *reliable.* (His work may be depended on.)
> 4. The secretary is *trustworthy.* (He is worthy of trust.)

remember. Do not say 'remember of' for *remember*:

> I *remember* having seen him at the museum.

respectively. *Respective* and *respectively* are seldom needed except in geometry and the like:

> They took their seats. (Not 'their respective seats'.)

revolver, gun. Do not use 'gun' for *revolver*. Avoid obscurity.

rise. Do not use *up* with *rise* or *arise* (the noun *uprising* is proper):

> 1. The bird *rose* from its nest.
> 2. He *arose* and began to speak.
> 3. They could not quell the *uprising*.

same. *Same* is an adjective, and is frequently used as a noun; in comparisons it is usually followed by *as* or *that* (the choice being a matter of idiom or euphony), sometimes by *with*; in legal documents *the same* is often used for a personal pronoun (*he, she, it, they*), and in commercial language with reference to things (neither of these uses is now literary):

> 1. This is the *same* horse *that* I had yesterday.
> 2. He wrote at the *same* time *as* (or *with*) Byron.
> 3. He was in exactly the *same* predicament *as* I had been.
> 4. Write it in the *same* way *that* he wrote it. (Not 'Write it the same as he wrote it'.)
> 5. He would defend you on the *same* grounds *that* he did me.
> 6. My wish is the *same as* his; the *same* answer *as* before.
> 7. It's all the *same* to him and to me.
> 8. I shall go just the *same*. (Adverbial; § 51.)
> 9. The books are here; we are sending *them* to you by post. (Not 'the same'.)

say, tell. Do not use the active voice of *say* with the infinitive; do not use 'says I' for *say I* or *said I*:

> 1. He *said* that I should wait. (Not 'He said to wait'.)
> 2. He *told* me to wait; I was *told* to wait.
> 3. He is *said* to be traveling in the Orient.
> 4. He did not *say* what we were to do.
> 5. He did not *tell* us what to do.
> 6. "I don't care if I do", *say I* to myself. (Not 'says I'.)

sense. *Sense* (= ' feel instinctively ') for *understand* or *comprehend* is colloquial (U.S.):

1. The herd *sensed* the danger and made off.
2. Queen Mary watched her closely, *sensing* an enemy.
3. He *comprehended* the situation. (Better than ' sensed '.)

set, sets. The plural of the noun *set* is *sets* (not ' set '):

A *set* of furniture; two *sets* of china.

settle. Do not use ' up ' or ' down ' with *settle* (§ 413):

1. The estate has been *settled*. (Not ' settled up '.)
2. The bird *settled* on the roof. (Not ' settled down '.)
3. Why doesn't he marry and *settle*? (Not ' settle down '.)
4. You will succeed when you *settle* to work. (Not ' settle down '.)

sewed, sown. Use *sewed* preferably as the past participle of *sew*, and *sown* as the past participle of *sow* (§ 654):

1. The sleeves were *sewed* with linen thread.
2. Light is *sown* for the righteous. — THE BIBLE.

ship. The transitive verb *ship* means to send or transport by ship; do not use it for *send* (by rail, post, etc.), *carry*, *convey*, *transport*, or the like (similarly, *shipment*, *aboard*, *board*, and *on board* should be used of ships, not of cars and the like; § 369):

1. The goods were *shipped* to England.
2. The goods were *sent* by express.

sit, set. Do not use the verb *set* for *sit* (§ 173):

1. The boy *sits* at work; a hen *sits*; the coat *sits* well. (Not ' sets '.)
2. The sun *sets* late now; the woman *set* the hen yesterday.
3. Food of this kind does not *sit* well on the stomach. (Not ' set '.)

size, sized. Do not use the noun *size* for the adjective *sized*; do not use ' size up ' (slang, U.S.) for *form an opinion of*, *judge*, and the like:

1. *Large-sized* models; *medium-sized* type. (See § 502.)
2. He quickly *took the measure of* his opponent. (Not ' sized up '.)

skilled, skillful. *Skillful* means more than *skilled*, implying natural ability in addition to acquired knowledge:

    1. A *skilled* workman. (He knows his trade, but may be dull.)
    2. A *skillful* workman. (He knows his trade, and has ability.)
    3. *Skilled* labor; a *skillful* physician; *skillful* artists.

skyscraper. ' Skyscraper ' applied to a tall building is slang.

smart. *Smart* usually means vigorous, pertinent, witty, intelligent (do not use it for ' keen ', ' shrewd '); do not use ' right smart ' as an adjective or noun meaning considerable, many, a great deal, and the like:

    1. A *smart* blow with the whip; a *smart* skirmish.
    2. A *smart* (pertinent) reply; a *smartly* turned compliment.
    3. My father was a *capable* man. (Not ' smart '.)
    4. A *considerable* distance. (Not ' right smart '.)
    5. A *large* crop of cotton. (Not ' right smart '.)

snap. The use of *snap* for *energy*, *life*, *vigor*, and the like is colloquial and inelegant; its use for *easy study*, *easy job*, and the like is slang.

so. *So* has important idiomatic uses (see § 305 also); its use as a mere intensive (as in the eighth example, below) is chiefly colloquial:

    1. It rained *so* hard *that* we stayed indoors. (§ 262, 4.)
    2. She was *so* ill (*that*) she could hardly speak. (*That* is often omitted.)
    3. Hetty was blushing *so*, [*that*] she didn't know whether she was happy or miserable. — GEORGE ELIOT.
    4. I think *so* (= I am of that opinion). I don't think *so*.
    5. The roof had fallen in; *so that* the hut was useless. (§ 303, 5.)
    6. It rained hard, *and so* we stayed indoors.
    7. *So* Abraham departed. (§ 262, 6.)
    8. A man is *so* in the way in the house. (Colloquial.)

some. *Some* (meaning *about*, *nearly*, *approximately*, etc.) may be used as an adverb with numerals, but not otherwise; the use of ' some ' as an adjective meaning *good*, *excellent*, *deserving of consideration*, and the like is slang:

1. There were *some* (*about, perhaps*) fifty cases of fever.
2. She is *rather* (or *somewhat*) better. (Not ' some '.)
3. Those are *good* pictures ; *large* elephants. (Not ' some '.)

specialty. Do not say ' speciality ' for *specialty* :

We make a *specialty* of athletic goods. (§ 423.)

start, begin. Do not use *start* or *start in* with the infinitive as its object :

1. They *started* down the river.
2. The doorbell *started* ringing.
3. We *began* to raise the sail. (Not ' started ' or 'started in '.)

stay, stop. Do not use the verb *stop* for *stay* or *remain* (avoid obscurity) :

1. They are *staying* at the hotel. (Not ' stopping '.)
2. He *stayed* (or *remained*) there a month. (Not ' stopped '.)
3. He *stopped* at the store on his way home.

struck, stricken. *Stricken* means to be smitten, wounded, or injuriously affected ; do not use it for *struck* :

1. *Struck* by lightning ; *struck* with amazement.
2. Their names were *struck* from the roll. (Not ' stricken '.)
3. The *stricken* animal leaped from the cliff.
4. *Stricken* with palsy (or grief) ; *stricken* in years.

stunning. ' Stunning ' for *astonishing, striking, remarkable,* and the like is slang :

1. He dealt me a *stunning* blow. (Correct.)
2. Her verses are *remarkable*. (Not ' stunning '.)

stylish, ultrafashionable. The word ' swell ' for *stylish, ultrafashionable, rich, influential,* and the like is slang :

A *stylish* turnout ; a *rich* man's club ; the *ultrafashionable* set.

such, another such, such as, such . . . that. Do not use ' such another ' for *another such* :

1. She will not be pleased with *such* results.
2. *Another such* victory means ruin. (Not ' Such another '.)
3. They will give you *such* work *as* you can do.
4. There was *such* a crowd *that* we had to stand.

summons. *Summons* is a noun in the singular (§205,19); do not use it as a verb for *summon* :

    1. A *summons* had already been sent to him.
    2. The witnesses were *summoned*. (Not 'summonsed'.)

sunrise, sunset. Avoid using 'sunup' (local, chiefly U.S.) and 'sundown' (chiefly dialectal and U.S.) for *sunrise* and *sunset* :

    We were on our way before *sunrise*.

surely. Do not use the adjective *sure* for the adverb *surely* (§ 260); the phrase *sure enough* is colloquial :

    1. They felt *sure* that she would succeed.
    2. Will you meet me at three? *Surely*.
    3. *Sure enough*, they were looking for us. (Colloquial.)

take. *Take* may mean to undertake, perform, take in hand; do not use 'take in' for *visit*; 'take in' for *impose on* is colloquial; do not use 'take on' for *act*; do not use 'take up' for *begin, study,* or *make* :

    1. Will you *take* the alto?
    2. She would *take* the grammar class at ten.
    3. Did you *visit* Niagara Falls? (Not 'take in'.)
    4. I was easily *taken in* by his appearance. (Colloquial.)
    5. He *acted* as if he were demented. (Not 'took on'.)
    6. It *took up* (= occupied) his time and bored him.
    7. School *begins* at nine o'clock. (Not 'takes up'.)
    8. I shall *begin* French next year.
    9. They *made* a collection. ('Took up' is colloquial, U.S.)

taste, taste of. *Taste of* may mean simply to taste, but it usually means to take a taste of, to eat or drink a little of, and hence to feel or experience :

    1. We *tasted of* the bread; it was dry, but not unpleasant.
    2. When he had *tasted of* it, he would not drink.
    3. The population had already *tasted of* oppression.

tasteful. Do not use 'tasty' for *tasteful*, or for *appetizing, savory* :

    1. It was a *tasteful* style of pottery.
    2. The rooms were furnished *tastefully*. (Not 'tastily'.)
    3. The food was *appetizing* and wholesome. (Not 'tasty'.)

teach, learn. The use of *learn* for *teach* is vulgar; say *teach in a school* rather than ' teach school ' (" now dialectal and U.S." — Oxford English Dictionary):

    1. They soon *learn* to speak correctly.
    2. She *teaches* them to read distinctly.
    3. He *teaches in a school* in the South. He *teaches* history.

team, three team. *Team* means a group of two or more animals harnessed together; do not use it of one animal, or of a vehicle (do not say ' a horse and team', which is nonsense); after a numeral the collective plural *team* (§ 30) is used:

    1. That is a fine *team* of horses.
    2. A thousand *team* of cattle. (But, The two *teams* play today.)
    3. They came in a *carriage*. (Not ' team'.)

telephone. The use of ' phone ' for *telephone* is colloquial and inelegant.

that, to. Do not use ' in order that ' for *that*, or ' in order to ' for *to* (see § 310). Do not use *when* for *that*:

    1. It was late *when* they arrived. (Correct.)
    2. It was night *when* they arrived. (Correct.)
    3. It was on Saturday *that* we went to town. (Not ' when '.)

this, that. Do not say ' this here ' for *this*; ' these here ' for *these*; ' that there ' for *that*; ' those there ' or ' them ' for *those*; *this* and *that* are sometimes used colloquially as adverbs, in expressions like ' that far ', but the use is objectionable; do not use ' that ' for *so*; do not use ' at that ' for *too* or the like:

    1. Are *those* your books? (Not ' those there '.)
    2. He didn't go *so far as that*. (Not ' that far '.)
    3. I remember when you were *knee-high*. (Not ' this high '.)
    4. I have never thought it was *so* bad. (Not ' that bad '.)
    5. A shoemaker, and a poor one *into the bargain*. (Not ' at that'.)

this, thus. *This* and *thus* usually refer to something near and already spoken of; do not use them for *the following* or *as follows* unless the reference is made clear by the form of the sentence or by the punctuation (a comma or a colon following *this*; avoid ambiguity):

1. *This* was our last day together. (Already mentioned.)
2. *Thus* he had wasted his opportunities. (As described.)
3. He had *this* aim, namely, to be somebody. (Not 'This was his aim. He wished to be somebody'.)
4. His one aim was *this*, to be somebody.
5. *This* above all: to thine own self be true. — SHAKESPEARE.

toward, etc. On the ground of smoothness (§ 373) *toward*, *upward*, *downward*, and the like are preferable to the forms with *s* ('towards', etc.):

The bear ran *toward* me.

truth, veracity. *Truth* and *truthfulness* are used of things or of persons ; *veracity* is generally used of persons :

1. The *truth* of this story can be proved.
2. Some people doubt the boy's *veracity*.
3. He is a man of *truth* ; his *truthfulness* is well known.

try to. Do not say 'try and' for *try to*. See § 251.

twins. *Twins* denotes *two* ; do not say 'a pair of twins'.

ugly. *Ugly* means offensive, hideous, repulsive ; do not use it for *disagreeable*, *ill-natured*, *quarrelsome*, and the like :

1. We have the *ugliest* house in the village.
2. *Ugly* crimes ; *ugly* manners.
3. He has a *disagreeable* temper. (Not 'ugly'.)

unique. *Unique*, from the Latin word for *one*, means 'alone of its kind', 'without an equal', and should not be used if there are more than one of the same kind :

They occupy a *unique* position in history.

unknown. Do not say 'unbeknown' or 'unbeknownst' for *unknown* :

He was *unknown* to all of them.

unless, if . . . not. Do not say 'without', 'without that', or 'except' for *unless* or *if . . . not* :

1. We shan't go *unless* you do. (Not 'without' or 'except'.)
2. We shan't go *if* you *don't* go with us.
3. They would not have gone *without* you.

until, before. *Until* (or *till*) means *to the time that*; do not use it
for *before*:

    1. We will wait *until* you return.
    2. Hardly a week passes by *before* the pupils feel benefited.
       (Not 'until'.)

up. The adverb *up* is often used in the sense of *completely*, but it
should not be used redundantly (§ 413):

    1. To burn *up*; to eat *up*; to drink *up*.
    2. To *finish* a letter; *open* a door. (Not 'finish up', etc.)
    3. To *settle* an account; to *write* a description.

up to date. "This detestable phrase", says the *Westminster
Gazette*. Avoid 'up to date' and such expressions as 'bank on'
(= *depend on*) and 'take stock in' (= *trust*):

    1. That book has *just been revised*.
    2. This history extends *to the present time*.
    3. The narrative has been *brought down* to the present.
    4. Only *the most modern appliances* are used.
    5. His machine is *of the latest type*.
    6. This play is *up to the present standard*.

used to. Do not omit the infinitive after *used to*; do not pronounce
used to or *use to* yōos'tŭ :

    He *used to* go. He *used not* (or, colloq., § 380, *didn't use*) to go.

useless, worthless. Do not use 'no good' or 'no use' for *good
for nothing*, *useless*, or *worthless*:

    1. The old watch was *worthless*. (Not 'no good'.)
    2. It was *useless* to ask him. (Not 'no use'.)

valuable, valued. A thing (or person) is *valuable* which commands
a good price or has considerable worth in any other respect; a
person is *valued* who is highly regarded:

    1. A *valuable* horse; a *valuable* invention; *valuable* advice.
    2. A *valued* friend; our most *valued* fellow townsman.

verbs. Do not use *can* for *may* (§ 184); *will* for *shall* (§ 178);
would for *should* (§ 187). Do not make verbs at random; see
handwritten.

vex, irritate. Do not say 'rile' for *vex, irritate, annoy*, and the like:

    1. He was *vexed* (*irritated, disturbed*) by the news.
    2. They began to *muddy* the water. (Not 'rile'.)
    3. The water was *muddy* (or *turbid*). (Not 'rily'.)

want, wish, desire. *Want,* used colloquially, may be followed by an infinitive, but not by a clause; *wish* or *desire* may be followed by either; do not say 'I want in', 'I want out', and the like; *want* in the sense of *ought to* or *should* is colloquial:

    1. They may *want* bread and water; she *desired* to go.
    2. He *wished* (wanted) me to go. (Not 'wanted that I go'.)
    3. They *desire* her *to remain* (or *that* she remain, or *that* she should remain).
    4. She *wants* (colloquial) to come in. (Not 'wants in'.)
    5. You don't *want* to do that. (Colloquial.)

was, were. Do not use *was* for *were* (§§ 335, 339):

    1. If he *was* there, I did not see him.
    2. If he *were* here, I should be glad.
    3. If you *were* to go away, I should be sorry. (Not 'was'.)

way. Do not use 'ways' for *way*; nor 'way' for *away* (see *away*); to denote manner, use *in that way*:

    1. The river is a long *way* off. (Not 'ways'.)
    2. They live *away* down the valley. (Not 'way'.)
    3. Do not use your pen *in that way*.

we, you, etc. Do not use 'one' for *we, you*, etc. See § 106.

weekly, biweekly, etc. The words *weekly, semiweekly, biennial, triennial*, and so on, have distinct meanings, and are good words. *Biweekly* is objectionable, because it may mean 'twice a week' or 'every two weeks'; use *semiweekly* in the first case, and *semimonthly* in the second. Similarly, *triweekly* may mean 'three times a week' or 'every three weeks'; unless the meaning is clear (as in 'semiweekly and triweekly newspapers') use the longer expressions, 'three times a week', 'every three weeks'.

well, good. Do not use 'good' for *well* (§ 239).

when, where. Do not use as a definition a clause beginning with *when* or *where* (see *because*):

1. The interesting event of the day was the arrival of the mail. (Not ' was when the mail arrived '.)
2. A hospital is a place for the care of the sick and injured. (Or, ' is a *place where* the sick and injured are cared for '; but not ' is where the sick and injured are cared for '.)

whereabouts. *Whereabouts* is singular (§ 205, 24).

while. *While* means ' during the time that '; then it often has an adversative sense approaching *although*; do not use it for *whereas* or a mere *and*:

1. He studies *while* the rest of us sleep.
2. *While* we condemn the act, let us not condemn the man.
3. They claimed victory, *whereas* they were defeated.
4. The piano was in a corner of the room, *and* a lamp stood near it. (Not ' while '.)

-wise, -ways. Use *endwise, lengthwise, sidewise,* etc., rather than ' endways ', etc.

with regard to, etc. Say ' *in* or *with* regard to ', ' *with* reference to ', ' *with* respect to '. See § 287.

within. Do not use ' inside of ' for *within* or *in less than* :

He will be at home *within* a week.

woman, woman's, etc. See §§ 149, 151.

wonderful. *Wonderful* means *astonishing, marvelous* (§ 415); its general use for *good, excellent, interesting, instructive, successful, beautiful,* and the like should be avoided :

1. A *wonderful* view ; a *wonderful* piece of machinery.
2. A *good* dinner ; an *excellent* specimen ; an *interesting* talk.

worst kind. Do not use *the worst kind* for *greatly* or *much* :

1. It was *the worst kind* of day for fishing. (Correct.)
2. The change is needed *greatly*. (Not ' the worst kind '.)

would rather. Do not say ' would better '. See § 244 and N.

write-up. ' Write-up ', for *account, description,* or the like, is American journalistic cant.

you were. Do not say ' you was ' for *you were*. See §§ 59, 196.

CHAPTER VII

WORDS OFTEN MISPRONOUNCED

A man's character is known from his conversation. — MENANDER.

Such rackers of orthography, as to speak *dout* fine, when he should say *doubt*; *det*, when he should pronounce *debt*; d e b t, not *det*: he clepeth a calf *cauf*; *half*, *hauf*. — SHAKESPEARE.

418. Value of correct pronunciation. If we agree with the Greek poet Menander that a man's character is known from his conversation, ought we not to be particular not only about the choice and use of words, but about their pronunciation? Correct pronunciation, like correct grammar and graceful style, adds charm to any personality.

419. Common words mispronounced. Most of the words in § 423 are in common use. Most of them have but one correct pronunciation. Most of them are mispronounced every day. Some of the commonest of them are often mispronounced even by educated people.

420. Words varying in pronunciation. Some of the words in the list have two or more accepted pronunciations. These words are followed by *W* (Webster), or *O* (Oxford), or *W-O* (Webster-Oxford), to indicate that the pronunciation given is preferred in Webster's New International Dictionary, or in the Oxford English Dictionary, or in both these authorities, as representing the best present usage in the United States and the south of England. When these two authorities do not agree on the preferred pronunciation of a word, the pronunciation preferred by the one is usually the second choice of the other; thus the reader usually has before him the first and second choices of both these authorities. For example, *illustrate* is pronounced ĭ-lŭs'trāt or ĭl'ŭs-trāt in Webster, and ĭl'ŭs-trāt or ĭ-lŭs'trāt in the Oxford English Dictionary. The abbreviations *a.*, *n.*, *v.*, *adv.*, stand for *adjective*, *noun*, *verb*, *adverb*.

421. Typical words. The list contains certain typical words which are intended to be a guide in the pronunciation of similar words. For example, many words which have the sound of *u* in *use* are commonly pronounced as if they had the sound of *oo* in *bōot*: tūne (pronounced tyōon; not tōon); *dew* and *new* rime with *few* (not with ' do '). Words ending in a long *o*-sound (*ō*) should not be pronounced as if they ended in *ŭ*: fŏl'lōw, mĕad'ōw, wĭn'dōw (not fŏl'ŭ, mĕad'ŭ, wĭn'dŭ). Short *e* (*ĕ*) should not be pronounced like *u* in *ŭp* or in *ûrn*: gov'-ern-mĕnt (not gov'er-mŭnt), A-mĕr'i-ca (not a-mûr'i-ca).

422. Words ending in *ide*, *ine*, *ile*. The pronunciation of the ending *ide* in chemical terms varies between īd and ĭd; but usage is decidedly in favor of īd, especially in words of long standing. The pronunciation of *ine* is threefold, īn, ēn, and ĭn; in most words the Oxford English Dictionary gives īn only, whereas Webster gives ēn as the usual pronunciation of chemists in the United States. The ending *ile* is usually pronounced īl in British usage, and ĭl in the United States (as, fer'tīle, fer'tīle ; hos'tīle, hos'tĭle).

423. Acquiring correct pronunciation ; caution. To acquire the correct pronunciation of the words in the list below, pronounce each word aloud several times, with exaggerated stress on the accented syllable. Learn to write the words with their diacritical marks ; this will help you to use the dictionary. Be careful not to add or omit letters or syllables, or to transpose them. For example, *idea* is pronounced ī-dē'à (not ī'dĕ-à or ī-dē'àr) ; *really* is pronounced rē'ăl-ĭ (not rē'lĭ) ; *casualties* is pronounced kăzh'ŭ-ăl-tĭz (not kăzh-ŭ-ăl'ĭ-tĭz).

LIST OF MISPRONOUNCED WORDS

KEY TO PRONUNCIATION

ā as in fāce
ȧ as in sur'fȧce
â as in câre
ă as in ăm
ȧ as in ȧffect'
ä as in fär
ȧ as in ȧf'ter
à as in àfire'
ã as ē in o'vẽr
au as in au'thor
c as in cat
ç as in çell
ch as in chair
ch as in cho'rus
ē as in bē
ēē as ē in bē
ĕ as in bĕgin'
ĕ as in mĕn
ĕ as in mo'mĕnt

ẽ as in o'vẽr, hẽr
g as in get, go
ġ as in ġem
ī as in pīne
ĭ as in pĭn
ì as ẽ in o'vẽr, hẽr
ŋ as n in ink
N (see Note 1)
ō as in pō'et
ȯ as in pȯet'ic
ô as in bôr'der
ŏ as in bŏn'net
ŏ as in cŏnnect'
ŏ as in sŏft
õ as ẽ in o'vẽr
ȯ as ŭ in cir'cŭs
oi as in oil
ōō as in bōōt
ŏŏ as in bŏŏk

ou as in out
ph as in Phil'ip
qu as in quest
s as in this
ş as in theşe
ū as in ū'nit
ủ as in ủnite'
û as in ûrn
ŭ as in mŭst
ŭ as in cir'cŭs
ü (see Note 2)
th as in thin
th as in then
y as in yet
ȳ as in bȳ
ў as in near'lў
ỹ as ẽ in o'vẽr
zh as z in az'ure

NOTE 1. The small capital letter N represents nasal *n*, as in French *son*. To make this sound, pronounce *son* as in the word *song* (omit no sound but that of *g*).

NOTE 2. The letter ü represents French *u*. To make this sound, hold the lips rounded as if to pronounce *ōō*, and try to pronounce *ē*.

NOTE 3. The endings *cious* and *scious* and *tious* are pronounced shŭs, as in *pre'cious*, *con'scious*, and *conscien'tious*; *sion* and *tion* are pronounced shŭn, as in *inver'sion* and *ac'tion*.

NOTE 4. Vowels not marked are silent. For example, *read* is pronounced rēd; *read*, rĕd; *Cai'ro*, kā'rō; *Cai'ro*, kī'rō; *ous*, ŭs.

NOTE 5. For the letters *W*, *O*, *W-O*, *a.*, *n.*, *v.*, *adv.*, see § 420.

Aar'on (âr'ŭn)
ăb'ȧ-cŭs
ăb-dō'mĕn
ăb-dŏm'ĭ-nȧl

ȧ-bey'ȧnçe (-bā'-)
Ăb'ĭ-gāil
ăb'jĕct
ăb-jĕc'tion

ăb'jĕct-lў
ăb'jĕct-nĕss
ăb-lū'tion (§ 421)
ăb'sĕnt (*a.*)

ăb-sĕnt′ (v.)

ăb′sŏ-lūte

ăb-stē′mĭ-oŭs

ăb′străct (a., n.)

ăb-străct′ (v.)

ăb′străct-lў

ăb-struse′ (-strōōs′)

à-cā′cia (-shà)

ăc′çĕnt (n.)

ăc-çĕnt′ (v.)

ăc-çĕpt′

ăc′çĕss (W-O)

ăc-çĕs′sŏ-rў (W;
    ăk′sĕ-sĕr-ĭ, O)

ăc-clī′măte

à-çē′tĭc (W-O)

À-chā′tēṣ

À-chĭl′lēṣ

à-cous′tĭcs (-kōōs′-;
    W-O)

ăc-quĭ-esce′ (-ĕs′)

à-crŏss′

à-cū′mĕn

à-dä′gio (-jō)

ăd-à-măn′tĭne

ăd-drĕss′ (n., v.)

ăd-drĕss′ēē′

ăd-dūçe′

ăd′ē-noid

à-dĕpt′ (a., n.)

à-dieu′ (-dū′)
    (French à-dyû′)

ăd ĭn-fī-nī′tŭm

ăd′mĭ-rà-ble

ăd nau′se-am
    (nô′shē-ăm)

à-dō′bĕ

À-dō′nĭs

à-dŭlt′ (a., n.)

ăd và-lō′rĕm

ăd′vērse

ăd′vērse-lў

ăd′vēr-tīṣe (W;
    ăd-vēr-tīz′, O)

ăd-vēr′tĭṣe-mĕnt
    (W-O)

æ′gis (ē′jĭs)

Æ-nē′ăs (-ĕ-)

Æ-nē′ĭd (-ĕ-)

Æ′ŏ-lŭs (ē′-)

ā′ĕr-āte

ā-ē′rĭ-àl

ā′ĕr-ŏ-naut (W-O)

ā-ĕr-ŏ-nau′tĭcs

ā′ĕr-ō-plāne

æs-thĕt′ĭc (ĕs-; W-O)

af′flu-ence
    (ăf′lōō-ĕns)

ā fôr-ti-ō′rī (-shĭ-)

à-gain′ (-gĕn′; W-O)

à-gainst′ (-gĕnst′;
    W-O)

Ă′găs-siz (-sē)

aged (ā′jĕd, as in
    aged men; ājd, as
    in much aged, mid-
    dle-aged, aged five
    years)

ăg′grăn-dīze

ăg-grăn′dīze-mĕnt
    (W-O)

ăġ′īle (W-O)

ai-grette′ (ā-grĕt′, W;
    ā′grĕt, O)

āi-lăn′thŭs

Ăl-à-bä′mà

ăl′à-bàs-tĕr (W-O)

à la carte′ (à là kärt′)

À-lăd′dĭn

ăl-bū′mĕn

ăl-bū′mĭn

Ăl-çĭ-bī′à-dēṣ

al′dĕr (ôl′-)

Ăl′dīne (W; ôl′-, O)

Ăl′frĕd

ā′lĭ-às

ăl′ĭ-bī

āl′ien (-yĕn)

ăl′kà-līne (W-O)

Ăl-lē′ghe-nў (-gā-)

ăl-lē′giance (-jàns)

äl-le′grō (-lā′-)

ăl-lŏ-păth′ĭc

àl-lŏp′à-thў

àl-loy′ (-loi′)

àl-lūde′

àl-lў′ (n., v.)

Ăl′mà Mā′tĕr

ăl-păc′à

Ăl′pīne (W; -pīn, O)

ăl′tĕr-nāte (v.; W-O)

ăl-tĕr′năte (a., n., W;
    -nĕt, O)

ăl-tĕr′năte-lў

ăl-tĕr-nā′tion (W-O)

ăl-tĕr′nà-tĭve (W-O)

ăl′tĭ-tūde

ăl-ū̆-mĭn′ĭ-ŭm

à-lū′mĭ-nŭm

ăm-à-teûr′ (W-O)

ăm′bĕr-gris (-grēs)

à-mē'nà-ble

à-měn'ĭ-tў

A-mēr'ĭ-cà (§ 421)

Ăm'herst (-ẽrst)

ăm-mō'nĭ-à

ăm-pere' (-pâr')

ăm'phŏ-rà

ăn-ăch'rŏ-nĭṣm

A-năc'rĕ-ŏn

à-næ'mĭ-à (-nē'-)

à-năth'ĕ-mà (curse)

ăn-chō'vў

Ăn-drŏ-nī'cŭs (in Shakespeare -drŏn'ĭ-)

à-nĕm'ŏ-nĕ

à-new' (-nū'; § 421)

ăn'ġĭ-nà pĕc'tŏ-rĭs

an-gō'rà (ăŋ-)

ăn'ĭ-līne (W; -līn, O; § 422)

ăn-ĭ-măl'cūle

ăn'nà-līne (W)

ăn-nĕx' (n., v.; W-O)

ăn'nō Dŏm'ĭ-nī

ăn-nŭn'ci-āte (-shĭ-)

ăn-nŭn-ci-ā'tion (-sĭ-; W-O)

ănt-ärc'tĭc

ăn-tĕ-pē'nŭlt (W; -pĕ-nŭlt', O)

ăn'thrà-çīte (§ 417)

ăn'tĭ- (§ 408)

ăn'tĭ-dōt-ăl (W-O)

Ăn-tĭg'ŏ-nĕ

ăn-tĭp'ŏ-dēṣ

ăn-tĭ-tŏx'ĭn

anx'ious (ăŋk'shŭs)

an'y (ĕn'ĭ)

an'y-bŏd-ў (ĕn'ĭ-)

Ăph-rŏ-dī'tĕ

A-pŏl'lō Bĕl-vĕ-dēre' (or bĕl'và-dā'rā)

ăp-ŏ-thē'ŏ-sĭs (W-O)

Ăp-pà-lăch'ĭ-ăn (W)

ăp-pà-rā'tŭs

ăp-pâr'ĕnt (W-O)

ăp-pĕn-dĭ-çī'tĭs

ăp-pĕn'dĭx (§ 39); pl. ăp-pĕn'dĭ-çēṣ

ăp'plĭ-cà-ble

ăp-prē'ci-āte (-shĭ-)

ā'prī-côt (W-O)

ā prī-ō'rī (W-O)

ā'pron (-prŭn; W-O)

ăp-rŏ-pos' (-pō')

ăp'tĭ-tūde

ā-quà-mà-rine' (-rēn')

à-quăt'ĭc

ăq'uĕ-dŭct

ā'quĕ-oŭs

ăq'uĭ-līne (W-O)

Ăr'ăb

Ăr'à-bĭc

är-bĭt'rà-mĕnt

är'bĭ-trà-rĭ-lў

är'bŭ-tŭs (W-O)

ärch'ān'ġĕl

Är-chĭ-mē'dēṣ

är-chĭ-pĕl'à-gō

är'chĭ-tĕct

är'chive (W-O)

ärc'tĭc

ā'rĕ-à (W; âr'ĕ-à, O)

ä'rĭ-à (W-O)

är'ĭd

Ā'rĭ-ēṣ

Ăr-ĭs-tī'dēṣ

Ăr-ĭs-tŏph'à-nēṣ

Ăr'kăn-sas (-sô)

Är-kăn'ṣàs Çĭt'ў (in Kansas)

är-mā'dà

är'mĭ-stĭçe

à-rō'mà

ăr-raign' (-rān')

är-tē'sian (-zhăn)

är-tĭf'ĭ-çēr

är'tĭ-ṣăn (W; är-tĭ-zăn', O)

är'tiste' (-tēst')

as-çĕt'ĭc (ă-)

Ā'sia (-shà)

Ā-si-ăt'ĭc (-shĭ-; W-O)

à-skănçe'

asked (àskt; not ăst)

ăs'phălt (W-O)

ăs-pīr'ănt (W-O)

ăs'pĭ-rāte (v.; -răt, a., n.)

ăs-sĕnt' (n., v.)

ăs'sĕt

ăs-sign-ee' (-ĭ-nē')

ăs-sō'ci-ate (-shĭ-āt, v.; -ăt, a., n.)

ăs-sō-çĭ-ā'tion (W; -shĭ-, O)

ăs-sūme'

ăs-sŭmp'tion

asth'mȧ (ăz'-, W ; ăsth'-, O)

asth-măt'ĭc (ăz-, W ; ăsth-, O)

ăs-tūte'

ăth-ĕ̇-næ'ŭm (-nē'-)

ăth'lēte

ăth-lĕt'ĭc

ȧ-tŏm'ĭc

ȧ-trō'cious

ȧ-trŏç'ĭ-tў

ăt'rŏ-phied (-fĭd)

ăt'rŏ-phў

ăt'tȧ-che' (-shā')

ăt-tacked' (-tăkt')

ăt'tĭ-tūde

ȧt-tūne'

au-dā'cious

Au-ġē'ăn

aug'mĕnt (n.)

aug-mĕnt' (v.)

Auld Lăng Şӯne

aunt (änt)

au'rĕ̇-ōle

au re-voir' (ō rĕ-vwȧr')

au-rō'rȧ bō-rĕ̇-ā'lĭs

au-tŏ-mō'bĭle (W ; not in O)

au'tŏp-sў

aux-il'ia-ry (ôg-zĭl'yȧ-rĭ)

ăv'ĕ̇-nūe

ȧ-vēr'sion

ā-vĭ-ā'tion

ā'vĭ-ā-tŏr

ăv-oir-dŭ̇-poiş' (-ēr-)

ăx'ĭ-om (-ŭm)

Ăx'mĭn-stēr

aye (ā, ever ; ī, yes)

ȧ-zā'lĕ̇-ȧ

Á-zores' (-zōrz')

az'ure (ăzh'ŭr, W ; -ēr, O)

băc-chȧ-nā'lĭ-ȧ

băc'chȧnt

bac-chante' (bȧ-kȧnt' ; W-O); pl. -chantes' (-kȧnts')

Băc'chŭs

bȧ-çĭl'lŭs ; pl. bȧ-çĭl'lī

băc-tē'rĭ-ŭm ; pl. băc-tē'rĭ-ȧ

bade (băd)

bȧ'dĭ'nage' (-dē'näzh' ; W-O)

Bȧ-hä'mȧ

Bā'iæ (-yē)

Bai-käl' (bī-)

băl-brĭg'găn

băl'cŏ-nў

bal'dēr-dăsh (bôl'-)

Băl-ĕ̇-ăr'ĭc

balm (bäm)

Băl-mŏr'ăl

bal'săm (bôl'-)

băl-ŭ̇s-trāde' (W-O)

Bȧl'zȧc'

bäm-bi'nō (-bē'-)

băm-boō'

băn'ăl (W ; bā'năl, O)

bȧ-nä'nȧ (W-O)

Băn'crŏft

băn-dăn'nȧ

băn'dĭt, băn-dĭt'tĭ

ban'quĕt (băŋ'-)

băp'tĭs-tēr-ў

Băr-bā'dōş

bär-băr'ĭc

bär'cȧ-rōle

Bär'nȧrd (college)

bȧ-rouche' (-roōsh')

bȧr'rage' (-räzh' ; English bär'ăj)

bär'rĕl

Bär-tĭ-mæ'ŭs (-mē'-)

bȧ-salt' (-sôlt' ; W-O)

bȧ-sĭl'ĭ-cȧ

bas'-re-lief' (bä'rĕ̇-lēf', W ; bȧs'rĕ̇-lēf', O)

băs-tĭ-nā'dō

bȧ'ton' (-tôɴ', W ; băt'ŭn, O)

Bá'yeux' (-yû')

bay'ou (bī'oō)

bē-ȧ-tĭf'ĭc

bĕ-ăt'ĭ-fў

bĕ-ăt'ĭ-tūde

Beau'rĕ̇-gärd (bō'-)

beau'tĕ̇-oŭs (bū'-)

bĕ-cauşe'

bĕ-dew' (-dū')

Bĕd'ou-in (-oō- ; -ĭn, W ; -ēn, O)

Bĕ-ĕl'zĕ̇-bŭb

been (bĭn, W ; bēn, O)

Bē-ēr-shē'bȧ (W)

Bee'tho-ven (bā'tō-věn)

bĕ-gŏ'nĭ-ȧ

bĕ-grīmed'

bĕl'dȧme

Bĕl'gĭ-ăn

Bĕl'gĭ-ŭm

Bē'lĭ-ȧl

Bĕl-lēr'ŏ-phŏn

belles'-let'tres (bĕl' lĕt'r)

bĕl'lōw (§ 421)

bĕ-nēath' (W-O)

bĕn-ĕ-fĭ'ci-a-ry (-fĭsh'ĭ-ȧ-rĭ, W; -fĭsh'ȧ-rĭ, O)

bĕ-quēath'

bĕs'ti-al (-chȧl, W; -tĭ-ȧl, O)

bĕs-ti-al'ĭ-tȳ (-chăl'-, W; -tĭ-ăl'-, O)

bête' noire' (bât' nwär')

bī'çȳ-cle

bī-ĕn'nĭ-ȧl

bĭl'let-doux' (-ĕ-dōō'; French bē'yĕ'dōō'); pl. bĭl'lets-doux' (-ĕ-dōōz'; Fr. bē'yĕ'dōō')

bī'nȧ-rȳ

bī-ŏg'rȧ-phēr

bī-ŏ-grăph'ĭc

bī-ŏg'rȧ-phȳ

bī-ŏl'ŏ-ġȳ

bĭs'cuit (-kĭt)

bĭ-tū'měn (W-O)

bĭv'ouac (-wăk; W-O)

bĭ-zärre'

black'guard (blăg'ärd)

Blăck'stŏne

blanc-mange' (blȧ-mänzh'; W-O)

blȧ'sé' (-zā')

blȧs-phēme'

blȧs'phĕ-moŭs

blȧs'phĕ-mȳ

blā'tȧnt

blĕss'ĕd (a.)

Bō-äb-dil' (-dēl')

Bō-ȧ-dĭ-çē'ȧ

bōat (not bŏt)

bōat'swāin (nautically bō's'n)

Boc-cac'cio (bŏ-kä'chō)

Boer (bōōr)

Boise (city, boi'zȧ)

bois'tĕr-oŭs

Bol'eyn (Anne) (bŏŏl'ĭn)

Bŏ-lō'nyȧ

Bŏl'shĕ-vi-ki' (-vĕ-kē', W)

Bŏl'shĕ-vĭşm

bomb (bŏm; W-O)

bŏm'bȧst

bō'nȧ fī'dĕ

bon' mot' (bôN'mō');

pl. bons' mots' (bôN' mōz')

bon' vo'yage' (bôN' vwȧ'yȧzh')

bŏr'rōw (§ 421)

bos'om (bŏŏz'ŭm; W-O)

Bŏs'pŏ-rŭs

bou'doir (bōō'dwär)

bought (bôt)

bou'illon' (bōō'yôN', W; bōō'lyŏN, O)

bound'ȧ-rȳ

boun'tĕ-oŭs

bou-quet' (bōō-kā'; W-O)

bour'geoi'sie' (bōōr'zhwȧ'zē')

bourn(e) (bōrn; W-O)

bō'vīne (W-O)

bow (of ship, bou)

Bōw'doin (-d'n)

bōw'ie (-ĭ, knife) (W-O)

bōw'sprĭt (W-O)

brȧ-vä'dō (W; -vā'-, O)

brä'vō (W-O)

breech'ĕş (brĭch'-)

brĕth'rĕn

brĕ-vĕt' (W; brĕv'ĕt, O)

brē'vĭ-ȧ-rȳ (W; -ȧ-rĭ, O)

Brī-ā'rḗ-ŭs
brĭg'ănd
brĭg'ănd-ăġe
Brī-sē'īs
brŏ-chure' (-shür')
brō'mīde (W-O)
brō'mĭne (W-O)
bron-ehĭ-ăl (brŏṇ'-)
bron-ehī'tĭs (brŏŋ-)
Brŏn'të (-tĕ)
brŏnze
brooch (brōch ; W-O)
brōōm
brough'am (brōō'ŭm, W ; brōōm, O)
brusque (brōōsk, W ; brŭsk, O)
bŭ-çĕn'taur
bŭ-cŏl'ĭc
Bud'dha (bōōd'á)
Bud'dhism (bōōd'ĭz'm ; W-O)
buf-fet' (bōō-fā', W ; bŭf'ĕt, O)
bŭg'á-bōō
buoy (boi ; W-O)
buoy'ănt (boi'- ; W-O)
bŭ-reau'crá-çў (-rŏ'- ; W-O)
bū-reau-crăt'ĭc (-rŏ-)
burgh'er (bûr'gĕr)
bûr-lesque' (-lĕsk')
bur'y (bĕr'ĭ)
busi'nĕss (bĭz'-)
bus'tle (bŭs''l)
butch'ĕr (bōōch'-)

Bysshe (Shelley ; bĭsh)
Bў-zăn'tĭne (W ; -tīn, O)

cá-băl'
căb'á-lá
căb'á-rĕt (W ; kà'bà-rĕ', O)
Căb'ot (-ŭt)
cá-dā'vĕr (§ 402)
cá-dăv'ĕr-oŭs
Cæd'mon (kăd'mŭn)
cá'fé' (-fā')
căf'fĕ-ĭne (W ; -īn, O)
Caï'rō (U. S. ; Egypt, kī'-)
cāis'sŏn (W ; -sŭn, O)
Căl'chăs
cā'lĭph (W ; kăl'ĭf, O)
Căl-lī'ŏ-pĕ
calm (käm)
cá-lŏr'ĭc
căl'ŏ-rie (-rĭ)
Cá-lўp'sō
cá-mĕl'lĭ-á (W-O)
cá'mou'flage' (-mōō'fläzh')
căm-pä-ni'le (-nē'lā, W ; -pà-nē'lā, O)
Camp'bĕll (kăm'-)
cá-nā'rў
căn-dĕ-lā'brŭm ; pl. -lā'bra (§ 402)
cá-nīne' (W-O)
ca'ñon (kăn'yŭn ; W-O)

cănt (jargon)
căn't
căn'tá-loupe (-lōōp ; W-O)
căn-tä'tá (W-O)
căn-tēēn'
căn'tŏn-mĕnt (W ; căn-tŏn'-, O)
căp'-á-pie' (-pē')
cá-price' (-prēs')
cá-prī'cious
Căp'ŭ-chĭn (W-O)
cā'pŭt (W ; kăp'ŭt, O) ; pl. căp'ĭ-tá
cá-ràfe'
căr'ăt
căr'bīne
căr'ĕt (W-O)
Căr-ĭb-bē'ăn
căr'ĭ-cá-tûre (n., v.)
cär'mĭne (W-O)
Cär-nĕg'ie (-ĭ)
cär-nĭv'ŏ-rá
Cär-ŏ-lī'ná
cá-rŏt'ĭd
căr'riage (-ĭj)
cärte' blanche' (blänsh')
cär'trĭdġe
cäs'cá-rä (W-O)
cas'ŭ-ăl-tў (kăzh'-) (pl. -ăl-tĭz)
cā'sŭs bĕl'lī
căt'á-lŏgue
căt'á-lŏgu-ēr (see demagoguism)
căt'á-lŏgu-ĭng

catch (kăch; *not* kĕch)

Cau-cā′sian (-shăn, W; -shĭ-ăn, O)

Cau′cȧ-sŭs

cāy-ĕnne′ (W-O)

çĕl′ĭ-bȧ-çў̆ (W-O)

cel′lo (chĕl′ō)

Çĕlt′ĭc, Kĕlt′ĭc

çĕ-mĕnt′ (*n., v.*; W-O)

çĕm′ĕ-tĕr-ў̆

çĕn-tĕn′nĭ-ăl

cen′time′ (säɴ′tēm′; W-O)

çĕ-răm′ĭc

Çĕr′bĕr-ŭs

çĕr′ĕ-brăl

çĕr′ĕ-brŭm

Çē′rēṣ

çĕr′tain (-tĭn)

çĕ-ru′lē-ăn (-rōō′-)

Çĕy-lŏn′

chaise (shāz)

Chăl-dē′ăn

cha-let′(shȧ-lā′; W-O)

chăl′ĭçe

chȧ-mē′lĕ-on (-ŭn)

cham′ois (shăm′ĭ, W; shăm′oi, O)

Champs′ É′ly′sées′ (shäɴ′zā′lē′zā′)

chăn′tĭ-clēer

chā′ŏs

chȧ-ŏt′ĭc

chap′er-on (shăp′ĕr-ōn, W; shăp′ĕr-ŏn, O)

cha-ri-va′ri (shä-rĕ-vä′rĕ, W; -rĭ-vä′rĭ, O)

char′lȧ-tăn (shär′-)

Chā′rŏn

châr′ў̆ (W; chā′rĭ, O)

Chȧ-rўb′dĭs

chās′ten (-′n)

chăs-tīṣe′

chăs′tīṣe-mĕnt

châ′teau′ (shä′tō′)

Cha′teau′-Thier′ry′ (shä′tō′ tyĕ′rē′)

chauf′feûr′ (shō′-)

Chau-tau′quȧ (shȧ-tô′-)

chef (shĕf)

chef′-d′œu′vre (shĕ′dû′vr)

Chē′ŏps

Chĕph′rĕn

chĕ-ru′bĭc (-rōō′-)

Che-ru-bi′ni (kā-rōō-bē′nē)

Chĕṣ′ȧ-pēake

chest′nŭt (chĕs′-)

chev-ȧ-lier′ (shĕv-)

Chey-ĕnne′ (shī-)

chic (shĕk)

Chi-ca′go (shĭ-kô′gō)

chi-cān′ĕr-ў̆ (shĭ-)

chĭ-mē′rȧ (W-O)

chĭ-mĕr′ĭ-căl

chĭm′ney (-nĭ)

chī-rŏg′rȧ-phў̆

Chĭ′rŏn

chĭ-rŏp′ŏ-dĭst

chiv′al-rĭc (shĭv′-ăl-, W; shĭ-văl′-, O)

chiv′ăl-rў̆ (shĭv′-; W-O)

chŏck′-full (-fŏŏl)

chŏl′ĕr

chŏl′ĕr-ĭc

chris′ten (krĭs″n)

Christ′mȧs (krĭs′-)

chute (shōōt)

çī-cā′dȧ

çī-cā′trĭx (W-O); *pl.* çĭc-ȧ-trī′çēṣ

ci-ce-ro′ne (*n.*, chē-chā-rō′nä; W-O)

Çĭn-cĭn-nȧ′tĭ (*not* -tŭ)

çĭn′ĕ-mȧ

çĭn-ĕ-măt′ŏ-grȧph

cir′ca (sûr′kȧ)

Cir′ce (sûr′sē)

çĭt′rāte

çĭt′ron (-rŭn)

clăn-dĕs′tīne

clan′gor (klăŋ′gĕr; W-O)

clĕan′lў̆ (*a.*; *adv.* klēn′-)

clĕm′ȧ-tĭs

Clē-ŏ-pā′trȧ

clī-ĕn-tĕle′ (W; -tēl′, O)

clique (klēk)

clothes (klōthz)

Clў′ti-e (klĭsh′ĭ-ē)

cṓ-ad′ju-tănt (-ăj′o͞o-)

cō-ad-ju′tor (-ă-jo͞o′tĕr)

cōat (*not* kŏt)

cō′cȧ-ĭne (W ; -ĭn, O ; § 422 ; *not* kṓ-kān′)

cŏc′cŭs ; *pl.* -çī (§ 402)

cō′gnac (-nyȧk)

cŏg′nĭ-zănçe (W-O)

cŏg-nō′mĕn

coif′fure′ (kwȧ′für′ ; W-O)

cŏl-lāte′

cŏl′lier-y̆ (-yĕr-)

cȯ-lō′nĭ-ăl

Cŏl-ȯ-rä′dō

Cŏl-ŏs-sē′ŭm

cŏl′umn (-ŭm)

cŏm′ȧ-tōse (W ; kō-mȧ-tōs′, O)

cŏm′băt (*n.,v.*; W-O)

cŏm′băt-ănt (W-O)

cŏm′băt-ĭng (W-O)

cŏm′bȧ-tĭve

come′ly̆ (kŭm′-)

cŏm-mȧn-dänt′

cŏm-mĕn′su-răte (-sho͞o-)

cŏm′mĕnt (*n., v.*; W-O)

cŏm′mŭ-năl (W ; kȯ-mū′năl, O)

cŏm′păct (*n.*)

cȯm-păct′ (*a., v.*)

cŏm′pȧ-rȧ-ble

cŏm-pā′trĭ-ot (-ŭt)

cŏm-pēer′

cŏm′pĕn-sāte (W ; -pĕn-, O)

cŏm′plȧ′çĕnçe

cŏm′plȧi-şȧnçe (W-O)

cŏm′plȧi-şȧnt (W-O)

cŏm-plĕx′ (*a., n.*)

cŏm-pŏş′īte (*a., n.*, W ; kŏm′pŏ-zĭt, O)

cŏm′pound (*a., n.*)

cŏm′pound′ (*v.*)

cŏm′prĕss (*n.*)

cŏm-prĕss′ (*v.*)

comp-trōl′lĕr (cŏn-)

cŏm′răde (W ; -răd, O)

cȯn ä-mō′re (-rā)

cŏn′cāve (*a., n., v.*)

cŏn′çĕn-trāte (W-O)

cȯn-cer′tō (-chĕr′- ; W-O)

con′côrd (kŏŋ′-, W ; kŏn′kŏrd, O)

Con′côrd (kŏŋ′-, *town, grape*)

cŏn′crēte (*a., n.*; W-O)

cŏn-dō′lĕnçe

cŏn′duit (-dĭt)

cŏn-fĭ-dȧnt(e)′

cŏn′fīneş

cŏn′fĭs-cāte (W-O)

con′frère′ (kôɴ′frâr′)

con′gé′ (kôɴ′zhā′)

cŏn-ġē′rĭ-eş

cō′nĭ-fĕr

cŏn-jure′ (-jo͞or′, *entreat*)

con′jure (kŭn′jĕr, *summon*)

con-nois-seur′ (kŏn-ĭ-sûr′, W ; kŏ′nŏ′sûr′, O)

con′quĕst (kŏŋ′-)

cŏn-sci-ĕn′tious (-shĭ-)

cŏn′sĕr-vā-tŏr

cŏn-sĕrve′ (*n., v.*; W-O)

cŏn-sĭd′ĕr-ȧ-ble

cŏn-sŏl′ȧ-tȯ-ry̆

cŏn-spīr′ȧ-çy̆

con′stȧ-ble (kŭn′- ; W-O)

cŏn′stĭ-tūte

cŏn-stĭ-tū′tion

cŏn′strue (-stro͞o ; W-O)

cŏn-sūme′

cŏn-sŭm′măte (*a.*; W-O)

cŏn′sŭm-māte (*v.*; W-O)

cŏn′tĕm-plāte (W ; -tĕm-, O)

cŏn-tĕm′plȧ-tĭve

cŏn′tĕnts (W ; kŏn-tĕnts′, O)

cŏn-tĭ-nū′ĭ-ty̆

cŏn′tour(-to͞or; W-O)

cŏn′trȧ-rĭ-ly̆

cŏn'trȧ-rў

cŏn'trīte

cŏn'trīte-nĕss

cŏn'tŭ-mȧ-çў

cŏn'tŭ-mĕ-lў

cŏn'vẽr-sȧnt

cŏn'vĕx

cōōp (*not* kŏŏp)

cŏpse

cō'quet-rў (-kĕt-)

cŏ-quette' (-kĕt')

côr'dial (-jȧl, W ; -dĭ-ȧl, O)

côr-dĭl-le'ra (-yā'rȧ, W ; -yâ'rȧ, O)

Côr'dṑ-vä

côr'nĕt (W-O)

corps (kōr) ; *pl.* corps (kōrz ; § 39)

cŏr-răl' (*n., v.,* W ; kŏ-, O)

côr'tège' (-tĕzh')

cŏs'tūme (*n.,* W ; kŏs-tūm', O)

cou'gȧr (kōō'-)

coup' de grâce' (kōō' dĕ gräs')

coup' d'é'tat' (kōō' dā'tȧ')

cou'pŏn (kōō'-)

cou'rĭ-ẽr (kōō'-, W ; kŏŏ'-, O)

course (kōrs)

coûr'tĕ-oŭs (W ; kōrt'yŭs, O)

cour'te-san (kōr'tĕ-zȧn, W ; -zän, O)

court'ier (kōrt'yẽr)

cov'e-tous (kŭv'ĕ-tŭs)

cow'ard-ice (kou'ẽr-dĭs)

cowl (koul)

Crea'sў (krē'-)

crĕ-dū'lĭ-tў

crēēk (*not* krĭk)

crĕ-māte' (W-O)

crĕm'ȧ-tṑ-rў (W ; -tẽr-ĭ, O)

cre-scen'dō (krĕ-shĕn'-, W ; krȧ-shĕn'-, O)

Crĭ-mē'ȧ

crī-tē'rĭ-on (-ŭn)

crois' de guerre' (krwä' dĕ gâr')

cru'cial (krōō'shȧl)

crўs'tȧl-līne (W-O ; § 422)

cuck'ōō (kŏŏk'-)

cui bō'nō (kī)

cui-rass' (kwĕ-rȧs', W ; kwĭ-răs', O)

cui-sine' (kwĕ-zēn')

cul'-de-sac' (kü'd'-sák')

cū'lĭ-nȧ-rў

cŭ-nē'ĭ-fôrm (W-O)

cup'board (kŭb'ẽrd)

cū'pṑ-lȧ (*not* -pȧ-lō)

cŭ-rā'tŏr

cu'ré' (kü'rā')

Çўc'lȧ-dēṣ

çўc'lȧ-mĕn

Çȳ-clṑ-pē'ȧn

Çȳ'clŏps ; *pl.* Çȳ-clō'pēṣ

çȳ'nṑ-sure (-shōōr, W ; sĭn'ṑ-sŭr, O)

dȧ-guerre'ṑ-tȳpe (-gĕr'-)

dahl'ia (däl'yȧ, W ; dä'lĭ-ȧ, *properly* dä'-, O)

dai'rў (dā'-, W ; dâr'-, O)

dăm'nȧ-ble

damn'ĭng (dăm'-; W-O)

Dăn'ǡ-ē

dăn'dĕ-lī-on (-ŭn)

Dān'ĭsh

Där-dȧ-nelles' (-nĕlz')

dā'tŭm ; *pl.* dā'tȧ (§ 402)

Dau'det' (dō'dĕ')

daugh'tẽr (dô'-)

dä Vin'ci (vēn'chē)

deaf (dĕf)

deaf'en (dĕf''n)

dĕ-bä'cle (W-O)

dĕ-bāte' (*n., v.*)

dé'bris' (dā'brē', W ; dā'brē, O)

dé'but' (dā'bü'; W-O)

dé'bu'tante' (dā'bü'täɴt')

dĕc'āde

dĕ-cā'dĕnçe (W ;
  dĕk'a-dĕns, O, *as*
  more scholarly ; *so*
  dĕc'a-dĕn-cў)

dé'col'le-té'
  (dā'kŏl'-tā')

dĕc'ŏ-rå-tĭve

dĕ-cō'roŭs (W-O)

dĕ-cō'rŭm

dĕ-crĕp'ĭt

dĕ-dūçe'

dē-făl'cāte

dē-făl-cā'tion (W-O)

dĕ-fĕct'

dĕf'ĭ-çĭt

dĕ-file' (*n.*, W ;
  dē'fĭl, O)

dĕ-file' (*v.* ; W-O)

Dĕl'hi (-ĕ ; *India*)

dĕ-lĭr'ĭ-oŭs

dĕ-lĭv'ĕr-ў

dĕ-lūde' (§ 421)

dĕ-lū'sion (-zhŭn)

dĕ lüxe'

dĕm-a-gŏg'ĭc

dĕm'a-gŏgue

dĕm'a-gŏg(u)-ĭşm [1]

dĕm'a-gŏg-ў (W ;
  -gŏg, O)[1]

dĕ-mesne' (-mān' ;
  W-O)

Dĕ-mē'tĕr

dĕ-mĭşe'

dĕ-mŏ'nĭ-ăc

dē-mŏ-nī'a-cál
  (W-O)

dĕm'ŏn-strāte (W ;
  dĕ-mŏn'-, O)

dĕ-mў' (*not* dĕm'ĭ)

dé-noue'ment
  (dā-nōō'mäⁿ ;
  W-O)

dē nō'vō

de'pot (§ 417)
  (dē'pō, W ;
  dĕp'ō, O)

dĕ-prē'ci-āte (-shĭ-)

dĕpths

dĕ-rī'sĭve

dĕ-sĭd-ĕr-ā'tŭm

Des Moines'
  (dĕ moin')

dĕs-pĕr-ā'dō

dĕs'pĭ-ca-ble

des-sert' (dĕ-zûrt')

dĕs'tĭne

dĕs'ue-tūde (-wĕ-)

dĕs'ŭl-tō-rў

dĕ-tāil' (*n., v.* ; W-O)

dĕ-tour' (-tōor')

Deū-tĕr-ŏn'ŏ-mў

dew (dū ; § 421)

dĕx'tĕr-oŭs

dī-a-bē'tēş

dī'a-mond (-mŭnd)

Dī-ăn'a (W-O)

dī-ăs'tŏ-lē

dĭc-tā'tŏr

dĭf'fĕr-ĕnçe

dĭf-fūse' (*a.* ;
  -fūşe', *v.*)

dĭ-ġĕs'tion (-chŭn)

dĭġ-ĭ-tā'lĭs

dĭl-ĕt-tăn'tĕ (W-O)

dĭ-ŏç'ĕ-sän (W-O)

dī'ŏ-çēse (W ; -sĕs, O)

Dī-ŏġ'ĕ-nēş

Dī-ŏ-nў'sŭs

dĭph-thē'rĭ-a (W-O)

dĭph'thŏng (W-O)

dĭ-plō'ma

dĭ-plō'ma-cў

dĭp'lŏ-măt

dĭ-rĕct'

dĭ-rĕc'tion

dĭş-ás'tĕr

dĭş'çī-plĭne

dĭs'count (*n., v.*, W ;
  v., dĭs-kount', O)

dĭs-cōurse' (*n., v.*)

dĭs-crēēt' (W-O)

dĭs-crĕp'ån-cў (W-O)

dĭs-crē'tion

dĭs-dāin'

dĭs-ha-bille'
  (-a-bēl' ; W-O)

dĭ-shĕv'eled (-ĕld)

dĭs-ĭn'ter-ĕst-ĕd

dĭs'pū-ta-ble (W-O)

Dĭş'rae'lĭ (-rā'-)

dĭ-văn'

dī'vĕrş

[1] *Demagoguism* and *pedagoguism* are more properly spelled with *u*, to indicate the hard sound of *g*; *demagogy* is more properly pronounced with the second *g* soft before *y*; see § 402.

dĭ-vẽrse' (W-O)

dĭ-vẽrt'

Dī'vē̦ṣ

do (dōō ; see due)

dŏç'ĭle (W ; dō'sĭl, O ; § 422)

doge (dōj)

dŏl'ce fär nien'te (-chä ; nyĕn'tā)

dŏll (not dôl)

dŏl'ŏr-oŭs

dŏl'ŏr-oŭs-lў

dŏ-māin'

dŏm'ĭ-çĭle (W-O)

dŏm'ĭ-nĭe (W-O)

don'key (dŏŋ'kĭ ; W-O)

Dŏn Quïx'ōte (Spanish dŏn kĕ-hō'tä)

Dŏr'ĭc

dôr'mouse

Dŏr-ŏ-thē'ȧ

Dos-to-ev'ski (dȧs-tȧ-yĕf'skĕ)

dŏt'ȧge

dō'tȧrd

doth (dŭth)

Do'the-boys (Hall) (dōō'thĕ-boiz)

douche (dōōsh)

drä'mȧ (W-O)

drăm'ȧ-tĭs pẽr-sō'næ (-nē)

draught (drȧft)

drought (drout)

drowned (dround)

Drȳ'burgh (-bŭr-ð)

dū'ȧl (§ 421)

dū'bĭ-oŭs

dŭc'ȧt

dŭc'tĭle (W-O)

due (dū ; § 421)

dū'ȧl (§ 421)

dŭ-ĕt' (§ 421)

dūke (§ 421)

Dü'mas' (-mä)

Dŭm-fries' (-frēs')

dū-ŏ-dĕç'ĭ-mō

dūpe (§ 421)

dŭ-plĭç'ĭ-tў

Du-quesne' (dōō-kān')

dū'rȧ-ble (§ 421)

dūr'ĭng (§ 421)

dū'tĭ-ȧ-ble (§ 421)

dū'tў (§ 421)

dȳ'nȧ-mīte (W-O)

dȳ'nȧs-tў (W ; dĭn'ȧs-, O)

dȳs-pĕp'sĭ-ȧ (W-O)

ĕb-ŭl-lī'tion

ĕ-ҫhī'nŭs ; pl. -nī

é'clat' (ā'klä')

ē-cŏ-nŏm'ĭc (W-O)

ĕc-ŭ-mĕn'ĭ-cȧl

ĕc'zĕ-mȧ

Ed'in-burgh (ĕd''n-bŭr-ð)

é'di'tion' de luxe' (ā'dē'syôN' dĕ lüks')

ĕd'ŭ-cāte

ē-dūçe'

ĕgg (not āg)

ĕg'lȧn-tīne (W-O)

ē-grē'gious (-jŭs ; W-O)

Eif'fel' (Tower, ĕf'ĕl')

ēi'thĕr (W-O)

Ĕl Dŏ-rä'dō

ĕ-lē'ġĭ-ăc (W ; ĕl-ē̦-jī'-, O)

Ĕl'gĭn (Marbles ; not -jĭn)

Ē'lĭ-ȧ (Essays of)

ē-lĭç'ĭt

é'lite' (ā'lēt')

Ē-lĭz-ȧ-bē'thȧn (W-O)

ĕlm (not ĕl'ŭm)

ē-lūde'

ē-lū'sĭve

Ē-lys'ĭ-ŭm (-lĭzh'-, W ; -lĭz'-, O)

ē-mā'ci-āte (-shĭ-)

Ĕm-mā'ŭs (W)

ĕm-ploy-ēē' (-ploi-) •

en'core' (adv., äN'kŏr', W ; -kŏr', O)

en-core' (v., äŋ-kōr', W ; äN-kŏr', O)

ĕn'dīve (W-O)

ĕn-dūr'ȧ-ble

ĕn'ẽr-vāte (v.; W-O)

ē-nẽr'vȧte (a.)

ĕn-gȧġe'

ĕn'ġĭne

en' màsse' (äN')
en'nui' (än'nwē')
en' pas'sant' (än' pä'sän')
en' rap'port' (än' rà'pŏr')
en' route' (än' root')
ĕn'sign (-sīn)
ĕn-sue' (-sū'; § 421)
en'tente' (än'tänt')
ĕn-thū'sĭ-ăsm
ĕn-tīre'
en'trée' (än'trā')
ē-nŭn'ci-āte (-shĭ-; W-O)
ē-nŭn-çi-ā'tion (W; -shĭ-, O)
ĕn'vĕ-lōpe (W-O)
Ĕp-ĭc-tē'tŭs
Ĕp-ĭ-cū-rē'ăn
Ē-pī'rŭs
ē-pĭt'ŏ-mē
ĕp-ĭ-zŏ-ŏt'ĭc
ĕp'ŏch (W-O)
ĕp'ŏch-ăl
ē'quà-ble (W-O)
ē-quà-nĭm'ĭ-tў
ē-quā'tion (W-O)
ē-quā'tŏr (§ 451)
ē-quà-tō'rĭ-ăl
ē-quĭ-lĭb'rĭ-ŭm
ē'quīne (W-O)
ē'quĭ-nŏx
ĕq'uĭ-pàge
ē'quĭ-poişe
ĕq'uĭ-tà-ble
ē-quĭv'ŏ-căl

ē-rāse'
ē-rā'sure (-zhŭr)
Ēr'à-tō
ere (âr; W-O)
ēr'mĭne
ērr
ĕr-rā'tŭm (§ 39)
ĕrr'ĭng (W-O)
ĕr'u-dīte (-ŏŏ-)
ĕr-u-dī'tion (-ŏŏ-)
ĕr-ў-sĭp'ē-làs
ĕs-cà-pāde'
ĕs'côrt (n.)
ĕs-côrt' (v.)
ĕs'pĭ-ŏ-nàge (W-O)
ĕs-plà-nāde'
es'prit' de corps' (ĕs'prē' dĕ kŏr')
Ēs'qui-mau (-kĭ-mō)
é'tude' (ā'tüd')
Eū-rō-pē'ăn
Eū-rўd'ĭ-çē
ēve'nĭng (W-O)
ĕv'ĕr-ў (W-O)
ĕv'ĕr-ў-bŏd-ў
ē'vil (-v'l)
ĕv-ŏ-lū'tion (W-O)
ex-ag'ger-āte (ĕg-zăj'ĕr-)
ĕx cà-thē'drà (W-O)
ĕx-cŭl'pāte (W; ĕks'kŭl-, O)
ex'em-pla-rў (ĕg'zĕm-plà-, W; ĕg-zĕm'plà-, O)
ĕx-ĕm'plī grā'ti-a (-shĭ-à; abbr. e.g.)

ex'it (ĕk'sĭt)
ĕx ŏf-fi'ci-o (-fĭsh'ĭ-ō)
ĕx-pē'rĭ-ĕnçe
ĕx-pĕrt' (a.)
ĕx'pĕrt (n.; W-O)
ĕx-ploit' (n., v.)
ĕx-pō'nĕnt
ĕx'quĭ-şĭte
ĕx'tănt (W; -tănt, O)
ĕx-tĕm'pŏ-rĕ
ĕx'tir-pāte (-tĕr-; W-O)
ĕx-tŏl' (W-O)
ĕx'trà (not -trĭ)
ĕx-traor'dĭ-nà-rў (-trôr'-, W; -nà-, O)
ex-ū'bĕr-ănçe (ĕgz-)
ex-ū'bĕr-ănt (ĕgz-)
Eyre (Jane; âr)

fà-çàde' (W-O)
fā'cial (-shăl, W; -shĭ-àl, O)
făç'īle
făc-sĭm'ĭ-lē
făc'tŏ-rў
fair'ў (fâr'-)
fal'chion (fôl'chŭn, W; -shŭn, O)
fal'con (fô'k'n, W; fôl'k'n, O)
fàn-tà-sī'à (-zē'-, W; -tà-zē'à, O)
fà-tigue' (-tēg')
faux' pas' (fō'pä')

fē′brĭle (W-O)

Fĕb′ru-à-rȳ (-rōō-)

fĕd′ĕr-ăl

fĕl′lōw (§ 421)

fête (fāt, W ; fât, O)

fĕt′ĭd (W-O)

fē′tĭsh (W ; fĕt′ĭsh, O)

fia′cre (fyà′kr)

fi′an-cé(e)′ (fē′äɴ′sā′)

fi-às′cō (fĕ-)

fief (fēf)

fi′ēr-ȳ (W ; fĭr′ĭ, O)

fĭl′lĕt

fĭlm

fi-na′le (fĕ-nä′lā)

fĭ′năl-lȳ

fĭ-nănçe′ (W-O)

fĭn-ăn-cier′ (-sēr′, W ; fĭ-năn′sēr, O)

fĭ-nĕsse′

fĭ′nĭs

fiord (fyôrd, W ; fyōrd, O)

flăc′çĭd

flăg′on (-ŭn)

fleur′-de-lis′ (flûr′dĕ-lē′); pl. fleurs′-de-lis′ (flûr′dĕ-lē′)

flŏr′ĭd

flō′rĭst (W ; flŏr′ĭst, O)

Foch (fŏsh)

fō′lĭ-ō (W-O)

Fon′taine′ (fôɴ′tĕn′)

fōōd (not fŏŏd)

fŏr-băde′

fŏr-beârs′ (W-O)

fōre′beârs (W-O)

fore′head (fŏr′ĕd ; W-O)

fōrġe (W-O)

fŏr′ġer (W-O)

fŏr′ġer-ȳ (W-O)

fôr′mĭ-dà-ble

fôrt′night (-nīt ; W-O)

fŏr-tū′ĭ-toŭs

fō′rŭm

foy′er′ (fwà′yā′)

Frán′çĕs

Frán′çĭs

frank′ĭn-çĕnse (frăŋk′-)

frăt′ĕr-nīze (W-O)

frḛ-quĕnt′ĕr

frŏn′tiēr (W-O)

Froude (frōōd)

fuch′si-a (fū′shĭ-à, W ; fū′shà, O)

fugue (fūg)

fŭl′crŭm

fŭl′some (-sŭm)

fun′gŭs (fŭŋ′-) ; pl. fŭn′gī, § 39

fū-ṣĭl-lāde′

Gael′ĭc (gāl′-)

gā′là

găl′ăx-ȳ

Găl-ĭ-lē′ō

găl′lănt (-lȳ)
brave (-lу) (W-O)

găl-lănt′ (-lȳ)
polite (-lу) (W-O)

găl′lows (-ōz ; W-O)

Găl′vĕs-ton (-tŭn)

găm′ŭt

gan′grēne (găŋ′-)

gan′grḛ-noŭs (găŋ′-)

gaol (jāl)

gäpe (W ; gāp, O)

gà′rage′ (′-räzh′)

gâr′ĭsh

găr′ru-loŭs (-ōō-)

găs′ḛ-oŭs (W-O)

gas′ō̇-line (-lēn ; W-O)

găs-trī′tĭs

găth′ēr

Gä-tun′ (Dam ; -tōōn′)

gaunt (gänt, W ; gônt, O)

Gei′kĭe (gē′-)

gen′därme′ (zhäɴ′- ; W-O)

ġĕn-ḛ-ăl′ō̇-ġȳ (W-O)

ġĕn′ĕr-ăl-lȳ

ġḛ′nĭ-ī

ġḛ′nĭ-ŭs (god ; W-O)

ġĕn′ius (ability ; -yŭs, W ; ġē′nĭ-ŭs, O)

Ġĕn′ō̇-à

gen′re (zhäɴ′r)

ġĕn′û-ĭne

ġē′nŭs ; pl. ġĕn′ḛ-rà

Geof′frey (jĕf′rĭ)

geor′gic (jôr′jĭk)

ġĕr′ŭnd

gĕt (*not* gĭt)

gey′sĕr (gī′-, W ;
  gā′-, O)

Ghent (gĕnt ;
  not jĕnt)

gher′kĭn (gûr′-)

ghet′to (gĕt′ō)

ghoul (gōōl)

giaour (jour)

ġĭb′bĕr (W-O)

ġĭb′bĕr-ĭsh (*not* jĭb′-)

ġĭb′bĕt

ġĭb′boŭs (*not* jĭb′-)

ġībe, jībe

ġĭb′lĕt

Gil Blas (zhēl bläs)

gil′ly-flow-ĕr
  (jĭl′ĭ-flou-)

ġĭ-ráffe′

ġĭst

glā′cial (-shăl,
  W ; -sĭ-ăl, O)

glā′cier (-shĕr, W ;
  glăs′ĭ-ĕr, O)

glăd′ĭ-ā-tôr

glȧ-dĭ′ŏ-lŭs (W ;
  glā-, O)

Glăd′stone (-stŭn)

glăm′our (-ĕr)

glŏb′ūle

Glouces′tĕr (glŏs′-)

glow′ĕr (glou′-)

glўç′ĕr-ĭn

gneiss (nīs)

gnome (nōm)

Gŏl′gŏ-thȧ

Gȯ-lī′ȧth

gŏn′dȯ-lȧ

goose′bĕr-rỹ (gōōz′-;
  W-O)

gôr′geous (-jŭs)

Gŏt′ham (-ăm ; *often,
  improperly,
  gō′thăm, O ; as
  applied to New
  York, gō′thăm or
  gŏth′ăm is usual
  in America*)

gov′ẽrn-mĕnt (gŭv′-;
  § 421)

Grȧ-mĕr′çỹ (Park)

grăn′ȧ-rỹ

grăn′deur (-dŭr)

grăn′dĭ-ōse (*not* -ōz)

grā′tĭs (*not* grăt′-)

grăt′ĭ-tūde

grȧ-tū′ĭ-toŭs

grēaṣ′ỹ (W-O)

Green′wich
  (grĭn′ĭj)

griēv′ănçe

griēv′oŭs

grĭ-māçe′ (*n., v.*)

grīm′ỹ

grīpe

grĭppe

grōat (W-O)

grŏv′el (-′l)

guar-ȧn-tēē′ (găr-)

guard (gärd)

guar′dĭ-ăn (gär′-)

guide (gīd)

guile (gīl)

guil′lo-tine (gĭl′ŏ-tēn,
  W ; gĭl-ȯ-tēn′, O)

guin′ea (gĭn′ĭ)

Güi′se′ (-ēz′)

Gui′zot′ (gē′zŏ′)

gŭm ăr′ȧ-bĭc

gŭn′wale (-ĕl ; W-O)

Guy de Mau′pas′-
  sant′ (gē dĕ
  mō′pȧ′säN′)

Gy′ges (jī′jēz)

ġўm-nā′ṣĭ-ŭm

hä′bĕ̀-ȧs côr′pŭs

Hä′dēṣ

Hague (hāg)

Hai-dēē′ (hī-)

Hăl-çỹ′ŏ-nē

hăl′ĭ-bŭt (W ; -bŭt,
  O)

halve (häv)

hand′kĕr-chĭef
  (hăŋ′-)

hand′some
  (hăn′sŭm ; W-O)

han′gär (häŋ′- ;
  French äN′gär′)

hăr′ăss (*not* hȧ-räs′)

hăr′ăss-ĭng

hä′rĕm (W ; härĕm,
  O)

här′lĕ-quĭn (W-O)

hăr′rōw (§ 421)

häṣ, hăve

häs′ten (-′n)

haunch (hänch, W ;
  hônsh, O)

haunt (hänt, W ;
   hônt, O)
hau-teur′ (hŏ-tûr′)
hĕad mȧs′tẽr
hearth (härth)
heav′en (hĕv′'n)
Hē′bĕ
Hĕc′ȧ-tē
hĕc′ȧ-tomb (-tŏm ;
   W-O) .
Hĕc′ụ-bȧ
hĕ-gĕm′ŏ-nў (W-O)
hĕg′ĭ-rȧ (W-O)
height (hīt)
hei′noŭs (hā′-)
hē′lĭ-ŏ-trōpe
hĕlm
hĕl′ŏt (W-O)
Hĕm′ȧnş (Mrs.)
Hĕr-ȧ-clē′ȧn
Hĕr-ȧ-clē′ŭm
hĕ-răl′dĭc
Hĕr-cū′lĕ-ȧn
hĕ-rĕd′ĭ-tȧ-ble
hĕr-ĕ-dĭt′ȧ-mĕnt
Hĕr′ĕ-fôrd
Hĕr-mĭ′ŏ-nē
Hĕ-rŏd′ŏ-tŭs
hĕ-rō′ĭn (drug)
hĕr′ŏ-ĭne
Hē′sĭ-ŏd
hĕş′ĭ-tāte (W-O)
Hĕs-pĕr′ĭ-dēş
hī-ā′tŭs
Hī-ȧ-wa′thȧ
   (-wô′-, W)
hĭc′cough (-ŭp)

hĭ′ẽr-ŏ-glўph′ĭc
hī-lā′rĭ-oŭs (W ;
   hĭ-lâr′ĭ-, O)
hī-lăr′ĭ-tў (W ; hĭ-,
   O)
Hī-mä′lȧ-yȧ
Hĭp-pŏc′rȧ-tēş
hĭs′tŏ-rў
hoarse (hōrs)
hoist (hoist)
hŏl′lō (not hŏl′ẽr)
hŏl′lōw (§ 421)
hŏl′ŏ-caust
Hōl′yōke
hŏm′ȧge
hō-mĕ-ŏ-păth′ĭc (W ;
   hŏm-, O)
hō-mĕ-ŏp′ȧ-thў (W ;
   hŏm-, O)
Hō-nō-lu′lu (-lōō′lōō)
hon-ŏ-rā′rĭ-ŭm (ŏn-)
hoof
hoop
hoo′poe (hōō′pōō ;
   W-O)
hŏ-rī′zon (-zŭn)
hors′ de com′bat′
   (hôr′ dĕ kôn′bä′,
   W ; hōr dĕ kŏn′-
   bä′, O)
hors′ d′œu′vre
   (hôr′ dû′vr)
hôrse′-răd-ĭsh
Hŏ-şē′ȧ
hŏs′pĭ-tȧ-ble
hŏs′tȧge
hŏs′tẽl-rў

hŏs′tler (-lẽr, W ;
   ŏs′lẽr, groom, O ;
   hŏst′lẽr, host, O)
hŏv′ĕl (W-O)
hov′ẽr (hŭv′- ; W-O)
Hū′gue-not (-gĕ-nŏt)
hŭm′ble
   (pronounce h)
hū′mĭd
hū′mŏr (W-O)
hŭn′drĕd
hus-sär′ (hŏŏ-)
Hў′ȧ-dēş
hў-drăn′gĕ-ȧ
hў′gĭ-ēne (W-O)
hў-gĭ-ĕn′ĭc (W-O)
hў-mĕ-nē′ȧl
hў-pĕr′bŏ-lē
hў-pŏc′rĭ-sў
hў-pŏt′ĕ-nūse
hўs′sop (-ŭp)
hўs-tē′rĭ-ȧ

ĭ-bī′dĕm (abbr. ĭb′ĭd.)
-ide, § 422
ĭ-dē′ȧ (not ĭ′-dĕ-ȧ)
ĭ-dĕn′tĭ-cȧl
ĭ-dĕn′tĭ-fў
ĭd-ĭ-ŏ-syn′crȧ-sў
   (-sĭŋ′- ; not -sĭn′-)
ī′dўl
ĭ-dўl′lĭc
ĭg-nŏ-rā′mŭs
Īk Mär′vĕl
-ile, § 422
Ĭl′ĭ-ȧd
ĭl-lĭç′ĭt

Ĭl-lĭ-nois' (-noi')
ĭl-lū'mĭ-nāte
ĭl-lū'sion (-zhŭn)
ĭl-lū'sō-rў
ĭl-lŭs'trāte (W; ĭl'ŭs-trāt, O)
Il Pĕn-sĕ-rō'sō (ĕl)
ĭm'åge-rў
ĭm'bĕ-çĭle (W-O)
ĭm-bro'glio (-brŏl'yō)
ĭm-mē'dĭ-āte-lў
ĭm-pē'rĭ-ăl
ĭm'pĭ-oŭs
ĭm'pĭ-oŭs-lў
ĭm-plā'cå-ble (W-O)
ĭm-pŏr-tūne' (W-O)
ĭm'pŏ-tĕn-çў
ĭm'pŏ-tĕnt
ĭm-prŏmp'tŭ
ĭm-prŏv'ĭ-sā'tion (W; -zā'-, O)
ĭm-prŏ-viṣe'
ĭn-aug'ŭ-rāte
ĭn'chŏ-āte (a.)
ĭn-çī'sĭve
ĭn-cŏg'nĭ-tō
ĭn-cŏm'på-rå-ble
ĭn-crĕ-dū'lĭ-tў
ĭn'cŭl-pāte (W-O)
ĭn-dĕ-cō'roŭs (W-O)
ĭn-dĕ-cō'rŭm
Ĭn'dĭ-ăn
ĭn-dict' (-dīt')
ĭn-dĭg'ē-noŭs
ĭn-dĭs'pŭ-tå-ble (W-O)
ĭn-dĭs'sŏ-lŭ-ble (W-O)

ĭn-dĭ-vĭd'ŭ-ăl
ĭn-dūçe'
ĭn'dūs-trў
-ine, § 422
ĭn-ēr'ti-å (-shĭ-)
ĭn-ĕv'ĭ-tå-ble
ĭn-ĕx'ō-rå-ble
ĭn-ĕx'plĭ-cå-ble
ĭn'få-moŭs
ĭn'făn-tīle (W-O)
ĭn'fī-nīte
ĭn'flu-ĕnçe (-floo-)
in'gŏt (ĭŋ'-; W-O)
ĭn-hŏs'pĭ-tå-ble
ĭn-lāid' (W; ĭn'lād, O)
ĭn'lāy'(n.,W; ĭn'lā,O)
ĭn-lāy' (v.)
ĭn-lāy'ĭng (W-O)
ĭn-quīr'ў (not ĭn'-kwĭr-ĭ)
ĭn'sect (-sĕkt)
ĭn-sīd'ĭ-oŭs
ĭn stā'tū quō
ĭn-stĕad'
ĭn'stĭ-tūte
ĭn-stĭ-tū'tion
ĭn'sŭ-lår
ĭn'sŭ-lāte
ĭn'tĕ-ġĕr
ĭn'tĕ-grål
ĭn-tĕr'cå-lå-rў
ĭn'tĕr-ĕst-ĕd
ĭn'tĕr-ĕst-ĭng
ĭn-tĕr-lŏc'ŭ-tŏr
ĭn-tĕr-mez'zō (-mĕd'-)

ĭn-tĕr'stĭçe (W-O; pl. -tĕr'stĭ-çĕṣ)
ĭn'trĭ-cå-çў
ĭn-trigue' (n., v., -trēg'; W-O)
ĭn-trō'ĭt
ĭn'ŭn-dāte (W-O)
ĭn'vå-lĭd (W; ĭn-vå-lēd', O)
ĭn-văl'ĭd (not valid)
ĭn-veigh' (-vā')
ĭn-vei'gle (-vē'-)
ĭn'vĕn-tŏ-rў
Ī'ō-wå
Ī'ō-wăn
Ĭph-ĭ-ġĕ-nī'å
ĭ-rāte' (W-O)
Ī-rene' (-rēn', W)
Ī'rĭs
ĭ-rī'tĭs
ĭ'ron (-ŭrn)
ĭr-rĕc-on-çĭl'å-ble (-ŭn-; W-O)
ĭr-rĕf'rå-gå-ble
ĭr-rĕ-fūt'å-ble (W-O)
ĭr-rĕl'ĕ-vånt
ĭr-rĕ-mē'dĭ-å-ble
ĭr-rĕp'å-rå-ble
ĭr-rĕv'ō-cå-ble
I-sa'iah (ī-zā'yå, W; -zī'å, O)
ĭ'sŏ-lāte (W-O)
ī-sŏ-lā'tion (W-O)
ī-sŏ-thĕr'măl
ĭs'sue (ĭsh'ŭ)
isth'mŭs (ĭs'-, W; ĭsth'-, O)

Ĭ-tăl′ian (-yăn)

ĭ-tăl′ĭc

ĭ-tăl′ĭ-çīze

ĭ-tĭn′ĕr-ȧ-rȳ

-ĭ′tĭs (*not* -ē′tĭs; tŏn-
   sĭl-lī′tĭs, *etc.*)

ĭ′vȯ-rȳ

Ĭx-ĭ′ŏn

Jā′nᴜ̆s

Jā′phĕth

jar′di-nière′
   (zhȧr′dē′nyȃr′)

jăs′mĭne

jăve′lĭn (W; jăv′ĕ,
   O)

Jean Val′jean′ (zhäɴ
   vȧl′zhäɴ′)

jĕ-june′ (-jōōn′; W-
   O)

Jē′kȳll (Doctor)

Joan (jōn)

Joa-quin′ (wä-kēn′)

jŏc′ᴜ̆nd (W-O)

jōwl (W-O)

Jŭg′gĕr-naut

ju′gŭ-lᴀ̆r (jōō′-)

ju′jut′su
   (jōō′jōōt′sōō)

Ju′lĭ-ĕt (jōō′-)

ju′rȳ (jōō′-)

jŭs′tĭ-fī-ȧ-ble

ju′vĕ-nīle (jōō′-, W;
   -nĭl, O; § 422)

Kĕn-nĕ-bĕc′

Kĕn-tŭck′ȳ

kĕpt (*not* kĕp)

kĕr′chief (-chĭf)

kĕr′ȯ-sēne

kha′ki (kä′kĕ̇)

kiln (kĭl; W-O)

kĭl′ȯ-mē-tēr

knew (nū; § 421)

knoll (nōl)

knowl′edge (nŏl′ĕj;
   W-O)

Kȯ̇-rän′ (W-O)

Kos-ci-ŭs′kō (kŏs-ĭ-)

kraal (krăl; W-O)

lăb′ȯ-rȧ-tŏ-rȳ

lȧ-cŏn′ĭc

L′ Al-le′grō (läl-lā′-)

lăm′ĕn-tȧ-ble

lăn′dau (-dô; W-O)

lan′guid (lăŋ′gwĭd)

lan′guish (lăŋ′gwĭsh)

lan′guor (lăŋ′gĕr;
   W-O)

Lă-nier′ (Sidney)

Lȧ̇-ŏc′ȯ-ŏn

Lȧ̇-ŏd-ȧ-mī′ȧ

Lȧ̇-ŏd-ĭ-çē′ȧ

lȧ-pĕl′

lā′pĭs lăz′ᴜ̇-lī (W;
   lăp′ĭs, O)

lăp′sᴜ̆s lin′guæ
   (lĭŋ′gwē)

lā′rēṣ

lăr-ȳn-ġī′tĭs

lȧ-ryn′go-scope
   (-rĭŋ′gȯ̇-skōp)

lăr′ȳnx (W-O)

lȧst (*not* lăs)

lā′tĕnt

Lăt′ĭn

lăt′tĭçe

lä′vȧ

leaped (lēpt)

leapt (lĕpt)

lĕg (*not* lāg)

lĕg′ȧte

le-gä′tō (lā-)

lĕg′ĕnd (W-O)

lĕg-ĕr-dĕ-māin′

lĕg′ĭs-lȧ-tĭve

lĕg′ĭs-lȧ-tᴜ̆re

lĕg′ᴜ̆me (W-O)

Leices′tĕr (lĕs′-)

lei′sure (lē′zhᴜ̆r, W;
   lēz′ᴜ̆r, O)

lĕngth

lē′nĭ-ĕnt (W-O)

Lĕ̇-ŏn′ĭ-dᴀ̆s

lē′ȯ̇-nīne

leop′ärd (lĕp′-)

Les Mi′sé′rables′
   (lā mē′zä′rȧ′bl)

lĕ̇-thär′ġĭc

Lē′thē

lĕt′tuce (-ĭs)

Lĕ̇-vănt′

lĕv′ee (-ĕ̇, *embank-
   ment*, W; lĕ̇-vē′,
   O)

lĕv-ēē′ (*reception*,
   W; lĕv′ĕ̇, O)

lē′vĕr (W-O)

lĭb′ĕr-tĭne

lĭ′brȧ-rў
lĭ′chĕn (W-O)
lĭc′ŏ-rĭçe
lief (*not* lēv)
lĭ′ĕn (lē′-; W-O)
lieu (lū, W; lōō, O)
lieu-tĕn′ȧnt (lŭ-, W;
   lĕf-, O)
lĭ′lăc
li-mou-sine′ (lē-mōō-
   zēn′)
lĭn′ē-ȧ-mĕnt
lin′guĭst (lĭŋ′-)
lĭn′ĭ-mĕnt
Lĭn-næ′ȧn (-nē′-)
lĭn′ŏ-tӯpe (W-O)
lĭs′ten (-′n)
lĭt-ė̇-rā′tī
lĭt-ė̇-rā′tĭm
lĭt′ēr-ȧ-tŭre
līthe
līthe′some (-sŭm)
lĭ-thŏg′rȧ-phēr
lĭ-thŏg′rȧ-phў
lit′té′ra′teur′
   (lē′tā′rȧ′tûr′)
lĭve′lŏng
lōath, lōth
lōathe
lŏn-ġĕv′ĭtў
lŏng′līved
lŏ-quā′cious
lŏ-quăç′ĭ-tў
Lōs An′ġĕl-ĕs (ăŋ′-,
   W)
Lou′is-vĭlle (lōō′ĭs-,
   W)

Lou′vre (lōō′vr)
lōw′ēr (*v.*, *let down*)
low′ēr (lou′-, *frown*)
lū′çĭd
Lū′çĭ-fēr
Lū′çў
lū′dĭ-crous
lŭ-gū′brĭ-ous
Lūke
lŭll′ȧ-bӯ
lū′nȧ-tĭc (§ 421)
lūre
lū′rĭd
lūte
lŭx-ū′rĭ-ous (W-O)
lӯ-çē′ŭm
Lӯ-cûr′gŭs
ly′on′naise′ (lē′ŏ′-
   nâz′; *Anglicized*,
   lĭ-ŏ-nāz′)

Mä-chia-vel′li
   (-kyä-vĕl′lē)
Măch-ĭ-ȧ-vĕl′lĭ-ȧn
măch-ĭ-nā′tion
Mȧ-dei′rȧ (-dē′-)
mȧ-drȧs′
mael′strŏm (māl′-)
Mae′ter-linck
   (mä′tēr-lĭŋk)
măg-ȧ-zine′ (-zēn′)
Mag′da-len (*college*;
   môd′lĭn, *current*
   in England)
Mā′ġī
Măg′nȧ €härtȧ
măg′nĭ-tūde

măg-nō′lĭ-ȧ
Mag′yar (mŏd′yŏr,
   W; mȧd′yȧr, O)
Mȧ-hŏm′ĕt
māin-tāin′ (W-O)
māin′tė-nȧnçe
mȧ-lā′rĭ-ȧ
mȧ-lign′ (-līn′)
mȧ-lĭg′năn-çў
mȧ-lin′gēr (-lĭŋ′-)
mall (môl; *see* Pall
   Mall)
mȧm-mä′ (W-O)
Măn-chu′ (-chōō′)
măn-dā′mŭs
mā′nēṣ
măn′gў
mā′nĭ-ȧ
mȧ-nĭ′ȧ-căl
măn-ŭ-mĭt′
măr-ȧ-schi′nō (-skē′-)
măr′chion-ĕss
   (-shŭn-)
Măr-cō′ni (-nē)
Măr′di gras′ (-dĕ
   grä′)
măr′ĭ-tīme (W-O)
măr′mȧ-lāde
măr′quĭs
măr-quise′ (-kēz′)
Măr-sĕ-illaise′ (-lāz′;
   French măr′sĕ′yâz′)
măr′vĕl
măs′sȧ-cre (-kĕr)
măs′sȧ-cred (-kĕrd)
mas-sage′ (mȧ-säzh′,
   W; mă-säzh′, O)

Măs′sȧ-soit

măt′ĭn

mat-i-née′ (măt-ĭ-nā′,
  W; măt′ĭ-nā, O)

mā′tron (-trŭn)

mau-sŏ-lē′ŭm

měad′ōw (§ 421)

Mě-dē′ȧ

Měd′i-ci (-ĕ-chē)

mě-dĭç′ĭ-nȧl

mē-dĭ-ē′vȧl (W;
  měd-ĭ-, O)

mē′dĭ-ŏ-cre (-kĕr)

mē-dĭ-ŏc′rĭ-tȳ

mě′dĭ-ŭm

Mě-dū′sȧ

mě′lée′ (mā′lā′)

měl′lōw (§ 421)

Měl-pŏm′ě-nē

měm′oirs (-wŏrz, W;
  -wŏrz, O)

mě-năg′ěr-ĭe (W-O)

Měn-ě-lā′ŭs

měn-ĭn-gĭ′tĭs

měn′ū (W; mě′nü′,
  O)

měr′căn-tĭle (W;
  -tĭl, O; § 422)

mé′sal′liance′
  (mā′zȧl′yäns′)

Mes′dames′
  (mā′dȧm′; § 529)

měṣ′měr-ĭṣm

Mes′sieurs
  (měs′yĕrz; abbr.
  Messrs., but pron.
  as before; § 529)

mět′ȧl-lûr-ġȳ

mět′rĭc

mě-trŏp′ŏ-lĭs

mět-rŏ-pŏl′ĭ-tăn

měz′zȧ-nĭne (W;
  -nēn, O)

mez′zo (měd′zō)

mez′zō-sŏ-prä′nō
  (měd′-)

mez′zō-tĭnt (měd′-;
  W-O)

Mī′chael (-kĕl)

Mĭch′ael-mȧs (-ĕl-)

mĭ′crō-cŏṣm (W-O)

mī-crŏm′ě-tĕr

mĭ-crŏs′cŏ-pȳ (W-O)

Mī′dȧs

milch (mĭlch)

mĭl′ĭ-tă-rĭṣm

mĭ-li′tia (-lĭsh′ȧ)

mĭn′ȧ-rět

mĭn-ēr-ăl′ŏ-ġȳ

mĭn′ĭ-ȧ-tŭr (W-O)

mĭn′-ute (n., v., -ĭt)

mĭ-nūte′ (a.; W-O)

mĭ-nū′ti-æ (-shĭ-ē)

mĭ-răc′ŭ-loŭs

mi-rage′ (mē-räzh′)

mĭs-ȧl-li′ȧnçe

mĭs′ăn-thrōpe

mĭs-ăn-thrŏp′ĭc

mĭs′chief (-chĭf)

mĭs′chie-voŭs (-chĭ-)

mĭs-cŏn′strue
  (-strōo; W-O)

mĭṣ′ĕr-ȧ-ble

mĭ-sŏġ′ȳ-nĭst

mĭs′sile (-ĭl)

Mĭs-sou′rĭ (-sōō′-)

mĭs-tle-tōe (-′l-; W;
  mĭz′-, O)

mne-mŏn′ĭc (nē-)

mō′bĭle (W-O)

mō′bĭ-līze (W-O)

mō′dŭs ŏp-ĕ-răn′dĭ

mō′dŭs vĭ-věn′dĭ

mŏ-gŭl′

Mŏ-hăm′měd-ȧn

Mŏ-hī′căn (-hē′-)

mois′ten (-′n)

mŏ-lěc′ŭ-lȧr

mŏl′ě-cūle (W-O)

Mŏn′ȧ-cō

mŏn′ăd

mŏ-när′chȧl

mŏ-när′chĭ-ȧl

mŏ-när′chĭc

mŏ-när′chĭ-cȧl

mŏn′är-chȳ

mŏn′ě-tȧ-rȳ (W;
  -tȧ-, O)

Mon-gō′lĭ-ȧn (mŏŋ-)

mon′grĕl (mŭŋ′-)

mŏn′ŏ-grăm

mŏn′ŏ-gráph

mŏn′ŏ-lŏgue

mŏn-ŏ-mā′nĭ-ȧ

mŏn-si′gnor
  (-sē′nyôr, W;
  mŏn-sě-nyôr′, O)

Mŏn-tä′nȧ

Mont′Blanc′ (môn′
  blän′)

mŏ-rále′

mŏr'ĭ-bŭnd
Môr'pheus (-fūs)
mort'găge (môr'-)
Mŏs'cōw
moun'tain (-tĭn)
mŭlch (W; mŭlsh, O)
mulct (mŭlkt)
mŭl'tĭ-tūde
mŭl'tʉm ĭn pär'vō
Mŭ-rĭl'lō (Spanish
  moo-rēl'yō)
mŭr'rain (-ĭn)
mŭ-ṣē'ʉm
mŭsh'rōōm
mū-ṣĭ-càle'
mŭsk'mĕl-on (-ʉn)
mʉs-tache' (-tàsh',
  W; mōōs-, O)
mȳs-tē'rĭ-oʉs
mȳ-thŏl'ŏ-gȳ

nā'iad (-yăd, W;
  -ăd, O); pl. nā'ia-
  dēṣ (-yà-, W;-à-, O)
na-ïve' (nä-ēv')
na'ïve'té' (ná'ēv'tä')
Nā'ŏ-mī (W)
nāpe (not năp)
năph'thà (W-O)
när'g(h)ĭ-lĕ
năr-rāte' (W-O)
năr'rōw (§ 421)
năs'cent (-ĕnt)
năs-tûr-tium (-shʉm,
  W; -shĭ-ʉm, O)
nā-tà-tō'rĭ-ʉm
nā'tà-tō-rȳ

nā'tion
na'tion-ăl (năsh'ʉn-)
naught (nôt)
nau'se-à (-shĕ-; W-O)
nau'seous (-shʉs;
  W-O)
Nau-sĭc'ä-à
nĕç'ĕs-sà-rĭ-lȳ
née (nā)
né'gli'gé'
  (nā'glē'zhä'; W-O)
nĕg-lĭ-gee' (-zhā', W)
nei'thĕr (nē'-; W-O)
Nĕm'ĕ-sĭs
neph'ew (nĕf'ū, W;
  nĕv'ū, O)
nē plŭs ŭl'trà
nĕp'ŏ-tĭṣm
Nē'rĕ-ĭd
nĕs'tle (-'l)
nĕst'lĭng (W-O)
neu-răl'gĭ-à (nŭ-)
neu-rī'tĭs (nŭ-)
neu'tĕr (nū'-)
neu'trăl (nū'-)
Nĕ-vä'dà
new (nū; § 421)
New'found-lănd
  (n., nū'fʉnd-)
New-found'lănd
  (dog; a., nŭ-)
New Ôr'lĕ-ănṣ (nū)
news'pā-pĕr (nūz'-)
Nī-ăg'à-rà
nī'çĕ-tȳ
niche (nĭch)
nī'hĭl-ĭst

Nĭn'ĕ-veh (-vĕ)
Nī'ŏ-bĕ
Nō-bĕl' (prizes)
nŏ'blĕsse' ŏ'blige'
  (-blēzh')
nō'bŏd-ȳ
nŏm'ăd (W-O)
nŏ-mäd'ĭc
nom' dĕ plüme'
  (nôN')
nō'mĕn-clā-tʉre
  (W-O)
nŏn'cha-lànçe
  (-shà-; French
  nôN'shà'läNs')
nŏn-pà-reil' (-rĕl')
nŏs'trʉm
nō'tà bē'nē
nō'tà-rȳ
nŏv'ĕl
nŏv'ïçe
nō-vŏ-cā'ïne (W)
nox'ious (nŏk'shʉs)
Nū'bĭ-à
nūde (§ 421)
nui'sànçe (nū'-)
nū'mĕr-ăl
nū'mĕr-oʉs
nŭp'tial (-shăl)
nŭ-trī'tion
nū'trĭ-tĭve

ō-ā'sĭs (W-O)
ōat'mēal
ŏb-bli-gä'tō (-blĕ-)
ŏb'lĭ-gà-tō-rȳ (W;
  -tĕr-ĭ, O)

ŏb-lique′ (-lēēk′;
  W-O)
ŏb-nox′ious
  (-nŏk′shŭs)
ŏb-scen′ĭ-tўĭ (-sĕn′-)
ŏb′sĕ-quies (-kwĭz)
ŏb-sē′quī-oŭs
ŏb-tūse′
ŏc-cŭlt′
ŏc-cŭlt′ĭşm
Ŏ-çē′à-nŭs
ŏc-tā′vō (W-O)
ŏc′tŏ-pŭs (W ;
  ŏk-tō′-, O ; ŏk-
  tō′pŭs *is etymo-
  logically correct*)
ọ̆-dē′ŭm
Ŏ-dўs′seus (-ūs)
Ŏd′ys-sey (-ĭ-sĭ)
Œd′ĭ-pŭs (ĕd′-, W ;
  ē′dĭ-, *in England*)
ŏf′ten (-′n)
ō′gle (-g′l)
Ŏ-hī′ō
Ō-klà-hō′mà
ō-lĕ-ăn′dẽr
ō-lĕ-ọ̆-mär′gà-rine
  (-rēn; *not* -jẽr-)
ŏl-fäc′tŏ-rў
ŏl′ĭ-gär-chў
Ō′màr Khay-yam′
  (khī-yäm′, W)
ọ̆-mē′gà (W ; ō′mĕ-
  gà, O)
ŏn′ẽr-oŭs
on′-ion (ŭn′yŭn)
ōn′lў

ŏn′ўx (W-O)
ŏp-pō′nĕnt
ŏp-pŏr-tūne′ (W-O)
ôr′chĕs-trà
ŏr-chĕs′trăl (W-O)
ôr′chĭd
ôr′dĕ̆-ăl (W-O)
ôr′dĭ-nă̆-rĭ-lў (W ;
  -nà-, O)
Ō′rĭ-ĕnt
ŏr′ĭ-fîçe
Ŏ-rī′ŏn
ŏr-nāte′ (W-O)
ō′rŏ-tŭnd (W-O)
Ôr′pheus (-fūs)
ôr′thŏ-ĕ̆-pў (W ; -ē-,
  O)
ō′sier (-zhẽr)
Ŏ-sī′rīs
ŏs′tĕ-ọ̆-păth
ŏs-tĕ-ŏp′à-thў
Ō-tà-hei′tĕ̆ (-hē′-)
ō′ti-ōse (-shĭ-; *not*
  -ōz)
ō′vẽr-alls (-ôlz)
ō′vẽrt
ō′vẽr-tŭre
Ŏv′ĭd

păch′ў-dẽrm
păç-ĭ-fĭ-cā′tion (W-
  O)
Păc-tō′lŭs
păg′ẽant (W-O)
păg-ĭ-nā′tion
pà-lā′tial (-shăl)
Pà-lăt′ĭ-nāte

Păl′ĕs-tīne
păl′ĕtte
pal′frey (pôl′frĭ; W-
  O)
Pal′grāve (pôl′-)
păl′lĭ-à-tĭve
Pall Mall′ (pĕl mĕl′)
păn-à-çē′à
Păn-à-mä′
păn-ĕ-gўr′ĭc
păn-ŏ-rä′mà (W-O)
păn-thē′ŏn (W ; -ŏn,
  O)
păn′tŏ-mīme
pà-pä′ (W-O)
pā′pà-çў
pa′pier′-mâ′ché′(pà′-
  pyä′mä′shä′, W ;
  pà′pyä-mä′shä, O)
pä′pri-kà (-prĕ-)
pà-pў′rŭs; *pl.* -rī
păr′à-chute (-shōōt)
păr′à-digm (dĭm; W-
  O)
păr′ăf-fín
pâr′ĕnt
pâr′ĕn-tăġe
păr′ĕ-sĭs (*not* pà-rē′-)
pär ex′cel′lence′
  (ĕk′sĕ′läns′)
pä′rī-àh (W ; pâr′ĭ-,
  O)
pà-rī′ĕ-tăl
pär′lia-mĕnt (-lĭ-)
pär-quet′ (-kā′, W ;
  -kĕt′, O)
pär′tial (-shăl)

pär-ti-ăl'ĭ-tў (-shĭ- ;
  W-O)
pär'tial-lў (-shăl-)
pär'tĭ-çĕps crĭm'ĭ-nĭs
pär-tĭc'ŭ-lȧr-lў (W ;
  pȧr-, O)
pärt'nẽr
pär'trĭdġe
pȧ-shä' (W ; pȧsh'ȧ,
  O)
Pȧs'teur' (-tûr')
pȧs'tẽur-īze (W-O)
pā'tĕnt (O, in all
  senses ; = open, W)
păt'ĕnt (right, W)
păt'ent (n., v., W)
pȧ-tẽr'năl
pā'thŏs
pȧ'tois' (-twä', W ;
  -twà', O)
pā'trĭ-ŏt (W-O)
pā-trĭ-ŏt'ĭc (W-O)
pā'trĭ-ŏt-ĭşm (W-O)
pā'tron (-trŭn ; W-
  O)
păt'ron-age (-rŭn-āj,
  W ; rŏ-nĕj, O)
păt'ron-ize (-rŭn-īz,
  W ; -rŏ-nīz, O)
pē-căn' (W-O)
pĕd-ȧ-gŏg'ĭc
pĕd'ȧ-gŏgue
pĕd'ȧ-gŏg(u)-ĭşm
  (see footnote on
  page 273)
pĕd'ȧ-gō-ġў (W ;
  -gŏj-ĭ, O)

pĕd'ĕs-tăl
Pĕg'ȧ-sŭs
Pē'lĕg
pĕl-lū'çĭd
pē'năl
pē'năl-īze
pĕn'ăl-tў
pē-nā'tēş
Pē-nĕl'ŏ-pē
pĕn-ĭn'sŭ-lȧ
pĕn-ĭ-ten'tia-rў
  (-tĕn'shȧ-)
pĕn'knife' (-nīf')
Pĕnn-sўl-vā'nĭ-ȧ
pĕn-tăm'ē-tẽr
pē'nŭlt (W ; pē-
  nŭlt', O)
pē'ŏ-nў
Pepys (pēps, W)
pẽr ăn'nŭm
pẽr căp'ĭ-tȧ
pẽr'cŏ-lā-tŏr
pẽr dĭ'ĕm
pẽr'ĕmp-tŏ-rĭ-lў (W ;
  -ĕmp-tẽr-ĭ-lĭ, O)
pẽr'ĕmp-tŏ-rў (W ;
  -ĕmp-tẽr-ĭ, O)
pẽr'fĕct (v.; W-O)
per'fĕct-ĕd (W-O)
pẽr'fĕct-ẽr (W-O)
pẽr'fĕct-ĭng (W-O)
pẽr-fūme' (v.)
pẽr'fūme (n.; W-O)
pẽr'gō-lȧ
pẽr-ĭm'ē-tẽr
pē'rī-ŏd
pẽr-ĭ-tŏ-nē'ŭm

pẽr-ĭ-tŏ-nī'tis
pẽr'mĭt (n.)
pẽr-mĭt' (v.)
Pẽr-sĕph'ŏ-nē
Pẽr'seus (-sūs, W)
Per'sian (pûr'shăn ;
  W-O)
pẽr-sĭst' (not -zĭst')
pẽr-sĭst'ĕnçe
pẽr-sŏn-nĕl' (W-O)
pĕt'ăl
pet'it (jury, pĕt'ĭ)
pĕt'rĕl
Pet-ro-grad'
  (pyĕ-trŏ-grät')
pē-tū'nĭ-ȧ
Phæ'dō (fē'-)
Phā'ē-thŏn
phā'lanx (-lănks,
  W; făl'-, O)
Phā'raoh (-rō, W ;
  fâr'ō, O)
Phī Bē'tȧ Kăp'pȧ
Phĭd'ĭ-ȧs
phĭ-lăn'thrŏ-pў
Phĭ-lē'mŏn
Phĭ-lĭs'tĭne (W ;
  fĭl'ĭs-tīn, O)
Phĭl-ŏc-tē'tēş
phĭ-lŏl'ŏ-gў
phŏn'ĭcs (W; fō'nĭks,
  O)
phŏs'phŏr-ŭs
phŏ-tŏg'rȧ-phẽr
phŏ-tŏ-grȧ-vūre'
  (W-O)
phthi'sĭs (thĭ'-)

phỹ-sique′ (-zēk′)

pĭ-ăn′ĭst (W ; pē′a̍-
 nĭst, O)

pièce′ de ré′sis′-
 tance′ (pyĕs′ dĕ
 rā′zēs′täns′)

pĭ-lăs′tēr

pĭl′lōw (§ 421)

pĭn′çĕr̯s

pi′quan-çỹ (pē′kăn-)

pi′quant (pē′kănt)

Pĭ-sĭs′tra̍-tŭs

pĭs-tā′chi-o (-shī-ō ;
 W-O)

plā′ca̍-ble (W-O)

plăc′ärd (n., W ;
 -a̍rd, O)

plāgue (not plĕg)

plăid (W ; plād, O)

plāit (W-O)

plĕ̍-bē′ian (-yăn)

plĕb′ĭ-scite (-sĭt)

plĕb̯s

Ple′ia-dēs̯
 (plē′ya̍-, W ; plĭ′a̍-,
 O)

plē′na̍-rỹ (W-O)

Plȳm′outh (-u̍th)

pneu-mō′nĭ-a̍ (nŭ-)

pō′ĕm

poign′ănt (poin′-)

pō-lŏ-nāis̯e′ (W ;
 pŏl-ŏ-, O)

pŏ-māde′ (W-O)

pom′mĕl (pŭm′-)

pŏm′pa̍-dour (-dōͦr)

Pŏm-pe′ii (-pā′yē)

pŏn′iard (-ya̍rd)

pōor

pôr′çĕ-lȧin (W ;
 pōr′sĕ-, O)

pōrch

pôr′poise (-pu̍s)

Pôr′sĕ-na̍

pŏrte′-cŏ′chère′
 (-shâr′)

pŏr′tière′ (-tyâr′)

Pōrt Sä-id′ (-ēd′)

pōr′trăit

pōr-trāy′

pōr-tŭ-lā′ca̍ (W-O)

Pŏ-sei′dŏn (-sī′-)

pos-sess′ (pŏ-zĕs′ ;
 W-O)

post′hu-mou̯s
 (pŏs′tŭ- ; W-O)

pōst-pōne′

pōst′scrĭpt

pō-tā′tō

pot′pour′ri′
 (pō′pōͦ′rē′ ; W-O)

pŏt′shĕrd

pŏt′tĕr-ĭng (pŭt′tĕr-
 ing is dialectal ;
 common in U. S.)

poul′trỹ (pōl′-)

Pow-ha̍-tăn′ (pou-)

prāi′rĭe (W ; prâr′ĭ,
 O)

Prăx-ĭt′ĕ̍-lēs̯

prĕ̍-çēd′ĕnçe

prĕ̍-çĕd′ent (a.)

prĕç′ĕ̍-dĕnt (n.)

prĕ̍-çīse′

prĕ̍-cō′cious

prĕ̍-cŏç′ĭ-tỹ

prĕd′a̍-tŏ-rỹ

prĕd-ĕ̍-çĕs̯′sŏr (W ;
 prē-dĕ̍-, O)

prĕ̍-dīc′a̍-mĕnt

prĕf′açe (n., v.)

prĕf′ĕr-a̍-ble

prē′fĭx (n.)

prĕ̍-fīx′ (v.)

prĕl′a̍te

prĕl′ūde (n.; W-O)

prĕ̍-lūde′ (v., W ;
 prĕl′ūd, O)

prē-ma̍-tūre′ (W-O)

prē′mĭ-ĕr (W ;
 prĕm′ĭ-, O)

prĕm′īse (n.)

prĕ̍-mīse′ (v.)

prē-mŏ-nī′tion

prĕp-a̍-rā′tion

prĕ̍-păr′a̍-tŏ-rỹ

prĕ̍-pŏs′tĕr-ou̯s

prĕs′a̍ge (n.; W-O)

prĕ̍-sāge′ (v.)

prē′sci-ĕnçe (-shĭ- ;
 W-O)

prĕs̯-ĕn-tā′tion

prĕ̍-sĕn′tĭ-mĕnt
 (not -zĕn- ; W-O)

prĕs̯-tige′ (-tēzh′ ;
 W-O)

prĕ̍-s̯ūme′

prĕ̍-s̯ŭmp′tŭ-ou̯s

prĕ̍-tĕnse′, prĕ̍-tĕnçe′

prē′tĕxt

pret'tў (prĭt'-)

prĕ-vĕn'tĭve (*not*
pre-ven'ta-tive)

pri'ma dŏn'na (prē'-;
W-O)

prī'ma fā'ci-e (-shĭ-ē)

prī'mă-rĭ-lў

prĭm'ẽr

prĭs'tĭne (W-O)

prĭth'ee (-ĕ)

prĭv'ĕt

prĭv'ĭ-lў

prŏb'a-blў

prŏb'ĭ-tў (W-O)

prŏç'ĕss (W-O)

Prŏ-crŭs'tĕ-ăn

prŏc'ŭ-rā-tŏr

prŏ-di'gious (-dĭj'-ŭs)

prŏd'ūçe (*n.*)

prŏ-dūçe' (*v.*)

prō'fīle (W ; -fēl, O)

prŏ-fūse' (*not* -fūz')

prō'grăm (*not* -grăm;
W-O)

prŏg'rĕss (*n.*, W ;
prō'grĕs, O)

prŏ-grĕss' (*v.* ; W-O)

prŏj'ĕct (W-O)

prō'lĭx (W-O)

prŏm-ĕ-näde' (W-O)

Prŏ-mē'theus (-thūs)

prŏ-nŭn-çĭ-ā'tion
(W-O)

prŏ-pin'quĭ-tў (-pĭŋ'-)

prŏ-pĭ'ti-āte (-shĭ-)

prŏ-pĭ-ti-ā'tion (-shĭ-)

prō rā'ta

Prŏ-sẽr'pĭ-na

Prŏs'ẽr-pĭne

prŏs'pĕct (*n.*, *v.*)

Prō'tĕ-ăn (W-O)

prŏ'té'gé(e)'
(-tā'zhā')

prō'tĕ-ĭd

prō'tĕ-ĭn

prō tĕm'pŏ-rē

prŏt-ĕs-tā'tion

Prō'teus (-tūs)

prŏ-vī'şō

prŏ-vŏc'a-tĭve (W-
O)

prŏv'òst (W-O)

prŭs'sĭc

psalm (säm)

Psal'tẽr (sôl'-)

pseu'dŏ-nўm (-sū'-)

Psy'chĕ (sī'-)

psy'chĭc (sī'-)

Ptol'ĕ-mў (tŏl'-)

pto'ma-īne (tō'-, W ;
-īn, O ; *not* tō'mān)

Puc-ci'ni (pōōt-
chē'nē)

pud'ding (pŏŏd'ĭng)

pueb'lō (pwĕb'-)

pū'ẽr-īle (W ; -ĭl, O ;
§ 422)

pū'ĭs-sănçe (W-O)

pū'ĭs-sănt (W-O)

pŭmp'kĭn

pū'nĭ-tĭve

pŭ-rĭf'ĭ-ca-tŏ-rў

pûr'pōrt (*n.*, *v.*, W ;
v., pûr-pōrt', O)

păr-sue' (-sū')

păr-suit' (-sūt')

put (pŏŏt)

Pўl'a-dēş

pў-răm'ĭ-dăl

pў-rī'tēş

pў-rŏ-tech'nĭcs (W-
O)

Pў-thăg'ŏ-răs

Pў-thăg'ŏ-rē'ăn

quad-rī'ga (kwŏd-)

quad'ru-ple
(kwŏd'rŏŏ-)

quăg'gў

quăg'mīre

quar'an-tine (*n.*, *v.*,
kwŏr'ăn-tēn ; W-
O)

quash (kwŏsh)

quā'sī

quay (kē)

quẽr'u-loŭs (-ŏŏ-, W ;
-yŏŏ-, O)

quē'rў

ques-tion-naire'
(kwĕs-chŭn-âr',
French kĕs-
tyŏ'nâr' ; W)

qui'nĭne (W ; kwĭ-
nēn', O)

Quĭr'ĭ-năl

Quĭ-rī'năs

Quĭ-rī'tēş

qui vive' (kē vēv')

quĭx-ŏt'ĭc

quoit (W ; koit, O)

răb'bī (W-O)

rā'bī-ĕş

rā'cial (-shǎl, W; -shī-ǎl, O)

răd'ĭsh (*not* rĕd'-)

rȧ-gout' (-gōō')

rāil'lĕr-ў (W-O)

rai'son' d'ê'tre (rĕ'zôɴ' dâ'tr)

Răm'ĕ-sēş

rămp'ǎnt

ran'cŏr (răŋ'-)

Răph'ā-ĕl (W)

răp'ïne

rȧth'ĕr (W; răth'-, O)

rā'ti-ō (-shĭ-; W-O)

rā'ti-ŏç'ĭ-nā'tion (răsh'ĭ-)

rā'tion (W-O)

ră'tion-ǎl

rē'ǎl (*not* rēl)

rē'ǎl-īze

rē'ǎl-lў

rĕ-bāte' (*n., v.*)

rĕ-call' (*n., v.,* -kôl')

rĕ-cĕss' (*n., v.*)

rĕç'ĭ-pē

rĕç'ĭ-tȧ-tive' (*n.,* -tēv')

rĕc-lȧ-mā'tion

rĕ-cluse' (*a., n.,* -klōōs')

rĕc'ŏg-nīz-ȧ-ble

rĕ-cŏg'nĭ-zǎnçe (W-O)

rĕc'ŏg-nīze

rē-cŏl-lĕct' (*collect again*)

rĕc-ŏl-lĕct' (*call to mind*)

rĕc'ŏn-çĭl-ȧ-ble

rĕc'ŏn-dīte (W-O)

rĕ-cŏn'nois-sance (-ĭ-sǎns; W-O)

rĕc-ŏn-noi'tĕr

rē-cōurse'

rēc'rē-ǎnt

rĕc'rē-āte (*refresh*)

rē-crē-āte' (*create again*)

rĕc'tĭ-tūde

rĕ-drĕss' (*n., v.*)

rĕ-dūçe'

rĕf'ĕr-ȧ-ble

rĕf'ĕr-ĕnçe

rē'flĕx (*a., n.;* W-O)

rĕf'lu-ĕnt (-lōō-)

rĕf'ūse (*n.; not* -ūz)

rĕ-fuse' (-fūz')

rĕ-fūt'ȧ-ble

rĕ-gǎt'tȧ (*not* -gĕt'-)

ré'gime' (rā'zhēm')

rĕg'ǔ-lǎr

Reims, Rheims (rēmz; *French* rāɴs)

rĕ-lāy' (*a., n., v.;* W-O)

rĕ-lin'quĭsh (-lĭŋ'-)

rĕ-mē'dĭ-ȧ-ble

rĕ-mŏn'strāte

rĕn-ais-sance' (-ĕ-säns', W; rĕ-nā'sǎns, O)

ren'dez-vous (räɴ'dĕ-vōō, W; rĕn'dĕ-vōō, O)

rĕ-new' (-nū')

rĕ-nŭn-çĭ-ā'tion (W-O)

rĕp'ȧ-rȧ-ble

rĕp-ȧr-tēē'

rĕ-pȧst'

rĕp'ĕr-toire (-twär)

rĕp'ĕr-tŏ-rў

rĕp-ĕ-tĭ'tion

rĕp'lī-cȧ

ré'pon'dez' s'il vous plait' (rā'pôɴ'dā' sēl vōō plē'; *abbr.* R.S.V.P.)

rĕp'rĭ-mȧnd (*n., v.,* W; *v.,* rĕp-rĭ-mȧnd', O)

rĕp'tĭle (W-O)

rĕp'ǔ-tȧ-ble

rē'quĭ-ĕm (W-O)

rĕ-quĭt'ǎl

rere'dŏs (rēr'-)

rĕ-sēarch' (*n., v.*)

rĕş'ĕr-voir (-vwôr, W; -vwär, O)

rĕş'ĭ-dūe

rē-şil'ĭ-ĕnçe

rē-şil'ĭ-ĕn-çў

rĕş'ŏ-lūte

rĕş-ŏ-lū'tion

rĕ-sōurçe'

rĕ-spīr'ȧ-tŏ-rў (W; -tĕr-ĭ, O)

rĕs'pīte (*n., v.*)

rĕs′tau-rănt (-tŏ-,
 W ; -tŭ-, O)
ré′su′mé′ (rā′zü′mā′)
rĕ-ṣŭmp′tion
rē′tāil (a., n.)
rĕ-tāil′ (v.)
rĕ-tāil′ĕr (W-O)
rĕt′ĭ-çĕnçe
rĕt′ĭ-çĕnt
rĕt′ĭ-nūe
rĕ-trĭb′ŭ-tĭve
rĕt′rŏ-çēde (go back ;
 W-O)
rĕt′rŏ-grāde (W-O)
rĕ-trŏ-gres′sion
 (-grĕsh′ŭn ; W-O)
rĕt′rŏ-spĕct (W-O)
rĕ-veil′le (-vāl′yà ;
 W-O)
rĕv′ĕ-nūe
rĕv′ŏ-cà-ble
rĕ-vōlt′ (n., v. ; W-O)
rĕv-ŏ-lū′tion
Rheims (see Reims)
rĭb′àld
rĭg′ĭd
rĭnd (not rīn)
rĭnse (not rĕns)
Ri′ō Grän′de (rē′-,
 -dā)
Rĭp′ŏn
rĭṣe (n., v. ; W-O)
rĭṣ-ĭ-bĭl′ĭ-tў
rĭṣ′ĭ-ble
Ri-vie′ra (rĕ-vyâ′rä)
Rŏb′särt (Ā′mў)
rŏ-bŭst′

Rŏ-get′ (-zhā′)
roil′ў (not rīl′-)
rôle (rōl)
rŏ-mănçe′ (a., n., v.)
Rŏm′ŏ-là
Rŏm′ŭ-lŭs
rōof (not rŏŏf)
rōom (not rŏŏm)
rōot (not rŏŏt)
Rouen (rwäN)
Rous′seau′ (rōō′sō′)
rout (rout)
route (rōōt ; W-O)
rou-tine′ (rōō-tēn′)
rŭf′fĭ-ăn (W-O)
ruse (rōōz)
Rus′sia (rŭsh′à)
Rus′sian (rŭsh′ăn)
rŭs′tle (-′l)
Ruy Blas′ (rwē bläs′)

săb′à-ŏth (W)
sà′bot′ (-bō′)
sà′bŏ′tage′ (-täzh′)
săc′ehà-rīn (W ;
 -rīn, O)
săç-ĕr-dō′tăl
sā′chĕm (W-O)
Sa′cō (sô′-)
săc′rà-mĕnt
săc′rĭ-fĭçe (n. ; W-O)
săc′rĭ-fice (v., -fīz,
 W ; -fīs, O)
săc′rĭ-lege (-lĕj)
săc-rĭ-lē′ġioŭs (not
 -lĭj′ŭs)
săc′rĭs-tăn

săc′rĭs-tў
sà-gā′cious
Sà-hä′rà
said (sĕd)
Sầint Au-gŭs′tīne
 (person ; W)
Sầint Au′gŭs-tine
 (-tēn ; town)
Sầint Lou′is (lōō′ĭs,
 W)
Saint′-Mi′hiel′
 (săN′ mē′yĕl′)
Săl′à-dĭn
săl′à-rў
Săl′ĭc
săl-ĭ-çўl′ĭc
sā′lĭ-ĕnt
sā′line (W-O)
săl′ĭ-và-rў (W ; -và-,
 O)
salm′on (săm′ŭn)
sà′lon′ (-lôN′)
sà-lū′brĭ-oŭs
sà-lū′tà-tŏ-rў (W ;
 -tĕr-ĭ, O)
salve (n., säv)
sang′-froid′ (säN′-
 frwä′)
san′guĭne (săŋ′-)
sā′pĭ-ĕnt
Sap′phic (săf′ĭk)
Sap′pho (săf′ō)
sär-cō′mà
sär-cŏph′à-gŭs; pl.-ġī
Sär′dà-nà-pā′lŭs
sär-dine′(-dēn′; W-O)
sär-dŏn′ĭc

sär'dŏ-nȳx

sär-s*a*-p*a*-rĭl'l*a*

sā'ti-āt-ĕd (-shĭ-)

s*a*-tī'ĕ-tȳ

săt'ĭn

săt'īre (W-O)

sā'trăp (W-O)

Săt'*u*r-d*a*̇y

săt'ȳr (W-O)

sau'çȳ

s*a*̇'vant' (-vän');
pl. -vants' (-vän')

says (sĕz)

scal'loped (skŏl'*u*pt;
W-O)

scăr'*a*b

sce-nä'rĭ-ō (shā-;
Anglicized, sė-)

sce'nĭc (sē'-; W-O)

scep'tĕr (sĕp'-)

schĕd'ûle (W; shĕd'-,
O)

Sche-he'r*a*-zä'dĕ
(shĕ-hā'-)

Schĕ-nĕc't*a*-dȳ

schĕr'zo (-tsō)

schism (sĭz'm)

schist (shĭst)

schot'tische (shŏt'ĭsh,
W; shŏ-tēsh', pre-
vailing pronuncia-
tion, but having no
justification, O)

Schuyl'kĭll (skōōl'-)

sci-ăt'ĭ-c*a* (sī-)

scil'ĭ-çĕt (sĭl'-; abbr.
scil., sc.)

scin'tĭl-lāte (sĭn'-)

sci'on (sī'*u*n)

Scit'*u*-āte (sĭt'-)

scle-rŏt'ĭc (sklĕ-)

Scyl'la (sĭl'*a*)

scythe (sīth)

sēam'-strĕss

sé'änçe (sā'-, W;
sā'äns', O)

Sė-ăt'tle

sĕck'el (-'l; pear)

sĕc'rė-t*a*-rȳ (W;
-t*a*-, O)

sė-crē'tŏ-rȳ (W;
-tĕr-ĭ, O)

sĕd'*a*-tīve

seis'mĭc (sīs'-, W;
sīz'-, O)

seis'mŏ-grăph (sīs'-,
W; sīz'-, O)

seis-mŏg'r*a*-phȳ (sĭs-,
W; sīz-, O)

Sĕm'ė-lē

Sė-mír'*a*-mĭs

Sĕm'īte

sē'nīle (W-O)

sĕp'*a*-rāt-ĕd

sĕp-*a*-rā'tion

Sĕp'tŭ-*a*-gĭnt

sĕp'*u*l-chĕr

sĕp'*u*l-tûre

sē'quĕnçe

se-ragl'io (sė-răl'yō,
W; sė-räl'yō, O)

Sĕr-*a*-pē'*u*m

sė-răph'ĭc

Sė-rā'pĭs

sér'geant (sär'jĕnt)

sē'ries (-rēz, W; -rĭ-
ēz, O)

sĕr'pĕn-tīne (W-O)

sĕr'vīle (W; -vĭl, O;
§ 422)

sĕr'vĭ-tūde

sĕs'*a*-mė

sĕv'ĕr-*a*l

sew'*a*̇ġe (sū'-)

shăd'ŏw (§ 421)

Shăng-hä'ĭ

shän't

Shē'chĕm

sheik (shēk, W;
shāk, O)

shĕk'el (-'l,W; -ĕl, O)

shew (show, shō; in
the Bible)

shĭb'bŏ-lĕth

shōne (W; shŏn, O)

shrewd (shrōōd; pro-
nounce h)

shriek (shrēk)

shrill (shrĭl)

shrine (shrīn)

shrink (shrĭŋk)

shŭt (not shĕt)

sĭb'ȳl

sĭb'ȳl-līne (W-O)

sĭd'ĕr-īte (W-O)

Sien-kie'wicz (shĕn-
kyä'vĭch)

sī-ĕs't*a*

sĭg'n*a*-tûre

si'gnor (sē'nyŏr)

si-gno'ra (sė-nyō'rä)

sĭl-hou-ĕtte' (-ōō-)
sĭm'ĭ-làr
sĭm'ĭ-lē
sī-mŭl-tā'nĕ-oŭs (W; sĭm'ŭl-, O)
sĭnçe (*not* sĕns)
sī'nĕ-cūre
sī'nĕ dī'ē
sī'nĕ quā nŏn
sĭn'ew (-ū)
sĭn'ĭs-tēr
Sinn Fein (shĭn fān)
Sioux (sōō)
sī'rĕn
Sïr'ï-ŭs
sī-rŏc'cō
sïr'ŭp, sўr'ŭp
Sïs'ў-phŭs
sĭt (*not* sĕt)
skein (skān)
ski, ski'ĭng (skē-, W; shē-, O)
slāke (*not* slăk)
slāv'ēr-ў
slēa'zў (W-O)
slēek (*not* slĭk)
slĕpt (*not* slēp)
slōth (W-O)
slōth'ful (W-O)
slough (*skin*, slŭf)
slough (*v.*, slŭf)
slough (*bog*, slou)
sluice (slōōs)
snout (*not* snōōt)
so'brĭ'quet' (sŏ'brē'kā', W; sō'brĭ-kā, O)

sō-cia-bĭl'ĭ-tў (-sha-; W-O)
sō'cia-ble (-sha-; W-O)
sō-ci-ŏ-lŏg'ĭc (-shĭ-)
sō-ci-ŏl'ŏ-gў (-shĭ-)
sŏf'ten (-'n)
soi'rée' (swa'rā'; W-O)
sō'joûrn (*n., v.*, W; sŭj'ērn, O)
sŏl'åçe (*n., v.*)
sol'der (sŏd'ēr, W; sŏl'dēr, O)
sōl'dier (-jēr)
sŏl'ĕ-çĭşm (W-O)
sŏl'emn (-ĕm)
sŏl-ĭ-tâire'
sŏl'ĭ-tūde
sŏl'stĭçe
sọ̆-lū'tion
sŏm-bre'rō (-brā'-)
some'bŏd-ў (sŭm'-)
sŏm-năm'bŭ-lĭst
sọ̆-nä'tà
sọ̆-nō'roŭs
sōōn (*not* sŏŏn)
sŏŏt (W-O)
Sŏph'ĭst
sŏph'ĭst-rў
sō-pŏ-rĭf'ĭc (W-O)
sŏr'rŏw (§ 421)
sōt'tō vō'ce (-chä)
sough (*n., v.*, sŭf; W-O)
soup (sōōp; *not* sŏŏp)

soûth'ēr-lў
sou-ve-nir' (sōō-vĕ-nēr'; W-O)
sŏv'ēr-eign (-ĭn, W; sŏv'rĕn, O)
spăn'iel (-yĕl)
spăr'rŏw (§ 421)
spe'cial-tў (spĕsh'ăl-)
spē'cie (*coin*, -shĭ; W-O)
spē'cies (-shēz; W-O)
spĕc-tā'tŏr
spĕc-trŏs'cŏ-pў (W-O)
spĕc'ū-lāte
spēr-mà-çē'tĭ (W-O)
sphe'roid (sfē'-)
spĭn'ach (-ảj; W-O)
spī-ræ'à (-rē'-)
spīr'ĭt
splĕ-nĕt'ĭc (W-O)
Spō-kane' (-kăn')
spō'lĭ-à ŏ-pī'mà
spŏn-tà-nē'ĭ-tў
spōōn (*not* spŏŏn)
squal'ĭd (skwŏl'-)
squal'ŏr (skwŏl'-; W-O)
stàc-cä'tō
stàff; *pl.* stāveş, stàffs (W-O; § 26, N.)
stà-lăc'tīte
stà-lăg'mīte
stā'mĕn; *pl.* stăm'ĭ-nà, stā'mĕnş (§ 39)

stăt′ĭcs

stȧ-tĭs′tĭcs

stā′tŭs ĭn quō

stăt′ūte

stĕad′ў̄

stĕ-ăr′ĭc

stē′ȧ-rĭn

stĕppe

stĕr-ĕ-ŏp′tĭ-cŏn (W ;
  -cŏn, O)

stĕr′ĕ-ŏ-tȳpe (W-O)

stĕr′īle (W ; -ĭl, O ;
  § 422)

stew (stū)

stew′ărd (stū′-)

stĭr′rŭp (W-O)

stō′ĭ-çĭşm

stŏl′ĭd

stom′ach (stŭm′ŭk)

stom′ach-er
  (stŭm′ŭk-ĕr, W ;
  -ȧ-chĕr, O)

stŏ-măch′ĭc

stōne (*not* stŭn)

stŏn′ў̄

Strā′bō

strȧ-tē′gĭc (W ;
  -tĕj′ĭc, O)

străt′ĕ-gĭst

străt′ĕ-gў̄

Străt′fŏrd-ŏn-Ā′vŏn

strā′tŭm (§ 402)

strĕngth

striped (*participle,*
  strīpt)

striped (*a.*, strīpt; W-
  O)

stripped (strĭpt)

strўch′nĭne (W ;
  -nēn, O)

Stū′ȧrt (§ 421)

stū′dĕnt

stū′dĭ-ō

stū′dĭ-o*ŭ*s

stū′pĕ-fȳ

stū-pĕn′do*ŭ*s

stū′pĭd

stū-pĭd′ĭ-tў̄

stū′pŏr

suave (swāv ; W-O)

suave′nĕss (swāv′-)

suav′ĭ-tў̄ (swăv′-)

sŭb-dūe′ (§ 421)

sŭb-lū′nȧr

sŭb′lŭ-nȧ-rў̄ (W ;
  -nȧ-, O)

sŭb-sīd′ĕnçe (W-O)

sŭb′tīle (W ; sŭt′ĭl,
  O)

sub′tle (sŭt′′l)

sub′tly (sŭt′lĭ)

sŭb′ûrb

sŭb-ûr′bȧn

sŭc-cinct′ (-sĭŋkt′)

sŭch (*not* sĭch)

sūe (§ 421)

suède (swād ; *French*
  swĕd)

Sue-tō′nĭ-*ŭ*s (swē-)

sŭf-fīçe′ (W-O)

sŭg-gĕst′ (W ; sŭ-
  jĕst′, O)

sū′ĭ-cīd-ȧl

sū′ĭ ġĕn′ĕ-rĭs

suit (sūt; § 421)

suit′ȧ-ble (sūt′-)

suite (swēt)

sŭl′phāte

sŭl′phĭde (W-O)

sŭl′tȧn

sū′măc (W-O)

sŭmp′tŭ-o*ŭ*s

sŭ-pĕr′flu-o*ŭ*s (-floō-)

sŭ-pīne′ (*a.*; W-O)

sŭ-pīne′nĕss

sŭp′ple

sŭr-mīşe′ (*n., v.*)

sŭr-prīşe′ (*not* sŭ-
  prīz′)

sûr′vey(*n.,*-vā; W-O)

sŭr-vey′ (*v.,* -vā′)

sŭs-pĕct′ (*n., v.*)

sū′tŭre

swal′low (swŏl′ō ;
  § 421)

swath (swôth ; W-O)

swāthe (*v.*)

swĕpt (*not* swĕp)

sword (sōrd)

sў̄c′ō-phănt

sў̄l-lăb′ĭc

Sym′onds (J. A. ;
  sĭm′*ŭ*nz, W)

Sў̄m-plĕġ′ȧ-dēş

sў̄m-pō′şĭ-*ŭ*m

syn′chrŏ-no*ŭ*s (sĭŋ′-)

syn′cŏ-pāte (sĭŋ′-)

sў̄n′dĭ-cȧl-ĭşm

sў̄n′dĭ-cȧl-ĭst

sў̄n′od (-*ŭ*d)

sў̄n′ō-nўm

sȳ-rĭn'gȧ (-rĭn̄'-)
sȳr'ĭnġe
sȳs'tŏ-lē

tăb'leau (-lō, W ;
    tȧ'blō', O) ; *pl.*
    -leaux (-lōz, W ;
    tȧ'blōz', O)
ta'ble d'hôte'
    (tá'bl dōt', W ;
    tä'bl, O)
tăç'ĭt
tăç'ĭ-tûrn
Tä-gä'lŏg
Tä'hi-ti (-hē-tē)
Tä-hi'tĭ-ăn (-hē'-)
Täm-pi'cō (-pē'-)
Tăn'ȧ-grȧ
Tăn'tȧ-lŭs
tăp'ĕs-trȳ
tä'pir (-pēr)
tȧ-răn'tŭ-lȧ
tär-pau'lĭn
Tär-pē'ia (-yȧ)
Tär-pē'ian (-yăn)
tär-tär'ĭc
Tär'tȧ-rŭs
Tăṣ-mä'nĭ-ȧ
tăs'sel (-'l)
tau-tŏl'ŏ-ġȳ
tăx'ĭ-dẽr-mĭst
tēat (*not* tĭt)
tĕch-nique' (-nēk')
Tē Dē'ŭm
tē'dĭ-oŭs (W-O)
tē'dĭ-ŭm
tēeth'ĭng

Tĕl'ȧ-mŏn
tĕ-lĕg'rȧ-phẽr (W ;
    tĕl'ĕ-grȧf-, O)
tĕ-lĕg'rȧ-phȳ (W-O)
Tĕ-lĕm'ȧ-ċhŭs
tĕl-ĕ-păth'ĭc (W-O)
tĕ-lĕp'ȧ-thȳ (W-O)
tĕ-lĕph'ŏ-nȳ (W-O)
tĕ-lĕs'cŏ-pȳ (W-O)
tĕm'pẽr-ȧ-mĕnt
tĕm'pẽr-ȧ-tŭre
tĕm'pŏ-rȧ-rĭ-lȳ (W ;
    -rȧ-, O)
tĕ-nä'cious
tĕn'ĕt
tĕn'ūre
tē'pēē (W-O)
tĕp'ĭd
Tẽrp-sĭċh'ŏ-rē
tẽrp'sĭ-ċhŏ-rē'ăn
tẽr'rȧ cŏt'tȧ
tẽr-rāin' (W-O)
Tẽr'rē Haute' (hōt')
tẽr'rĭ-ble
tẽr'rŏr
tĕs-tä'tŏr
tĕt'ȧ-nŭs
tête'-à-tête' (tāt'ȧ-
    tāt', W ; -ȧ-, O)
tĕt-răġ'ŏ-nȧl
tē'träreh (W ;
    tĕt'rärk, O)
tĕt'rärch-ȳ
Teu'çẽr (§ 421)
tĕx'tĭle (W-O)
Thȧ-lī'ȧ
Thames (tĕmz)

thanks-gĭv'ĭng
    (thăŋks-)
thē'ȧ-tẽr
Thē'mĭs
Thē-mĭs'tŏ-clēṣ
thĕnçe
Thē-ŏċ'rĭ-tŭs
Thẽr-mŏp'ȳ-læ (-lē)
thē-sau'rŭs
Thĕs'sȧ-lŏ-nī'cȧ
Thē'tĭs
thĭs'tle (-'l)
thĭ'thẽr
thought (thôt)
Thrăs-ȳ-bū'lŭs
three'-lĕg-gĕd (W ;
    -lĕgd, O)
three'pence
    (thrĭp'ĕns ; W-O)
three'pen-ny
    (thrĭp'ĕn-ĭ ; W-O)
thrĕsh
thrĕsh'ōld
Thŭ-çȳd'ĭ-dēṣ
thyme (tīm)
tĭ-ā'rȧ (W ; tē-ä'-, O)
tĭ'nȳ
tĭ-rāde' (W-O)
tis'sue (tĭsh'ŭ)
tīthe
Tī'tian (tĭsh'ăn)
tŏl'ẽr-ȧ-ble
Tol-stoy' (-stoi')
tŏ-mä'tō (W ; -mä'tŏ,
    O)
to-mŏr'rŏw
    (tŏŏ-; § 421)

tŏn-sĭl-lī'tĭs

tŏp-ŏ-grăph'ĭc

tŏ-pŏg'rȧ-phў

tŏr-nā'dō

tôr'toise (-tŭs; W-O)

tŏt'tĕr-ĭng

tour (tōōr)

tour' de force'
(tōōr' dĕ fôrs')

tour'nȧ-mĕnt (tōōr'-;
W-O)

tō'ward (-ẽrd; W-O)

trä'chē-ȧ (W; trȧ-
kē'ȧ, O, etymo-
logically correct)

Trăf-ăl-gär' (cape)

Trȧ-făl'gȧr (Square;
in London)

trăg'ȧ-cănth

tran'quil (trăn'-)

trăn'sient (-shĕnt)

trăns-lū'çĕnt

trăns'mĭ-grāte

trăns-mĭ-grā'tion

trăns-pâr'ĕnt

trăv'ail (-ăl)

trăv'ail-ĭng (-ăl-)

trăv'ĕl

trăv'ĕl-ẽr

trăv'ẽrse (a., n., v.)

trea'cle (trē'k'l)

trĕ'ble (not trĭ'-)

trĕk

trĕ-mĕn'doŭs

trē'mŏr (W; trĕm'ŏr,
O)

trȇ-păn'

trĕs'tle (-'l)

Trī-ăs'sĭc

trī-bū'năl

trĭb'ūne

trī-chī'nȧ

trĭch-ĭ-nī'ȧ-sĭs

trĭch-ĭ-nō'sĭs

trī'çў-cle

trī-ĕn'nĭ-ăl

trĭm'ĕ-tĕr

trī'ō (trē'-; W-O)

trī-pär'tīte (W-O)

trī'pŏd

Trī'tŏn

trĭv'ĭ-ăl

trōpe

trō'phў

trŏth (W; trōth, O)

trous'seau' (trōō'sō')

trōw (not trou)

trŭc'ŭ-lĕnt (W;
trōō'kŭ-, O)

trŭf'fle (W-O)

trŭst'wor-thў (-wûr-)

trŷst (W; trĭst, O)

tūbe'rōs̟e' (W; in-
correct, says O;
tū'bĕr-ōs, O)

Tūes̟'dăy

tū'lĭp (§ 421)

tū'mŏr (§ 421)

tū'mŭlt (§ 421)

tūne (§ 421)

tûr'bĭne (W-O)

tûr'gĭd

tŭr-quoise' (-koiz';
W-O)

tū'tĕ-lȧ-rў (W; -lȧ-,
O)

tū'tŏr (§ 421)

tut'ti-frut'ti (tōōt'tĕ-
frōōt'tĕ)

two'pence (tŭp'ĕns;
W-O)

two'pen-ny (tŭp'ĕn-ĭ;
W-O)

Tŷn'dăle

tŷ-răn'nĭ-căl (W;
tī-, O)

tŷr'ăn-nīze

tŷr'ăn-nў

tŷ'rō

Ū-lўs'sēs̟

ŭm-bĭ-lī'cŭs (W-O)

ŭm-brĕl'lȧ

ŭm'pīre

ŭn-ăc-çĕnt'ĕd

ŭn-ăs-sūm'ĭng

ŭn-bāt'ĕd

ŭn-çĭv'ĭl

ŭn'dĕr-ground

ŭn'dĕr-hănd-ĕd

ŭn-dĕr-nēath'

ŭn-dĕr-signed'
(-sīnd')

ŭn'dŭ-lȧ-tŏ-rў (W;
-tĕr-ĭ, O)

ŭn-ĕn-dūr'ȧ-ble

ŭn-ẽrr'ĭng (W-O)

ŭn-frē-quĕnt'ĕd

ŭn-ĭn'tĕr-ĕst-ĭng

ŭn-jŭs'tĭ-fī-ȧ-ble

ŭn-prĕç'ē-dĕnt-ĕd

ŭn-tū'tŏred
ŭn-wā'rў (W; -wâr'ĭ, O)
ŭp'mōst
ŭp'right (-rīt)
ŭp-rĭş'ĭng
Ū'rȧ-nŭs
ûr'băn
ûr-bāne'
ûr-băn'ĭ-tў
Ûr'sŭ-lȧ
ūşed to (too̅; *not* ūs tŭ)
ū'su-ăl (-zhŭ-)
ū'su-ăl-lў (-zhŭ-)
ū'şŭ-frŭct
ů-şûrp'
Ū-tō'pĭ-ȧ
ŭt'tĕr-ănçe

văc'çĭne (W; -sīn, O)
vȧ-cū'ĭ-tў
văc'ŭ-ŭm
vā'dĕ mē'cŭm
vȧ-gā'rў
văl'ĕn-tīne
văl'ĕt (W-O)
văl'ŭ-ȧ-ble
van'quĭsh (văŋ'-)
văp'ĭd
văr'ĭ-cōse (*not* -cōz)
vā'rĭed (W; vâr'ĭd, O)
vā'rĭ-ĕ-gāt-ĕd (W; vâr-ĭ-, O)
vȧ-rī'ŏ-lȧ

vā'rĭ-ŏ-loid (W; vâr'ĭ-, O)
vā'rĭ-oŭs (W; vâr'ĭ-, O)
vā'rў (W; vâr'ĭ, O)
vāse (W; văz, O)
văs'ĕ-līne (W; -ĕ-lēn, O)
vaude'vĭlle (vōd'-; W-O)
vĕg'ĕ-tȧ-ble
vē'hĕ-mĕnçe (W; vē'ĕ-, O)
Ve-lás'quez (vā-läs'kāth)
vĕn'ēr-ȧ-ble
vē'nī, vĭ'dī, vĭ'çī
vē'nĭ-ăl
Vĕn'īçe
vĕn'ĭ-son (-z'n, W; vĕn'z'n, O)
vē'noŭs
vĕn-trĭl'ŏ-quĭşm
vĕ-rā'cious (W; vĕ-, O)
vĕ-răç'ĭ-tў (W; vĕ-, O)
vĕ-răn'dȧ (W; vĕ-, O)
vĕr-bā'tĭm
vĕr'bĭ-âge
vĕr-bōse' (*not* -bōz')
vĕr-bŏs'ĭ-tў
vĕr'dĭ-gris (-grēs, W; -grĭs, O)
vĕr'dŭre
vĕr-mi-çĕl'lĭ (-mĕ-, W; -mĭ-, O)

vĕr-mĭl'ion (-yŭn)
Ve-ro-ne'se (Paul; vā-rŏ-nā'sā)
Vĕr-sailles' (-sālz'; *French* vĕr'sä'y')
vĕr'sȧ-tīle (W; -tīl, O; § 422)
vĕr'sion (*not* -zhŭn)
vĕr'tĕ-brȧ; *pl.* -bræ (-brē)
vĕr'tĕ-brăl
vĕr'tĕ-brāte
vĕr'tĕx (§ 39); *pl.* vĕr'tĭ-çĕş
vĕr'tĭ-gō (W-O)
vĕt'ĕr-ĭ-nȧ-rў
vĭ'ȧ (W-O)
vĭ'ȧ-dŭct
vĭc'är
vĭçe (president)
vĭçe'roy (-roi)
vĭ'çĕ vĕr'sȧ
vĭç'ĭ-nȧge
vĭ-çĭn'ĭ-tў (W-O)
vĭ'cious
vĭ-çĭs'sĭ-tūde
vĭc'tĭm
vĭc'tŏ-rў
vict'uals (vĭt''lz)
vĭ'dĕ (*abbr.* v., vid.)
vĭ-dĕl'ĭ-çĕt (*abbr.* viz.)
vĭg'ĭl
vi-gnette' (vĭn-yĕt'; W-O)
vĭl'lain (-ĭn)
vĭl'lein (-ĭn)
vĭn-ȧi-grĕtte'

vĭn-dĭc′a̍-tĭve (W-O)
vĭn′dĭ-ca̍-tŏ-rȳ (W ;
  -kā-tēr-ĭ, O)
vĭn-dĭc′tĭve
vĭne′ya̍rd
vi-ō′la̍ (vĕ- ; W-O)
vĭ-ȯ̍-lĭn′ (W-O)
vĭ-ȯ̍-lŏn-cel′lō
  (vē-,-chĕl-, W ; vĭ-,
  -sĕl′-, O)
vĭ-rā′gō (W-O)
Vĭr-ġĭn′ĭ-a̍
vĭr′ĭle (W ; -ĭl, O ;
  § 422)
vĭ-rĭl′ĭ-tȳ (W-O)
vĭr-tu-ō′sō (-tōō-, W ;
  vûr-tū-, O) ; pl. -si
  (-sē), -sōṣ (§ 39)
vĭr′u-lĕnçe (-ōō-, W ;
  -ū-, O)
vĭr′u-lĕnt (-ōō-, W ;
  -ū-, O)
vĭṣ′a̍ge
vis′-à-vis′
  (vē′za̍-vē′, W ;
  vĭz′a̍-, O)
vĭs′cer-a̍ (-ẽr-)
vĭs′cid (-ĭd)
vis′count (vĭ′-)
vĭṣ′ĭ-tŏr
vis′or, viz′or (vĭz′ẽr,
  W ; vĭz′ẽr, O)
vis′u̍-a̍l (vĭzh′-)
vĭ-tăl′ĭ-tȳ
vī′ta̍-mĭn (W)
vi′ti-āte (vĭsh′ĭ-)
vĭt′rĭ-ol (-u̍l)

vī-tū′pẽr-āte
vī-vā′cious (W-O)
vī-văç′ĭ-tȳ (W-O)
vĭ′va̍ vō′çĕ̍
vĭv′ĭd
vĭ-zier′ (-zēr′ ; W-O)
vŏc′a̍-tĭve
vogue (vōg)
vŏl′a̍-tĭle (W ; -tĭl, O ;
  § 422)
vȯ-lĭ′tion
vŏl′plāne
vōlt
vōlt′a̍ge
vŏl-tā′ĭc
vŏl′ūme
vȯ-lū′mĭn-ou̍s
vŏl′u̍n-ta̍-rĭ-lȳ
vȯ-rā′cious
vȯ-răç′ĭ-tȳ
vouch-sāfe′
vŏx hŭ-mā′na̍
vŭl′ga̍r
vŭl-găr′ĭ-tȳ
Vŭl′ga̍te

wāin′scŏt (W-O)
wāist′cōat (W-O)
Wal-lā′chĭ-a̍n (wŏ-)
wan′dẽr-ẽr (wŏn′-)
was (wŏz)
wa′tẽr (wô′-)
wāy-lāy′ (W-O)
wēal
wĕap′on (-u̍n)
wēa′rĭ-nĕss (W ;
  wēr′ĭ-, O)

wēa′rȳ (W ; wēr′ĭ, O)
Wednes′da̍y
  (wĕnz′- ; W-O)
wēir
wēird
wĕll′-bē′ĭng
wĕll′-bôrn
wĕll′-brĕd
Welles′leẙ (wĕlz′-)
wĕll′-known (-nōn)
wĕll′-nigh (-nī)
wĕll′-rĕad
wĕll′-to-do′
  (-tōō-dōō′)
were (wûr, W ;
  wâr, O)
Wĕst′mĭn-stĕr
Wĕst Point′
Wĕst Point′ĕr
whale (hwāl)
  (pronounce h)
wharf (hwôrf)
what (hwŏt)
wheat (hwēt)
wheel (hwēl)
when (hwĕn)
where (hwâr)
wheth′ĕr (hwĕ**th**′-)
which (hwĭch)
whiff (hwĭf)
while (hwĭl)
whip (hwĭp)
whirl (hwûrl)
whis′tle (hwĭs″l)
whole (hōl)
whol′lȳ (hōl′-)
whoop′ĭng (hōōp′-)

why (hwī)
wĭd'ōw (§ 421)
wĭnd'mĭll
wĭn'dōw (§ 421)
wĭnd'pīpe
wĭth (W-O)
withe (*n.*, wĭth, W ; wĭth'ī, O)
with'ў̆ (*a.*, *n.*, wĭth'-, W ; wĭth'-, O)
wont (*a.*, *n.*, *v.*, wŭnt, W ; wōnt, O)
Worces'tĕr (wŏŏs'-)
worst'ĕd (*defeated*, wûrst'-)
wor'sted (*yarn*, wŏŏs'tĕd ; W-O)
wound (wōŏnd ; W-O)
wraith (rāth)
wreak (rēk)
wreath (rēth ; *pl.* rēthz)
wreathe (rēth)
wres'tle (rĕs'l)
wres'tler (rĕs'lĕr)
wroth (rŏth, W ; rŏth, O)
wry (rī)
Wȳ'ăn-dŏtte
Wўc'liffe
Wȳ-ō'mĭng (W)

Xan-thĭp'pē̆ (zăn-)
Xan-tĭp'pē̆ (zăn-)
Xe-nŏc'ra̅-tē̆ş (zē-)
Xe-nŏph'a̅-nē̆ş (zē̆-)
Xen'ŏ-phŏn (zĕn'-)
Xerx'es (zûrk'sēz)
xy'lŏ-phōne (zī'-)

yacht (yŏt)
Yä'qui (-kē)
ў-cleped', ў-clept' (-klĕpt')
ye *for* ' the ' (thē ; § 139, N.)
yea (yā)
yĕast (*not* ēst)
yĕl'lōw (§ 421)
yeŏ'măn
Yĕr'kē̆ş
yĕs'tĕr-dȧy
yew (yōō)
yō'del, yō'dle (-d'l)
yōke
Yō'kŏ-hä'ma̅
yolk (yōk ; W-O ; *not* yĕlk *or* ĕlk)
Yŏm Kĭp'pur (-ōŏr)
Yŏ-sĕm'ĭ-tē̆
your (yōŏr)
Y'pres (ē'pr)
Ў̆p-sĭ-lăn'tĭ
Yu-cä-tän' (yōō-)

yule (yōōl)

Zac-chæ'ŭs (ză-kē'-)
Zā'ma̅ (*battle*)
zeal (zēl)
zeal'ot (zĕl'ŭt)
zeal'oŭs (zĕl'-)
Zĕb'ē̆-dēē
zē'nĭth (W ; zĕn'ĭth, O)
zĕph'ȳr
Zĕph'ў̆-rŭs
zeug'ma̅ (zūg'-)
Zeus (zūs ; § 421)
zinc (zĭŋk)
zinc'ĭc (zĭŋk'-)
zinc'ĭ-fȳ (zĭŋk'-)
zinck'ȳ, zink'ў̆ (zĭŋk'-)
Zĭp-pō'ra̅h (W)
zĭth'ĕr
zō'dĭ-ăc
zŏ-dī'ȧ-căl
zōō (*colloq.* ; § 380)
zŏ-ŏ-lŏğ'ĭ-căl
zŏ-ŏl'ŏ-ğĭst
zŏ-ŏl'ŏ-ğȳ
Zō-rŏ-ăs'tĕr
Zou-äve' (zōō-, W ; zōō-, O)
zoundş
Zu'lu (zōō'lōō)

CHAPTER VIII

CAPITAL LETTERS

Then there's an M, and a T, and an S, but whether the next be an izzard, or an R, confound me, I cannot tell. — GOLDSMITH.

424. Alphabet. The letters of the Greek alphabet, from which most of our own letters are derived through the Latin, were originally all capitals. They were made with straight lines, being usually cut into some hard material, such as stone or metal. After writing materials came into use, the letters gradually became rounded, and connected letters were made small. Thus in our alphabet there are two kinds of letters. The interesting history of the alphabet will be found in any large encyclopedia.

In the writing of English, until recently, capital letters have been used with a good deal of freedom, chiefly for emphasis or distinction, at the pleasure of the writer. Nowadays they are used as little as possible, and their usage is determined by certain rules. To write accurately and most effectively, it is essential to know these rules.

NOTE. This chapter is based on Webster's New International Dictionary and on Rules for Compositors and Readers at the University Press, Oxford.

GENERAL RULES

425. Sentence, line of poetry, etc. Every sentence, every line of poetry, and every line in the conclusion of a letter (§§ 524, 540, 545) begins with a capital letter:

1. That would be difficult, would it not?
2. He is correct, is he not, in this?
3. The question is, What shall we do?
4. The sun is warm, the sky is clear,
    The waves are dancing fast and bright.

426. Series of sentences. In a series of distinct interrogative or exclamatory sentences each sentence begins with a capital letter:

1. Who is he? *Where* does he live? *What* does he do?
2. Where shall we go? *When? How?*
3. What a piece of good luck that is! *How* fortunate you are!

When interrogative or exclamatory sentences are closely connected in thought, or, when abbreviated, if they may be substituted in the predicate of preceding sentences, they do not begin with a capital letter:

1. Why art thou wroth? *and* why is thy countenance fallen?
2. How long, ye simple ones, will ye love simplicity? *and* the scorners delight in their scorning, and fools hate knowledge?
3. How is the gold become dim! *how* is the most fine gold changed!
4. What did you think of him? *of* his brother? *of* his father?

427. After a colon; after *whereas*, etc. The first word after a colon receives a capital letter when it begins a complete quotation or what is equivalent to a complete quotation; after *whereas* and *resolved* in resolutions, contracts, and the like the first word begins with a capital letter:

1. His next question was this: " How shall we find the necessary means? "
2. My next question is this: How shall we find the necessary means? (See *this, thus,* § 417.)
3. Whereas, It has pleased . . . ; therefore be it
    Resolved, That we do . . .

428. Quotation. A quotation begins with a capital letter if it is complete; otherwise not:

1. My aunt looked up and said, "*What* do you think of him?"

2. His pathetic words, "*on* my pallet of straw", were ringing in my ears.

3. She ended with a quotation from Shakespeare:

> "for he is given
> To sports, to wildness, and much company".

429. *I, O.* The pronoun *I* and the interjection *O* are capitalized.

430. Emphatic capitals. In textbooks important words in definitions or the like sometimes begin with capital letters, called emphatic (or topical) capitals:

An *Infinitive* or a *Clause* may be used as an appositive.

PROPER NAMES

431. Proper noun with title. A proper noun (or proper name) and a title used with it begin with a capital letter:

1. Miss Polly Boynton; Aunt Mary; Father Whitman.

2. Professor and Mrs. W. W. Goodwin.

3. The Very Reverend Thomas Browne, D. D.

NOTE. A common noun derived from a proper name retains the capital: Spain, *Spaniard*; Plato, *Platonist*.

432. Title used as name. A title used in address or as the short form of a well-understood name begins with a capital letter:

1. Well, *Captain*, what do you think of the weather?

2. A little party at the *Doctor's*. — DICKENS.

3. The *President* received them (= the president of the United States now in office).

4. The *King* has returned to London (= the present king of England).

5. The *Pope* (= the present head of the Roman Catholic Church).

6. The *Lakes* (= the Great Lakes); the *Gulf* (= the Gulf of Mexico); the *Continent* (= the continent of Europe).

7. The *Chamber* (= the Chamber of Commerce); the *Club* (= the Golf Club, the Union Club, the University Club, etc.).

8. An *Act* (= an Act of Parliament); the *Acts* (= the Acts of the Apostles); the *Constitution* (= the constitution of the United States), *Amendments XI* and *XII* (referring to the constitution of the United States); the *Fourteenth Amendment*.

433. Months, days, sects, events, etc. Proper nouns include the names of the months and the days of the week, holidays and days of special observance, the names of sects and parties, and important historical events; the names of the seasons begin with a small letter (when personified, they usually begin with a capital; §§ 22, 434):

1. January, August, November, Sunday, Tuesday.

2. Thanksgiving Day, the Fourth of July, Labor Day, Christmas Eve, New Year's Day, Ash Wednesday, Good Friday, Commencement Day.

3. The Catholic Church (either the group of believers or the name of a building), the Baptist Church, the Church of the Holy Sepulcher, Presbyterian, the Friends (= the Quakers), Democrat, the Republican party.

4. The Deluge, the Christian Era, the Middle Ages, the Reformation, the Wars of the Roses, the French Revolution, the War of 1812, the Civil War, the Congress of Vienna, the Treaty of Paris.

5. The Battle of the Giants, the Battle of the Standard, the Battle above the Clouds. (But, the *battle* of Waterloo, the *battle* of Bunker Hill; the word 'battle' is not a part of the title when a geographical name locates the battle.)

6. The spring, summer, autumn, winter; Come, gentle Spring, ethereal mildness, come. (See § 434.)

434. Personification. In personification (§ 22) any abstract name may begin with a capital letter; capitalization usually makes the meaning clearer:

1. Ah, how unjust to *Nature* and himself
   Is thoughtless, thankless, inconsistent man!
2. Scared at thy frown terrific, fly
   Self-pleasing *Folly's* idle brood,
   Wild *Laughter*, *Noise*, and thoughtless *Joy*,
   And leave us leisure to be good.

435. Proper name as common noun. A proper name may denote, not an individual, but merely the qualities of a person so named, and be used as a common noun ; but it retains its capital letter :

1. A *Demosthenes* ; no *Cicero* ; our *Napoleon*.
2. He was a young *Hercules*.

PREPOSITIONS IN PROPER NAMES

436. *Ex-*. The prefix (preposition) *ex* does not receive a capital unless it begins a sentence :

1. The meeting was attended by *ex-President* Adams.
2. *Ex-President* Adams attended the meeting.
3. *Ex-senators* were not invited.

437. *Da, de,* etc. In foreign names of persons such words as *da, de, (d'), del, della, di, du, la, le, van,* and *von* receive a capital letter when they begin a sentence. Elsewhere the word *von* is not capitalized ; the other words vary, and the usage of the persons themselves should be followed :

1. *Da* Vinci painted it ; by *da* Vinci ; by Leonardo *da* Vinci.
2. *D'*Ailly, Pierre *d'*Ailly ; *Della* Robbia, Luca *della* Robbia.
3. *La* Fontaine, *De La* Fontaine, Jean *de La* Fontaine.
4. *Van* Dyck, Henry *van* Dyke, Anthony *Van* Dyck.

438. Proper adjective, verb, adverb. A proper adjective (adjective derived from a proper name, § 117, or proper noun used as an adjective), or a verb or an adverb derived from it, usually begins with a capital letter unless the original meaning is remote or lost, in which case the proper name itself ceases to be written with a capital (the Oxford University Press does not capitalize *anglicize, christianize, frenchified, latinize, pasteurize*) :

1. The *Latin* language, *Latinized* races ; *California* fruit ; *French* literature, *Frenchified* style ; *Pasteurized* milk ; *Parisian* manners ; the *American* Indians ; a *Turkish* rug ; *Castile* soap ; *Chinese* blue ; *Turkey* red ; *India* ink ; *Wedgewood* ware ; *Presbyterian* seminary ; *Benedictine* order.

2. America, *American*, *Americanize*, *un-American*, *non-American* ; the Orient, *Oriental*, *Orientalize*, *non-Oriental* ; the West, *Western*, *Westernize*, going *West* (= *to the West*) ; the Continent (= Europe), *Continental* alliances ; the Bible, *Biblical* ; Christ, *Christian*, *Christianize*, *non-Christian* races (see Note 1).

3. The *Philippics* of Demosthenes ; *Philippize.*
    He delivered a *philippic.* (Like a Philippic of Demosthenes.)

4. The severe *Laconic* discipline. (Of Laconia, or Sparta.)
    A *laconic* reply. (Like that of the Laconians.)
    He wrote startling *laconics.*

5. Some *Italic* tribes. (Of Italy.)
    A kind of *italic* type. (Like that invented in Italy.)

6. A *China* rose. (Name of a particular rose.)
    A *china* cup. (Like that made in China.)

7. Why do you *tantalize* me ? (From *Tantalus*.)
    He can *mesmerize*. (From *Mesmer*.)

8. A *galvanic* battery ; galvanism. (From *Galvani*.)
    They use *galvanized* iron.

9. That is *macadam*. (From *McAdam*.)
    The road is *macadamized.*

10. If we are to govern *Asiatics* well, we must govern them *Asiatically*. — MARQUIS OF SALISBURY (1869).

NOTE 1. We should also say 'un-Christian' ; but *unchristian*, which has been long used, still retains its old form. Similarly, when we refer to the *Constitution*, meaning the constitution of the United States, we should use the adjectives 'Constitutional' and 'un-Constitutional' ; but here again the words are still generally used without capitals, *constitutional, unconstitutional.*

The prefixes *non* and *un*, when used before a capital letter, take the hyphen.

Note 2. In French, German, Italian, Spanish, and various other modern languages proper adjectives do not begin with a capital letter: la langue *anglaise*.

439. For proper adjectives denoting the species of plants and animals, see § 455.

COMMON NOUN AND ADJECTIVE

440. Common noun; adjective. When a common noun or an adjective becomes a proper name, or part of a proper name, it begins with a capital letter (but see § 441):

1. In what *street* do you live? I live in Beacon *Street* (*Third Avenue, Twenty-first Street, Buckeye Lane, Adams Square, Bradford Road*). (See § 293.)

2. Do you go to *school* or *college*? I attend the Girls' Latin *School*. Next year I shall go to Washington *University*. The *Senior Class* (of a particular institution); Seniors (§ 431, N.).

3. The Ohio *River*, *Lower* Canada, the Panama *Canal*, Polk *County*, *Lake* Erie, Sioux *City*, New York *City* (but, the *city* of New York), New York *State* (or, the State of New York; § 453), Franklin *Park*, the Garden of *Eden*, the *Friends* (= Quakers), the Orthodox Friends, the First National Bank, Bellevue Hospital.

But, the *river* Charles, the *river* Saint Lawrence, the *city* of Chicago.

4. Cooper Union, the University Club, the North Station, the Royal Geographical Society, Knights of the Round Table, Volume III, Chapter XV, Rule 3, Figure 99, Plate VII.

5. Richard the *Second*, James the *Less*, Alfred the *Great*, Charles the *Bold*, Pliny the *Younger*.

6. The United States (§ 205, 22), the District of Columbia, the French Republic, the Roman Empire.

7. His name shall be called Wonderful, Counsellor, The mighty God, The everlasting Father, The Prince of Peace. — The Bible. (See § 445.)

8. The Book of Job, the Lord's Prayer, the Last Supper, the Prodigal Son, the parable of the Sower, the Apostles' Creed, the Methodist Church (either the group of believers or the name of a building), the Catholic Church, the Church of the Holy Sepulcher.

NOTE 1. Do not capitalize *church* or *state* in such expressions as 'the church and the state'. But, the High Church, the Low Church, which represent parties in the church.

NOTE 2. The custom of printing the words *street*, *river*, and the like without a capital letter in proper names arose at a time when type-setters had few capitals. Typesetting machines have now removed this difficulty, and the newspapers should, as a guide to their readers, follow the literary style. But see § 441.

NOTE 3. In French, Spanish, and various other modern languages the word for *street* (French *rue*, Spanish *calle*) precedes the name, and is not capitalized except at the beginning of a sentence : She lives in *rue* de Rivoli.

441. Plurals. When common nouns used with proper names are put in the plural, they do not begin with a capital letter unless they precede the proper names :

1. He lives at the corner of Cleveland and Dartmouth *streets*.

2. The Ohio and Mississippi *rivers*.

3. There are *Generals* Greene and Morgan ; *Lakes* Huron and Michigan.

4. The Stamp *Act*, the Navigation *Act* ; but, the Stamp and Navigation *acts*.

442. Academic degrees. The names of academic degrees and their abbreviations are capitalized :

The degree of Bachelor of Arts (A.B.); Doctor of Laws (LL.D.); Doctor of Dental Surgery (D.D.S.).

TITLES OF HIGH OFFICIALS; DEPARTMENTS

443. High officials ; departments. The titles of high officials and of departments in a national government begin with a capital letter; in hyphened compound words both parts are capitalized :

1. The President, the Vice President, Congress, the Senate, the Administration (= the United States Government), the Secretary of State, the Secretary of the Interior, the Department of Commerce and Labor, the Supreme Court, the King of England, the Prince of Wales, Parliament, the House of Lords, the Cabinet (in England), the Speaker.

Similarly, in colleges and other institutions, the Department of English, the Department of Mathematics, and so forth.

2. *Attorney-General* Wade; the *Postmaster-General*; the *Post-Office* Department.

NOTE 1. When the meaning of *president* and *vice president* is made clear by the context, these words are commonly not capitalized (except as a matter of uniformity, emphasis, or personal taste):

1. The *president* and *vice president* of the United States are elected every four years.

2. The *President* was there (= the president of the United States).

NOTE 2. *Presidential, Congressional, Senatorial, Parliamentary,* and the like begin with a capital letter when they refer to a particular President, Congress, Parliament, and so forth. Similarly, *Federal,* when referring to the United States: the *Federal* government.

444. *Grace, highness,* etc. Words like *grace, highness, majesty,* and *duke,* when used as titles, begin with a capital letter, and the adjectives accompanying them also begin with a capital letter (§ 545):

1. I saw His Grace; Her Highness; Your Royal Highness; Their Royal Highnesses; Her Imperial Majesty; His Most Gracious Majesty.

2. The Duke of York; the Earl of Warwick; His Grace, the Duke of Buckingham.

TITLES OF THE TRINITY; THE VIRGIN MARY; *GOD, SATAN,* AND OTHER SPECIAL NAMES

445. The Trinity. Titles of the Trinity (God, Christ, and the Holy Ghost) and of the Virgin Mary begin with a capital letter:

The Lord, the Father, Master, the Holy Ghost, the Supreme Being, the Godhead, the Son, the Son of the Highest, the Saviour, the Holy One of Israel, the Blessed Virgin, Saint Mary the Virgin.

446. God, Satan, etc. The word *god* begins with a capital letter when it refers to the Supreme Being; *heaven* begins with a capital letter when it refers to the Deity (see the fifth example); *hell* and *purgatory* do not begin with a capital letter; *Hades* begins with a capital letter; *paradise* begins with a capital letter when it means the Garden of Eden; *Satan* and *Beelzebub* begin with a capital letter; *devil*, as a specific name of *Satan*, begins with a capital letter:

1. The *god* of war; a pantheistic *god*.
2. Thou shalt have no other *gods* before me.
3. In the beginning *God* created the heaven and the earth.
4. Nothing in *heaven* or earth would have stayed her.
5. May *Heaven* prosper you.
6. Thou wilt not leave my soul in *hell*.
7. Adam and Eve dwelt in *Paradise*.
8. Then the *devil* leaveth him.
9. That old serpent, called the *Devil*, and *Satan*.

447. Pronouns and possessive adjectives. In hymns and the like the personal and possessive pronouns (§§ 59, 68) and the possessive adjectives (§ 69), if referring to the Trinity, usually begin with a capital letter; but this style is not followed where it would result in much capitalization, as in the Bible, the Book of Common Prayer, and works on theology:

1.　　All my trust on *Thee* is stayed,
　　　　All my help from *Thee* I bring;
　　Cover my defenceless head
　　　　With the shadow of *Thy* wing. — CHARLES WESLEY.

2. And it came to pass the day after, that *he* went into a city called Nain; and many of *his* disciples went with *him*, and much people. — THE BIBLE.

TITLES OF BOOKS, PLAYS, STORIES, ETC.

448. Books, plays, etc. The titles of books, plays, stories, or the like may be written in several different styles :

1. A TALE OF TWO CITIES. (Capital letters ; for the method of indicating capitals in manuscript, see § 515.)

2. A TALE OF TWO CITIES. (Capitals and small capitals, the first word and the other more important words beginning with a capital ; see § 515.)

3. A Tale of Two Cities. (Capitals and lower-case letters, the first word and the other more important words beginning with a capital ; see § 515.)

NOTE 1. When a title is quoted in connected writing, the third form above is generally used : Have you read Shakespeare's As You Like It ? (For the use or omission of quotation marks, see § 492 ; for the use of italics, see § 512, N.)

NOTE 2. When a title contains a hyphened compound word, the second part of the compound word is usually capitalized if it is a noun :

1. The *Record-Herald* ; *Secondary-School* Dictionary ; *Post-Office* Department (§ 443) ; *Eighteenth-Century* Verse ; Living on a *Man-of-War.* (Exceptions, *Seventh-day* Adventists ; Red *Riding-hood.*)

2. The *Star-spangled* Banner (§ 502) ; *Broad-bottomed* Administration ; *Thirty-nine* Articles ; Our *Black-and-tan* Pup.

NOTE 3. The French neglect capitals in titles, their usual practice being to capitalize only the first important word. As a guide for compositors, the Oxford University Press has adopted a working rule, according to which the first word of a title begins with a capital letter ; if the first word is *le, la, les, un,* or *une,* and it is immediately followed by a noun or by a noun preceded by an adjective, the noun and the adjective also begin with a capital letter :

1. *Autre* étude de femme.

2. *De* la terre à la lune. (The preposition *à,* when capitalized, does not take the grave accent : DE LA TERRE A LA LUNE.)

3. *Un Mariage* d'amour.

4. *Le Petit Chose* ; but, *Les Femmes* savantes.

449. Titles beginning with *the*. *The* at the beginning of the title of a book, play, story, poem, or the like should be capitalized when the title needs to be quoted in its exact form (as in encyclopedias and other books of reference); but when a work is merely referred to, either as being familiar to the reader or as having been already mentioned, *the* should not be capitalized except at the beginning of a sentence (for the use of *the* with the names of newspapers and other periodicals, and of ships, see § 513):

1. *The* Vicar of Wakefield; *The* Traveler; *The* Pilgrim's Progress; *The* Life of Samuel Johnson.

The subject of the poem called *The* Royal Progress was the arrival of the king. — MACAULAY.

2. Goldsmith published *the* Vicar of Wakefield in 1766. — MACAULAY.

It is quoted from *the* Bible (§ 450); *the* Iliad; *the* Æneid; *the* Oxford English Dictionary; *The* Oxford English Dictionary is indispensable.

NOTE. In the spoken language, or in connected writing, *the* or *a* (*an*) at the beginning of a title may be omitted after a noun in the possessive case or after a possessive adjective (§ 118), to avoid clumsiness (on the other hand, 'The Will, by Barrie', for example, is far better than 'Barrie's Will' or 'Barrie's The Will'):

1. I remember a passage in *Goldsmith's* 'Vicar of Wakefield'. —JOHNSON.

2. Goldsmith published *his* Vicar of Wakefield. — MACAULAY.

3. *Boswell's* Life of Samuel Johnson.

4. *A* Tale of Two Cities; Charles *Dickens's* Tale of Two Cities.

450. The Bible, etc. 'The Holy Bible' and 'The Book of Common Prayer' may be formally so quoted, but they are usually shortened to the familiar names *the Bible* and *the Prayer Book*. In such phrases as 'my Bible' and 'your Prayer Book' they are common nouns, but retain their capitals.

The names of the Bible (including its divisions, versions, etc.) and of other sacred books begin with a capital letter:

The Bible, the Book, the Scriptures, the Old Testament, the Gospels, the Authorized Version (or King James Bible), the Revised Version (1881, 1885), the Koran, the Vedas.

GEOGRAPHIC AND OTHER SCIENTIFIC NAMES

451. Lines and points ; areas. The imaginary lines and points on the earth's surface, and other terms that are not felt to be crystallized as proper names, do not begin with a capital letter (*Equator* is capitalized by the Oxford University Press) ; similarly, geographical terms used in a general sense ; but when the names denote specific areas of the earth's surface, they begin with a capital letter :

1. The arctic circle, the north pole, the equator, the horizon, the tropic of Capricorn, Mason and Dixon's line, Newton's first law of motion, Boyle's law, Joule's equivalent.

2. The *arctic* regions, the *northern* cities, the Pacific *coast* (in a general sense; but, the Pacific Coast, with definite boundaries), the Arctic *coast* (coast of the Arctic Ocean).

3. The Arctic Ocean, the Gulf of Mexico, the Northwest Territory, the Northern and Southern delegates (= of the North and the South), the Western Highland, the Atlantic Coast Plain, the Cotton Belt, the Corn Belt.

452. Regions. The important regions (more or less definite in their area) of a country or of the earth's surface begin with a capital letter :

The North, the South, the East, the West, the Northwest, the Orient, the Far East, the Levant, North Africa, Western New York, the Western Hemisphere, the New World, the Old World.

453. *State, territory,* etc. The words *state, territory, dominion, province,* and the like, when denoting specific geographical divisions, begin with a capital letter (for ' church and state ', see § 440, N. 1) :

The North Central *States*, the Western *States*, the Southern *States* (south of Mason and Dixon's line and the Ohio River), the Gulf *States*, the *State* of Arizona, New York *State*, the *Territory* of Alaska.

454. Heavenly bodies. The heavenly bodies and constellations begin with a capital letter (*sun*, *earth*, and *moon* have long been written without capitals; but they are proper names, and should be capitalized. *Sun* and *Earth* are now capitalized by the Oxford University Press):

1. Is *Jupiter* or *Venus* the evening star now?
2. Which is the constellation of *Canis Major*?
3. The *North Star* is in the constellation of the *Little Bear*, or *Ursa Minor*.
4. The *Milky Way* (or the *Galaxy*); the *Dog Star*; the *Lesser Dog*.

455. Geology; plants and animals. The names of ages and strata in geology begin with a capital letter; so, also, the Latin names of genera, families, and higher classifications of plants and animals, but not the adjectives denoting the species, nor the English nouns derived from the Latin names:

1. This belongs to the *Triassic* period; *Upper Cretaceous*.
2. Man is of the genus *Homo*.
    A plant of the family *Rosaceæ* of the order *Rosales*.
3. The Rosa *chinensis* ('the China rose'); Lynx *canadensis*.
4. The *Insecta* (Latin); the *insects* (English).

NOTE. When botanical names are used as the common names of plants, flowers, and the like, they are not capitalized: the *Geranium* (genus); a *geranium* (a single plant or flower).

PARENTHETIC MATTER

456. Parentheses; brackets. Matter enclosed in parentheses or brackets does not begin with a capital letter unless it is preceded by a period:

1. A noun (page 4) is the name of a person or a thing.
    A noun is the name of a person or a thing. (Page 4.)
2. Hastings (so ran the tradition) had been picked up at sea.
3. They [the father and son] had not yet returned.

BILLS AND ACCOUNTS

457. Bills ; accounts. In making out bills, or in keeping
accounts, capitalize proper names and proper adjectives only :

April 21	3 cans Hodge's cocoa	@ 36¢	$1.08
	1 doz. pencils	@ 30¢	.30
	10 yd. Turkey red	@ 55¢	5.50
			$6.88

NOTE. Some writers prefer to use emphatic capitals (§ 430).

ABBREVIATIONS

458. Abbreviations. The abbreviations of proper names
and of titles used with them (§ 529) are capitalized ; abbreviations consisting of the initial letters of words or phrases which
are not proper names or titles are usually capitalized :

1. Mr. John *P.* Jones, *Jr.*
2. *E.* (east), *W.*, *N.*, *S.*, *MS.* (manuscript), *MSS.* (manuscripts).
3. The abbreviations *A. D.* and *B. C.* are usually printed in small
capitals (see § 417); the abbreviations for forenoon and afternoon
are put in small capitals (A. M., P. M.) or in lower-case letters (*a.m.*,
p. m. ; this is the style at the Oxford University Press); *f. o. b.* (' free
on board ') in lower-case letters ; so also some common abbreviations
of Latin words, such as *e.g.* (= *exempli gratia*, ' for example '), *i.e.*
(= *id est*, ' that is '), *etc.* (= *et cetera*, ' and the rest ').

NOTE. In writing abbreviated forms do not use both the period
and the apostrophe (§ 510) : *Bldg.* (not ' B'ld'g.') ; *acct.* (not ' ac'ct.') ;
recd. ; *Mfg.*

459. For the use of abbreviations see § 529. The usual
abbreviations will be found in most dictionaries. Many libraries,
business houses, and the like have special lists for their own
use. (Exercise XLI, § 586.)

CHAPTER IX

PUNCTUATION AND OTHER MARKS

Why, gentlemen, if you know neither the road you are going, nor where you are, nor the road you came, the first thing I have to inform you is, that — you have lost your way. — GOLDSMITH.

460. Punctuation. An era of intense study of grammar has been followed by the present violent reaction. But ignorance of grammar produces faulty punctuation, as can be seen on every side. If we try to read present-day English aloud, we meet so many perplexities and annoyances that we quickly give up this useful practice (§§ 361, 364). Teachers complain not only that they spend much of their time in helping students over difficult passages, but that frequently they themselves are not sure of the author's meaning. Students, when reading alone, often receive vague or erroneous impressions, and do not derive the aid which they should to enable them to present their own thought more clearly. In writing and in punctuating, we should seek and keep before us the point of view of the reader, especially of the young reader, and try to express ourselves in such a way as not to increase the difficulties of what we have to say by the manner in which we say it. (Exercise XLI, c, § 586.)

Marks of punctuation, like guideposts, are intended to point out the way, that the traveler may continue his journey without having to retrace his steps. Furthermore, as guideposts stand only at the intersections of the roads, so marks of punctuation should stand only at the turning points of the thought; otherwise they distract the attention, and waste time and strength.

On the other hand, written language should be so constructed and so arranged that its meaning depends on the order of the words, not on the marks of punctuation; for although marks of punctuation play an important part as a device for saving the time of the reader, they should not be used to encourage or to cloak slovenliness on the part of the writer by bolstering up his ill-constructed and ill-arranged English.

Marks of punctuation are often not a matter of grammar, but of rhetoric; that is, they are often used to slacken the reader's pace, and to produce other rhetorical effects.

To learn the uses of comma, semicolon, and colon, we need to study sentences of different types; for these marks of punctuation have changing values, according to the length and complexity of the sentence.

NOTE. This chapter is based on the following books: Webster's Collegiate Dictionary; Rules for Compositors and Readers at the University Press, Oxford; The King's English (Oxford University Press), by H. W. Fowler and F. G. Fowler, compilers of The Concise Oxford Dictionary of Current English; and Spelling and Punctuation, by Henry Beadnell (examples followed by ' — B.' are taken from Beadnell's manual).

THE PERIOD

461. Period. The period (.) is used at the end of declarative sentences (whether complete or elliptical, § 347); after abbreviations (§§ 458, 529); and before decimals. The Roman numerals (I, II, etc.) are not abbreviations, and should not be followed by the period except at the end of a sentence; *per cent* is now written without the period (§ 289):

1. The ship will sail before daybreak.
2. Tell me an interesting experience. Impossible.
3. Heaven be with you. Would that I could go.
4. Mr., Mrs., MSS., LL.D., a. m., C.O.D., 10.6 ft., $1.25.
5. Edward VII; Volume XXIV; It was Philip II.

NOTE 1. "*Mr.*, *Mrs.*, *Dr.*, etc., must be printed with a full point, but not *Mme*, *Mlle*." — Oxford University Press.

NOTE 2. Such forms as *1st*, *2d* (or *2nd*), *3d* (or *3rd*), *4th*, used in designating the days of the month, are not abbreviations, and do not take the period; similarly, *4to*, *8vo*, *12mo*, and so on.

NOTE 3. Do not use a period at the end of an interrogative sentence. See § 463, N.

462. Period omitted. The period is usually omitted at the end of words or lines in display work, a style of printing in which words or groups of words are usually centered in a given space, after the manner of inscriptions. Display work includes the lines on the title-pages of books and pamphlets, headings (of pages, chapters, and other divisions), lists of words, and the like, and a great variety of work in advertising. For the period at the end of the address in letters, see § 528.

THE INTERROGATION MARK

463. Interrogation mark. The interrogation mark (?) is used at the end of an interrogative sentence, whether the sentence is complete or elliptical (§ 347); it is no longer used at the end of an indirect question (§ 77):

1. When did he go? You met him? Where?
2. "Why don't you go?" he inquired.
3. She asked, "Where does he live?"
4. She asked where he lived. (Indirect question.)

NOTE. Do not put a period at the end of an interrogative sentence. Say either ' In case of delay will you please notify us?' or ' In case of delay please notify us.'

THE EXCLAMATION MARK

464. Exclamation mark. The exclamation mark (!) is much abused. Properly, it is used only after real exclamations, and to express the writer's surprise, incredulity, disgust, ridicule, or other emotion at what somebody else has said.

Real exclamations include interjections (§§ 316, 318); words or expressions which are not complete sentences (§ 317); and sentences containing an exclamatory word (*how*, *what*):

1. But ah! so pale, he knew her not.
2. Milton! thou shouldst be living at this hour. — WORDSWORTH.
3. Alas! the happy day! the foolish day!
4. Ne'er to behold thee again!
5. That it should come to this! — SHAKESPEARE.
6. What a piece of work is a man! — SHAKESPEARE.
7. O Lord, how great are thy works! — THE BIBLE.

As a means of expressing the writer's surprise, incredulity, and the like (§ 323, N.), the exclamation mark is particularly effective:

1. He expressed the wish that the whole race might be purified by fire and fagot!
2. Entomb'd within this vault a lawyer lies,
   Who, fame assureth us, was just and wise! — B.

465. Improper use. The exclamation mark is often used, improperly, after simple declarative sentences, or after sentences that are interrogations; this confuses statement, question, and exclamation:

1. "We have won", he shouted. (Not 'won!'.)
2. I would have died rather than surrender. (Not '!'.)
3. Who would not envy you? (Not '!'.)
4. What had she not sacrificed? (Not '!'.)

NOTE. This use of the exclamation mark is frequent in the less careful writers, and sometimes makes its way into the works of the better class, including historians. If Walter Savage Landor were living today in the United States, he would doubtless include most of us in his observation on the misuse of the exclamation mark: "I read warily; and whenever I find the writings of a lady, the first thing I do is to cast my eye along her pages, to see whether I am likely to be annoyed by the traps and spring-guns of interjections; and if I happen to espy them, I do not leap the paling."

THE COMMA

466. Coördinate words, etc. The comma is used to separate coördinate words, phrases, and clauses (see §§ 467, 476. Exercise XLI, *d*, § 586):

A. In series.

    1. A cold, gray, cheerless afternoon; a cold, gray, and cheerless afternoon. (The comma before *and* prevents obscurity.)

    2. I followed him down the stairs, out of the door, and across the street.

    3. The rain descended, and the floods came, and the winds blew.

    4. Scott, Brown, and Company. (But the Oxford University Press does not use a comma before ampersand in the name of a firm : ' Longmans, Green & Co.')

B. In compound sentence.

    1. One vessel was driven upon the rocks, and twenty-six men were drowned. — PARKMAN. (The change of subject makes the comma before *and* necessary.)

    2. Virtue is the highest proof of a superior understanding, and it is the only basis of greatness. (There is no change of subject, but the comma adds clearness and emphasis.)

    Seek peace, and pursue it. — THE BIBLE.

NOTE 1. In sentences like ' Come and see ' the thoughts are too closely associated to be separated by the comma.

NOTE 2. In sentences like ' It was his first, and he hoped it would be his last attempt ' it is better not to add a comma after *last*. (It is often best to recast the sentence : ' It was his first attempt, and he hoped it would be his last '.) In ' He was in communication with and under the guidance of the government ' use no comma ; but it is better English to say ' He was in communication with the government, and was under its guidance '. (The comma shows that *and* does not connect *government* with what follows ; see § 466, *D*, 2.)

C. In compound subject.

  1. Industry, honesty, and temperance are essential to happiness. (In this type of sentence, with *and*, there is now generally no comma before the verb; but see 2.)

  2. Fights, conquests, and revolutions, lie thick together. — ADDISON. (An illustration of the comma before the verb. This punctuation avoids confusion; the authors of The King's English, § 460, N., unhesitatingly recommend it as the best.)

  3. Love, desire, hope, rise in the pursuit. (The omission of *and* before *hope* makes the comma before the verb necessary.)

     Old and young, rich and poor, helped in the cause.

  4. Mr. Jobling, Mr. Guppy, and Mr. Smallweed, all lean their elbows on the table. — DICKENS. (The use of *all* to sum up the subject does not change the punctuation. Do not add a dash to the comma before *all*.)

     Love, desire, hope, all the pleasing motions of the soul, rise in the pursuit. — ADDISON.

D. In compound predicate.

  1. She suddenly bowed her head, and wept. (The comma is necessary; for *suddenly* modifies *bowed* only.)

     They found the town well fortified, and defended by two hundred soldiers.

  2. Hope makes pain easy, and labor pleasant. — ADDISON. (The comma adds clearness and emphasis.)

     The good man admired her prudence, and followed her advice. — ADDISON.

467. *And, or, nor.* When words are connected throughout by *and*, *or*, or *nor*, the comma is not necessary; but it may be used for the sake of clearness (§ 466) or rhetorical emphasis (§ 460):

  1. A cold *and* gray *and* cheerless afternoon; a cold, *and* gray *and* cheerless afternoon.

2. I have just cause, being her uncle, *and* her guardian. — SHAKESPEARE. (See § 474.)

3. There is no man that has left house, *or* brethren, *or* sisters, *or* father, *or* mother, . . . — THE BIBLE.

4. For I am persuaded, that neither death, *nor* life, *nor* angels, *nor* principalities, *nor* powers, . . . — THE BIBLE.

468. Comma omitted. When two or more adjectives in a series are not of the same kind, they are not separated by the comma :

1. A handsome old man.
2. A live electric wire.
3. A great rough Newfoundland dog. — B.
4. A kind-hearted old Irish policeman.

469. Illiterate comma. One of the worst errors is the use of the comma between independent clauses which are not joined by a connective :

1. He was not admitted, for he had no ticket. (Not 'He was not admitted, he had no ticket'.)

2. He was not admitted ; for he had no ticket. (§ 476.)

3. He was not admitted ; he had no ticket.

470. Parenthetic or independent matter. The comma is used to set off words, phrases, or clauses used parenthetically or independently (see §§ 471 and 472 also) :

1. Tell me, then (therefore), what you wish.

2. Indeed (however, moreover, besides, well), it was anything but a gloomy prospect. (For *however* as a subordinating conjunction, see § 303, 8.)

3. To put the matter frankly, what does she intend to do?

4. Having missed the train, they returned on foot.

5. This road is, I fear, too steep.

6. His difficulties, and great difficulties they were, found a speedy solution. (Parentheses may be used for the commas ; § 490. Do not use dashes for commas ; §§ 488, 489.)

Note. In the following sentence from James Russell Lowell all the commas are necessary; but, as the authors of The King's English remark, "the crowd of commas ought to have told the writer how bad his sentence was; it is like an obstacle race": "Shakespeare, it is true, had, as I have already said, as respects England, the privilege which only first-comers enjoy."

471. Nominative of address. The comma is used to set off words in the nominative of address (this is the proper punctuation after the salutation in letters; §§ 527, 534, 542, 544, 545):

1. Mother, will you go with me?
2. It is not possible, my boy, for me to go.

Note. When the words of address express emotion, they may be followed by the exclamation mark (§ 464): My dear boy! you have done too much.

472. Nonessential words, etc. The comma is used to set off nonessential words, phrases, and clauses (§§ 50, 92, 270):

1. Mr. John Adams, the vice president, was absent. (§ 50.)
2. Mr. and Mrs. Henry Jackson, of Springfield, were not there. (But, 'The Jacksons of Springfield were not there'.)
3. Refreshed by sleep, she continued her journey.
4. The poor boy, wearied and sad, paused by the wayside.
5. Such a book is called a manual, or handbook.
6. James Scott, D.D., LL.D., editor in chief.
7. The weather, which had long been stormy, now began to moderate. (§ 92.)

473. Direct quotation. The comma is used to set off a direct quotation (§ 176) or the like:

1. He then said, "This can be done at once."
2. She exclaimed, "How fortunate!" (But, '"How fortunate!" she exclaimed'.)
3. "We shall be early", I replied.
4. The question is, Can it be done?

When a quotation is formal, or consists of several paragraphs, the colon is used instead of the comma (§ 486) :

1. The stranger replied : " Do not think ", etc.
2. He arose and addressed them : " Gentlemen, this is ", etc.

474. Added thought. The comma is used to set off a thought added at the end of the sentence ; the position and the punctuation give the added thought unusual emphasis :

1. 'Twas certain he could write, and cipher too. — GOLDSMITH.
2. The master beat the scholar, with a strap. (" A strap, we are to understand from the comma, is a barbarous instrument." — The King's English.)
3. " Why is it best, sir ? " returned Richard, hastily. — DICKENS. (In this usage the principal verb, *returned*, usually precedes the subject, *Richard*; but if the subject is a pronoun, the pronoun is unemphatic and should precede the verb, where it is less emphatic than at the end of the clause : " Why not ? " he asked, with a grin.)
4. He stood by the window, looking out into the night.

475. Unusual order. The comma is used to set off words, phrases, or clauses that are out of their normal position ; but short prepositional phrases at the beginning of a sentence need not be set off by a comma unless a following clause or phrase makes the punctuation necessary :

1. Suddenly, before he could prevent it, his hands were seized from behind.
2. In the rear of the house an old shed was visible.
   In the rear of the house, where an old shed had stood, was a flower garden.
3. To avoid getting into trouble, I went home. (When an infinitive phrase expresses purpose, § 615, it is regularly followed by a comma, for clearness ; compare ' To avoid getting into trouble was difficult ', in which the infinitive phrase is the subject of *was*.)
4. But if we will be useful to the world, we must take it as we find it. — ADDISON. (In this type of sentence the comma is not needed after *and*, *but*, or *for* followed by *although*, *if*, *when*, etc.)

5. He then called together the most faithful of his counsellors, and acquainting them with the secretary's crime, asked their advice. — ADDISON. (The omission of a comma after *and* is ungrammatical, but here rhetoric is more important than grammar.)

6. What the answer is, I leave you to discover. (But, I leave you to discover what the answer is.)

476. Coördinating conjunctions.

The coördinating conjunctions *but* and *for* are usually preceded by the comma, semicolon, or period ; in the older language (as in the Bible), by the colon also; when mere words or phrases are contrasted, the comma may be omitted before *but* :

1. He called, but nobody answered.

2. He did not return ; for he had lost his way.

3. But they had not forgotten him.

4. Blessed are the merciful : for they shall obtain mercy. — THE BIBLE.

5. Goldsmith published the Vicar of Wakefield, not in 1761, but in 1766. — MACAULAY. (Observe the comma before *not*.)

Thus he accomplished, not what he had planned, but what he had despaired of.

6. He is not only bright, but studious. (§ 298.)

7. He is a wise but melancholy old man.

477. Subordinating conjunctions.

The subordinating conjunctions, if their clauses are nonessential (§ 270), are preceded by the comma or the semicolon (for *but*, see § 312) :

1. We did not stop, since it was already late. (But, We have not seen him since you went away.)

2. Arise and eat ; because the journey is too great for thee.

478. Ellipsis.

The comma is often used to denote an ellipsis (§ 347) :

1. To err is human ; to forgive, divine. (The comma after *forgive* indicates the omission of the verb *is*.)

2. He was always silent about what he himself had done ; but of what his friends had done, never.

479. Ambiguity. The comma may be used to avoid ambiguity; but, as a rule, sentences that would be ambiguous without the comma should be rewritten:

1. Faulty: In the valley below, the villages looked small. (Say 'Down in the valley the villages looked small'.)

2. Faulty: To John, Henry was always friendly. (Say 'Henry was always friendly to John', 'John always found Henry friendly', or the like, according to the sense.)

3. It rained *so* hard *that* we waited. (Not 'It rained *so that* we waited'; nor 'It rained so, that we waited'.)

480. *Also, too; namely, that is.* The words *also* and *too* at the end of a sentence or clause should not be set off by a comma; nor should they be set off in the middle of a sentence, unless they are parenthetic and refer to the whole sentence; put a comma (not a colon or a dash) before and after *namely* and *that is* (unless *that is* is followed by a principal clause, when it is usually preceded by a semicolon):

1. The works that I do shall he do *also*. — THE BIBLE. (Avoid using *also* at the beginning of a sentence or clause; use *and, furthermore, moreover, besides,* or the like; see § 273, 6.)

2. That ye *also* love one another. — THE BIBLE.

3. Our ship was an excellent sailor *too*. — DEFOE.

4. Like twilight's, *too*, her dusky hair. — WORDSWORTH.

5. If we look into the second rule which Socrates has prescribed, *namely*, that we should apply ourselves to the knowledge of such things as are best for us . . . — ADDISON.

6. It is briefly comprehended in this saying, *namely*, Thou shalt love thy neighbour as thyself. — THE BIBLE.

7. Be what you are, *that is*, a woman. (Be what you are; *that is*, be a woman.)

None is good save one, *that is*, God. — THE BIBLE.

But sell not all thou hast, except thou come and follow me; *that is*, except thou have a vocation wherein thou mayest do as much good with small means as with great. — LORD BACON.

481. Comma in numbers. In ordinary numbers of four or more figures the comma is usually inserted after the digits expressing thousands, millions, and so forth; but in numbers indicating dates, pages, lines of poetry, and library numbers, the comma is not used :

3,216; 24,213,216; in the year 1918; p. 2437; l. 1132; No. 23187.

482. *Etc.* The abbreviation *etc.* (§ 417) is not permissible in literary style. When *etc.* (or *&c.*) is used (as in footnotes and other abbreviated matter), it should be set off from the rest of the matter by a comma or commas ; this punctuation tends to prevent obscurity, and is particularly useful after a quotation (for example, '*That he was*, etc., is a subordinate clause '). But when ampersand (*&*) is used in the name of a firm, it is not set off by a comma (for example, ' Longmans, Green & Co.'; see § 466, *A*, 4). (Exercise XLI, *e*, § 586.)

THE SEMICOLON

483. Phrases and dependent clauses. The semicolon denotes a longer pause than the comma. It is regularly used to group a series of phrases and dependent clauses which are of the same general kind, but which are less closely associated than those taking the comma :

1. To give an early preference to honor above gain, when they stand in competition ; to despise every advantage which cannot be attained without dishonest arts ; to brook no meanness, and stoop to no dissimulation, are the indications of a great mind, the presages of future eminence and usefulness in life.

2. He expresses a hope that the competition of other nations may drive us out of the field ; that our foreign trade may decline ; and that we may thus enjoy a restoration of national sanity and strength. — Macaulay.

484. Independent clauses. The semicolon is used to group a series of independent clauses (with or without connectives) which are parallel in thought and arrangement (§ 375). Study the following commas and semicolons :

a. ——, and ——. (§ 466, *B.*)

1. The rain descended, and the floods came.

2. He goes early, and he returns late.

b. —— ; and ——.

1. Wisdom is better than rubies ; and all the things that may be desired are not to be compared unto her. — THE BIBLE.

2. Of the rural life of England he knew nothing ; and he took it for granted that everybody who lived in the country was either stupid or miserable. — MACAULAY.

3. The temperate man's pleasures are always durable, because they are regular ; and all his life is calm and serene, because it is innocent. — B.

4. What I do about slavery and the colored race, I do because I believe it helps to save the Union ; and what I forbear, I forbear because I do not believe it would help to save the Union. — LINCOLN.

5. He turned his house into a place of refuge for a crowd of wretched old creatures who could find no other asylum ; nor could all their peevishness and ingratitude weary out his benevolence.

6. Keep thy heart with all diligence ; for out of it are the issues of life. — THE BIBLE.

c. —— ; ——.

1. Truth ennobles man ; learning adorns him. — B.

2. Never speak concerning what you are ignorant of ; speak little of what you know ; whether you speak or say not a word, do it with judgement.

3. They bought pictures of him [Byron] ; they treasured up the smallest relics of him ; they learned his poems by heart, and did their best to write like him, and to look like him. — MACAULAY.

4. Histories make men wise ; poets, witty ; the mathematics, subtle ; natural philosophy, deep ; moral, grave ; logic and rhetoric, able to contend. — LORD BACON. (Exercise XLI, *f,* § 586.)

THE COLON

485. Colon. The colon was formerly used to mark the balance, or turning point, of the sentence. It informs the reader that the thought is not finished, and invites him onward with the promise that what he has just read will be explained, illustrated, or concluded in what follows. A knowledge of this use of the colon is essential in the reading of the older literature, such as Shakespeare and the Bible. (For the modern usage, see § 486.)

When, at the beginning of "Hamlet", Francisco is relieved from the watch, he answers,

> " For this relief much thanks : 'tis bitter cold,
> And I am sick at heart."

The colon in this passage informs the reader that the clause before and after it are not independent, but related to each other; the thought ends with the period; what follows the colon explains what precedes it. To change the colon to the period, as has frequently been done in this and many other passages in Shakespeare (particularly in recent editions), not only breaks the connection, but alters, obscures, or destroys the meaning. It also changes what may be called the legato style of Shakespeare to the choppy, staccato style of modern English. Thought and punctuation go hand in hand, and neither can be disturbed without disturbing the other. In Shakespeare the original punctuation is not only grammatical, but rhetorical; thus it is an aid to the understanding of the text, and should be made a means of interpretation. We may all study the punctuation of the Bible, which is contemporary with that of Shakespeare and practically identical with it.

486. Modern use. The colon is now used chiefly as a means of introduction (see Examples 1-3); more rarely it is used (instead of the semicolon and a conjunction) to indicate a following antithesis or explanation (see Examples 4–7 ; for the misuse of the colon after the salutation in letters, see §§ 527, 542):

1. Please give me your opinion of the following sentence: " Dear Father, I am ", etc. (Not ' What do you think of the following sentence ? " Dear Father, I am " ', etc.)

Ask yourself this question: What can I do without? (See *this, thus,* § 417.)

2. There are eight parts of speech. These are as follows: noun, pronoun, etc. (Not ' These are: noun, pronoun ', etc.; use a complete sentence, or its equivalent, before the colon.)

3. A noun is the name of a person or thing: Alice, violet.

4. Man proposes: God disposes. (But, Man proposes; but God disposes.)

5. Study to acquire a habit of thinking: no study is more important. — B. (But, ' of thinking; for no study ', etc.)

6. In business there is something more than barter, exchange, price, payment: there is a sacred faith of man in man. — B.

7. Think not that I am come to destroy the law, or the prophets: I am not come to destroy, but to fulfil. — THE BIBLE.

THE DASH

487. Slang in punctuation. With unthinking writers the dash has become what may be termed slang in punctuation. Such writers use it indifferently for almost any kind of stop; this robs the dash of its distinct meaning, and puzzles the reader. Carelessness and obscurity in writing indicate carelessness and obscurity in thinking.

Henry Beadnell, an English writer on punctuation, says, " The dash is frequently employed in a very capricious and arbitrary manner, as a substitute for all sorts of points, by writers whose thoughts, although, it may be, sometimes striking and profound, are thrown together without order or dependence; also by some others, who think that they thereby give emphasis and prominence to expressions which in themselves are very commonplace, and would, without this fictitious assistance, escape the observation of the reader, or be deemed by him hardly worthy of notice."

" It [Beadnell's comment on the dash] is all only too true; these are the realms of Chaos, and the lord of them is Sterne, from whom modern writers of the purely literary kind have so many of their characteristics. . . . The modern newspaper writer who overdoes the use of dashes is seldom as incorrect as Sterne, but is perhaps more irritating." — The King's English.

The dash should not be allowed to take the place of other punctuation. Its use does not tend to clear thinking or clear writing. When it has to be resorted to as a means of avoiding ambiguity, the sentence should be rewritten. In the entire Bible there is but one dash (Exodus, xxxii, 32); it is used to denote an interrupted thought.

488. Proper use. The proper use of the dash is to denote hesitancy, sudden change in the thought or construction, or interruption of speech:

1. " It — can't — be ", muttered Sydney Carton.
2. She — have you seen her, Doctor?
3. No, I was not a shoemaker by trade. I — I learnt it here. I taught myself. I asked leave to —

NOTE. A writer sometimes uses the dash to announce to the reader an unexpected or humorous ending to a sentence. This practice is both needless and dangerous; for the unexpected is most effective, and humor, if announced, falls flat unless it satisfies the reader's anticipation. See the quotation at the beginning of this chapter.

The dash is used properly to denote a change of speaker in a dialogue reported in a single paragraph; or to set off the author's name from a quotation:

1. The following dialogue ensued: Where do you live? — In Cambridge. — Have you been there long? — Three years. — Have you no home? — No, sir.

2. Hitch your wagon to a star. — EMERSON.

The dash is used properly to denote the omission of a word or of letters in a word:

I hope you have met Mrs. ——— (Miss K———, Mr. B———n).

A short dash is used in tabulations, references, and the like to denote the omission of figures or letters in a series (§ 131):

Reports for 1907–1918; pp. 21–343; sec. a–f.

489. Objectionable use. The dash denotes the interruption of thought; its use for the comma, semicolon, or colon, which denotes the continuation of thought, is a contradiction, and often bewilders the reader. The dash, or the comma followed by the dash, should not be used for the comma or the colon (see § 50):

1. Faulty: There was one whom he did not forget — his aged mother. (Use a comma.)

2. Faulty: Anybody might be an accuser, — a personal enemy, an infamous person, a child, a parent, a brother, or a sister. (Use a colon; or, preferably, change the dash to *whether.*)

3. I have taken a general view of it under these four heads, the fable, the characters, the sentiment, and the language. — ADDISON. (The comma after *heads* might, formally, be a colon; § 486.)

4. London had only one commercial rival, the mighty and opulent Amsterdam. — MACAULAY. (Do not add a dash to the comma.)

5. Lord Byron could exhibit only one man, a man proud, moody, cynical. — MACAULAY.

6. The proverb of old Hesiod, that half is often more than the whole, is eminently applicable to description. — MACAULAY.

Two dashes, or two commas followed by two dashes, are often used, instead of commas or parentheses, to set off parenthetic matter (§§ 470, 490); but foreign matter introduced parenthetically destroys the unity of the sentence, and should be avoided (§ 355):

1. Objectionable: His difficulties — and great difficulties they were — found a speedy solution. (Use commas; § 470.)

2. Objectionable: The sailors nibbled what little bread was not water-soaked, — for they had lost all their bacon, — and caught rain water to drink. (Use parentheses, and put a comma before *and*; or, better still, recast the sentence: 'Having lost all their bacon, the sailors nibbled what little bread was not water-soaked, and', etc.)

NOTE. Oftentimes the reader does not know whether the first dash is followed by a second, and reads with uncertainty. "If two single independent dashes are placed near each other, still more if they are in the same sentence, the reader naturally takes them for a pair constituting a parenthesis, and has to reconsider the sentence when he finds that his first reading gives nonsense." — The King's English.

PARENTHESES

490. Parentheses. Parenthetic words, phrases, or clauses are set off lightly by the use of commas (§ 470); formally, and often with the force of an effective aside, by the use of parentheses, but this should not be overdone:

1. This, you see, is his present plan.

2. But (I ask you, sir), what was I to do?

3. I have seen charity (if charity it may be called) insult with an air of pity. — B.

4. Left now to himself (malice could not wish him a worse adviser), he resolves on a desperate project. — B.

NOTE 1. "The occasional use of parentheses may add liveliness and spirit to a discourse, but their frequent employment is very injudicious: for nothing so much weakens the force of language as the continual dropping of the voice, and the consequent diversion of the attention from the main object of inquiry, which a constant recurrence of parenthetical observations necessitates." — BEADNELL.

QUOTATIONS 331

Note 2. When parentheses are used, any accompanying punctuation should be so placed that if the parentheses and all they inclose were removed, the sentence would still be properly punctuated (as in Examples 2 and 4, above; here the comma stands after the parenthesis because the parenthesis explains what precedes).

BRACKETS

491. Brackets. Brackets are used to denote that the matter inclosed by them is inserted, and is not a part of the text:

1. Go you and tell her of it. [Enter Attendants.] Cousins, you know what you have to do.

2. Under him [Pericles] Athens had become the most powerful naval state in the world.

3. He wrote that under Pyrocles [*sic*] Athens had become, etc. (The Latin word *sic*, meaning *thus*, is used to indicate that the faulty or anomalous expression before it is quoted correctly.)

QUOTATION MARKS

492. Quotations; titles of books, etc. Quotation marks (" " or ' ') are used to inclose quotations and titles of books, poems, and the like; titles which are made plain by the capitalization do not need quotation marks, and look better without them; short titles are sometimes put in italics (§ 512, N.), or if well known, are often unmarked:

1. I do not like your " if " (or ' if ').

2. He replied, " Do not act hastily." (Or ' Do not act hastily.')

3. Dickens wrote A Tale of Two Cities (or " A Tale of Two Cities "; or ' A Tale of Two Cities ').

4. Kingsley's *Hypatia*; Homer's Iliad (or *Iliad*); Vergil's Æneid (or *Æneid*).

Note 1. Double quotation marks are still in general use in the United States. The Oxford University Press uses single marks. The single marks are sufficient, and save space. For quotations within quotations, see § 494.

NOTE 2. Single (or double) quotation marks are often used to call attention to a word or group of words, as is done in this book.

493. The Bible. In the Bible no quotation marks are used, but quotations begin with a capital letter.

494. Quotation within quotation. When a quotation contains a quotation, the double quotation marks are used with one quotation, the single marks with the other:

He said, " Dickens wrote ' A Tale of Two Cities '." (Or ' Dickens wrote " A Tale of Two Cities ".' The latter is the practice at the Oxford University Press.)

495. Quoted punctuation. At the Oxford University Press no sign of punctuation is included within quotation marks unless it is a part of the quotation (as in quoted dialogue, standing alone); after ? and ! the period is omitted. With regard to the almost universal custom of quoting the comma and the period at the end of an extract the Oxford University Press says, " There seems to be no reason for perpetuating a bad practice." The following examples illustrate the Oxford usage:

1. " It is late." " It is late ", she says. She says, " It is late." (The period in the last example is a part of the quotation.)

2. " Is it late? " she asks. Will she say, " It is late "?

3. Do not say, " It is late "; say nothing.

4. " Yes, it is late." She replied, " Yes, it is late."
   " Yes," she replied, " it is late." (The comma after *Yes* is a part of the quotation; *she replied* is parenthetic, and has no effect on the period.)

5. " But it is late." " But ", she replied, " it is late." (The comma after *But* is not a part of the quotation.)

6. " How late it is! " she cried.
   How foolish it was to cry, " It is late "!

7. " Why does she say, ' It is late '? " (See Note 2.)

8. Such phrases as ' now and then ', ' in and out ', ' by and by ', ' to and fro '. (So with isolated words, phrases, or clauses.)

Note 1. Similarly, marks of punctuation should not be italic or boldface unless they are a part of the subject matter: *To err is human; to forgive, divine*; Did she say *at last* or *alas?*

Note 2. Do not use such forms as " Does she ask, ' Is it too late?'?" Make the second question indirect: " Does she ask if it is too late?"

Note 3. A superior figure (referring to a footnote) is placed after the word which is to be commented on in the footnote; if an entire sentence or clause is to be commented on, the figure is placed at the end of the sentence or clause, after the punctuation: *Thou* [1], *ye*, and *you* are of the second person; [2] but *ye* and *you* are plural. [3]

496. Two or more paragraphs. When the quoted matter runs into more than one paragraph, each paragraph begins with quotation marks, but only the last paragraph ends with them.

497. Needless quotation marks. Care should be taken not to use quotation marks where they are not needed. For example, it is better not to quote familiar proverbial expressions; not to quote terms that are known to the reader; not to quote good colloquial words as an apology for using them; and not to quote words or expressions used ironically or playfully:

1. But I felt it was better late than never. (Not ' But I felt that it was " better late than never " '.)

2. They tried to corner the market. (Not ' to " corner " the market '.)

3. He said he didn't want to be bamboozled. (Not ' to be " bamboozled " '.)

4. Such kind-heartedness I did not relish. (Not ' Such " kind-heartedness " '.)

THE HYPHEN

498. Noun phrases. In the hyphening of noun phrases usage among writers and publishers is not uniform. Webster does not use the hyphen except for the sake of clearness (see the New International Dictionary, page lxxx, Use of the Hyphen). When in doubt, consult the dictionary.

499. Disunited words. In general, noun phrases in which the words keep their meaning, whether hyphened or not, may be written as separate words; if their meaning changes, they should be united by the hyphen (for example, a ' man of peace ' is a man who is disposed to have peace; a ' man of war ' is a man who fights, a warrior, a soldier; a 'man-of-war' is a warship; see § 549, *c*):

1. Post office, water wheel, dining room, hymn book, fellow creature, letter writing, machine shop, lightning rod, high school, oak tree, apple pie, drawing paper, tax collector, pen filler, life preserver, school committee, proof reader, commander in chief, secretary treasurer, actor manager, head master (but, head-mastership), lieutenant colonel (but, lieutenant-colonelcy).

2. But, drawing-room (= reception room; compare ' drafting room ' = a room for drafting), bull's-eye, jack-o'-lantern, son-in-law, man-of-war, forget-me-not.

NOTE. When the phrases are in the possessive (genitive) case, the hyphen sometimes adds clearness: *proof-readers'* marks; the *commander-in-chief's* headquarters.

500. United words. When words are to be united, being felt as single words, Webster omits the hyphen if the compound forms are familiar or not confusing to the eye:

1. Textbook, railroad, grandfather, masterpiece, nutshell, manservant, onlooker, officeholder, windowpane, fireproof, homelike, doorstep, anybody, everybody, sometimes, plowboy, schoolgirl, schoolhouse, nonconductor, nonessential, nonresident, anticlimax, prehistoric, aircraft.

2. But, ex-president (ex-President Adams; § 436), passer-by, lookers-on, self-preservation, non-Quaker, anti-imperialist, pre-Homeric, helter-skelter.

NOTE. When the second part of a noun phrase is an adjective, the words are generally united by the hyphen: *court-martial* (§ 34), *attorney-general*, *postmaster-general*, *knight-errant* (§ 34); but, *notary public* (§ 34).

501. *Today*, etc. The familiar words *today*, *tonight*, and *tomorrow* are still hyphened very generally. The Concise Oxford Dictionary gives the preference to the unhyphened form. " It seems absurd to keep any longer the division in *to-day* and *to-morrow.*" — The King's English.

502. Compound adjectives. Compound attributive (or adherent) adjectives (§ 113, N.) are readily formed by the union of two or more words. Such forms are hyphened to avoid ambiguity (otherwise a compound adjective might be mistaken for two single adjectives) :

1. The *post-office* employees, *dining-room* furniture, *machine-shop* methods, *high-school* pupils.

2. An *olive-green* coat, *deep-blue* sea, *bright-eyed* girl, *doll-faced* boy, *would-be* captain, *two-handled* cup, *ten-foot* pole, *two-gallon* jars, *long-distance* telephone, *first-year* studies, *nineteenth-century* literature, *right-hand* road, *one-man* power, *five-cent* fare, *five-minute* talks, *deep-sea* fishing, *twenty-four-pound* shot, *hand-to-mouth* existence, *long-talked-of* arrangement, a *silk-and-cotton* fabric, *North-American* Indians, *South-African* rubies ; ' in those *East-Indian* seas ' (DICKENS).

NOTE 1. In such phrases as 'a *sad day's* work ', 'a *two weeks'* voyage ', no hyphen is used. Ordinary phrases, when used as predicate adjectives (§ 113, N.), are not hyphened : ' It is an *out-of-the-way* place '; but, ' The place is *out of the way* '.

NOTE 2. Proper names, having the nature of a unit, do not require hyphens : *Bunker Hill* Monument; *Peter Bent Brigham* Hospital.

503. Misuse of hyphen. Avoid using the hyphen in German fashion :

1. *Sitting-room* and *dining-room* furniture. (Not ' Sitting- and dining-room furniture '.)

2. *Grammar-school* and *high-school* teachers. (Not ' Grammar- and high-school teachers '.) Still better, ' Teachers in the grammar school and the high school '.

3. A *three-year* or *four-year* course. (Not ' A three- or four-year course '.)

Note. Do not use the hyphen to form uncouth compounds:

1. Methods of teaching foreign languages. (Not ' Foreign-language-teaching methods '.)

2. A clerk in the Bank of Commerce. (Not ' A Bank-of-Commerce clerk '.)

504. Adverbs. A participle used as an attributive (adherent) adjective (§ 113, N.) may be modified by an adverb without the use of the hyphen; but such adverbs as *best, better, ill, long, loud,* and *well,* which may be mistaken for adjectives (§ 258), are joined to the participle:

1. A *gently flowing* brook crossed the meadow; a *never ending* day; a *somewhat troubled* look.

2. The *best-laid* plans; a *better-looking* house; a *hard-boiled* egg; a *long-pointed* pencil; a *much-needed* reform; a *well-trained* dog; a *picked-up* supper; a *played-out* method; *ill-humored* people.

3. *Half-baked* measures; but, *half past* five (without hyphen).

505. Hyphen omitted. When the participle is used either appositively or predicatively (§ 113, N.), the adverb and the participle are not joined:

1. The messenger, *well instructed*, answered no questions.
2. The letter was *long forgotten*.

506. Cardinal numbers. The cardinal numbers from *one* to *nine*, and the ordinals from *first* to *ninth*, inclusive, are joined by the hyphen to the words *twenty, thirty,* and so forth, up to *ninety* inclusive:

1. Twenty-one, forty-nine, ninety-seven, one hundred and sixty-five; but, one hundred and one, one thousand and one.
2. Twenty-first, forty-ninth, ninety-seventh.

507. Ordinal numbers. In the writing of ordinal numbers above one hundred the cardinal forms *hundred, thousand,* and so forth are used as ordinals, and only the last number takes the ordinal form:

One hundred and first; the one hundred and twenty-first Psalm. (It is not customary to hyphen the entire adjective, ' one-hundred-and-twenty-first ', as some writers do; see § 128, *a*, 2, *b*.)

508. Fractions. Words representing fractions need not be hyphened unless they form compound adjectives:

1. We ate *two thirds* of the melon. (*Thirds* is a noun, modified by the adjective *two*.)

2. The law was passed by a *two-thirds* vote.

509. End of line. The hyphen is used to divide a word at the end of a line (do not use a hyphen at the beginning of a line). Do not divide a word unless it has two or more syllables; do not divide it when there is a syllable of only one or two letters to be carried to the next line:

1. Scream, seemed, could, tripped. (Incapable of division.)

2. Adjec-tive, book-case, sing-ing, posi-tion.

3. Many, needed, proper, only. (Not to be divided.)

Note. Avoid such divisions as ' star-vation ', ' obser-vation ', ' gene-ration ', ' happi-ness '; write ' starva-tion ', and so forth. " The principle is that the part of the word left at the end of a line should suggest the part commencing the next line." — Oxford University Press.

THE APOSTROPHE

510. Apostrophe. The apostrophe is used in forming the possessive case (§ 41); and in forming the plurals of letters, signs, and the like (§ 35). It is also used in marking the omission of a letter or letters in contracted words (do not confuse contractions with abbreviations, § 458); do not space between words except to distinguish *'s* (= *is*) from the sign of the possessive case (§ 41):

1. Isn't, doesn't, 'tis, can't, don't, they're, I'll (= I will), ne'er (= never), o'er (= over), o'clock (= of the clock). See *isn't*, § 417.

2. The *boy 's* right; *that 's* it; *what 's* the matter?

ITALIC

511. Italic. Italic mars the looks of the page, and should be used as sparingly as possible. It is seldom necessary to italicize words for the sake of emphasis; ordinarily the sentence should be rewritten. In the Bible the italicized words are not emphatic; they are so printed because they do not occur in the original manuscripts. In mathematical works the theorems and the like are usually in italic. (For the method of indicating italic in manuscript, see § 515.)

512. Titles of books, plays, etc. For the titles of books, plays, and the like, see § 448.

NOTE. "In many works it is now common to print titles of books in italic, instead of in inverted commas [quotation marks; § 492]. This must be determined by the directions given with the copy, but the practice must be uniform throughout the work." — Oxford University Press.

513. Names of newspapers, etc.; ships. The names of newspapers and other periodicals, and of ships, are usually in italic; as a rule, do not italicize or capitalize *the*; do not italicize the name of the city or town where a periodical is printed unless it is a part of the title:

1. He takes the London *Daily News*; the *New York Times*; the *Outlook*.

2. We visited the *Philadelphia*; the *King George*; the *Revenge*. (Ships.)

514. Foreign words, etc. Foreign words and phrases, unless Anglicized, should be in italic. The following illustrative words and phrases (selected from the manual of the Oxford University Press) will be found pronounced in § 423:

a. Words and phrases not Anglicized:

adagio	*au revoir*	*bourgeoisie*
ad nauseam	*billet-doux*	*carte blanche*

chef-d'œuvre	*en rapport*	*noblesse oblige*
circa (abbrev. *c.*)	*en route*	*par excellence*
con amore	*esprit de corps*	*pro tempore*
coup de grâce	*ex cathedra*	*raison d'être*
coup d'état	*ex officio*	*résumé*
dénouement	*hors de combat*	*sang-froid*
dolce far niente	*mêlée*	*sine qua non*
édition de luxe	*modus operandi*	*sotto voce*
élite	*multum in parvo*	*tête-à-tête*
en masse	*naïveté*	*tour de force*
en passant	*ne plus ultra*	*vis-à-vis*

b. Words and phrases Anglicized:

alibi	menu	rendezvous
apropos	morale	savant
bona fide	per annum	sobriquet
débris	personnel	soirée
début	prestige	via
dilettante	prima facie	vice versa
ennui	protégé	virtuoso
entrée	régime	viva voce

NOTE. "Ad loc., cf., e. g., et seq., ib., ibid., id., i. e., loc. cit., op. cit., q. v., s. v., viz., not to be in italic."— Oxford University Press.

515. Manuscript ; proof-readers' marks. In preparing manuscript (called "copy" by the printer), use entire sheets of ordinary typewriting paper. On the left-hand side of the paper leave a margin not less than an inch in width. Indent the first line of each paragraph not less than half an inch. Write legibly, preferably with a typewriter, spacing well and uniformly between the lines. Write on one side of the paper only. When you have finished writing the manuscript, revise it with great care to see that it is correct in pagination, capitalization, punctuation, spelling, and paragraphing. Do not fold or roll the manuscript.

Proof-readers' marks. The following marks are used in correcting proof :

✣	= apostrophe	#	= space (or more space)
,	= comma	⊃	= less (or no) space
/=/	= hyphen	*out; see copy*	= matter omitted
⊙	= period	?	= query (to the author)
⅋ ⅋	= quotation marks	*stet* (····)	= let it stand
¶	= paragraph	*tr.*	= transpose
no ¶	= no paragraph	*w.f.*	= wrong font of type
l.c.	= lower-case letters	⌞	= move to the left
rom.	= roman type	⌟	= move to the right
ital. (——)	= italic	⌐	= raise
s. c. (＝＝)	= small capitals	⌐⌐	= lower
caps. (＝＝＝)	= capitals	＝	= straighten
⌁	= bold-faced type	✗	= broken type
◿	= delete (take out)	9	= reverse
◿	= delete and close up	⊥	= quadrat (or space)

NOTE. For the use of italic and bold-faced marks of punctuation, see § 495, N. 1.

The paragraph below shows how a printer's first proof appears after being marked by a proof reader :

¶/◿ ✣/ I no sooner come in⌒to the *library*, but I bolt the ⊃/*rom.*
lust/ door to me, excluding, ambition, avarice, and all such
◿/ vice, whose nurse is ⫯ idleness the mother of Igno- ◿/*cap.*
,/; rance and Melancholy herself/⌐
no ¶/l.c. And in the very lap of eternity, amongst so many *w.f.*
9/⌞ divine souls, I take my seat, with a spirit so lofty *tr.*
stet and sweet content, that I pity all great ones, and *out/*＝
⊥ rich men, that know not this happiness.— Heinsius, *s.c.*
keeper of the library at Leiden. ✗/◿

The first proof of a book or the like is usually taken from the type while it is on the printer's galley, and is called " galley proof ". Proof taken when the type is made up into pages is called " page proof ". The revised proof of the matter at the bottom of the preceding page would appear as follows :

> I no sooner come into the library, but I bolt the door to me, excluding lust, ambition, avarice, and all such vices, whose nurse is Idleness the mother of Ignorance, and Melancholy herself ; and in the very lap of eternity, amongst so many divine souls, I take my seat, with so lofty a spirit and sweet content, that I pity all our great ones, and rich men, that know not this happiness. — HEINSIUS, keeper of the library at Leiden. (From Burton's Anatomy of Melancholy.)

CHAPTER X

LETTER WRITING

Letters should be easy and natural, and convey to the persons to whom we send them just what we would say to those persons if we were with them. — LORD CHESTERFIELD.

Nothing is so vulgar as haste. — EMERSON.

516. Letters in general. Letters not only play a leading part as a branch of literature, but in daily life they are the most general, interesting, and practical kind of writing. Being personal in their nature, they reveal the writer's real self, and hence they should be made to reveal his best self ; for what is written is written, and must stand with all its imperfections, regardless of protest or apology. Letters are so indicative of education and character that many a splendid opportunity is won or lost by the literary or the mechanical style of a single epistle. " Style ", Lord Chesterfield wrote to his son, " is the dress of thoughts ; and let them be ever so just, if your style is homely, coarse, or vulgar, they will appear to as much disadvantage, and be as ill received, as your person, though ever so well-proportioned, would be if dressed in rags, dirt, and tatters."

517. Business letters. Business letters should be written with even greater care than social letters, that by their form they may testify to the esteem in which the writer holds his patron, and may extend to him the courtesy dictated by good breeding. Such letters are a tonic to both recipient and writer. On the other hand, ignorance and bad taste may be displayed as quickly by improper abbreviations, for example, as by bad spelling or bad grammar.

518. Models. School libraries should be provided with collections of letters, such as may now be purchased at a small cost.

In writing letters imitate the best models. Avoid repetition (study the outlines in § 359). When you go out into the world, maintain your self-respect by not permitting the rush of business to tempt you to adopt the ill manners of short cuts and slovenly methods. Read your work aloud ; see § 364.

THE INFORMAL PERSONAL (OR FRIENDLY) LETTER

519. Informal personal letter. The personal letter may be informal or formal. Study the following informal personal letters written by Charles Dickens and James Russell Lowell :

Broadstairs, Kent, September 28, 1842.

My dear Longfellow,

How stands it about your visit, do you say? Thus : your bed is waiting to be slept in ; the door is gaping hospitably to receive you. I am ready to spring towards it with open arms at the first indication of a Longfellow knock or ring. And the door, the bed, I, and everybody else who is in the secret, have been expecting you for the last month.

. . . .

I have decided, perhaps you know, to publish my American Visit. By the time you come to me I hope I shall have finished writing it. I have spoken very honestly and fairly ; and I know that those in America for whom I care will like me better for the book. A great many people will like me infinitely the worse, and make a devil of me straightway.

Rogers is staying here, and begs me to commend him to you, and to say that he has made me pledge myself, on pain of non-forgiveness ever afterward, to carry you to see him without loss of time when you come.

Faithfully your friend,
Charles Dickens.

Elmwood, May 3, 1876.

Dear Longfellow,

Will you dine with me on Saturday at six? I have a Baltimore friend coming, and depend on you.

I had such a pleasure yesterday that I should like to share it with you to whom I owed it. J. R. Osgood & Co. sent me a copy of your Household Edition to show me what it was, as they propose one of me. I had been reading over with dismay my own poems to weed out the misprints, and was awfully disheartened to find how bad they (the poems) were. Then I took up your book to see what the type was, and before I knew it I had been reading two hours or more. I never wondered at your popularity, nor thought it wicked in you; but if I *had* wondered, I should no longer, for you sang me out of all my worries. To be sure they came back when I opened my own book again — but that was no fault of yours.

If not Saturday, will you say Sunday? My friend is a Mrs. ——, and a very nice person indeed.

Yours always,

J. R. L.

520. Address and date. In the informal personal letter the address of the writer and the date of the composition are usually put at the top of the letter, at the right (as in § 519). They may also be put at the bottom of the letter, at the left (for the business letter see § 536; for the punctuation, see § 528):

Dear Longfellow,

Will you dine with me on Saturday at six? I have a Baltimore friend coming, and depend on you.

.   .   .   .

If not Saturday, will you say Sunday? My friend is a Mrs. ——, and a very nice person indeed.

Yours always,

J. R. L.

Elmwood, May 3, 1876.

521. Salutation. The salutation of a letter should be what the writer would naturally say to the person to whom he is writing, with *Dear* or *My dear* before it (for the punctuation, see § 527 ; for *Dear* and *My dear*, see § 544) :

1. Dear Mother, Dear Frank, Dear Polly, Dear Boy.
2. Dear Mr. Brown, Dear Miss Brown, Dear Mr. President (§ 545).
3. My dear Archbishop, Dear Father Reed, Dear Sister Superior (§ 545).

NOTE 1. Observe that *dear* does not take a capital letter unless it begins the salutation.

NOTE 2. The word *Friend*, as a common salutation for letters, is improper. It should be used between intimate friends only ; even then it should be restricted to acts involving their friendship : ' Dear old Friend, I am a thousand times obliged to you ', etc. The conclusion, too, should be in harmony with the thought : ' Most gratefully yours ', ' Gratefully and affectionately yours ', or the like. (Not ' Yours sincerely '.)

522. First paragraph. The first paragraph of a letter should have the same indention as the following paragraphs, and no more.

523. Body of letter. A letter should be as easy and natural in expression as if the writer were talking to the person to whom he is writing.

524. Conclusion. The conclusion of a letter should be in harmony with the salutation (§§ 544, 545) ; if the conclusion consists of not more than three or four short words, it should begin a little to the right of the middle of the page (as in Lowell's letter, § 519 ; compare Lincoln's letter to Mrs. Bixby, § 531) ; for the capitalization, see § 425 :

With love, With love to all, Affectionately yours, Yours always, Sincerely yours, Faithfully yours, Ever sincerely yours, Yours most sincerely, Ever faithfully yours, Most affectionately yours.

NOTE. Observe that only the first word of the conclusion begins with a capital letter (see § 425). For the punctuation, see § 528.

346 ENVELOPE AND PAPER

525. Envelope and paper ; stamp. As much pains should
be taken with the envelope of a letter as with the letter itself,
that the recipient may be pleased with the courtesy of his
correspondent. The Post-Office Department says, "Do not

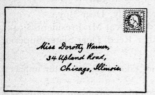

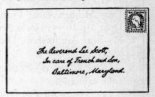

abbreviate or use lead pencil." See § 529. The stamp should
be placed neatly (not upside down or at an angle) in the upper
right-hand corner of the envelope.

The paper used for the personal (or friendly) letter should
be white (the ink being black), of the same quality and style
as the envelope. It should be a folded sheet of four pages,

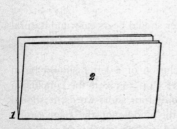

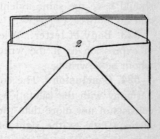

which will fit the envelope when folded once more from side
to side. The letter should be placed in the envelope with the
transverse fold (1) at the bottom of the envelope, and the back
of the letter (2) next to the back of the envelope ; thus, when
the recipient opens the envelope with a paper knife, and takes
out the letter, he will open the letter right side up.

526. Cards. If the letter or note is written on a card that matches the envelope, the card should be inserted in the envelope with the top of the card at the top of the envelope, and the face of the card toward the back of the envelope.

527. Punctuation after salutation. The proper mark of punctuation after the salutation in a letter is the comma; for the salutation is in the nominative of address (§ 471). The comma has been in use for hundreds of years; the colon and other marks of punctuation recently coming into practice in the United States are illogical American innovations.

The salutation, like any other nominative of address, should be read with the rising inflection. This brings the writer and the recipient face to face, as it were, and their letters will grow in courtesy.

NOTE. The salutation in a letter is now usually placed above the body of the letter, to catch the eye of the reader, the following word being capitalized. In the reprinting of letters space is sometimes saved either by omitting the salutation or by putting it at the beginning of the first line of the body of the letter, a dash sometimes being added to the comma, rather unreasonably, to separate the salutation from what follows.

It is surprising with what frequency and seeming carelessness American editors, in quoting letters from English literature, change the original comma to some other mark of punctuation.

528. Omission of punctuation in address, etc. The omission of punctuation in the address (whether in the letter or on the envelope) and in the conclusion, as sometimes seen, is less to be recommended. It is not in general use; it is not in harmony with the rest of the letter; it might seem to indicate haste, and hence a lack of courtesy. See § 529.

NOTE. Partial punctuation in the address or elsewhere should be avoided; it is likely to give the impression that the writer would omit it all if he could. For example, write 'Yours sincerely, Bob.' (Do not omit the period after *Bob*; it ends the sentence. See § 347.)

529. Abbreviations. Most abbreviations are not used in literature, but are confined to mathematical and similar scientific books, dictionaries, tables, memoranda, footnotes, and the like. Good taste avoids them in both personal and business correspondence, for they not only look badly, but give the impression of haste, and hence of a lack of courtesy. See §543.

Do not abbreviate the names of states, cities, towns, streets, months, and days of the week. For numbers, see §§ 127–131.

Do not abbreviate such titles as *Captain*, *Doctor*, *Esquire*, *General*, *Governor*, the *Honorable* (§ 417), *President*, *Principal*, *Professor*, and the *Reverend* (see *honorable*, § 417). The abbreviated titles *Mr.*, *Mrs.*, *Messrs.* (= *Messieurs*, §§ 423, 544, I), *Mmes* (= *Mesdames*, §§ 423, 544, II, III), *Jr.*, and *Sr.*, and such abbreviations as *A.B.*, *D.D.*, *M.D.*, *LL.D.*, *Ph.D.*, are correct when used with proper names (but see § 544, I, N. I); in connected writing, however, *Messrs.*, *Mmes*, *Jr.*, and *Sr.* should not be abbreviated (*Messieurs, Mesdames, Junior, Senior*):

1. " Quite so ", said *Doctor* Parker Peps. — DICKENS.
2. The Right *Honorable* William Buffy. — DICKENS.
3. The *Reverend* Josiah Cargill. — SCOTT.
4. Wilkins Micawber, *Esquire*, presented himself. — DICKENS.
5. *Messrs.* Fraser and Fraser.
   I dined with him at *Messieurs* Dillys. — BOSWELL.
6. *Mmes* Scott and Brown.
   Mesdames Scott and Brown were patronesses.
7. Tom Brown, *Jr.*, Treasurer.
   ' Pray come in ', said M. Pocket, *Junior*. — DICKENS.
8. He has received his bachelor's degree (not his ' A.B.').

NOTE. The abbreviations of titles, such as *A.B.*, *D.D.*, *Litt.D.*, *LL.D.*, are not spaced between the letters. The title *Esquire* is used loosely in the United States; it is given to Federal and state officials not entitled to ' Honorable ' (§ 545, IV–VI), lawyers, justices of the peace, and leading men who have no other title. The abbreviation *Co.* (= *Company*) should be used if it is the form adopted by the firm: Longmans, Green & *Co*. See § 466, *A*, 4.

530. Order of pages. In the personal letter written on a four-page sheet of paper it is simpler and clearer to write on the pages in their regular order, as if they were pages in a book, without regard to whether the message is to fill two, three, or four pages.

THE FORMAL PERSONAL LETTER

531. Formal personal letter. The following letters written by Washington and Lincoln illustrate the formal personal letter:

General Washington having been informed, lately, of the honor done him by Miss Kitty Livingston in wishing for a lock of his Hair, takes the liberty of inclosing one, accompanied by his most respectful compliments.

Camp, Valley Forge,
    18th March, 1778.

                Executive Mansion,
                   Washington, November 21, 1864.

Mrs. Bixby,
    Boston, Massachusetts.
Dear Madam,

I have been shown in the files of the War Department a statement of the Adjutant General of Massachusetts that you are the mother of five sons who have died gloriously on the field of battle. I feel how weak and fruitless must be any word of mine which should attempt to beguile you from the grief of a loss so overwhelming. But I cannot refrain from tendering you the consolation that may be found in the thanks of the republic they died to save. I pray that our Heavenly Father may assuage the anguish of your bereavement, and leave you only the cherished memory of the loved and lost, and the solemn pride that must be yours to have laid so costly a sacrifice upon the altar of freedom.

                Yours very sincerely and respectfully,
                    A. Lincoln.

532. Address and date. Washington's letter to Miss Livingston is a formal note rather than a letter. The address of the writer is placed at the bottom, at the left; the address of the addressee is omitted. The day of the month would now usually be written out: 'March the eighteenth' (or 'The eighteenth of March'); the year would ordinarily be omitted. The note is written in the third person, and hence has no salutation or conclusion. A formal invitation omits not only the salutation and conclusion, but the address and date; the answer to a formal invitation should be equally formal: 'Mr. and Mrs. Charles Browne request the honor of Mr. and Mrs. James Scott's presence at', etc.; 'Mr. and Mrs. James Scott accept with pleasure (regret that they cannot accept) Mr. and Mrs. Charles Browne's invitation to', etc.

Lincoln's letter to Mrs. Bixby illustrates the formal personal letter. The name of the addressee (with title, §§ 529, 544, 545) would now usually be placed at the bottom of the letter, at the left, the residence (street, city, and state) being omitted:

Executive Mansion,
Washington, November 21, 1864.

Dear Madam,

    I have been shown in the files of the War Department a statement of the Adjutant General, etc.

Yours very sincerely and respectfully,
A. Lincoln.

    Mrs. Bixby.

533. Salutation; conclusion. For the salutations and conclusions of the formal personal letter, see §§ 544, 545; for the capitalization of the conclusion, see § 425. For the punctuation after the salutation, see § 527.

534. Paragraphing, etc. For the paragraphing, envelope and paper, stamp, punctuation after salutation, and abbreviations, see §§ 522, 525, 527–529.

THE BUSINESS LETTER

535. Business letter. The business letter should be natural, and as brief as possible (§ 518). Avoid using hackneyed expressions, such as 'your esteemed favor', 'has come to hand', 'contents duly noted', ' your communication of yesterday's date' (business jargon), 'unforeseen circumstances', ' enclosed please find', ' beg to advise', ' pleased to inform', ' as per' (§ 289), 'earliest convenience', 'in compliance with your request ', 'assuring you of our best attention ', 'awaiting your further orders ', 'trusting this will be satisfactory '.

In addressing a letter, use only one title (' Superintendent David Warren ', not 'Mr. David Warren, Superintendent '; ' Henry Jackson, Treasurer ', not ' Mr. Henry Jackson, Treasurer '. See § 544, I, N. 1). Write out ' In care of '; use it only when writing to a person at a temporary address.

Study the following letters (for dates, see § 128, *b*, 2):

50ᴬ, ALBEMARLE STREET,
LONDON, W.1.
24th March, 1916.

Messrs. ———&———,
    Boston.
Dear Sirs,
    I am in receipt of your letter of March 6th, in reference to copies of "The Classical Review" and "Quarterly" for Miss Hurst. I understand that your London House is despatching the January and February numbers direct, and I have noted that in the case of future re—subscriptions your London House is to be notified in the first instance.

Yours faithfully,
JOHN MURRAY.

                              34 Washington Street,
                                   Montclair, New Jersey,
                                        July 1, 1920.
Mr. John A. Brown,
      216 Jefferson Street,
            Salem, Oregon.
Dear Sir,
      The goods ordered by you in your letter of
June 25th were sent [see 'ship', § 417] by express
today.
      If you do not receive them promptly, please
let us know.
                              Yours very truly,
                                   Tomson and French.

NOTE. In general, typewritten letters should have double spacing.
Single spacing, which arises from a desire to save space and paper,
should be confined to informal interdepartmental letters and the like.
In either case the spacing should be uniform throughout.

536. Address and date. In the business letter, for the sake
of convenience of reference, the address of the writer, the
date of composition, and the address of the person written to
(addressee) are usually placed at the top. In England, and
sometimes in the United States, a comma is placed after house
numbers : ' 27, Beacon Street '.

NOTE. The so-called block arrangement (without indention) is not
to be recommended. It is not established by good usage ; it lacks symmetry, and hence is not pleasing to the eye ; it is less legible ; it is not
approved by the Post-Office Department.

537. Salutation. The salutation in the business letter
should be what the writer would naturally say to the addressee
if speaking to him, with or without *Dear* or *My dear* before it
(§§ 544, 545):

Dear Sir, Dear Sirs, Dear Mr. Senator, Sir, Sirs, Dear Madam,
Dear Mother Superior, Mesdames. See §§ 521, 524, 540, 544, 545.

538. First paragraph. The first paragraph should have the same indention as the others, and no more (§ 522).

539. Body of letter. The business letter should be as easy and natural in expression as if the writer were talking.

540. Conclusion. The conclusion in the business letter should be in harmony with the salutation (§§ 544, 545); for the capitalization, see § 425:

Very truly yours, Sincerely yours, Faithfully yours, Most respectfully yours, Your obedient servant.

541. Envelope and paper; stamp. The envelope and the paper should be of the same quality and style. As much pains should be taken with the envelope as with the letter itself, that the recipient may be pleased with the courtesy shown him. Abbreviations should be avoided (§ 529); they cause the loss

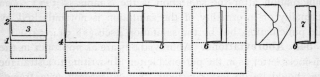

of much mail matter; the Post-Office Department says, "Do not abbreviate or use lead pencil." For the stamp, see § 525.

If the paper is a narrow sheet of a width that matches the length of the envelope, and needs to be folded but once, transversely, it should be folded as in § 525. If it needs to be folded twice transversely, it should be folded first from the bottom, on a line about one third of the way to the top of the paper; the top edge of the paper should then be brought down and laid about half an inch above the first fold, and held there while the second fold is being made (see 1 and 2 in the diagram above); the letter should be inserted in the envelope with the first fold (1) at the bottom of the envelope, and the folded top (3) next to the back (the sealed side) of the envelope.

If the paper needs to be folded three times, it should be folded first transversely, with the bottom edge of the paper carried up and laid about half an inch from the top of the sheet (see 4, above); then it should be folded vertically, from the right, on a line about one third of the way across the sheet (5); the left-hand edge should then be brought over and laid about half an inch to the left of the first vertical fold (5), and held there while the second vertical fold (6) is being made. The letter should be inserted in the envelope with the second vertical fold (6) at the bottom of the envelope, and the folded top (7) next to the back of the envelope. When the recipient opens the envelope with a paper knife, and takes out the letter, he will open the letter right side up.

542. Punctuation after salutation. The proper mark of punctuation after the salutation is the comma (§ 527). The formality or informality of the salutation is not indicated by the punctuation, but by the salutation itself (§§ 544, 545).

543. Abbreviations. Abbreviations are as improper in the business letter as in the personal letter. In writing to a stranger we should be no less courteous than in writing to a friend. For the use of abbreviations, see § 529.

ADDRESSES AND SALUTATIONS IN ORDINARY LETTERS

544. Ordinary letters. In the United States the salutation with ' My dear ' (see § 521, N. 1) is generally less intimate than that with ' Dear '; in British usage the reverse is true; this distinction should be observed in foreign correspondence (see the letters in § 519). In business letters it is courteous, in referring to patrons and friends, not to call them Scott, Brown, and so forth, but to give to each his proper title: Mr. Scott, Professor Brown, the Reverend Doctor Dow.

I. To Men

Singular 1. *Address :* Mr. (Professor, etc. Use the higher form of a person's title : as, Professor; not 'Associate Professor' or 'Assistant Professor') John Scott.

2. *Informal salutation :* Dear Jack (intimate); Dear Mr. Scott (less intimate); My dear Mr. Scott (least intimate).

3. *Formal salutation :* Dear Sir; My dear Sir (more formal); Sir (most formal; see § 545).

Plural 1. *Address :* Messrs. Scott and Brown; Messrs. Ginn and Company; Messrs. Brown, Shipley, and Company, Ltd. But with such impersonal forms as G. and C. Merriam Company, The Macmillan Company, The Whittier Paper Company, *Messrs.* is not used.

2. *Formal salutation :* Dear Sirs (or, Gentlemen; see Note 2); My dear Sirs (more formal); Sirs (most formal; see § 545).

NOTE 1. It is best not to use more than one title in an address: as, *Professor* James Scott (not 'Professor James Scott, Ph.D.'); *The Right Reverend* James Scott (not 'The Right Reverend James Scott, D.D.'). See § 545, XI, N., and § 535.

NOTE 2. In ordinary letters both 'Dear Sirs' and 'Gentlemen' are now in common use, with the tendency in favor of 'Dear Sirs'.

Originally, the salutation in the singular was the formal 'Sir', the plural of which was 'Sirs' or, more commonly, 'Gentlemen'. After a while the singular 'Sir' progressed to the less formal 'Dear Sir'; but the corresponding plural 'Dear Gentlemen' was not felt to be proper, and the formal 'Gentlemen' continued for some time to be used much more frequently than the less formal 'Dear Sirs'. More recently, however, there has been an increasing use of 'Dear Sirs', as being the appropriate plural to 'Dear Sir'. " It is easy to prophesy that 'Dear Sirs' will oust 'Gentlemen' before long ", says Mr. H. W. FOWLER (see § 460, N.).

NOTE 3. Firms composed of both men and women are addressed 'Messrs.', with the salutation 'Dear Sirs'. The masculine forms include the feminine; see § 60, 6, § 118, N., and § 120. For firms composed of women, see § 544, II, III.

II. To Unmarried Women

Singular 1. *Address :* Miss Edith Scott (younger daughter); Miss
Scott (elder or eldest daughter, without initials).

2. *Informal salutation :* Dear Edith (intimate); Dear
Miss Edith (less intimate); My dear Miss Edith
(least intimate). Dear Miss Scott; My dear Miss
Scott (less intimate).

3. *Formal salutation :* Dear Madam; My dear Madam
(more formal); Madam (most formal).

NOTE. An unmarried woman should ordinarily sign her name in
full, 'Edith Scott'; if she is writing to a stranger, she may put
'(Miss)' before it, although this is not necessary. But see 'To Married
Women', Note 1, below.

Plural 1. *Address :* The Misses Scott ('The Miss Scotts' is
common in conversation, but is not permissible as
an address); The Misses Scott and Brown.

2. *Formal salutation :* Mesdames (§ 423. This salutation is most formal, and may not be preceded by
'My dear' or 'Dear').

III. To Married Women

Singular 1. *Address :* Mrs. John Scott.

2. *Informal salutation :* Dear Mrs. Scott; My dear
Mrs. Scott (less intimate).

3. *Formal salutation :* Dear Madam; My dear Madam
(more formal); Madam (most formal).

Plural 1. *Address :* Mmes Scott and Brown. (Mmes = Mesdames, §§ 423, 461, N. 1.)

2. *Formal salutation :* Mesdames. (This salutation is
most formal, and may not be preceded by 'My
dear' or 'Dear'.)

NOTE 1. In social correspondence a married woman signs herself
by her own name, 'Emily Randolph Osgood' (not 'Mrs. James B.
Osgood ').

In business correspondence, if writing to a stranger, she should add, below her own name, ' (Mrs. James B. Osgood.) '. She is usually addressed ' Mrs. James B. Osgood '. If she is a widow, she signs herself by her own name, with ' (Mrs.) ' before it when writing to a stranger; she is usually addressed by her own name, ' Mrs. Emily Randolph Osgood '.

In signing a legal document, a woman (single, married, or widow) uses her own name, ' Emily Randolph ', ' Emily Randolph Osgood '.

NOTE 2. On her calling card a married woman has ' Mrs. James Barr Osgood ' (use the full name; not ' Mrs. James B. Osgood '); a widow may have ' Mrs. James Barr Osgood ' or ' Mrs. Emily Randolph Osgood ' (the latter avoids confusion).

NOTE 3. A business woman should have two kinds of cards : for calling, ' Miss Jane Day Brown '; for business, ' Jane Day Brown, M.D.' In business Miss Brown should be addressed ' Doctor Jane Day Brown '.

ETIQUETTE IN FORMAL LETTERS TO HIGH OFFICIALS

545. Formal letters. In formal letters to high officials certain points of etiquette should be observed. For example, to begin a letter with ' Sir ' and end it with ' Yours sincerely ' or the like displays a lack of propriety. The position of the name of the addressee is shown in § 532. For the capitalization of the conclusion, see § 425. (If acquaintance or intimacy warrants, high officials are addressed less formally, or informally ; §§ 544, 519–521, 524.)

I. To a Duke (or a Duchess)

Address : To His Grace, the Duke (or, To Her Grace, the Duchess) of Buckingham.

Salutation : My Lord Duke (or, Madam).

Reference : Your Grace. (This means that in the body of the letter ' Your Grace ' is used instead of ' you ', and ' Your Grace's ' instead of ' your '.)

Conclusion : I have the honor to be, my Lord Duke (or, Madam),
Your Grace's most devoted and most obedient
servant (to a duchess, Your Grace's most humble
and most obedient servant),

Charles Kingsley.

II. To an Earl (or a Countess)

Address :   The Right Honorable the Earl——(or, To the Right
Honorable the Countess of——).
Salutation : My Lord (or, Madam).
Reference : Your Lordship (or, Your Ladyship). (See 1, above.)
Conclusion : I have the honor to be, my Lord (or, Madam),
Your Lordship's (or, Your Ladyship's) obedient
and humble servant.

III. To a Foreign Ambassador

Address :   His Excellency,
The Ambassador of Great Britain (of the French
Republic, etc.).
Salutation : Sir.
Reference : Your Excellency. (See 1, above.)
Conclusion : I have the honor to be, Sir,
Your Excellency's obedient servant.

IV. To a Governor

Address :   The Honorable
The Governor of Tennessee,
Nashville. (By law in Massachusetts and New
Hampshire, and by courtesy in some other
states, 'His Excellency, The Governor of——.')
Salutation : Sir.
Reference : Your Excellency (used only when the address has
'His Excellency'). (See 1, above.)
Conclusion : I have the honor to be, Sir,
Your obedient servant.

V. To a Mayor, Judge, Member of Congress, etc.

Here are included mayors (of cities), judges, heads of state departments, members of state senates, commissioners of bureaus, assistants to members of the cabinet, members of Congress (senators and representatives), lieutenant governors, and the vice president of the United States.

Address: The Honorable James Scott, Mayor of —— (Senator of ——; Commissioner of Education; etc.).

Salutation: Sir.

Conclusion: I have the honor to be, Sir,
Your obedient servant.

VI. To a Member of the Cabinet

Address: The Honorable
The Secretary of Agriculture (or, The Honorable
The Postmaster-General; etc.).

Salutation: Sir.

Conclusion: I have the honor to be, Sir,
Your obedient servant.

VII. To the President of the United States

Address: The President,
The White House,
Washington, D.C.

Salutation: Sir.

Conclusion: I have the honor to be, Sir,
Your most obedient servant.

VIII. To a Protestant Bishop

Address: The Right Reverend —— ——, D.D.,
Bishop of New Hampshire. (See xi, n.)

Salutation: Right Reverend Sir.

Conclusion: I have the honor to be, Right Reverend Sir,
Your obedient servant.

NOTE 1. In the Methodist Church a bishop, unless retired, is addressed The Reverend —— ——; salutation, Dear Sir; conclusion, Sincerely yours (or the like; § 524).

NOTE 2. In England a bishop is addressed The Right Reverend the Lord Bishop of ——; salutation, My Lord; reference, Your Lordship (see 1, above); conclusion, I have the honor to be, my Lord, Your Lordship's obedient and humble servant.

IX. TO A PROTESTANT CLERGYMAN OR A RABBI

Address: The Reverend Harry Wise.
Salutation: Reverend Sir.
Conclusion · I am, Reverend Sir,
           Your obedient servant.

X. TO A CARDINAL

Address: His Eminence James Cardinal Gibbons,
           Archbishop of Baltimore.
Salutation: Your Eminence (or, My Lord Cardinal).
Reference: Your Eminence. (See 1, above.)
Conclusion: I have the honor to be, my Lord Cardinal,
           Your Eminence's most devoted and obedient
           servant.

XI. TO A ROMAN CATHOLIC ARCHBISHOP

Address: The Most Reverend —— ——, D.D.,
           Archbishop of San Francisco.
Salutation: Your Grace (or, My Lord Archbishop).
Reference: Your Grace. (See 1, above.)
Conclusion: I have the honor to be, my Lord Archbishop,
           Your Grace's most devoted and obedient servant.

NOTE. "The addition of *D.D.*, or the prefixing of *Doctor* or *Dr.*, to the names of Catholic Archbishops or Bishops, is not necessary, and is not in conformity with the best usage." — The Catholic Encyclopedia. See § 544, 1, N. 1.

XII. To a Roman Catholic Bishop

Address :   The Right Reverend —— ——, D.D.,
             Bishop of Trenton. (See XI, N.)

Salutation :   Right Reverend and dear Bishop (or, My Lord ; or,
             Your Lordship ; see Note 1).

Reference :   Your Lordship. (See Note 1, below, and 1, above.)

Conclusion :   I have the honor to be,
             Right Reverend and dear Bishop (or, my Lord ;
             see Note 1),
                Your (or, Your Lordship's ; see Note 1) obedient
                and humble servant.

NOTE 1. In the United States the forms with ' Lord ' and ' Lordship ' are less usual.

NOTE 2. A bishop may also be addressed Monsignor : address,
The Right Reverend Monsignor —— ——, D.D., Bishop of —— ;
salutation, Right Reverend and dear Monsignor ; conclusion, I have
the honor to be, Right Reverend and dear Monsignor, Your obedient
and humble servant. (See XIII.)

XIII. To a Roman Catholic Monsignor

Address :   The Right (or, The Very, as the case may be)
             Reverend Monsignor —— ——.

Salutation :   Right (or, Very, as the case may be) Reverend and
             dear Monsignor.

Conclusion :   I have the honor to be,
             Right (or, Very, as the case may be) Reverend and
             dear Monsignor,
                Your obedient and humble servant.

XIV. To a Roman Catholic Priest

Address :   The Reverend —— ——.

Salutation :   Reverend and dear Father.

Conclusion :   I have the honor to be,
             Reverend and dear Father,
                Your obedient servant.

XV. To Men in Religious Orders

Address :   (*to a father superior*) The Reverend —— ——, Superior.
Salutation : Reverend and dear Father Superior.
Conclusion : I have the honor to be,
                Reverend and dear Father Superior,
                    Your obedient servant.

Address :   (*to a father*) The Reverend —— ——.
Salutation : Reverend and dear Father.
Conclusion : I have the honor to be,
                Reverend and dear Father,
                    Your obedient servant.

Address :   (*to a community of fathers*) The Franciscan Fathers.
Salutation : Reverend and dear Fathers.
Conclusion : I have the honor to be,
                Reverend and dear Fathers,
                    Your obedient servant.

Note 1. The head of an educational institution is addressed, at least by courtesy, The Very Reverend: address, The Very Reverend —— ——; salutation, Very Reverend and dear Father Rector (President, etc.); conclusion, I have the honor to be, Very Reverend and dear Father Rector, Your obedient servant.

Note 2. A brother in the various orders or congregations is addressed The Reverend Brother Alfred ——; salutation, Dear Brother Alfred; conclusion, I have the honor to be, Dear Brother Alfred, Your obedient servant.

XVI. To Women in Religious Orders

Address :   (*to a mother superior*) The Reverend Mother Camilla, Saint Joseph's Convent.
Salutation : Reverend and dear Mother Superior.
Conclusion : I have the honor to be,
                Reverend and dear Mother Superior,
                    Your obedient servant.

Address: (*to a sister*) Sister Mary Helen (or, Madam ——
             ——; see Note 1).

Salutation: Reverend and dear Sister (or, Reverend and dear
             Madam; see Note 1).

Conclusion: I have the honor to be,
             Reverend and dear Sister (or, Reverend and dear
               Madam; see Note 1),
             Your obedient servant.

Address: (*to a community of sisters*) The Sisters of the Sacred
             Heart (or, Mesdames of the Sacred Heart; see
             Note 1).

Salutation: Reverend and dear Sisters (or, Mesdames; see Note 1,
             and § 544, 11).

Conclusion: I have the honor to be,
             Reverend and dear Sisters (or, Mesdames; see
               Note 1),
             Your obedient servant.

NOTE 1. 'Sister' and 'Sisters' are generally preferable to 'Madam' and 'Mesdames', but in the case of a few communities who use the title 'Madam' (as most others use 'Sister') the address and the salutation have 'Madam' or 'Mesdames' instead of 'Sister' or 'Sisters'.

NOTE 2. If the sister addressed is known to be the superior of a school or convent, 'Superior' may well be added to the address and the salutation: address, Sister —— ——, Superior; salutation, Reverend and dear Sister Superior.

NOTE 3. The salutation 'Dear Sister' or 'Dear Sisters' is frequently used when acquaintance warrants the omission of the more formal title (§§ 521, 524, 537, 540).

XVII. To the Trustees of an Institution

Address: The Honorable and Reverend
            The Board of Trustees of —— College.

Salutation: Honorable and Reverend Sirs.

Conclusion: I have the honor to be,
            Honorable and Reverend Sirs,
               Your obedient servant.

CHAPTER XI

EXERCISES

The style of an author should be the image of his mind, but the choice and command of language is the fruit of exercise. — GIBBON.

546. Exercise I (Preface). *a*. **1.** Read the quotation on the title-page. **2.** Why is education necessary? **3.** Is the primary object of education to teach us how to make money, or how to be good citizens? **4.** Write your reasons for desiring an education.

b. **1.** How important is language to the progress of the world? **2.** What would happen if all the languages were lost? **3.** Why should we be careful about our dress? **4.** In what way is language like dress? **5.** What is meant by shabby dress? by shabby manners? by shabby language?

c. **1.** Is it usually easy to become an athlete? Why? **2.** Why are not more people successful in life? **3.** What are you willing to do to help yourself to get an education? **4.** Read aloud at least half an hour in the evening, several times a week, to your mother or father, sister or brother. Read good stories, books of travel and adventure, and biographies. Read carefully and patiently, and you will soon enjoy it and be helped by it.

d. **1.** What does Lord Bacon say about the value of reading? (For the use of *that* in the quotation from Bacon, see § 83, N.) **2.** What does he mean by *conference*? **3.** What does Lord Bacon say about the need of practice in writing? When you read aloud, ask questions and talk about what you read. In this way you will learn to speak freely and naturally.

When you write, at home or at school, be as natural as if you were talking, and your reader will feel as if you were with him, speaking to him.

547. Exercise II (page 1). 1. What power does music possess? 2. What, according to Plato, is the power of language? 3. What is meant by the proverb " The pen is mightier than the sword"? 4. Do you think that the sword is sometimes necessary? 5. Write your reasons for thinking that it is (or is not) essential for you to be a good writer as well as a good reader and a good speaker.

548. Exercise III (§§ 2–8, 361–364, 516–518). *a*. 1. Which is the easier method of making ourselves understood, speaking or writing? Why? 2. Why should we study words? 3. What does Chesterfield say about style? 4. Why do we need a great deal of practice in writing letters? 5. In applying to a stranger for a position, should you prefer to write to him, or to put on your best clothes and have a talk with him? 6. Which do you think he would prefer to have you do? Why?

b. 1. In writing a letter of any kind to anybody try to be as natural as if you were speaking. Read and discuss the letter of Charles Dickens in § 519. 2. Write to an imaginary person a letter on any of the subjects in § 587. Put the letter away for a few days; then read it aloud, to see how it looks and to hear how it sounds.

c. 1. What is the difference between a phrase and a clause? 2. Write five sentences containing principal and subordinate clauses. For adjective and adverb phrases and clauses, see §§ 557 and 571.

549. Exercise IV (§§ 9–22, 378–380, 498–509). *a*. 1. Why should we study grammar? rhetoric? 2. Learn to classify words by the way in which they are used in sentences (§§ 383, 585, *b*). 3. Write five sentences containing noun phrases; noun clauses.

b. Write five sentences containing compound words. If you are where you have no dictionary, and are in doubt about how to write the compound words, write them first as single words (without a hyphen; as, *schoolgirl, warship*); if they look odd and illegible, rewrite them as separate words (as, *boy scout*).

c. 1. A man of peace is a man who desires peace (§ 499). What is a man of war? 2. What is the difference between a *man of war* and a *man-of-war*? 3. What would *forget-me-not* mean without the hyphens? 4. What would *grandfather* mean if written as two separate words? 5. What is the difference between 'he has a son in law' and 'he has a son-in-law'? between 'eight pound boxes' and 'eight-pound boxes'? 6. Why does *commander in chief* need no hyphens?

550. Exercise V (§§ 588–603). *a.* 1. Who were our linguistic ancestors? 2. Where did they live? 3. Why did they separate? 4. Where did they go? 5. What did the Romans do for Britain? 6. How did England get its name? 7. Who were the Normans? 8. How did the Norman Conquest affect the English language? 9. Describe some of the elements in the English language of today.

b. 1. Choose some interesting topic in the history of the Indo-European languages, or in the early history of England, and read about it in the encyclopedia. 2. Write to a friend (real or imaginary), telling him what you have been doing, and ask him if he has any book on the subject.

551. Exercise VI (§§ 23–39, 402, 604–606). 1. Use the singular and plural of the words in §§ 23–28 in oral and written sentences. 2. How do you pronounce *c* and *g* in Latin and Greek words? Give examples. 3. Spell, pronounce, and define the words in § 39 (consulting the dictionary if necessary). 4. Use these words in oral and written sentences. 5. Spell, pronounce, and define the following Latin and Greek words,

and give their plurals (consulting the dictionary if necessary):
*amanuensis, apex, arcanum, axis, basis, dogma, effluvium, enco-
mium, erratum, focus, medium, metamorphosis, nucleus, spectrum,
vortex.* **6.** Point out the fault in each of the following words:
cherubims, candelabras, bandittis, seraphims, vertebræ.

552. Exercise VII (§§ 40–54). **1.** Write sentences containing the nominative (or objective) and the possessive case, singular and plural, of *child, deer, goose, mouse, sheep, woman,
Watkins, father-in-law, cash girl, man clerk.* **2.** Write sentences
containing the possessive case (or a phrase with *of*) of *Moses,
Socrates, Allen and Greenough, the Charles E. Osgood Company.*

553. Exercise VIII (review). **1.** Pick out the nouns in
§§ 588–594, and tell how they are used. **2.** Change singulars
to plurals, and plurals to singulars.

554. Exercise IX (§§ 56–64, 403). (*a*) How do you know
whether such words as *this, that, his, whose, which,* and *other*
are adjectives or pronouns? (§ 56.) (*b*) Write five sentences
containing personal pronouns as objects. (*c*) What is the difference between *daub* and *bedaub, moan* and *bemoan, thump*
and *bethump*? (*d*) Form some words with the prefixes *be-, mis-,
over-, un-, under-*. (*e*) Read and discuss Lowell's letter in § 519.
(*f*) Write a letter to an imaginary boy (or girl) accepting (or
declining) an invitation to a party. (*g*) From the following
parentheses select the proper forms; give your reasons:

1. She is no better than (I, me, he, him). 2. They invited you
and (I, me, she, her). 3. It couldn't have been (she, her, he, him,
they, them). 4. They sat in the same seat with you and (I, me).
5. What would you do if you were (she, her, he, him, they, them)?
6. What difference does it make to you and (I, me, he, him)? 7. Was
it (we, us, they, them)? 8. No, that's (she, her, he, him) over there.
9. They won't let you and (I, me) go. 10. Do you like her better
than (I, me, he, him, they, them)?

555. Exercise X (§§ 65–74, 520–522, 524, 527, 528). *a.* In the following sentences correct the faulty use of nouns and pronouns; rewrite the sentences:

1. His father became a sailor when he was ten years old. 2. When she rebuked her, she was very angry. 3. He ran into the house, and found him in the library with his mother. He asked him if he would meet him at the river, after school. 4. When he examined the wound, he said that he would recover. 5. It was at Rome, while Gibbon sat musing amidst the ruins of the Capitol, that Gibbon had his vision of the decline and fall of Rome. 6. Yesterday we found the boat. It was leaking, and it was so short a time till sunset that it was impossible to take it back to camp. 7. The thief followed the policeman until they reached the crowded part of the street, where he turned into a narrow alley. 8. At daybreak the wind blew harder and harder. I had been in Yarmouth when people said the wind blew great guns, but I had never known a wind like this wind. 9. Harry saw him watching him while he spoke to us, and he evidently thought he was a spy. 10. Mr. Arnold and his man Sam started toward the river. Sam looked at Mr. Arnold and saw that Mr. Arnold was very pale. 11. At a turn in the road they saw the figures of two men start up in front of them. They tried to cry out. One of them fell before he could utter a sound; the other had only time to cry for help.

b. Write five subjects for five compositions, and the first sentence of each composition. (See § 354, N.)

c. Write the beginning and the end of a letter to your mother or sister; to an old schoolmate; to a poor woman whose window you broke.

556. Exercise XI (§§ 75–91, 387–391). *a.* Fill the following blanks with *who* or *whom*, and give your reasons:

1. She invited those —— she said liked sailing. 2. He was a man —— there was reason to admire. 3. —— did you suppose me to be? 4. —— did you think she was? 5. Let them be —— they may. 6. There is a boy —— I suppose is suitable. 7. It depends on ——

they think ought to be sent. 8. —— did you discover to be the author? 9. Is there any question as to —— should be chosen? 10. —— do they say she is? 11. His associates are persons —— he feels sure are interested.

b. 1. Why do we easily understand the old English words? 2. Why is it essential to learn the fundamental meanings of Latin and Greek words? 3. What is the meaning of the Latin *fac-* (§ 407)? 4. See how many words you can write in five minutes by compounding *fac-* with the Latin prefixes in § 405. 5. Give the fundamental meanings of the words you have written.

557. Exercise XII (§§ 92–97, 375, 376, 472). *a.* In the following sentences pick out the adjective and adverb phrases and clauses, and tell what they modify (see § 571 also); explain why they are essential or nonessential (§ 472):

1. The water by the old mill is deep. 2. She lives in a smaller house, at the corner of the street. 3. They have built a new barn, which stands back from the road. 4. A path made by deer wound along the side of the glen. 5. We saw a young Italian girl, who was selling flowers. 6. Heavy winds which blow from the south cause a period of extreme heat. 7. The old trader, whom he met at the inn, told strange tales of the wilderness. 8. The bank which the canoe approached was covered with a growth of small trees. 9. Frank Thomson, of Charleston, did not attend the convention. 10. She likes pictures that have bright colors. 11. He lives with Charles Black, who was once a pupil of his. 12. In the hall of the old mansion stood a chair of even more ancient days. 13. He who perseveres will find a place in the world. 14. We boarded the larger ship, which was sailing for India. 15. She has one friend who will help her; she has one friend, who will help her.

b. In the following sentences place the pronouns where they ought to be; rewrite the sentences:

1. We rode in a carriage to the boat, which we found exceedingly uncomfortable. 2. There were masses of flowers in the booths along

the streets, which would have interested you. 3. The table was covered with books, at which he sat down to read. 4. I drew another large chair up to the fire, in which she quietly seated herself. 5. He was transferred to the island in a small boat, on which the prison was situated. 6. That is the son of James Scott, the multimillionaire, whom Dorothy is teaching to play the piano. 7. A basket of food was attached to a rope, which the prisoner needed. 8. There was a bird in a cage by a window, near which the cat crouched.

558. Exercise XIII (§§ 98–112). *a.* Fill the following blanks with *whoever* or *whomever*, and give your reasons:

1. Let him be —— he may. 2. They traded with —— came to their village. 3. She will trust —— you choose to send. 4. I will send —— you think should go. 5. He rewards —— he sees is faithful to him. 6. She will give a reward to —— will return the jewels. 7. They were kind toward —— chance brought to their door. 8. We will ask —— you think would like to come. 9. Choose —— it is easiest for you to do without. 10. I shall be satisfied with —— she thinks is trustworthy.

b. Improve the following paragraph; rewrite it:

It is surprising the amount of exercise one can get on board an airship of this size. The keel is about 600 [see § 128, *b*, 1] feet long and one is constantly running about from one end to the other. There are also steps in a vertical ladder to the top of the ship for those who feel energetic or have duty up there. By the time it comes one's turn to go to bed one generally finds one is very sleepy and the warmth of one's sleeping bag and hum of the engines soon send one to sleep.

c. Pick out the pronouns in § 377. Tell what they are, and how they are used. Change the singulars to plurals, the plurals to singulars, and use them in new sentences.

d. Correct the following sentences, and give your reasons:

1. Himself and wife were at the theater. 2. Yourself and friends will be welcome. 3. We saw herself and her cousin. 4. My uncle and self are now at the seashore.

559. Exercise XIV (§§ 113–138, 388). (*a*) Write five proper adjectives. Explain the use or omission of capital letters. (See §§ 117, 438, 455.) (*b*) Write five sentences with the adjective *each* ; with *either* ; with *neither*. Use these words as pronouns in the nominative case. (See § 568, *b*, also.) (*c*) Read in literary style the numbers 124, 1024, 10034; the years 1919, 1865, 1066. (*d*) Write five sentences containing *farther* ; *farthest* ; *further* ; *furthest* ; *little* ; *smallest* ; *oldest* ; *elder*. (*e*) When is the final consonant of a word doubled (§ 393)? When not? Give five examples of each. (*f*) Write ten words formed from the Latin *duc-*, § 407. (*g*) From the following parentheses select the proper forms ; give your reasons :

1. Neither he nor she (was, were) there. 2. Neither of them (has, have) a horse. 3. Every one of us (was, were) busy. 4. Neither of you (has, have) any reason to complain. 5. Every one of the elephants (wants, want) a drink.

560. Exercise XV (§§ 139–153). *a*. 1. What is the difference between ' I need a leader and adviser ' and ' I need a leader and an adviser ' ? 2. Write five sentences, each containing two or more ordinal numerals. (See §§ 121, 142.)

b. Write a letter on one of the subjects in § 587. Use as many adjectives as you can, but make your letter natural.

561. Exercise XVI (review). *a*. 1. Pick out the adjectives in § 375, and tell what they modify. 2. Use them in new sentences.

b. 1. Study the synonyms of *bad* and *good*, § 417. 2. Use them in sentences. 3. Give the comparative and the superlative of these synonyms.

562. Exercise XVII (§§ 154–167). 1. Write five sentences containing verbs (or verb phrases) used transitively. 2. If possible, write five other sentences with the same verbs used intransitively. 3. Write five sentences containing predicate adjectives ; five containing predicate nominatives.

563. Exercise XVIII (§§ 167–175). *a*. **1**. The irregular verbs are the old verbs of the language; new verbs added to the language are regular (see §§ 169, 170). Read aloud several times the verbs in § 172. **2**. Use these verbs in oral and written sentences. (From time to time read aloud some of the irregular verbs in § 654, and use them in sentences.) **3**. How are progressive verb phrases used? **4**. Write five sentences containing progressive verb phrases.

b. From the following parentheses select the proper forms; give your reasons:

1. We did not (lay, lie) there long. 2. He had (set, sat) by the fire all day. 3. Your dress (sets, sits) well. 4. The hens are now (setting, sitting). 5. The children were (laying, lying) in the grass. 6. The books have (laid, lain) here a long time. 7. They (laid, lay) in the sand. 8. She often (sets, sits) in that chair. 9. She had been (laying, lying) there an hour.

c. Use in sentences the present perfect and the past perfect of the following verbs : *bring, do, drink, eat, forget, get, ring, shake, swim, take.*

d. Read §§ 418–423. Read aloud the first column of words in § 423. (The teacher should pronounce the words to the class, and then have the class pronounce them.) Occasionally the students should write the words from dictation, and add the diacritical marks.

564. Exercise XIX (§§ 176–195). (*a*) Fill the following blanks with *shall* or *will*; then (*b*) change the principal verbs to the past, and use *should* or *would*; then (*a, b*) repeat the process with the first or second person changed to the third, and the third to the first :

1. I —— miss the train; —— you not help me? 2. He knows he —— be late. 3. Do you promise that you —— meet me? 4. Do you think we —— be able to find the road? 5. Jack says his sister —— be glad to see us; but he fears he —— be out of town.

6. —— you be obliged to wait? 7. Does she doubt that she —— be happy there? 8. Do you think you —— live here for some time? 9. Where —— I find the driver? 10. Do they say they —— have to start at once? 11. I cannot help you now, but I —— gladly do so tomorrow. 12. You say you —— be glad to help me?

(c) From the following parentheses select the proper forms; give your reasons:

1. (Can, may) he see you today? 2. (Could, might) we call this evening? 3. Ask mother if we (can, may) go to the beach. 4. Do you think you (can, could, may, might) drive a large car? 5. He said that we (could, might) take his boat. 6. (Can, may) I trouble you to open the door? 7. She says we (can, may) use her books. 8. It (can, may) be that we can go tomorrow. 9. It (can, could, may, might) not be possible. 10. I (can, could, may, might) not lift it now, but perhaps I (can, could, may, might) when I am older.

565. Exercise XX (§§ 176–181; 187–189). (a) Explain why either *shall* or *will* may be used in the following blanks; then (b) *should* or *would* (the principal verbs being changed to the past):

1. —— you answer the letter? 2. Do you say you —— answer it? 3. He says you —— receive a sealed package. 4. Do they write that they —— be here at ten? 5. I think I —— stay at home today. 6. He says he —— pay his own fare. 7. —— the finder be rewarded? 8. You say you —— not be gone long? 9. When —— you be at home? 10. —— you be at home by eight o'clock? 11. Jane is away; so I —— work alone until you come.

566. Exercise XXI (§§ 187–189). a. Fill the following blanks with *should* or *would*; then repeat the process with the first or second person changed to the third, and the third to the first:

1. We —— like to take you with us. 2. —— you like to come? 3. I —— gladly go with you, but it is impossible. 4. He —— be happy there, and I —— be so too. 5. They said they —— be late

if it rained. 6. —— you be good enough to read this? 7. —— you
have recognized her? 8. Did he say he —— have liked to remain?
9. She said she —— remain gladly if we needed her. 10. —— you
have been surprised? I ——n't, but he —— have been. 11. We
—— all enjoy having them here.

b. What is the difference between ' I should urge him to go
now ' and ' I would urge him to go now '? (See § 189, 6.)

c. What is the difference between ' if he would try ' and ' if
he should try '? (See § 194.)

567. Exercise XXII (§§ 178–181, 187–195). In the following sentences explain the faulty use of *shall*, *will*, *should*, or
would; give the direct form of the indirect quotations :

1. Jane said that I would be sick. 2. Harry says that he (Harry)
will be glad to go. 3. Would he and I be happy there? 4. She and
I shall wait gladly. 5. Did you say you would be sorry to miss them?
6. I said I should gladly write to him. 7. They think he and I would
get along well together. 8. Would you and he be willing to come again
tomorrow? 9. Do you think you and he will be troubled about the
delay? 10. He fears he would be too late, does he?

568. Exercise XXIII (§§ 196–207). *a.* Write five sentences containing the following subjects :

1. Collective nouns with singular verb ; with plural verb. 2. *Each,
either, neither.* See § 559, *g*, also. 3. Concrete numbers ; abstract
numbers. 4. Subjects connected by *or* or *nor*. 5. Subjects separated
from the verb. 6. *Percentage* ; numerals with *per cent.*

b. In the following sentences explain the faults :

1. Everybody has their troubles. 2. Neither of the girls have
found what they wanted. 3. Are either of you going to town?
4. Neither of them were necessary. 5. Neither of their farms were
large. 6. My profession, as well as the times in which we live, compel me to be severe. 7. Neither of you recognize the handwriting,
of course? 8. Are neither of the men at home? 9. Do either of
the girls wish to go with us this morning?

c. From the following parentheses select the proper forms; give your reasons :

1. The number of seats (was, were) not large. 2. Half the crew (was, were) seasick. 3. One or two (was, were) missing. 4. A series of pictures (was, were) exhibited. 5. Beside him (was, were) a boy and girl. 6. She (doesn't, don't) know what the name is. 7. There (is, are) only three of us. 8. The brother, as well as the sisters, (was, were) there. 9. The mother with her two children (was, were) lost. 10. There (is, are) his headquarters. 11. The number of failures (grows, grow) every day. 12. The greatest number of mistakes (occurs, occur) in this volume. 13. She is one of those who never (gives, give) up. 14. Each of the rooms (was, were) painted white. 15. The family (was, were) always together. 16. Neither of the men (was, were) to be found.

569. Exercise XXIV (§§ 208–214). 1. How is the passive voice formed? Give examples in sentences. 2. Which voice is usually to be preferred? Why? 3. Write five sentences containing the active voice ; change the active voice to the passive. 4. Write five sentences containing indirect objects. Rewrite the sentences twice, making first the direct and then the indirect object the subject. (See § 213.) 5. Explain *hot* in ' he heated the iron *hot* ' ; change *heated* to the passive voice. 6. Write five similar sentences in both voices. (See § 214.)

570. Exercise XXV (§§ 215–251). *a.* Correct the following sentences ; give your reasons :

1. Who did you take him to be? 2. It is not pleasant to hardly have a thing to do. 3. Whom were they thought to be? 4. To fully accomplish this requires time. 5. He was not able to wholly convince us. 6. They were willing to silently give their consent. 7. Let her be whom she may be. 8. My feet were too weary to think of going farther. 9. She has already done too much to ask her to do more. 10. To openly violate the law would have made them unpopular in their own town. 11. Your father had been too liberal in his giving to expect him to increase his subscription.

b. From the following parentheses select the proper forms; give your reasons:

1. I never thought of (his, him) doing so. 2. We couldn't prevent (your, you) staying if we wished. 3. There was a rumor of (Mr. Grey, Mr. Grey's) being ill. 4. He insisted on (me, my) paying for it. 5. She was in favor of (John, John's) going to Europe.

c. Correct the following sentences; give your reasons:

1. On climbing the mountain the view was extensive. 2. After sleeping well my appetite was improved. 3. By doing this his life was saved. 4. In learning to swim the boy's health was restored. 5. On ringing the bell the door was opened by an old man. 6. On coming of age his fortune was soon wasted.

d. Correct the following sentences; give your reasons:

1. Climbing the mountain, the view was extensive (in *c*, above, omit the prepositions *on*, *after*, etc., and then correct the sentences). 2. Giving him my ticket, he admitted me. 3. Looking out of the window, his face broke into a smile. 4. Lifting his voice, the President's speech was heard by all. 5. Running to catch the train, my hat blew off.

e. In the following selections tell whether the words ending in *ing* are gerunds or participles, and explain their use:

1. Clear *thinking* goes before clear *writing*.

2. By *promising* much and *performing* but little we become despicable.

3. Mrs. Rawson's *dashing* little carriage and ponies was *whirling* down the street.

4. Habits are soon assumed; but when we strive to strip them off, 'tis *being* flayed alive.

5. The man's love for his pets was *touching*.

6. Far up the *lengthening* lake we spied
Four *darkening* specks upon the tide.

7. He may live without books: what is knowledge but *grieving*?

8. The main object in our *undertaking* systematic exercise is to prepare us for the duties of life.

9. Generally *speaking*, his conduct is honorable.

10. For a long while I heard only the *scratching* of pens and the *shuffling* of feet.

11. And the women are *weeping* and *wringing* their hands
For those who will never come home to the town.

12. We saw a snow-white butterfly
Dancing before the fitful gale.

13. Before he was ten years old, he began *studying* the violin.

14. They made their way up the great river, *sailing* in the shade of the lofty trees, *hearing* no human voice and only the occasional *chirping* of strange birds.

15. I have no more pleasure in *hearing* a man *attempting* wit and *failing*, than in *seeing* a man *trying* to leap over a ditch and *tumbling* into it.

16. All day the gusty north-wind bore
The *loosening* drift its breath before;
Low *circling* round its southern zone,
The sun through *dazzling* snow-mist shone.

17. And the Raven, never *flitting*, still is *sitting*, still is *sitting*
On the pallid bust of Pallas just above my chamber door;
And his eyes have all the *seeming* of a demon's that is *dreaming*,
And the lamplight o'er him *streaming* throws his shadow on the floor;
And my soul from out that shadow that lies *floating* on the floor
Shall be lifted — nevermore!

f. 1. Form the present and perfect infinitives and gerunds of the following verbs, and use them transitively in sentences: *write, study, play, ride, sing, eat, build, see.* 2. Write sentences in which each of these present infinitives has a subject.

g. What is the difference between ' my friends have gone' and ' my friends are gone' ?

Write five sentences containing *good* (predicate adjective); *bad*; *well*; *badly.*

571. Exercise XXVI (§§ 252–281). *a.* In the following sentences pick out the adverb and adjective phrases and clauses, and tell what they modify (see § 557 also); explain why they are essential or nonessential (§ 472):

1. The morning sun peeped in at the garret window. 2. She lives up the street, where you see that pretty garden. 3. They will visit us when they return to the South. 4. He started toward the barn, when he saw the great dog. 5. The fire comforted us with its cheerful blaze. 6. They talked about it while they were walking through the meadow. 7. The little girl looked wistfully at the violets. 8. He will come with us, although he is tired. 9. The beautiful full moon rose before we started down the river. 10. We should begin our journey early, while the air is cool.

b. Write five sentences containing the predicate adjective *bad*; *sure*; *terrible*; *sudden*. Write five sentences containing the corresponding adverbs. From the following parentheses select the proper forms; give your reasons:

1. The girl looked (wistful, wistfully). 2. She looked (wistful, wistfully) at the flowers. 3. We came (near, nearly) missing the boat (see *near*, § 417). 4. He was (most, almost) exhausted (see *almost*, § 417). 5. Father is (some, § 417, somewhat) better. 6. That sounds (good, well). 7. Has the fruit kept (good, well)? 8. Your coat doesn't sit (good, well). 9. I feel (ill, bad, badly). 10. I feel (bad, badly) about it. 11. Will you come? (Sure, surely) we will. 12. She looks (good, well) in that dress.

c. Write five sentences containing the adjectives *good, better, best*; the adverbs *well, better, best*. (See §§ 238, 239.)

d. Write five sentences containing *also*; *too*; *only*; *quite*.

e. Write five sentences containing *first, secondly, thirdly*.

572. Exercise XXVII (§§ 282–296). *a.* Use a part of § 287 for drill in oral and written sentences. (This section should be studied and reviewed in small portions. It is useful for reference also.)

b. Write five sentences containing *in*; *into*; *in* with the names of streets and squares; *about*; *round*.

573. Exercise XXVIII (§§ 297–315). *a.* Write five sentences containing *no* followed by *or*; *no* followed by *nor*; *not* followed by *or*; *not* followed by *nor*; containing *so . . . as*.

b. **1.** Write five causal clauses with *because*; *since*; *inasmuch as*. **2.** Write five sentences containing *than* followed by personal pronouns. **3.** Write five sentences containing *that* (to express purpose); *to* (to express purpose); *but that*.

574. Exercise XXIX (§§ 320–350). **1.** Write five sentences containing a compound subject; a compound predicate. **2.** Write five sentences containing noun clauses; adjective clauses; adverb clauses. **3.** Write five ·elliptical sentences; telegrams (§§ 347–350). **4.** Analyze the sentences in § 66, 1–7 ; tell whether the sentences are simple, complex, or compound ; pick out the clauses, and tell what kind they are ; pick out the subjects and the predicates. In § 347 fill in the ellipses, and analyze the sentences in the same way. Analyze the sentences in § 570, *e.*

575. Exercise XXX (§ 355, *A*, 1, *a*). In the following sentences pick out the principal thought and make the other thoughts subordinate to it ; if necessary, use more than one sentence ; rewrite the sentences :

1. I heard the knock, and I opened the door, and I couldn't see anybody. 2. The game was to decide the championship of the school league, and there was a large crowd present, and there were no seats left when we arrived. 3. Jack looked worried because he was trying to qualify as a first-rank scout, and he had to light a fire in the open, using no matches, but it had rained the night before, and no dry wood was to be found, and Jack thought the chances were against him. 4. Not long after this Charles earned enough to pay his father's debts, and his father was released from prison, and Charles was once more sent to school. 5. The train was already moving, but

I ran faster than ever, and I think I might have caught it, but I stumbled and fell, and when I had picked myself up, everybody was laughing at me, and the train was just disappearing in the tunnel beyond the station. 6. A veritable forest as far as the eye can see covers the landscape from south to west, and this is broken only by the buildings of the Newton hospital and the Woodland Golf Club, which are situated in Washington Street, and this extends through the beautiful town of Wellesley.

576. Exercise XXXI (§ 355, *A*, 1, *b*). In the following sentences avoid *and* and the joining of unrelated thoughts; rewrite the sentences:

1. People waste a great deal of time and money on automobiles, and riding in automobiles tends to make them lazy. 2. These animals have sometimes been captured by hunters, and it has been found that they can be trained. 3. He leaves a wife and several children, and his land is valued at nearly a million dollars. 4. Only people who have lived in Maine know what good cooks the Maine women are, and I think the committee has secured all the best in the state to prepare the dinner for the carnival. 5. The heads of the native men are partly shaved, and they wear only a small girdle. 6. The Bolshevist menace will not be destroyed until the Russians discover that a dishonest government is in control, and then a new government by the people and for the people will be established. 7. This type of car is the cheapest to maintain, and you will also find it has plenty of power.

577. Exercise XXXII (§ 355, *A*, 2, *a*, *b*). Combine the following groups of words in single sentences without violating the principle of unity; pick out the principal thought, and make the others subordinate to it; rewrite the sentences:

1. The dancers stood beside the porch railing. Where they were eagerly waiting for the music to begin. All were dressed in masquerade costumes. The colors of their costumes appeared most effective under the soft light which came from the Japanese lanterns. 2. At last the coach stopped. The driver opened the door.

Because we found ourselves in front of a large tavern. 3. Some men were carrying casks into the wine shop. When they dropped one of the casks and spilled the wine. Women and children began to scoop up the wine with their hands and drink it. 4. There were hundreds of automobiles standing along the avenue. Many persons, resplendent in their fine clothes, were entering the churchyard. Because it was evident that there would be a throng of guests to witness the wedding. 5. All of us were frightened. A strong south wind had been blowing all the afternoon. We were returning from the fishing grounds. Huge waves were breaking on the shore. It was a hazardous undertaking for us to row to the beach.

578. Exercise XXXIII (§ 355, *B*, 1, 2). The following sentences illustrate the fault of change in the point of view; tell what the changes are, and then revise the sentences to secure unity:

1. The shell bursts under the aëroplane, which wavered, side-slipped, and fell. 2. The period of recitation in English should be lengthened for two reasons: first, we shall have more time for reading the classics; secondly, there would be more time for writing themes. 3. Everybody dislikes to be ridiculed, and they dislike those who cause the laugh to be on them. 4. If you keep on trying, you would see the difficulties vanish. 5. He decided to visit the beautiful estate, and that he would take several snapshots of the terraces and gardens. 6. Even if a person is very wealthy and does not save, they come to the end of their wealth sooner or later. 7. Whether a man be rich or poor, you should cultivate good habits, use good language, and strive to be true to the best ideals. 8. It has never been done imperfectly by him, and sometimes he does it with extraordinary skill. 9. The team used several trick plays, and soon the ball is advanced to their opponents' five-yard line. 10. Sometimes we had to carry the canoe, but one didn't mind that. 11. While we were going through the woods, Jack declared that he has had enough of the country. 12. If anybody is going with you to a game of baseball, they wouldn't keep one waiting for them. 13. Franklin lived to benefit his fellow men; and they were benefited by him in many

ways. 14. If one studied hard, Latin is not difficult, and it would
be unusually helpful to you. 15. The colt is so gentle that a child
could feed it; he never hurt anybody. 16. It gives one a chance
to develop himself, and you never know what is before you.
17. When he is being carried into the hospital, he said, " Well,
old boy, come soon."

579. Exercise XXXIV (§§ 356–358). Develop the following topic sentences into paragraphs; examine your work to
make sure that each paragraph contains but one central
thought, and that all the sentences in the paragraph aid in
presenting this thought:

1. My attempt to grow a garden was a succession of mistakes
and humiliating consequences. 2. A thick fog hung over the town
(the bay). 3. You would think that the famous Mr. Micawber of
Charles Dickens had come to life again. 4. A dozen times he heard
the strange noise. 5. I shall never forget Bartlett's country store.
6. The high cost of food is the problem which now perplexes every
housewife. 7. The farmer and the city gentleman watch the falling
snow with different emotions. 8. Young people of today should be
cautioned about extravagance. 9. A shopping excursion is a good
test of human nature. 10. It was the kind of day that drives people
to the shore. 11. Down with the billboards which line the country
roads. 12. Entering the woods, we came at last to a place which
appeared to be ideal for our camp. 13. Frantically I searched my
pockets. 14. Before her was the long, white road winding down
the hill. 15. At our camp the work came before play. 16. A large
crowd had gathered in front of the score board.

For other exercises in paragraphing, choose portions of this
or of another book, and copy them in single paragraphs. Put
the written work aside for a few days, and then rewrite it as you
think it ought to be. Compare your results with the originals.

580. Exercise XXXV (§ 359). Suitable prose for paraphrasing will be found in Irving (The Sketch Book), Addison
(essays on Sir Roger de Coverley), Carlyle (essay on Burns).

Carl Schurz (life of Lincoln). Suitable poetry will be found in Goldsmith (The Deserted Village, The Traveller), in Milton (Comus, sonnet on his blindness), and in Shakespeare. Alan Seeger's "I have a rendezvous with Death" is a favorite with students.

581. Exercise XXXVI (§§ 366, *A*, *B*, 2, *b*, 95). *a*. In the following sentences correct the faulty order of words; rewrite the sentences:

1. Do you expect to find science only in scientists? 2. I have only finished the first part. 3. She wanted us only (say *simply* or *merely*) to know that she had called at the office. 4. He gained an exalted vision of what his college had done for him as time passed. 5. The doctor said that the man would recover when he examined the wound. 6. I was often called from my study to receive the visit of some idle neighbors in the midst of an interesting work. 7. He recited a poem which he had happened to read while waiting at a station forty years afterwards. 8. He was transferred to the island on which the prison was situated in a small boat. 9. If you don't help a child that's been hit by the war at the first chance, you may never have another. 10. Mr. Burns was shot in the middle of his campaign. 11. It still poured, and Uncle Henry started out to feed the cows with an umbrella. 12. John Smith's back was strained by lifting the day before yesterday. 13. It is said that Lincoln wrote his famous address while riding to Gettysburg on a scrap of brown paper.

b. In the following sentences correct the faulty use of pronouns:

1. There are several parks in the city in which they play games. 2. We work on the farm when they need us. 3. He dwelt on his aches and pains, which I tried to prevent. 4. She could not understand his heartaches, but she knew that her own ached unceasingly. 5. It says that we should apply early. 6. They gently loosed his shoestrings, and took them off. 7. The boat will not run today; they have broken the steering gear. 8. I don't like to live where they don't treat you decently. 9. The chairs were broken, but they didn't need them. 10. It said that they had changed the regulations.

582. Exercise XXXVII (§ 370). *a.* In the following sentences improve the emphasis; rewrite the sentences:

1. We can learn the great man's career from this simple story. 2. He was growing inattentive to the people. 3. There could be no possibility of alarm to Jane herself. 4. There were two small portraits above the old fireplace, at the end of the room. 5. She used to talk a great deal about the sea when she was a child. 6. He burst into tears, overcome by sudden grief, and unable to retain his self-composure. 7. She sat thinking while it was being brought and being warmed at the fire. 8. He could do nothing but talk about Jessie all the way home. 9. My young brother was the only member of the party who refused to adapt himself to circumstances. 10. My meaning simply is that I have always been thoroughly in earnest in great aims and small. 11. There is no substitute for ardent, thoroughgoing, and resolute leadership. 12. I owe everything to this place, and to the kindheartedness of these people. 13. We are depending on you for the solution of this difficult problem. 14. The momentous issue of civil war is in your hands, my dissatisfied fellow countrymen, and not in mine. 15. Thales was a mathematician, astronomer, and philosopher in his later years, a statesman in middle life, and a merchant in his younger days.

b. Correct the following sentences by removing the unnecessary words:

1. They were filled with genuine pity for her. 2. The audience rose to their feet and applauded. 3. He is a man of many successful achievements. 4. He has discovered a panacea for all ills. 5. The effect was perfectly exquisite. 6. You should always scrutinize all your work very carefully. 7. You should practice this again and again. 8. The germs are not visible to the eye. 9. This machine is absolutely indispensable. 10. I often don't know where I'm at. 11. It is absolutely essential to study the rules. 12. We couldn't hardly believe him.

c. In the following sentences correct the voice and tense (see § 578 also):

1. At daybreak a few men are led out by Captain Mason to look for Indians. 2. "That traitor Girty", he reports, "is making his way up the Ohio." 3. "No, no!" is shouted by everybody. 4. A place is chosen by them at the foot of the mountain, where they cannot be reached by the wind. 5. "Board, board", orders Decatur, as he springs to the deck of the frigate. 6. The next two years do wonders for this awkward boy. 7. "How many are there of you?" asks a young girl. 8. "Enough", answers one of the riflemen, "to whip Ferguson, if we can catch him." 9. He briefly tells them what is wanted by General Washington, and volunteers are called for.

583. Exercise XXXVIII (§§ 375, 376; 96, 97). In the following sentences use parallel constructions; rewrite the sentences :

1. He likes to read, play tennis, and horseback riding. 2. This apple vender has fruit which will last longer, and possessing better qualities. 3. She had heard of the book, saw it, and had tried to buy it. 4. We were much diverted by the crowd of spectators, music, and by the play. 5. He was not only generous to his friends, but to strangers. 6. The poor old man neither could read nor write; and he could neither see or hear. 7. I neither had the time to examine the old documents nor the inclination to look at them. 8. We stopped to read the new announcements, and which we did not know had been published. 9. The old soldier whom you passed just now, who was in the late war, is looking for a position. 10. He could accomplish a great deal of hard work in a few hours, and which others would take a whole day for. 11. The doctor told him not to work so steadily or that he would have to give up his plans. 12. When the day was done, supper over, we gathered about the old fireplace. 13. We take pride in publishing the book, and hope that you may find pleasure in its use.

584. Exercise XXXIX (§ 378). The inability to recognize quickly the position of words in their alphabetical order in the dictionary is the source of much delay and inconvenience. As a rule, boys and girls who have reached the high school still appear bewildered when they try to find a new word. All this uncertainty might be avoided by a little study of the order of the letters. For example, the alphabetical order of a list of words beginning with *e* does not depend on the *e*, but on the alphabetical order of the letters following the *e*.

a. Arrange the following words in alphabetical order:

Eager, elude, error, emperor, ellipse, escape, element, earnest, embarrass, event, echo, episode, exact, elephant, emerald, excavate, effect, eagle, evening, emotion, effort, edge, embroider.

b. Arrange the following proper names in alphabetical order:

Palestine, Iceland, Toronto, Madras, Yucatan, Andes, Memphis, Illinois, Tunis, Liberia, Fiume, Russia, Ecuador, Granada, Lucerne, Finland, Ganges, Ryswick, Elba.

c. How do you distinguish the hyphen which indicates the division of syllables in a word from the hyphen which separates the parts of a compound word? (The latter is heavier; see Webster's New International Dictionary, page lxxx, Explanatory Notes.) Make a list of ten hyphened words, beginning with different letters of the alphabet (study §§ 499–508).

d. Observe that in Webster's New International Dictionary the pages of words are arranged in an upper and a lower division. What kind of words are given in the lower division? Which division contains most of the foreign words and phrases? historical names? names of characters famous in literature? Where should we look for foreign words and phrases, biographical names, terms in mythology, and so forth in Funk and Wagnalls's New Standard Dictionary?

e. Look up the meaning of the following foreign phrases:

Sine qua non, tertium quid, dolce far niente, obiter dictum, faux pas, laissez faire, ex cathedra, deo volente, noblesse oblige, coup de maître, carpe diem, hors d'œuvre, nom de plume, per se, serus in cœlum redeas. See § 514.

f. Cultivate the dictionary habit. When in your reading you come to an allusion which is unfamiliar, make a note of the word, and at the first opportunity look it up in the dictionary. Explain the following terms:

Boniface, Saracen, Pickwickian, veronica, palladium, Vinegar Bible, Sick Man of Europe, talisman, Mother Carey's chickens, Davy Jones's locker, marplot, Parnassus, bed of Procrustes, Malvolio, Wandering Jew, Darby and Joan, Brother Jonathan.

585. Exercise XL (§§ 381, 383). *a.* Look up the derivation of the following words:

Auction, bead, calico, canter, character, consider, constellation, currant, curfew, daisy, dandelion, dilapidate, dollar, dunce, epidemic, galaxy, hypocrite, infantry, jovial, laconic, martial, meander, milliner, opportune, orchestra, palliate, peninsula, person, privilege, rehearse, secretary, steward, tantalize.

b. In the following sentences tell what parts of speech the italicized words are:

1. They *brown* their arms in the sun. She wore a *brown* dress. I think *brown* is becoming to you. 2. The *floor* has not been swept today. They will soon *floor* the rooms in the new house. 3. They were in a *little* boat. You can *little* imagine my surprise. There was *little* to be said. 4. The moon cast a pale *light*. We will wait till they *light* the candles. Many hands make *light* work. 5. They swam *down* the stream. The ups and *downs* of life were many. The train was on the *down* grade. He could not come *down*. 6. They made an image out of *snow*. It was a *snow* image. It will probably *snow* before night. 7. Our long *fast* was now broken. He does not *fast* every week. He ran too *fast*. The cloth has *fast* colors. A *fast* day was appointed. 8. In *which* room is the picture? *Which* do you prefer? The fruit *which* you sent was delicious. 9. We sat *near* the open window. He is a *near* relative of mine. She did not go *near*. The boats *near* the shore. The children came from far and *near*. 10. I like the lamp *that* you selected. *That* is our flower garden. Did you see *that* bird in the hedge?

Do you think *that* the day will be pleasant? 11. Couldn't she wait a *while*? He returned *while* we were in town. What do you do to *while* the hours away? 12. I have seen the man *before*. How did he live *before* you came? We were standing *before* the window. 13. Take such *as* you like. You are *as* tall *as* he. 14. The cattle *low* in the evening. Do you not hear the *low* of the cattle? I was sitting in a *low* chair by the door. The birds flew *low*. 15. Use the following words in sentences: *gilt, guilt; hew, hue; its, it's; leaf, lief; mantel, mantle; peace, piece; pealing, peeling; ring, wring; right, rite, wright, write.*

c. Use the following words in oral and written sentences; the figures in parentheses indicate the number of ways in which each word is to be used (if necessary, consult the dictionary):

Red (2), clean (2), brush (2), paper (3), quick (3), fine (3), ship (2), wrong (4), below (2), paint (2), about (2), outside (4), calm (3), since (3), above (4), all (3), round (5).

586. Exercise XLI (§§ 418–423, 424–459, 460–515). *a.* The chapter on pronunciation (§ 418) may be used for oral or written work. Students should learn to write the words with the diacritical marks (§ 423 and notes).

b. Tests on capital letters and punctuation may be made by copying portions of this or of another book, without capital letters, punctuation, or paragraphs. Put the written work away for a few days, and then rewrite it as you think it ought to be. Compare your results with the originals.

c. Copy the following sentences; revise the punctuation (see § 460); in the fourth example the placing of a comma after *cars* or *sidetrack* involved the gain or loss of seven thousand dollars; in the ninth example the English needs revision:

1. Toward the end of the trip of the month before Gower had noticed the growing change in Shaddock. 2. If you know where this man is what do you mean by coming to me with such a proposal? 3. This, they for the most part, throw away as worthless.

4. An insurance policy read " grain in cars on sidetrack within one hundred feet of the elevator ". 5. Society to live and accomplish life's purpose must have bread. 6. To this we must add as another example of the same philosophy, that one influence counteracts another. 7. Last night the house was filled with guests and their children, as only children can, entertained them. 8. It was clear to me as I watched this great man in action, that in the cause he was defending he saw, with a vision unimpaired and a judgment un-clouded by prejudice far beyond the present. 9. As each cluster of flowers was set in place, roses that blossomed in France or England, that blossomed in Canada and South Africa; poppies that thrust their slender stems through blood-drenched Flanders fields; and flowers of every color and hue that blossom under American skies — the air grew heavy with the fragrance.

d. Copy the following sentences; add commas where neces-sary, and give your reasons:

1. Everything was to be forgiven to youth rank and genius. 2. He leaped up with a yell screamed that somebody was killing him and ran for refuge into the river. 3. Then Tom could not restrain himself and gave Maggie two smart slaps on the arm. 4. Everything that could stimulate and everything that could gratify the strongest propensities of our nature the gaze of a hundred drawing-rooms the acclamations of the whole nation the applause of applauded men the love of lovely women all this world and all the glory of it were at once offered to a youth to whom nature had given violent passions and whom education had never taught to control them.

e. Copy the following sentences; add commas where necessary, and give your reasons:

1. On the seventeenth of June they approached Montreal where the assembled traders greeted them with discharge of small arms and cannon. 2. Instantly all his companions sprang to their feet and hearing in fancy the Iroquois war whoop took to the water splashing diving and wading up to their necks in the blindness of their fright. 3. And yet this Christmas day in spite of Tom's fresh

delight in home was not he thought somehow or other quite so happy as it had always been before. 4. Through black mud spongy moss water knee-deep over fallen trees among slimy logs and entangling roots tripped by vines lashed by recoiling boughs panting under their steel headpieces and heavy corselets the Frenchmen struggled on bewildered and indignant. 5. A nation [Greece] once the first among nations preëminent in knowledge preëminent in military glory the cradle of philosophy of eloquence and of the fine arts had been for ages bowed down under a cruel yoke.

f. Copy the following sentences; add commas and semicolons where necessary, and give your reasons:

1. Menendez kissed the royal hand he had another petition in reserve. 2. The letters at least those which were sent from Italy are among the best in the language. They are less affected than those of Pope and Walpole they have more matter in them than those of Cowper. 3. Some stripped sheets of bark to cover their camp sheds others gathered wood the forest being full of dead dry trees others felled the living trees for a barricade. 4. The howl of contumely followed him across the sea up the Rhine over the Alps it gradually waxed fainter it died away those who had raised it began to ask each other what after all was the matter about which they had been so clamorous and wished to invite back the criminal whom they had just chased from them. 5. He had been guilty of the offence which of all offences is punished most severely he had been overpraised he had excited too warm an interest and the public with its usual justice chastised him for its own folly. 6. At one end stood an upright tablet or flattened post rudely carved with an intended representation of the features of the deceased. If a chief the head was adorned with a plume. If a warrior there were figures near it of a shield a lance a warclub and a bow and arrows if a boy of a small bow and one arrow and if a woman or a girl of a kettle an earthen pot a wooden spoon and a paddle. 7. Now like a wall bristling at the top with woody islets the Falls of the Chats faced them with the sheer plunge of their sixteen cataracts now they glided beneath overhanging cliffs where seeing but unseen the crouched wildcat eyed them from the thicket now through the maze of water-

girded rocks which the white cedar and the spruce clasped with serpentlike roots or among islands where old hemlocks darkened the water with deep green shadow. 8. He had no net hook or line and he could not be a fisherman his boat had no cushion for a sitter no paint no inscription no appliance beyond a rusty boat-hook and a coil of rope and he could not be a waterman his boat was too crazy and too small to take in a cargo for delivery and he could not be a lighterman or river-carrier.

587. Exercise XLII (§§ 516–545). The topics beginning on page 393 are intended for oral or written work. If you write a narrative, it will consist of three elements, the setting, the characters, and the plot; the outline in § 359 may therefore be divided into three parts, corresponding to these three elements:

$$\left.\begin{array}{l} \textit{Where ?} \\ \textit{When ?} \end{array}\right\} = \left\{\begin{array}{l} \text{the setting, which gives the background, atmos-} \\ \text{phere, or color;} \end{array}\right.$$

$$\textit{Who ?} \quad = \left\{\begin{array}{l} \text{the characters, whose names and actions should} \\ \text{be in keeping with the setting;} \end{array}\right.$$

$$\left.\begin{array}{l} \textit{What ?} \\ \textit{How ?} \\ \textit{Why ?} \end{array}\right\} = \left\{\begin{array}{l} \text{the plot, which tells the action, giving the} \\ \text{reason, the means, and the result.} \end{array}\right.$$

For example, the letter on page 153 may be analyzed in the following manner:

Setting :   Buck's Harbor, Maine, in the summer of 1922.

Characters :   Dick, a schoolboy.
             Jack, another schoolboy, Dick's chum.
             Other boys, Dick's cousins.

Plot :   Dick is spending a part of his vacation at Buck's Harbor, with his cousins. While out fishing alone in a boat, he is caught in a fog, and cannot find his way. By means of his wits and the aid of his cousins he reaches safety.

Similar to this would be the analysis of O. Henry's story
The Gift of the Magi:

Setting :   A furnished flat in New York City at eight dollars
                a week, on Christmas Eve.

Characters : Mr. James Dillingham Young, husband of Della.
                Mrs. James Dillingham Young, wife of Jim.

Plot :   Tomorrow is Christmas, and with the James Dil-
                lingham Youngs money is scarce. They have,
                however, two notable possessions: Jim's gold
                watch (an heirloom) and Della's beautiful hair.
                Jim sacrifices his watch to buy Della a set of
                combs; Della sacrifices her hair to buy Jim a
                chain for his watch. Like the Magi of old
                (Matthew, ii, 1, 11), they give the best that
                they possess.

In planning an original story, you may begin with whichever of the three elements you please. If, for example, you
have in mind some interesting place, begin with the setting,
and invent the characters and the plot to go with it; if you
have in mind an interesting or curious person (or animal), make
him the central character, and develop the setting and the plot;
if you have in mind some strange act or event, begin with the
plot, and work out the setting and the characters.

To obtain material for original work, you should keep a
notebook in your pocket, and at your leisure develop the outlines. Make a collection of interesting names. Balzac (§ 364)
walked the streets of Paris to obtain names for his characters.
When he made a good find, he went home radiant. " Matifat,
Cardot! What delightful names!" he exclaimed. " I see my
Matifat; he'll have the wan face of a cat, and a very little
corpulence."

Make your plot simple. Condense the action into a fairly
short space of time, usually not more than a day or a few

hours, avoiding a rambling chronicle of several days' adventures. Try to tell the story in scenes; that is, select certain episodes for detailed treatment, including conversation and specific action. End the story with a strong climax, and do not run on after you have reached the point of highest interest.

Read your work aloud every time that you rewrite it. Read good stories aloud. Nowadays collections of good stories are easily obtainable. The Gift of the Magi, outlined above, will be found in the volume entitled The Four Million. Read the story. In this same volume read and analyze the following stories: The Romance of a Busy Broker, By Courier, The Cop and the Anthem, Mammon and the Archer, and The Furnished Room. You should also read stories by Poe (The Cask of Amontillado, The Gold-Bug, The Fall of the House of Usher), by de Maupassant (The Necklace, The Piece of String), by Leonard Merrick (The Tragedy of a Comic Song, The Doll in the Pink Silk Dress, both of these being in the volume entitled A Chair on the Boulevard), by Stevenson (Markheim), and by other writers.

The following topics are intended to suggest places, persons, or actions which may be useful in creating settings, characters, and plots:

1. Our neighbor's dog. 2. How my dog trained me. 3. Why I like farm (city) life. 4. Two cousins. 5. At the bend of the road. 6. Caught in the rain (snow). 7. A beggar in disguise. 8. How I learned to swim. 9. My dog (horse, rabbits, doves). 10. The books I like best. 11. Training my sister (brother). 12. My first trip to the seashore (city, country, mill, river). 13. My new acquaintance. 14. Washing the dog (kittens). 15. Helping mother. 16. My country (city) cousins. 17. Reading after supper. 18. The friends I had for vacation. 19. What I like (dislike) to do. 20. How I tore (mended) my clothes. 21. In the zoölogical garden (museum, woods). 22. Making candy (cake, pies). 23. My fall on the ice (sidewalk, in

the mud, out of a tree). 24. Why I like (dislike) study. 25. My sister (brother) entertains. 26. Applying for a position. 27. Why I won (lost) the position. 28. The worst thing I ever did. 29. The birds in our trees. 30. Entertained by a tramp. 31. A whitewashed uncle (aunt). 32. How I directed the postman. 33. The way I lost (recovered) my temper. 34. My part in the play. 35. Picking cherries (apples, berries). 36. Animals (persons) I love. 37. The road to Rome. 38. How we use the old barn. 39. What I need for vacation. 40. What I can do without. 41. Making a kite (table, chair). 42. Finger prints on the window. 43. Sleeping outdoors. 44. An unexpected visitor. 45. Saved by a dog. 46. A dilemma. 47. My long-headed chum. 48. Riding the colt. 49. The organ grinder's monkey. 50. The absent-minded beggar. 51. Teaching my dog tricks. 52. Dancing for a burglar. 53. My scrap book. 54. The best joke on me. 55. Counting the cost. 56. Our new neighbor. 57. Introducing myself to the policeman (watchman). 58. A day with the gypsies. 59. How I got my nickname. 60. What a horse (dog, cow, toad, grasshopper) would say about us. 61. Farm machinery. 62. Life in camp. 63. The advantage (disadvantage) of being tall (short). 64. Cruelty to horses (dogs, cats, toads). 65. Kindness to people (animals). 66. The usefulness of birds (insects). 67. Caged birds (squirrels, lions, animals). 68. Thoughtfulness for people (animals). 69. The rights of dogs (cats, birds, horses, animals, my young brother, my young sister). 70. Writing for the newspapers.

CHAPTER XII

THE DEVELOPMENT OF ENGLISH

Histories make men wise. — LORD BACON.

The use of history is to give value to the present hour and its duties. — EMERSON.

588. Migrations. Nearly all the languages of Europe, and many of those of Asia, are kindred dialects, descended from a common ancestor. This ancient parent speech was in use, possibly five or six thousand years ago, among a pastoral people who seem to have lived in or near the great central plain of Europe and Asia. From time to time, because of the scarcity of food, water, or pasturage, or on account of their love of booty and conquest, they sought new territory. They gradually spread over Europe; they moved to the southeast into Persia and India; and they pushed westward as far as the British Isles and Iceland.

NOTE. We should be careful not to confuse language with race. These people used the same parent speech, but this does not mean that they belonged to the same race. For example, the great musical genius Richard Wagner, born and reared in Germany, was not a Teuton, but a Semite, a Jew.

589. Changes in language. When our linguistic ancestors scattered to these different parts of the world, the climate and other conditions changed their habits of living and their manner of speaking. The different groups of the family grew more and more unlike each other, and after many hundreds of years became separate peoples, each speaking a different form of their old language.

590. Britain ; Julius Cæsar. In the years 55 and 54 B.C. the great Roman general Julius Cæsar, who had conquered Gaul, twice invaded Britain, to make it a part of the Roman world. He found that the population consisted of numerous tribes of barbarian people called Celts, who were ruled by chieftains, or kings, and who were almost constantly at war with one another. The domestic life of these people was extremely simple. They raised swine, sheep, goats, and cows, and lived mostly on flesh and milk ; some had fields of wheat, oats, and barley. They dressed in the skins of animals, and lived in houses that were nothing but circular huts of clay and thatch. Although Cæsar accomplished but little in Britain, he opened the way for its conquest.

591. Roman conquest of Britain. In the first century of the Christian Era the Romans again invaded Britain, and began to subdue it. Their rule in the island continued nearly four hundred years (A.D. 43–409). They built towns, and constructed great walls, roads, and bridges. They cut down the dense forests, drained the marshes, and extended the fields. They taught the Britons to build better houses, and to adopt better ways of living. They introduced Roman civilization, Roman laws, Roman games, Roman religion, and the Latin language. During their government of the island Christianity also was introduced.

Early in the fifth century the Roman soldiers in Britain were gradually called home to protect Italy from barbarian invasion, and the Romano-British people were left to themselves. Now began a long period of confusion and increasing barbarism, which swept away almost every vestige of Roman civilization.

592. Saxons and Angles. In less than half a century after Roman government in Britain had ceased, the island began to be invaded by marauding hordes from Europe, from the shores of the North Sea. Some of these adventurers were called Jutes, but most of them were Saxons and Angles. They were related to each other, and spoke different forms of the same language. They took possession of the fertile plains and river valleys in the south and east. The Britons either fled into the mountainous and barren country to the west and the north, or mingled with their conquerors. The language spoken by the foreigners became the language of the country which they occupied.

593. Language of Saxons and Angles. The language of the ancient Saxons and Angles was simple, with short words. The expanding life of the people brought them new experiences and new ideas, and for these new ideas they created new names by uniting words already familiar. For example, their word for *sun* was *woruld-candel* (= *world-candle*); their word for *sea* was *hwæl-mere* (= *whale-lake*); and their word for *harp* was *gliw-beam* (= *singing-tree*; *gliw* is the English *glee*). See § 599.

594. Literature; England. Soon after their settlement in Britain the Angles began to use the Latin letters to write down their words. Thus they gave a written form to their language, which they called Englisc (that is, English), after their own name, and were able to preserve the poems and songs that had long existed among their people. There were war songs, tales of adventure, stories of fabulous heroes, giants, and monsters, and possibly of gods and goddesses personifying such forces of nature as sea and storm, wind and cloud, springtime and dawn. This written language spread among the neighboring kingdoms of the Saxons, who accepted its name also, and continued to call it Englisc. The name of the language was gradually given to the Saxon people, and England (that is, Engla land) became the name of this part of the country.

595. Romance languages. With the conquests of Rome spoken Latin had been carried into Gaul (now France), Spain, and other Roman provinces in Western Europe, and became the common tongue. Not being spoken distinctly by the different foreign peoples, it gradually changed in pronunciation and form, and developed into French, Spanish, and other modern languages. In France it came to be called *Romance*, from *Romania*, the name given in the Middle Ages to the Latin-speaking territory of the old Roman Empire. The term *Romance* is now commonly applied to all the languages descended from Latin. One of these Romance languages, the French, not only became the source of many English words, but altered the course of development of the English vocabulary (see § 599).

596. Spread of Latin. The recall of the Roman soldiers from Britain (§ 591) did not save Italy and Rome from the rapacity of the barbarians. The Roman Empire in the West crumbled to pieces, and Roman civilization declined and almost came to an end. Before the invasions of the barbarians began, however, Rome had abolished pagan worship in the empire, and in its place had established Christianity. With the downfall of the empire, and the cessation of government, the Christian church gradually gained the ascendancy, and Rome again arose in majesty, not as the capital of the world, but transformed into the capital of Christendom. Through the clergy and the monks the Roman Church subdued and civilized the barbarians, and ruled them for hundreds of years. The monks established themselves in monasteries throughout Western Europe and England. They read and spoke and wrote Latin, the official language of the church; and thus, in this part of the world, Latin came to be the common tongue of the educated classes. Many of the monks were eminent statesmen, scholars, and writers, and their influence was great; in England they aroused much enthusiasm for the literature and culture of Rome, and the English monasteries became famous centers of learning.

597. Normans. For many years Scandinavian sea rovers had plundered the people living along the shore of the North Sea. Early in the tenth century, after various raiding expeditions, a piratical band, led by the chief Rollo, received permission to settle peacefully in the northern part of France, about the mouth of the Seine River. These strangers came to be known as Normans (the name being a softened form of the Teutonic or Scandinavian word ' Northmen '), and their new country was called Normandy.

At first, quite naturally, the Normans continued to speak their Scandinavian language, and kept up the habits formed in their old home. After a time, however, they began to intermarry with the people about them, and gradually adopted from them the French language, French culture, and the Christian religion. The Normans became great builders in stone, and constructed splendid churches and castles. Their capital, Rouen, became one of the most enlightened centers of Europe. Other Norman towns, devoted to trade and manufacture, grew in population and wealth. Thus the Normans wielded a strong influence, and this influence made itself felt in England.

598. Norman Conquest. The Normans called their rulers dukes. About the middle of the eleventh century they had a duke named William, who was cousin to Edward, the king of England. William expected to succeed Edward; but when Edward died, Harold, the son of a Saxon nobleman, received the crown. William now gathered an army and crossed into England. He met and defeated the English in the great battle of Hastings (A.D. 1066), and was crowned king of England. Thus, for a time, the Norman-French tongue (§ 595) came to

be the language of the king of England and of his nobles, of
the bishops and of the government officials, and was spoken
by the Norman townspeople who came to England to engage
in trade. It was also introduced into the universities and
schools; but in the church service Latin continued to be used,
and the learned books were written in that ancient language.
English was looked on with contempt by the Normans.
Although English continued to be spoken by the great body
of the English people, it almost ceased to be written, and soon
began to deteriorate. The Normans built splendid churches
and castles. The towns became more important, and new trades
and better methods of doing business were established.

599. Result of Norman Conquest. The Norman Conquest
has been called the most important event in English history.
Through intermarriage with the French the Normans had
acquired the physical and mental activity of the south, and
from a horde of marauders became the most brilliant and culti-
vated people of Europe. " It was through the Normans ", says
James Russell Lowell, " that the English mind and fancy,
hitherto provincial and uncouth, were first infused with the light-
ness, grace, and self-confidence of Romance literature. They
seem to have opened a window to the southward in that solid
and somewhat sombre insular character, and it was a painted
window all aglow with the figures of tradition and poetry."

In their daily intercourse in the market, at church, and elsewhere the English and the Normans tried to aid each other in
the exchange of ideas. When an Englishman had to use a word
unfamiliar to the Norman, he endeavored to put with it the
corresponding French word ; the Norman did likewise ; and
the language soon swarmed with pairs of English and French
words. The poetry of Chaucer (in the latter part of the
fourteenth century) abounds in them. Some of these phrases

still survive, such as 'will and testament', 'act and deed', 'aid and abet', 'acknowledge and confess', 'dissemble and cloak'. A picturesque illustration of this bilingualism will be found at the end of the first chapter of Scott's *Ivanhoe*.

But, as we have seen, French is descended from Latin (§ 595), and the borrowing of French words led to the borrowing of Latin words also. In modern English more than half the words have come from these two sources. Some Latin words have furnished two different English words, one through the French, the other directly from the ancient form. For example, from the Latin word *histo'ria* (originally a Greek word) have come the English words *story* and *history*; from *fidelita'tem*, *fealty* and *fidelity*; from *oratio'nem*, *orison* and *oration*; from *traditio'nem*, *treason* and *tradition*.

NOTE. In the study of French words, and of Latin words which have come into English from the French, it is helpful to note the accent of the original Latin words; for the syllables following the accent have usually fallen away, or have coalesced with the preceding syllable. For example, the Latin word *humanita'tem* becomes French *humanité* and English *humanity*; *capi'tulum* becomes French *chapitre* (two syllables) and English *chapter*; *un'decim* becomes French *onze* (one syllable); *cor'pus* becomes French *corps* and English *corps* and *corpse*; *su'per* becomes French and English *sur-* (as in *sur-pass*).

Since the increase in importations had made it easier to accept the foreign names of new objects than to create other names by compounding English words, as had been the custom (§ 593), the growth of English words almost stopped. Furthermore, many English words formerly in good use gave way to other words, chiefly of Latin and Greek origin. The English word *book-house*, for example, was supplanted by the Latin word *library*; *finger-apple* (= *finger-shaped fruit*), by *date* (from the Greek word meaning *finger*); *rime-craft* (= *reckoning-art*), by the Greek word *arithmetic*.

For about three hundred years after the Norman Conquest
there was little literature of high quality written in English;
the upper classes of the people still spoke French, and the
scholars continued to use Latin.

600. Revival of Learning. In the year 1453 the Turks
captured and sacked Constantinople, the Eastern capital of the
Roman Empire, and the center of Greek learning and Greek
civilization. The famous libraries of the city were scattered or
destroyed. A hundred and twenty thousand manuscripts are
said to have disappeared. The Greek scholars hastily packed
up their own priceless literary treasures, and fled to Italy.
Many of these learned men found refuge at Florence, where
they became teachers of the ancient classics of Greece and
Rome. Their lecture rooms were crowded with eager students,
and their learning and system of education permeated the West.
An additional impulse to learning was soon imparted by the
invention of printing, and in a few years the cities of Italy
were rivaling each other in the number and the elegance of
their printed books.

In England one of the chief results of the study and translation of the classical authors of Greece and Rome was the
introduction, into English, of an immense number of new
words derived from these ancient sources. Such words were
needed not only for the expression of new ideas, but for the
reclassification of the old. From this time forward English has
continued to enrich itself by borrowing from Latin and Greek.

601. Periods of English language; inflection. The
development of the English language may be divided roughly
into three periods, Anglo-Saxon (or Old English), Middle
English, and Modern English. Anglo-Saxon was brought to
Britain by the Jutes, Saxons, and Angles, and continued until
about a century after the Norman Conquest (A.D. 449–1150).

In this period the nouns, pronouns, adjectives, verbs, and participles had a variety of endings or other changes of form, called inflection, to show their relation to each other in the sentence. Since the language was used by scholars and cultured people as well as by the masses, it kept most of its inflections. Middle English extended from about the year 1150 to about the year 1450. In the earlier part of this period the different endings of a word commonly became the same, and later were often dropped out of use. During this period many words were introduced from French. Modern English began about the year 1450 (a little more than a century before Shakespeare's time). In this period the language has almost no inflections. A large vocabulary has been acquired, not only from the languages of Europe, but from other foreign tongues.

602. Vocabulary. The language of the Jutes, Saxons, and Angles was spoken in England by a few thousand primitive people, and consisted of a few thousand words. Today English is spoken by a hundred and fifty million people, and has about two hundred thousand words. Of these words not more than a fourth or a fifth have come from the Anglo-Saxon (§ 389); the others have been borrowed or formed from foreign languages, chiefly Latin and Greek, or from languages descended from Latin (French, Italian, Spanish, and others).

603. Indo-European languages. Celtic, Anglo-Saxon, French, Spanish, German, Latin, and Greek, however much unlike each other they are today, are among the descendants of the ancient tongue already mentioned, spoken centuries ago by that nomadic people of Asia and Europe. This numerous family of languages, called the Indo-European (or, less properly, Aryan), is the most important in the world. Some of these languages, such as Sanskrit, Russian, Greek, and Latin, are highly inflected. English has the least inflection.

604. Inflection of nouns. Besides the four cases used in
English (§ 606) Latin has two others: the vocative (usually
like the nominative in form), corresponding to the nominative
of address (§ 471); and the ablative, which expresses cause,
manner, means, and the like. The Latin noun *victoria, victory,*
is declined as follows:

SINGULAR

Nom.	victo′ria	*victory*	(Subject)
Gen.	victo′riae	*of victory*	(Possession, etc.)
Dat.	victo′riae	*to* or *for victory*	(Indirect object)
Acc.	victo′riam	*victory*	(Direct object)
Abl.	victo′ria	*from, with, in, victory*	

PLURAL

Nom.	victo′riae	*victories*	(Subject)
Gen.	victoria′rum	*of victories*	(Possession, etc.)
Dat.	victo′riis	*to* or *for victories*	(Indirect object)
Acc.	victo′rias	*victories*	(Direct object)
Abl.	victo′riis	*from, with, in, victories*	

The Indo-European word *fish* is declined in several languages
as follows (in Middle English the endings commonly become
the same; in Modern English they almost disappear; § 601):

	LATIN	ANGLO-SAXON	MIDDLE ENG.	MOD. ENG.	GERMAN
Nom.	pis′cis	fisc	fishes	fish	Fisch
Gen.	pis′cis	fisces	fishes	fish's	Fisches
Dat.	pis′ci	fisce	fish(e)	fish	Fisch(e)
Acc.	pis′cem	fisc	fish	fish	Fisch
Abl.	pis′ce				
Nom.	pis′ces	fiscas	fishes	fishes	Fische
Gen.	pis′cium	fisca	fishes	fishes'	Fische
Dat.	pis′cibus	fiscum	fishes	fishes	Fischen
Acc.	pis′cis	fiscas	fishes	fishes	Fische
Abl.	pis′cibus				

605. Endings of Latin and Greek nouns. Latin and Greek nouns are declined in several different ways, according to the ending of the nominative singular. The following table contains endings of the nominative singular and the nominative plural, as illustrated by the nouns in § 39 ; the Latin ending *ae* is written *æ* in English :

N. Sing.	N. Pl.	Examples
Latin : -a	-ae	alumna, alumnæ ; larva, larvæ.
-us	-i	alumnus, alumni ; fungus, fungi.
-us	-us	apparatus, apparatus ; plexus, plexus.
-s	-es	crux (for 'crucs'), cruces.
-um	-a	datum, data ; stratum, strata.
—	-a	caput, capita ; genus, genera (for 'genesa').
-es	-es	species, species ; series, series.
Greek : -on	-a	phenomenon, phenomena.
—	-a	miasma (for 'miasmat'), miasmata.
-is	-es	crisis, crises ; ellipsis, ellipses.

606. Modern English ; cases. Although Modern English has lost nearly all the endings, the uses of four cases are still distinct :

The nominative = the subject (§ 40), predicate nominative (§ 158), or nominative of address (§ 471).

The genitive = possession and the like. (Commonly called the possessive case ; § 41.)

The dative = the indirect object (or, dative of reference or concern, denoting the person referred to or concerned). (Commonly called the objective case ; § 212.)

The accusative = the direct object. (Commonly called the objective case ; § 40. The predicate objective, § 214, may be called the adjunct accusative.)

The following examples illustrate certain uses of the cases :

1. The *sun* has set. (Subject ; § 40.)

His coming was a *surprise*. (Predicate nominative ; § 158.)

2. We fed the *animals*. (Direct object; § 156.)

3. The *boy's* hat blew away. (Possession; § 41.)

The *law's* delay (= delay connected with the law). (Genitive of connection.)

Boys' hats (= hats for boys). (Genitive of connection.)

Cæsar's conquests. (Genitive of connection.)

They won by a *boat's* length. (Genitive of measure.)

Two *hours'* time was enough. (Genitive of measure.)

The *boy's* temptation was great. (Objective genitive; the boy was the object toward which the temptation went.)

The *boy's* love for his sister grew. (Subjective genitive; the boy loved; that is, he was the source or subject from which the love came.)

4. He gave *me* a top. (Indirect object; § 212.)

Take *me* a picture of that horse. (Dative of reference.)

Pick *her* some flowers. (Dative of reference.)

It will last *them* a lifetime. (Dative of reference.)

I stared *him* in the face. (Dative of reference.)

607. Inflection. In Modern English the accusative-dative is like the nominative; but some pronouns have two forms: *I, me; he, him; who, whom.* (See §§ 59, 76, 83, 98.)

608. Genitive. Some of the possessive adjectives (§ 118) are originally genitives of the personal pronouns. In Shakespeare are still to be found examples of this original use as genitives, with relative pronouns referring to them:

1. And do you now strew flowers in *his* way

   That comes in triumph over Pompey's blood? (= in the way *of him that* comes, etc.)

2. *Her* prayers, *whom* heaven delights to hear. (= the prayers *of her, whom,* etc.)

3. Upon *their* woes *whom* fortune captivates. (= upon the woes *of them whom,* etc.)

609. Possessive adjective for genitive. A possessive adjective was sometimes used after a noun as a substitute for the ending of the genitive (-es, -s); this usage is found in literature from the Anglo-Saxon period down to recent times, and still exists among the uneducated:

1. *God his* nama (*God his* name). Instead of '*Godes* nama' (*God's* name).

2. Once in a sea-fight 'gainst the *count his* gallies, I did some service. — SHAKESPEARE.

3. *Abram his* name is changed. — Genesis, xvii, contents (King James Bible).

4. Martha *Wilkins her* book.

610. Apostrophe in genitive. On account of the similarity and identity in spelling, and the use of the apostrophe to indicate the omission of *e* in such forms as *fox's*, the ending of the genitive singular (-es, -is, -ys) came to be regarded as a shortened form of the possessive adjective *his* (*is, ys*), and the custom arose of using the apostrophe with all words in the genitive, to indicate the omission of a part of the word. The genitive plural likewise received the apostrophe, as if it also were a shortened form.

611. Adjectives. In adjectives in Modern English the endings have disappeared. In Anglo-Saxon the adjective was inflected for all three genders, masculine, feminine, and neuter, as is still done in German.

612. Inflection of verbs. In verbs in Modern English the endings have almost disappeared. The following inflections are the present indicative of the Indo-European verb *sit*:

	LATIN	ANGLO-SAXON	MIDDLE ENG.	MODERN ENG.	GERMAN
1.	se'deo	sitte	sitte	sit	sitze
2.	se'des	sitest, sitst	sittest	sittest	sitzest
3.	se'det	siteth, sit	sitteth, sit	sits, sitteth	sitzt
1.	sede'mus	sittath	sitteth, -en, -e	sit	sitzen
2.	sede'tis	sittath	sitteth, -en, -e	sit	sitzt
3.	se'dent	sittath	sitteth, -en, -e	sit	sitzen

In Middle English three forms of the language were in use, the Southern, the Midland, and the Northern. The plural *sitteth* is found in the Southern language, and is closest to the Anglo-Saxon. In the Midland language the plural was *sitten* or *sitte*. This is the language from which Modern English came. It was used in London, at the universities of Oxford and Cambridge, and by the first great English poet, Chaucer, who was born in London about 1340 and lived till 1400.

613. Northern plural in -*s*. In the Northern language (§ 612) the plural of verbs ended in -*s* (as, *sittes*). This plural is frequent in Shakespeare. Most of these words have unfortunately been altered by modern editors; when there is a rime, however, as in the second example below, the plural in -*s* cannot be changed :

1. Ill deeds *is* doubled with an evil word.
2. She lifts the coffer-lids that close his eyes,
   Where, lo, two lamps burnt out in darkness *lies*.

NOTE. The plural in -*s* is still found in Scotland and northern England : All my hopes *is* lost.

614. Infinitive. The present infinitive of *sit* (§ 612) is as follows : *sedere, sittan, sitten* (or *sitte*), *sit, sitzen*. The infinitive is a verbal noun (§ 215). In Anglo-Saxon and Middle English it had two forms. One of these forms was for the nominative and the accusative ; the other was for the dative (§ 606), which took the preposition *to* : as, *sittan* (Middle English *sitten* or *sitte*), *to sittanne* (Middle English *to sittenne, to sittene, to sitten*, or *to sitte*).

615. Dative infinitive. The dative infinitive (§ 614) is the origin of the infinitive used to express purpose, and of the adverbial infinitive :

1. We came *to see* you. (Infinitive of purpose ; see § 475, 3.)
2. That is easy *to do*. (Adverbial infinitive.)

616. Gerundial infinitive. The dative infinitive (§ 615) is frequently called the gerundial infinitive, being used somewhat like the gerund (§ 215). In Shakespeare's day this infinitive had a much greater variety of use:

1. I don't care *to go* (= *about going*). (Correct present use.)
2. We laughed *to see* (= *at seeing*) him run. (Correct present use.)
3. Eleven hours I spent *to write* (= *in writing*) it over.
4. But I shall grieve you *to report* (= *by reporting*) the rest.
5. Oh, who shall hinder me *to wail* and *weep* (= *from wailing and weeping*)?

617. Use of *to*. In Modern English *to* is ordinarily used with the nominative and the accusative of the infinitive also (see § 614), as a mere sign, without meaning; the infinitive without *to* is used only in a few idioms or after the modal auxiliaries (§ 183) and a few other verbs (§§ 216, 241–244, 248):

1. *To live* is *to learn*. (Nominative, §§ 606, 215.)
2. He wishes *to remain*. (Accusative, § 606.)
3. *Have* is *have*. (= *To have* is *to have*. Nominative.)
4. Better *dwell* in the midst of alarms,
   Than *reign* in this horrible place.

618. Syntax. That part of grammar which treats of the relations of words in sentences is called syntax, from two Greek words meaning 'put together in order' (see *syn-*, *tag-*, §§ 408, 410).

619. Inflections. When English had many inflections, its syntax was much more complex, and resembled that of Latin and Greek. For example, certain verbs and prepositions were followed by the accusative case, others by the genitive, and still others by the dative (§ 606); and some might be followed by two cases. Such uses are still common in German:

1. Ich gedachte *deiner*, I was thinking of you. (Genitive.)
2. Er folgte *mir*, he followed me. (Dative.)

When English lost its inflections, many of these distinctions disappeared; that is, the language became simpler. What was once the genitive or the dative after verbs and prepositions is now simply called the accusative (§§ 604, 606). Verbs of giving, refusing, and the like still take the accusative of the direct object (§ 40) and the dative of the indirect (§ 212):

1. He brought *me* here. (Accusative, §§ 604, 606.)
2. He brought *me* (dative) *a present* (accusative). (§§ 604, 606.)

620. Illustrations. The following illustrations of Latin, Anglo-Saxon, German, and English are taken from the Gospel of John, xxi, 3:

Vulgate, 384:	Dicit eis Simon Petrus: Vado piscari. (Says to them Simon Peter, I go to fish.)
Anglo-Saxon, 1000:	Tha cwæth Simon Petrus to him, Ic wylle gan on fixath. (Then quoth Simon Peter to them, I will go a fishing.)
Luther, 1534:	Spricht Simon Petrus zu ihnen: Ich will hin fischen gehen.
Wycliffe, 1382:	Symount petir seith to hem, I go to fische.
Tyndale, 1526:	Simon Peter sayde vnto them: I goo a fysshynge.
King James, 1611:	Simon Peter saith vnto them, I goe a fishing.

Observe how close the German of Luther is to the Anglo-Saxon. Compare your own Bible.

The following verses (Matthew, viii, 14–16) are also taken from the King James Bible of 1611:

14. And when Iesus was come into Peters house, hee saw his wiues mother laid, and sicke of a feuer:

15. And he touched her hand, and the feuer left her: and she arose, and ministred vnto them.

16. When the Euen was come, they brought vnto him many that were possessed with deuils: and hee cast out the spirits with his worde, and healed all that were sicke.

621. Inflections; principal parts. A few inflections of regular and irregular verbs will be found in §§ 623–653. The principal parts of the common irregular verbs will be found in § 654, at the end of the book, where they are convenient for reference and study.

The irregular verbs may be taken in groups and used for oral and written drill in constructing sentences. The past, present perfect, and past perfect tenses deserve particular attention. There should be frequent drill, also, in using the future and the future perfect of all verbs. The interrogative forms of the future and the future perfect are more difficult than the declarative forms, and they are inflected in full. *Shall, will, should,* and *would* should be used frequently in sentences in indirect quotation (§§ 176, 177) and indirect questions (§ 77).

622. Personal endings. In the earlier language the verb had endings to indicate mood, person, and number (§§ 601, 612). Most of these endings have been lost. The following table shows the personal endings of the indicative mood today (see §§ 160, 161, 171):

	Present Tense		*Past Tense*	
	Singular	*Plural*	*Singular*	*Plural*
1.	——	——	——	——
2.	-est, -st	——	-est, -st	——
3.	-s, -eth, -th	——	——	——

NOTE 1. The ending *-eth* (*-th*) is found in the older language (as in the Bible) and in poetry.

NOTE 2. The verbs *can, may, must, ought, shall,* and *will* (§ 653) do not take *-s* in the third person singular of the present indicative; for these forms were originally past tenses, and had the third person like the first.

NOTE 3. The subjunctive has now no personal endings except in the second person singular of the past and past perfect (§§ 624, 630, 636, 642, 648), and in *canst, mayest,* etc. (§ 653), in which the subjunctive has become like the indicative.

623. INDICATIVE MOOD OF *HAVE* (§§ 161, 169–172)

Principal Parts, have, had, had (§ 170)

Present

1. I have.
2. Thou hast.
3. He has.

1. We have.
2. You have.
3. They have.

Present Perfect

I have had.
Thou hast had.
He has had.

We have had.
You have had.
They have had.

Past

1. I had.
2. Thou hadst.
3. He had.

1. We had.
2. You had.
3. They had.

Past Perfect

I had had.
Thou hadst had.
He had had.

We had had.
You had had.
They had had.

Future (§ 178)

1. I shall have.
2. Thou wilt have.
3. He will have.

1. We shall have.
2. You will have.
3. They will have.

1. Shall I have?
2. Shalt thou have?
3. Will he have?

1. Shall we have?
2. Shall you have?
3. Will they have?

Future Perfect (§ 178)

I shall have had.
Thou wilt have had.
He will have had.

We shall have had.
You will have had.
They will have had.

Shall I have had?
Shalt thou have had?
Will he have had?

Shall we have had?
Shall you have had?
Will they have had?

624.   SUBJUNCTIVE MOOD (§§ 162, 169–172)

Present	*Present Perfect*
1. I have.	I have had.
2. Thou have.	Thou have had.
3. He have.	He have had.
1. We have.	We have had.
2. You have.	You have had.
3. They have.	They have had.

Past	*Past Perfect*
1. I had.	I had had.
2. Thou hadst.	Thou hadst had.
3. He had.	He had had.
1. We had.	We had had.
2. You had.	You had had.
3. They had.	They had had.

625.   IMPERATIVE MOOD (§ 164)

Present, Have (thou), Have (you).

626.   INFINITIVE (§§ 165, 215–222)

Present, to have.
Perfect, to have had.

627.   GERUND (§§ 215, 223–229)

Present, having.
Perfect, having had.

628.   PARTICIPLE (§§ 166, 170, 175, 230–236)

Present, having.
Past, had.
Perfect, having had.

629. INDICATIVE MOOD OF *BE* (§§ 161, 169–172)

Principal Parts, am, was, been (§ 170)

Present	*Present Perfect*
1. I am.	I have been.
2. Thou art.	Thou hast been.
3. He is.	He has been.
1. We are.	We have been.
2. You are.	You have been.
3. They are.	They have been.

Past	*Past Perfect*
1. I was.	I had been.
2. Thou wast (*or* wert).	Thou hadst been.
3. He was.	He had been.
1. We were.	We had been.
2. You were.	You had been.
3. They were.	They had been.

Future (§ 178)	*Future Perfect* (§ 178)
1. I shall be.	I shall have been.
2. Thou wilt be.	Thou wilt have been.
3. He will be.	He will have been.
1. We shall be.	We shall have been.
2. You will be.	You will have been.
3. They will be.	They will have been.
1. Shall I be?	Shall I have been?
2. Shalt thou be?	Shalt thou have been?
3. Will he be?	Will he have been?
1. Shall we be?	Shall we have been?
2. Shall you be?	Shall you have been?
3. Will they be?	Will they have been?

630. SUBJUNCTIVE MOOD (§§ 162, 169–172)

Present

1. I be.
2. Thou be.
3. He be.

1. We be.
2. You be.
3. They be.

Present Perfect

I have been.
Thou have been.
He have been.

We have been.
You have been.
They have been.

Past

1. I were.
2. Thou wert.
3. He were.

1. We were.
2. You were.
3. They were.

Past Perfect

I had been.
Thou hadst been.
He had been.

We had been.
You had been.
They had been.

631. IMPERATIVE MOOD (§ 164)

Present, Be (thou), Be (you).

632. INFINITIVE (§§ 165, 215–222)

Present, to be.
Perfect, to have been.

633. GERUND (§§ 215, 223–229)

Present, being.
Perfect, having been.

634. PARTICIPLE (§§ 166, 170, 175, 230–236)

Present, being.
Past, been.
Perfect, having been.

635. INDICATIVE ACTIVE OF *CALL* (§§ 161, 169–172, 208)

Principal Parts, call, called, called (§ 170)

Present	*Present Perfect*
1. I call.	I have called.
2. Thou callest.	Thou hast called.
3. He calls.	He has called.
1. We call.	We have called.
2. You call.	You have called.
3. They call.	They have called.

Past	*Past Perfect*
1. I called.	I had called.
2. Thou calledst.	Thou hadst called.
3. He called.	He had called.
1. We called.	We had called.
2. You called.	You had called.
3. They called.	They had called.

Future (§ 178)	*Future Perfect* (§ 178)
1. I shall call.	I shall have called.
2. Thou wilt call.	Thou wilt have called.
3. He will call.	He will have called.
1. We shall call.	We shall have called.
2. You will call.	You will have called.
3. They will call.	They will have called.
1. Shall I call?	Shall I have called?
2. Shalt thou call?	Shalt thou have called?
3. Will he call?	Will he have called?
1. Shall we call?	Shall we have called?
2. Shall you call?	Shall you have called?
3. Will they call?	Will they have called?

636.   Subjunctive Active (§§ 162, 169–172, 208)

Present

1. I call.
2. Thou call.
3. He call.

1. We call.
2. You call.
3. They call.

Present Perfect

I have called.
Thou have called.
He have called.

We have called.
You have called.
They have called.

Past

1. I called.
2. Thou calledst.
3. He called.

1. We called.
2. You called.
3. They called.

Past Perfect

I had called.
Thou hadst called.
He had called.

We had called.
You had called.
They had called.

637.   Imperative Active (§§ 164, 208)

Present, Call (thou), Call (you).

638.   Infinitive Active (§§ 165, 208, 215–222)

Present, to call.
Perfect, to have called.

639.   Gerund Active (§§ 208, 215, 223–229)

Present, calling.
Perfect, having called.

640. Participle Active (§§ 166, 170, 175, 208, 230–236)

Present, calling.
Past, called.
Perfect, having called.

641. INDICATIVE ACTIVE OF *KNOW* (§§ 161, 169–172, 208)

Principal Parts, know, knew, known (§ 170)

Present	*Present Perfect*
1. I know.	I have known.
2. Thou knowest.	Thou hast known.
3. He knows.	He has known.
1. We know.	We have known.
2. You know.	You have known.
3. They know.	They have known.

Past	*Past Perfect*
1. I knew.	I had known.
2. Thou knewest.	Thou hadst known.
3. He knew.	He had known.
1. We knew.	We had known.
2. You knew.	You had known.
3. They knew.	They had known.

Future (§ 178)	*Future Perfect* (§ 178)
1. I shall know.	I shall have known.
2. Thou wilt know.	Thou wilt have known.
3. He will know.	He will have known.
1. We shall know.	We shall have known.
2. You will know.	You will have known.
3. They will know.	They will have known.
1. Shall I know?	Shall I have known?
2. Shalt thou know?	Shalt thou have known?
3. Will he know?	Will he have known?
1. Shall we know?	Shall we have known?
2. Shall you know?	Shall you have known?
3. Will they know?	Will they have known?

642.   SUBJUNCTIVE ACTIVE (§§ 162, 169–172, 208)

Present	*Present Perfect*
1. I know.	I have known.
2. Thou know.	Thou have known.
3. He know.	He have known.
1. We know.	We have known.
2. You know.	You have known.
3. They know.	They have known.

Past	*Past Perfect*
1. I knew.	I had known.
2. Thou knewest.	Thou hadst known.
3. He knew.	He had known.
1. We knew.	We had known.
2. You knew.	You had known.
3. They knew.	They had known.

643.   IMPERATIVE ACTIVE (§§ 164, 208)

     Present, Know (thou), Know (you).

644.   INFINITIVE ACTIVE (§§ 165, 208, 215–222)

     Present, to know.
     Perfect, to have known.

645.   GERUND ACTIVE (§§ 208, 215, 223–229)

     Present, knowing.
     Perfect, having known.

646.   PARTICIPLE ACTIVE (§§ 166, 170, 175, 208, 230–236)

     Present, knowing.
     Past, known.
     Perfect, having known.

647. INDICATIVE PASSIVE OF *CALL* (§§ 161, 169–172, 208)

Principal Parts, call, called, called (§ 170)

Present	*Present Perfect*
1. I am called.	I have been called.
2. Thou art called.	Thou hast been called.
3. He is called.	He has been called.
1. We are called.	We have been called.
2. You are called.	You have been called.
3. They are called.	They have been called.

Past	*Past Perfect*
1. I was called.	I had been called.
2. Thou wast called.	Thou hadst been called.
3. He was called.	He had been called.
1. We were called.	We had been called.
2. You were called.	You had been called.
3. They were called.	They had been called.

Future (§ 178)	*Future Perfect* (§ 178)
1. I shall be called.	I shall have been called.
2. Thou wilt be called.	Thou wilt have been called.
3. He will be called.	He will have been called.
1. We shall be called.	We shall have been called.
2. You will be called.	You will have been called.
3. They will be called.	They will have been called.
1. Shall I be called?	Shall I have been called?
2. Shalt thou be called?	Shalt thou have been called?
3. Will he be called?	Will he have been called?
1. Shall we be called?	Shall we have been called?
2. Shall you be called?	Shall you have been called?
3. Will they be called?	Will they have been called?

648.   SUBJUNCTIVE PASSIVE OF *KNOW* (§§ 162,
169–172, 208)

Principal Parts, know, knew, known (§ 170)

Present	*Present Perfect*

Present

1. I be known.
2. Thou be known.
3. He be known.

1. We be known.
2. You be known.
3. They be known.

Present Perfect

I have been known.
Thou have been known.
He have been known.

We have been known.
You have been known.
They have been known.

Past

1. I were known.
2. Thou wert known.
3. He were known.

1. We were known.
2. You were known.
3. They were known.

Past Perfect

I had been known.
Thou hadst been known.
He had been known.

We had been known.
You had been known.
They had been known.

649.   IMPERATIVE PASSIVE (§§ 164, 208)

Present, Be (thou) known, Be (you) known.

650.   INFINITIVE PASSIVE (§§ 165, 208, 215–222)

Present, to be known.
Perfect, to have been known.

651.   GERUND PASSIVE (§§ 208, 215, 223–229)

Present, being known.
Perfect, having been known.

652. PARTICIPLE PASSIVE (§§ 166, 170, 175, 208, 230–236)

Present, being known.
Past, known.
Perfect, having been known.

653. INDICATIVE OR SUBJUNCTIVE MOOD OF *CAN, MAY, MUST, OUGHT, SHALL, WILL* (§§ 161–163, 183)

Principal Parts, can, could; may, might; must, must; ought, ought; shall, should; will, would.

Present

1. I can.	may	must	ought	shall	will
2. Thou canst.	may(e)st	must	oughtest	shalt	wilt
3. He can.	may	must	ought	shall	will
1. We can.	may	must	ought	shall	will
2. You can.	may	must	ought	shall	will
3. They can.	may	must	ought	shall	will

Past

1. I could.	might	must	ought	should	would
2. Thou could(e)st.	might(e)st	must	oughtest	should(e)st	would(e)st
3. He could.	might	must	ought	should	would
1. We could.	might	must	ought	should	would
2. You could.	might	must	ought	should	would
3. They could.	might	must	ought	should	would

For the personal endings of the indicative mood, see § 622. For the third person singular without *-s*, see § 622, N. 2. For the endings of the subjunctive, see § 622, N. 3.

For *can, may, must*, and *ought* used in verb phrases, see §§ 183–186; for *shall, will, should, would*, see the table of Contents, pages x and xi.

For emphatic verb phrases, formed by using *do* with the present infinitive, see § 174.

For progressive verb phrases, used to denote continuance of action or to picture scenes and events, see § 175; for the passive voice of progressive verb phrases, see § 209.

654. Principal parts of irregular verbs. The following list contains the principal parts of the common irregular verbs (§§ 169–172). When there are two forms having the same meaning, both forms are in good use, but the first form is sometimes preferable.

Present Indicative	Past Indicative	Past Participle
abide	abode	abode
am (§ 629)	was	been
arise	arose	arisen
awake	awoke	awaked
bear	bore	borne, born [1]
beat	beat	beaten
become	became	become
beget	begot	begotten
begin	began	begun
behold	beheld	beheld
bend	bent	bent
bereave	bereaved, bereft	bereaved, bereft
beseech	besought	besought
bespeak	bespoke	bespoke, bespoken
bet	bet	bet
bid (command)	bade	bidden
bid (offer)	bid	bid
bind	bound	bound
bite	bit	bitten
bleed	bled	bled
blow	blew	blown
break	broke	broken
breed	bred	bred
bring	brought	brought
build	built	built
burn	burnt, burned	burnt, burned
burst	burst	burst
buy	bought	bought

[1] *Born*, given birth to.

Present Indicative	*Past Indicative*	*Past Participle*
can (§ 653)	could	——
cast	cast	cast
catch	caught	caught
chide	chid	chidden, chid
choose	chose	chosen
cleave (split)	clove, cleft	cleft
cling	clung	clung
clothe	clothed, clad	clothed, clad
come	came	come
cost	cost	cost
creep	crept	crept
crow	crowed, crew	crowed
cut	cut	cut
deal	dealt	dealt
dig	dug	dug
do	did	done
draw	drew	drawn
dream	dreamed, drĕamt	dreamed, drĕamt
drink	drank	drunk
drive	drove	driven
dwell	dwelt	dwelt
eat	ate	eaten
fall	fell	fallen
feed	fed	fed
feel	felt	felt
fight	fought	fought
find	found	found
flee	fled	fled
fling	flung	flung
fly	flew	flown
forbear	forbore	forborne
forbid	forbade	forbidden
forget	forgot	forgotten
forgive	forgave	forgiven
for(e)go (give up)	for(e)went	for(e)gone

Present Indicative	*Past Indicative*	*Past Participle*
forsake	forsook	forsaken
forswear	forswore	forsworn
freeze	froze	frozen
get	got	got [1]
gird	girded, girt	girded, girt
give	gave	given
go	went	gone
grind	ground	ground
grow	grew	grown
hang	hung, hanged [2]	hung, hanged [2]
have (§ 623)	had	had
hear	heard	heard
heave	heaved, hove	heaved, hove
hew	hewed	hewn, hewed
hide	hid	hidden, hid
hit	hit	hit
hold	held	held
hurt	hurt	hurt
keep	kept	kept
kneel	knelt, kneeled	knelt, kneeled
knit	knitted, knit	knitted, knit
know (§ 641)	knew	known
lade	laded	laden, laded
lay	laid	laid
lead	led	led
leap	leaped, lĕapt	leaped, lĕapt
learn	learned, learnt	learned, learnt
leave	left	left
lend	lent	lent
let	let	let
lie (recline)	lay	lain
light	lighted, lit	lighted, lit
lose	lost	lost
make	made	made

[1] The form *gotten* is used in *ill-gotten*.   [2] *Hanged*, executed.

Present Indicative	*Past Indicative*	*Past Participle*
may (§ 653)	might	——
mean	meant	meant
meet	met	met
mow	mowed	mowed, **mown**
must	must	——
ought (§ 653)	ought	——
pay	paid	paid
put	put	put
quit	quitted, quit [1]	quitted, quit [1]
rēad	rĕad	rĕad
rend	rent	rent
rid	ridded, rid	rid
ride	rode	ridden
ring	rang	rung
rise	rose	risen
run	ran	run
saw	sawed	sawed, sawn [2]
say	said	said
see	saw	seen
seek	sought	sought
sell	sold	sold
send	sent	sent
set	set	set
sew	sewed	sewed, sewn
shake	shook	shaken
shall (§ 653)	should	——
shave	shaved	shaved, shaven
shear	sheared	sheared, shorn
shed	shed	shed
shine	shone	shone
shoe	shod	shod
shoot	shot	shot
show	showed	shown

[1] *Quit*, colloquial (§ 380) in the United States.
[2] *Sawn*, as adjective, is much the more common.

Present Indicative	Past Indicative	Past Participle
shrink	shrank	shrunk, shrunken [1]
shut	shut	shut
sing	sang	sung
sink	sank	sunk, sunken [1]
sit	sat	sat
slay	slew	slain
sleep	slept	slept
slide	slid	slid
sling	slung	slung
slink	slunk	slunk
slit	slit	slit
smell	smelt, smelled	smelt, smelled
smite	smote	smitten
sow	sowed	sown, sowed
speak	spoke	spoken
speed	sped, speeded	sped, speeded
spell	spelled, spelt	spelled, spelt
spend	spent	spent
spill	spilled, spilt	spilled, spilt
spin	spun	spun
spit	spit, spat	spit, spat
split	split	split
spoil	spoiled, spoilt	spoiled, spoilt
spread	spread	spread
spring	sprang	sprung
stand	stood	stood
stave	staved, stove [2]	staved, stove [2]
stay	stayed	stayed, staid [3]
steal	stole	stolen
stick	stuck	stuck
sting	stung	stung
stink	stank, stunk	stunk
strew	strewed	strewn, strewed

[1] Used as an adjective.   [2] *Stove*, chiefly nautical.
[3] Used as an adjective, 'settled', 'steady'.

Present Indicative	*Past Indicative*	*Past Participle*
stride	strode	stridden
strike	struck	struck, stricken [1]
string	strung	strung
strive	strove	striven
swear	swore	sworn
sweat	sweated, sweat	sweated, sweat
sweep	swept	swept
swell	swelled	swollen, swelled
swim	swam	swum
swing	swung	swung
take	took	taken
teach	taught	taught
tear	tore	torn
tell	told	told
think	thought	thought
thrive	throve, thrived	thriven, thrived
throw	threw	thrown
thrust	thrust	thrust
tread	trod	trodden, trod
wake	woke, waked	waked
wear	wore	worn
weave	wove	woven
weep	wept	wept
wet	wet, wetted	wet, wetted
will (§ 653)	would	——
win	won	won
wind	wound	wound
wring	wrung	wrung
write	wrote	written

[1] Used as an adjective (see *struck*, § 417).

INDEX

mathematics, 511; how indicated in manuscript, 515; in titles, 512 and N., 513; in foreign words, etc., 514; in punctuation, 495, N. 1.

Its, 59 (N.), 118 and N.; *it's*, 68; with collective noun, 197.

Itself, 110, 111.

Join issue, 417.
Join to, with, 287.
Judge, how addressed, 545, V.
Judgment, 394.
Junior, Jr., 529.

K, added in spelling, 402 (*C*).
Kidnapping, hobnobbing, 393, N.
Kind, sort, 72, 197; *kind (sort) of a*, 72; *kind (sort) of*, see *rather*, 417.
King James Bible (= Authorized Version), 450, 620.
King's English, The, 460 (N.), 474, 487, 501.
Knight Templar, 34.
Knight-errant, 34, 500, N.
Know, have known, etc., with infinitive, 417.

La, le, etc., in names, 437.
Lady, 150, 152; *ladies*, used in oral address only, 152.
Language, living, dead, 387.
Large. See *big*, 417.
Larva, -æ, 39.
Last, latest, 134; see *latest*, 417.
Late, 134; adj. or adv., 258.
Later (on), 417.
Latest, last. See *latest*, 417.
Latin, 387, 388, 390–392, 591, 595, 596, 603, 604, 612; spelling, 392; pronunciation, 402; prefixes, 391, 405; suffixes, 406; roots and stems, 407; accent of, as affecting French and English, 599, N.; spread of, 596; syntax, 618–620.

Latin nouns, 39, 604, 605.
Latin verbs, inflection, 612.
Latinize, latinize, 438.
Latter, 134; *the latter*, 104, N.
Lay, lie, 173.
Lay (lie), of the land, *plan, lay-out*. See *lay, plan*, 417.
Lay in, 290, N.
Le, la, etc., in names, 437.
Learn. See *teach*, 417.
Learn of. See *hear of*, 417.
Leave, leave alone, 417; see *quit*, 417.
Less, fewer, 148.
Less vivid future, 339.
Lesser, 134.
Let alone. See *leave*, 417.
Let's, let's us, etc., 417.
Letter writing, 516–545 (see Contents, p. xx); in general, 516; business, 516, 517, 535–545; personal, 516, 519–534; body of letter, 523, 539; conclusion, 524, 540, 545; envelope, paper and folding, stamp, 525, 534, 541; cards, 526; punctuation, 527, 528 and N., 534, 542; abbreviations, 529, 541, 543; order of pages, 530; single spacing, 535, N.; signature of married woman, widow, 544, III, N. 1; calling cards, 544, III, N. 2; business woman, 544, III, N. 3.
Letters, plural of, 35.
Liable, likely. See *apt*, 417.
Lie, lay, 173; see *lay, plan*, 417.
Lieutenant governor, how addressed, 545, V.
Like, love, admire, 417.
Like, should like, 187, 188, 192.
Like, unlike, etc., 417; misuse of *like* for *as*, see *like, unlike*, 417.
Likely, liable. See *apt*, 417.
Liking, verbs of, with *shall, should*, 192; adverbs of, with *will, would*, 193.

INDEX

INDEX

INDEX

To, have been, had been to, 245.
To, in order to, 310.
To be, with predicate pronoun, 219.
To home. See *home*, 417.
Today, tonight, tomorrow, 501.
Together with, does not affect verb, 201.
Too, also, 273, 480.
Too, very, 280.
Topic sentence, 357.
Topical (emphatic) capitals, 430.
Touch, get in touch with. See *pet expressions*, 417.
Touching, preposition, 283.
Toward, etc., 417.
Towns, with *at*, 293.
Tragedy, 415.
Transitional words, etc., 356.
Transitive verb, 156, 211.
Transpire. See *happen*, 417.
Transplant into, 287.
Transportation (shipping) department, 369 (9).
Treat for, etc., *treatise on*, 287.
Tri-, triweekly, etc. See *weekly*, 417.
Trinity, *God*, etc., 445.
Trite expressions, 66, 413; see *pet expressions*, 417.
Trousseau, -x, 39, 423.
Trust. See *hope*, 417.
Trustees of an institution, how addressed, 545, XVII.
Trustworthy. See *reliable*, 417.
Truth, veracity, 417.
Try to (not 'try and'), 251.
Turkoman, plural of, 34, N.
Twins, 417.
Typewritten letter, spacing, 535, N.

U, in French, 423, N. 2.
Ugly, 417.
Ultimo. See *instant*, 417.
Ultrafashionable. See *stylish*, 417.
Umpire. See *handwritten*, 417.
Un-, before capital letter, 438, N.1.
Unbeknown. See *unknown*, 417.

Uncertain that, etc., 295.
Unchristian, 438, N. 1.
Unconstitutional, 438, N. 1.
Under. See *from*, 417.
Uninterested. See *disinterested*, 417.
Unique, 417.
Unite to, with, 287.
United States, verb with, 205.
Unity, 352–359; in title, 354; in sentence, 355; 'and' habit, 355, A, 1; unrelated thoughts, 355, A, 1, b; subordinate clause, A, 2, a; independent sentences, 355, A, 2, b; changing point of view, 355, B; in paragraph, 356; in entire composition, 359; violation of, 489.
Universal statements, 414 and N.
Unlike. See *like, unlike*, 417.
Until, misused, 417.
Up, caution, 417.
Up to. See *duty*, 417.
Up to date, 417, 502, N.
Upon, on, 294.
Uprising. See *rise*, 417.
Upward. See *toward*, 417.
Usage, good, 360.
Use of words determines classification, 383.
Use to. See *used to*, 417.
Used to, etc., 417.
Useless, no good, etc., 417.
Uses and abuses of words, 411–417; multiplying words, 413; universal statements, 414; strong words weakened, 415; makeshifts for adjectives, 416; do's and don't's, 417.
Utterly, 414 and N.

Valuable, valued, 417.
Van, in names, 437.
Variety in style, 372.
Various, 119.
Veracity. See *truth*, 417.